The
Troubled
and Troubling
Child

Nicholas Hobbs

 AREA

AMERICAN RE-EDUCATION ASSOCIATION

Cleveland, Ohio   1994

THE TROUBLED AND TROUBLING CHILD
Re-Education in Mental Health, Education, and Human Services Programs
for Children and Youth
            by Nicholas Hobbs

1994 SECOND EDITION
Reprinted in paperback with permission from Mary Thompson Hobbs, copyright
holder since January, 1993, by: American Re-Education Association, Cleveland, Ohio.

Original hardback edition publishing information:

Copyright 1982 by: Jossey-Bass Inc., Publishers
                     433 California Street
                     San Francisco, California 94104
                              &
                     Jossey-Bass Limited
                     201 Banner Street
                     London EC1Y 8QE

Library of Congress Cataloging in Publication Data

Hobbs, Nicholas.
            The troubled and troubling child.
            Bibliography: p.
            Includes index.
            1. Problem children. 2. Problem children—
Services for. I. Bower, Eli Michael. II. Title.
HQ773.H63   371.93   81-20875
ISBN 0-87589-518-2   AACR2

FIRST EDITION

            First printing: April 1982
            Second printing: February 1987

      Code 8208

SECOND EDITION

      First printing: August 1994

Manufactured in the United States of America

Book Cover Design: Diane Q. Klann

Dedication

The reprinting of this classic work by The American Re-Education Association is dedicated to the memory of Re-ED's founder, Dr. Nicholas Hobbs. Dr. Hobbs was a true visionary whose thought was decades ahead of his time. His dynamic ideas for serving young people and their families are alive and functioning today. Nick's leadership and inspiration to teacher-counselors, and to those who support their important work, live on. Through them, Nicholas Hobbs' goal to "change the world, one child at a time" continues to be accomplished. We carry his spirit in our hearts.

The AREA logo is a drawing of the sculpture "Come Play" by Katharine Blackman Haven. The original was on Nicholas Hobbs' desk. An enlarged bronze casting stands in front of the Nicholas Hobbs Laboratory of Human Development at Vanderbilt University.

Nicholas Hobbs
1915 - 1983

Nicholas Hobbs is today best known as originator of the Re-ED approach to helping troubled and troubling children. Past-president of the American Psychological Association, he chaired the committee that first developed the Ethical Standards of Psychologists. He served on a number of regional and national bodies concerned with children, health, and education, and was a member of the Select Panel for the Promotion of Child Health established by Congress in 1979. Dr. Hobbs was the first Director of Selection and Research for the Peace Corps. He founded the Center for the Study of Families and Children as part of the Vanderbilt Institute for Public Policy Studies and he was also Professor Emeritus of Psychology and Provost of Vanderbilt University in Nashville, Tennessee.

Born on March 13, 1915, in South Carolina, young Nicholas was reared in a prominent, socially concerned Southern family which lost its wealth in the Depression. Aspiring to be a teacher but lacking money for college, he won a competitive scholarship to The Citadel where he earned a B.A. in English. After two years as a high school teacher, Hobbs began graduate work at the Ohio State University, where he studied with such eminent psychologists as Carl Rogers and Sidney Pressey. Following wartime service as a colonel in the Army Air Force Psychological Research Program, he was appointed in 1946 to the faculty of Teachers College, Columbia University, as director of the Clinical Psychology Training Program. In 1950, Dr. Hobbs and his wife, psychologist Dr. Mary Thompson Hobbs, returned to the South. He spent most of his professional and nationally prominent career in Nashville at George Peabody College for Teachers and Vanderbilt University.

In 1954, Hobbs directed a survey of the mental health needs of children for the Southern Regional Education Board. This study found children with serious emotional disturbance were receiving little help or were being incarcerated in large destructive institutions. Further, massive psychotherapy with scarce and expensive mental health professionals was not a viable solution. Instead, the study called for new cost-effective models utilizing existing pools of professionals trained to serve troubled youngsters in a variety of settings, including the public schools. Responding to the need, Hobbs, along with a small group of psychologists and educators from Peabody (including William Rhodes, Lloyd Dunn, Wilbert Lewis, Matthew Trippe, and Laura Weinstein) joined together to invent a new approach. In 1961, the National Institute of Mental Health granted Hobbs and his colleagues two million dollars to develop the Re-ED model.

After eight highly successful years of research and demonstration, in 1970 Project Re-ED received an unqualified endorsement from the Joint Commission on Mental Health of Children and similar accolades from experts in delinquency prevention. Although governmental funds were not forthcoming, the Re-ED concept continued to develop, serving exceptional youngsters of all ages in a variety of settings from public schools to residential treatment facilities. In 1982, Nicholas Hobbs spoke at the founding of the American Re-ED Association and was given the association's first Lifetime Membership Award. The following year, he died of cancer. His work lives on through the many individuals, agencies, and programs still using and re-inventing Re-ED, as well as through the efforts of The American Re-Education Association.

Hobbs' previously published books include *The Futures of Children* and *Issues in the Classification of Children*. Following *The Troubled and Troubling Child*, he published *Issues in the Care of Children with Chronic Illness*.

Edited by Dee Newman & Claudia Lann Valore

Foreword

Fifteen years have passed between Nicholas Hobbs' preparation of *The Troubled and Troubling Child* and this third printing of his book. The American Re-Education Association (AREA) expresses its sincere appreciation to Mary Hobbs, Nick's wife and lifelong colleague, for her permission to reprint this work, making it available to new readers. AREA is also appreciative to Jossey-Bass Publishers, who published and distributed the initial two printings (1982 & 1987), and who returned the rights to this book to Mary Hobbs, assisting AREA in printing this third edition. Our purpose in reprinting *The Troubled and Troubling Child* is to make this classic available to professionals, parents, and students in our field, as well as to provide this description of our heritage for AREA members and staff of AREA programs.

"Re-ED" began as Nick Hobbs' vision in the late 1950's. The first realization of that vision began with the arrival of the first students at Cumberland House Elementary School in Tennessee in November,

1962, and at Wright School in North Carolina in January, 1963. Since those beginnings, many individuals heard and responded to Nick's challenge to "change the world, one child at a time." They created services to operationalize the philosophy Nick expressed so well. Many of these individuals identified themselves openly as "Re-EDers." They gave and received mutual support and assistance, and sought to share the Re-ED philosophy with others. In 1980 representatives of this informal group met to establish the American Re-Education Association. Nicholas Hobbs was present and provided early support and inspiration for the organization's development.

As Nick Hobbs frequently said, Re-ED re-invents itself every day. The original Re-ED programs were short term residential treatment programs called "schools" to emphasize both their identification with our society's natural socializing agents and their orientation toward health rather than pathology. The programs described in this book have, of course, changed over time. Service entities are as dynamic as the living organisms they serve, always changing, growing, or declining. Many factors cause those changes: social, economic, legal, political, bureaucratic, leadership, and less frequently, insights presented by evidence and supportive data.

To date Re-ED programs have implemented the Re-ED philosophy through a wide variety of service options. Current AREA member programs each provide one or more of the following array of services:

> Early intervention services to pre-schoolers and their parents
> Liaison services to maintain at-risk students in public schools
> Public school support services, such as consultation and training
> Special classrooms for students, operating in public schools
> Day treatment/partial hospitalization programs
> Pre-vocational and vocational training
> Job coaching and supported employment
> Family preservation services
> Therapeutic and specialized foster care
> Group homes
> Independent living services
> Therapeutic camping and wilderness programs
> Intensive liaison services/case management
> Wraparound service programs
> Diagnostic centers
> Sex offender treatment

Crisis care and safe places
Runaway shelters
Residential treatment
Consultation, training, and research efforts

For over thirty years we have followed Nick Hobbs' example—looking for ways to meet the most difficult challenges, making a commitment to help in the toughest situations, and viewing success for our children and families as the responsibility of creative professionals who believe in collaborative endeavor.

Today, most of what you will read in this book is commonly accepted as the basis of good practice. When Re-ED programs were first envisioned and Re-ED philosophy was first taking shape, these same ideas and beliefs were seen as revolutionary. Few disturbed and disturbing children and youth were served at all, and fewer were served well. Service ordinarily meant placement in psychiatric hospitals or residential treatment facilities (often with adults) for long periods of time without family visitation or participation. For problems less severe, service generally meant verbal therapy sessions with a therapist or counselor, with the primary goal of building insights into causative events. Creating a therapeutic environment where "successful living" was seen as the therapeutic goal was only seldom attempted.

A few other pioneers of the 1960's demonstrated the power of this approach. William Morse began the Fresh Air Camp, as a therapeutic experience for disturbed children in Michigan, and piloted the "crisis teacher" role in Michigan schools. Nicholas Long established the Rose School in Washington, D.C., employing the psychoeducational approaches he had learned from and developed with Fritz Redl and his colleagues. Frank Hewett experimented with the "engineered classroom" in California, investigating the effects of a highly structured teaching environment for students with severe emotional and/or behavior problems. Frank Wood in Minnesota and others were quick to incorporate into special education teacher training what they saw as hopeful advances in the treatment of disturbed and disturbing students. These professionals are among the most important early contributors to Re-ED beliefs and strategies, along with those whose central contributions Nick described in this book, including Bill Lewis, Bill Rhodes, and Matt Trippe.

AREA has recognized the contributions, direct and indirect, of many of these individuals by asking them to accept its highest honor. The annual AREA Lifetime Membership award has been given to date to the following, each awarded at the Biennial Conference in the location given.

1981	Nicholas Hobbs	(First Biennial Conference
1982	Campbell Loughmiller	in Nashville, Tennessee)
1983	Frank Hewett	(Second Biennial Conference
1984	Charles MacDonald	at Lehigh University)
1985	Mary Hobbs	(Third Biennial Conference
1986	Wilbert W. Lewis	at U.C.L.A., Los Angeles)
1987	Nelle Wheeler	(Fourth Biennial Conference
1988	Nat Winston	in Cleveland, Ohio)
1989	Nicholas Long	(Fifth Biennial Conference
1990	Laura Weinstein	in Norfolk, Virginia)
1991	William C. Morse	(Sixth Biennial Conference
1992	Betsy Burke	in Pittsburgh, Pennsylvania)
1993	Jeanie Williams	(Seventh Biennial Conference
1994	Robert F. Cole	in Nashville, Tennessee)

During the years since 1960, others have read Nick's words and been inspired by their simple elegance and innate good sense. They assimilated what they read into their own work, or found that Hobbs had articulated their own ideas and values in unforgettable ways. In the last twenty years, the ideas and beliefs Nick fostered have grown to become the commonly accepted assumptions of many of our nation's service leaders. The American Re-Education Association has encountered many professionals who discovered that they too are "Re-EDers". Having read Nick Hobbs' writing, they recognize his work and accomplishments as part of their own heritage, an inheritance that may have been previously unknown to them. AREA welcomes anyone whose vision of helping troubled children and youth, and their families, is similar to the one Nick expressed. AREA members are also active in many other professional organizations serving troubled and troubling children and youth, and their families.

If you would like more information about AREA and AREA member programs, or would like to become an individual or program member, please contact the national office by calling (216) 231-0401 (ext. 11) or writing to the following address:

American Re-Education Association
Claudia Lann Valore, Assistant to the Board
1827 East 101 Street (c/o PEP)
Cleveland, OH 44106

The challenges and the importance of our collective mission have never been greater, and we can better meet those challenges together.

Written for the AREA Board
by Mary Lynn Cantrell
AREA Past President (1989-1991)

Preface

No one knows how many emotionally disturbed or mentally ill children there are in the United States. The President's Commission on Mental Health (1978) made a conservative estimate: from three to six million. The gross imprecision of the estimate suggests how uncertain is our nation's grasp of the problem. But of one thing we can be certain: These young people are not getting the help they desperately need. Nor are they getting the help the nation needs them to have in the interest of the common good, both for now and for the future. The thesis of this book is that the problem is grave and that it cannot be solved by conventional treatment strategies. The book proposes a fresh definition of the problem, and it describes in detail one way of dealing with it—not the only way, to be sure, but a way that has been tested for two decades and appears to hold high promise for the future.

We call our approach reeducation, and this gets shortened to "Re-ED," an acronym devised originally to refer to "the reeducation of emotionally disturbed children." Reeducation uses concepts and procedures derived largely from education but cast in an ecological framework and informed by the insights of the mental health disciplines. To describe the children we work with, we prefer the phrase *troubled and troubling* to other more familiar labels: emotionally disturbed, behavior disordered, mentally ill, delinquent. These latter terms imply that the painful and often perplexing difficulties of the child are largely intrapsychic; the phrase *troubled and troubling* implies that the difficulties are an expression of dynamic transactions between the child and other people who are important in his life—parents most centrally, then siblings, teachers, relatives, family friends, professional people perhaps. We refer to this as an ecological perspective for reasons that are made clear in the text. Suffice it here to say that casting the problem in ecological terms results in an approach to troubled and troubling children and youth that is substantially different from conventional treatment programs.

The French have a useful expression: "D'abord, il faut durer" ("First and foremost, it is necessary to endure"). Re-ED has endured. It started out in 1961 as an eight-year demonstration project supported by a grant of approximately two million dollars from the National Institute of Mental Health to George Peabody College for Teachers and the states of Tennessee and North Carolina. Peabody set up a program to train staff for two pilot schools, Tennessee established Cumberland House in Nashville, and North Carolina established Wright School in Durham. On termination of federal funds, the program survived—an infrequent occurrence; both Tennessee and North Carolina have continued and expanded their programs. Both schools faced political crises but successfully weathered them, largely as a result of strong support from citizen groups and from parents of children served by the schools. Initially designed to serve children six to twelve years old, Re-ED programs have been extended upward to serve adolescents and downward to serve preschoolers. Research studies, though limited in number, have demonstrated that the program is effective. Successful propagation is a stern test of capacity for survival; there are today twenty-three Re-ED programs scattered over the country. Re-ED has endured, and well.

Further, the program received the strong endorsement of the Joint Commission on Mental Health of Children (1970, p. 44):

Because of its proven effectiveness, in terms of both cost per child and success in restoring the child to home, school, and community, the commission recommends that the Re-ED model be adopted and extended as one of the many needed kinds of services for emotionally disturbed children. Specifically, the commission recommends that funds be made available to any state, community agency, or nonprofit corporation for the construction and operation of residential schools, patterned after the Re-ED plan. Funds should be sufficient to establish at least 100 schools, with at least one school in each state, to serve as models for other programs.

With such a record of success and such a strong and important endorsement, it is a reasonable question to ask why Re-ED ideas have not swept the country. The heavy hand of tradition and the resistance of established professions to innovation could be cited, but there is little evidence for the validity of such conjectures. On the contrary, when responsible mental health specialists have had an opportunity to examine Re-ED ideas and programs carefully, they have generally been quite positive in their responses. Nor would we discount for a moment the significance of the score of programs that have been established largely as a result of word-of-mouth communication. Initial contacts have often been followed by extended visits to existing programs and by a process of colonization in which experienced staff members from an operating program serve as a cadre for the establishment of a new program. One could even argue that the slow maturation of reeducation ideas has had its benefits in encouraging the creation and testing of new forms under favorable circumstances. The major impediment to the propagation of Re-ED is that little has been written about it.

We hope this book will repair that deficiency. It is written primarily as a guide for professional people, including advanced students, who work or plan to work with troubled children and youth and who need an understanding of the underlying principles of reeducation as well as of their daily application in the workings of a program. It is written for workers in mental health, health, education, social services, and corrections, and it should be of interest to teacher-counselors, special educators, psychiatrists, psychologists, social workers, pediatricians, and others who work with disturbed children. The book should also be useful to the shapers and makers of public policy concerning the mental health of children and youth; they may want to read selectively, concentrating on the underlying philosophy and skipping the copious illustrations of how the programs actually operate.

A brief comment on vocabulary. We have tended to use the terms *emotionally disturbed* and *troubled and troubling* interchangeably. Sometimes the word *child* is used generically to mean individuals from birth to eighteen, sometimes to mean younger children only; the context will make the intention clear. To avoid sexist language without using stylistically awkward ways of handling personal pronouns, we have used masculine pronouns in some sections and feminine pronouns in others, with generic meaning.

The following paragraphs provide the reader with a cognitive map of the intellectual terrain to be covered. They should enable readers to understand the structure of the book and allow them to choose selectively from its contents.

Chapter One introduces the problem of the mental health of children and youth in contemporary America. The account covers roughly a thirty-year period, and it sets the stage for understanding Project Re-ED and a number of other efforts to provide mental health services to young people and their families. The Prologue argues that—in spite of the work of a number of advisory commissions, of generous appropriations by the Congress over the years, of dedicated efforts on the part of many professional people from diverse disciplines, and even in spite of a substantial increase in knowledge—we, as a nation, are failing our troubled and troubling children and youth.

Chapter Two records the origins, the character, and the current status of Project Re-ED: it describes briefly the principles of reeducation, and it assesses the implications of reeducation for mental health, health, education, social services, and corrections.

Chapter Three tells what Re-ED programs are like—their organizational arrangements, staffing patterns, physical facilities, and costs. About a dozen actual Re-ED programs are described in an attempt to portray their great diversity, their shared commitment to common principles, their continuing vitality, and their ability to invent new forms in response to local contingencies, including both opportunities and restraints on resources.

Chapter Four describes the teacher-counselor. It accounts for the origins of the role of teacher-counselor in Western Europe, its transformation to meet the requirements of a new culture, and its emergence as a new mental health profession in the United States. The present roles of teacher-counselors and the ways people are selected and trained for these roles are described. In an effort to make teacher-counselors come alive to the reader, to show them as the real people they are, the chapter ends with four autobiographical sketches.

Chapter Five describes the important role of consultants in Re-ED programs. Conservatively estimated, 6.5 million children need assistance with mental health problems. Re-ED has pioneered in developing the idea that the most effective way, perhaps the only way, to meet this great need is to have scarce experts—psychiatrists, psychologists, special educators, pediatricians, social workers—multiply the impact of their knowledge and skill by working through highly talented but less extensively trained people, such as teacher-counselors. We illustrate the idea through biographical sketches of four successful Re-ED consultants.

Chapter Six deals with the kinds of children and adolescents served in Re-ED programs. Uninformed critics of Re-ED find it difficult to believe that teacher-counselors can work effectively with seriously disturbed youngsters. It is important to clear up this misunderstanding if Re-ED is to take its place along the continuum of services needed to provide adequately for disturbed children and youth. It is also important to note that there are a few limitations on the kinds of children who can appropriately be admitted to the relatively open settings of Re-ED schools. Finally, the chapter presents accounts of eight children in Re-ED programs, representing six successful experiences and two failures to help.

Chapter Seven, in its discussion of ecological strategies, begins the process of describing the principles that undergird the processes of reeducation. *Ecology,* a much misunderstood term, refers to the study of dynamic interactions of forces in a natural system, which is precisely the focus of reeducational efforts. The goal of Re-ED is not to "cure" the child but to enable an ecological system, of which the child is the defining member, to work reasonably well. This formulation obviously differs radically from traditional concepts of the problem of children and youth called emotionally disturbed, behavior disordered, or mentally ill.

Chapter Eight, describing the liaison function, makes clear the consequences of adopting an ecological perspective in working with troubled and troubling children and youth. Approximately one third of the professional resources of a Re-ED program are devoted to assessing the strengths and weaknesses of ecosystems and to helping its members work out ways to enable the system to function well. Then the liaison process is delineated, step by step, and illustrated by the story of one boy and the people and resources mobilized to help him.

Chapter Nine describes the process of reeducation from the perspective of working with individual children. Twelve principles are presented and illustrated. These principles were derived from actual experience in working with children and youth, mostly in the early years of the project, and have been revised from time to time on the basis of further experience and new theoretical knowledge. The empirical origins of the principles are evident in their substantial divergence from conventional approaches to either treatment or education of disturbed children. The chapter contains a number of vignettes illustrating the application of the principles.

Chapter Ten, on learning to learn, reflects our strong belief, supported by research, that the overcoming of academic deficits is an essential component in enabling the child to function effectively in a restructured ecosystem. We reject the conventional wisdom that emotional disturbance causes academic failure and that the child must be cured in order to resume learning. We maintain instead that the achievement of adequacy in academic skills is an essential step in the process of overcoming emotional problems. We describe several teaching and learning enterprises to emphasize the centrality of school learning in the process of reeducation.

Chapter Eleven considers procedures for helping children and adolescents get their behavior under their own control. It describes in some detail the two predominant methods for effecting change in Re-ED programs: (1) operant conditioning (or behavior modification) and (2) group process. Actually, most programs blend the two in varying proportions. Again, an effort is made to translate general concepts into meaningful practice by using illustrations drawn from actual experiences in Re-ED programs.

Finally, as an epilogue, Chapter Twelve presents the report of a panel of visitors who have been participant observers in Project Re-ED from its earliest days. Members of the panel were selected because they were outstanding leaders in the field of mental health whose professional judgment is highly respected. They were thus part of the plan for evaluating the effectiveness of the program. It has seemed to us that *t* tests and chi squares are important in evaluating programs but that ultimately a program will be accepted or rejected on the basis of informed professional judgment. The Epilogue provides a summary of the panel's findings in 1980.

Hundreds of people have contributed to the building of Project Re-ED and to the development of reeducation as a major resource for providing assistance to emotionally disturbed children and their families. The task of acknowledging contributors is formidable and the results will inevitably be unsatisfactory. Yet an effort to record the names of major contributors is imperative, for Re-ED is, above all else, people, their ideas, their caring for children. We have attempted to reflect their deep involvement in the project by including in the book many contributions from teacher-counselors. Their work is acknowledged appropriately in footnotes. Re-ED is truly the work of many minds and hearts.

The most important people to name have to be nameless simply because of their numbers: the teacher-counselors who made Re-ED and who re-create it every day in their work with children.

In 1957, I started discussions about a new type of residential school for disturbed children, with the Southern Regional Education Board providing first a forum and then a vehicle to move the ideas to the stage of a proposal to the National Institute of Mental Health. William McLaughlin and later Paul Penningroth and Harold McPheeters facilitated the process.

The staff of the National Institute of Mental Health—most notably, Robert Felix, Joseph Bobbitt, and Leonard Duhl—were extraordinarily responsive to our earliest expressions of intent to build residential schools for the reeducation of emotionally disturbed children.

Lloyd Dunn, William Rhodes, and I designed the original Re-ED proposal. We were joined later by Wilbert Lewis, Wayne Richard, Matthew Trippe, and Laura Weinstein. It was essentially this group that guided Re-ED through its eight years as a demonstration project. Each member of the group made distinctive contributions, but it was Rhodes who started us thinking of emotional disturbance as evidence of discord in ecological systems, a governing concept in Re-ED today.

Two commissioners of mental health, Joseph Baker of Tennessee and Eugene Hargrove of North Carolina, had the courage and the vision to commit their states to support the project. Subsequently, Frank Luton and Nat Winston, Tennessee commissioners, encouraged the expansion of reeducation into all the state hospitals. Over the years, state directors of children and youth programs played important, day-by-day roles in building a solid support structure for Re-ED in Tennessee and North Carolina; the names of Charles McDonald, Leon Joyner, Wilbert Lewis, Samuel Cornwell, and Lenore Behar should be recorded with appreciation. Three years ago, Dale Farabee, commissioner, took Re-ED to California, where the program is flourishing under the able leadership of Betsy Burke.

Cumberland House was the first Re-ED school to open, in 1962. James Cleary was named principal (followed by Charles McDonald, Bill Willis, Louis Semrau, Nelle Wheeler, and Alice Shannon). The initial consultants were Eric Chazen, pediatrician; Jennie Adams, social worker; Gus Bell, clinical psychologist; and Maurice Hyman, psychiatrist. The teacher-counselors were Neal Buchanan, Charlotte Clark, Charlotte Cook, Helen Lindsay, Alice Shannon, Robert Slagle, and Nelle Wheeler. Jane Bridgeman, social worker, and James Newman, teacher-counselor, began to create the role of liaison teacher-counselor, and Jeanie Williams subsequently contributed significantly to its theory and practice.

John Ball was the first director of Wright School, followed by Neal Buchanan and Richard Yell. The principal consultants for Wright School were John Fowler, psychiatrist; Ila Gehman, psychologist; Lloyd Borstelman, psychologist; and David Jones, pediatrician and psychiatrist. The teacher-counselors were Pauline Frazier, James Paul, Wayne Pyle, Frances Spencer, Patricia Staffen, and Richard Yell. Anne Parrish, social worker, joined the staff later. Wayne Pyle was the first liaison teacher-counselor at Wright School.

Current Re-ED programs, with the names of their directors or principals, are listed in Appendix A.

A number of people—including Betsy Burke, Gregory Granna, Roy Hutton, Wilbert Lewis, Clark Luster, Lee Maxwell, Judith Mearig, Rico Pallotta, Alice Shannon, Robert Slagle, Lawrence

Thompson, Matthew Timm, Nelle Wheeler, and Richard Yell—have contributed to the writing of this book through their criticism of earlier drafts.

We have purposefully written the book with a focus on the Re-ED experience as though it had no origins in intellectual history or contemporary mental health scholarship. But we owe many intellectual debts and would like to acknowledge them here briefly, again with an acute awareness of how inadequate and incomplete such an effort must inevitably be. We are thus indebted: for the importance of relationship and the significance of time in life to Otto Rank, Jessie Taft, Virginia Robinson, and Carl Rogers; for psychodynamic concepts in general to Sigmund Freud and Anna Freud and their many interpreters; for concepts of ecological systems to Kurt Lewin, Ludwig von Bertalanffy, Roger Barker, Phil Schoggen, James G. Miller, and, most recently, Urie Bronfenbrenner; for concepts and techniques of behavior management to Joseph Wolpe, especially, and also to B. F. Skinner and Sidney Bijou; for the importance of meaning and structure in learning to Sidney Pressey and Jerome Bruner; for the significance of role and of personal engagement to George Kelly; for the uses of metaphor and games in learning to Eli Bower; for specific techniques of working with disturbed children to Carl Fenichel, William Glasser, Norris Haring, Frank Hewitt, Nicholas Long, William Morse, and Fritz Redl; for the importance of purpose and of joy in the life of children to Anton Makarenko of the Soviet Union; for the theory and practice of reeducation to Robert Lafon, Henri Joubrel, and Robert Préaut of France, Catherine McCallum of Scotland, and Jeannine Guindon of Canada; for therapeutic camping and group process to Campbell Loughmiller; and for concepts of the malleability of intelligence to Reuven Feuerstein.

Letha B. Rowley served as special assistant to the project during its demonstration years and most recently assisted in the preparation of this manuscript. Her determination to get things right is evident throughout this volume. Louise C. Patton, administrative assistant, has patiently and expertly prepared numerous drafts and has otherwise assisted in rounding out Re-ED's second decade. Every page of the book is the better for the skill and good judgment of editor Dorothy Conway.

Funds to support Re-ED and the writing of this manuscript have come from numerous sources. The initial grant making the project possible was provided by the National Institute of Mental Health. Subsequently, funds were made available by the Bureau of Education of the Handicapped (for Laura Weinstein's evaluation). The writing of the book was made possible by my appointment (in 1966) as a fellow at the Center for Advanced Study in the Behavioral Sciences; a first draft of the book was completed at the time but has subsequently been completely rewritten to take advantage of additional years of experience in reeducation. Robert Lafon and Tina Rividi of the Association pour la Sauvegarde de l'Enfance et l'Adolescence opened up countless opportunities to learn from scholars, investigators, and leaders in reeducation in France. Elisabeth Necker graciously extended to me the hospitality of La Fondation Ripaille, Thonon-les-Bains, France, for a period of seclusion, reflection, and writing. The Ford Foundation, the Spencer Foundation, and Vanderbilt University have also contributed generously to the effort.

George Peabody College for Teachers provided an extraordinarily congenial and encouraging environment for carrying out Project Re-ED; in fact, we doubt that it could have been done elsewhere. Over the past six years, the Vanderbilt Institute for Public Policy Studies has provided an ideal setting for writing this account, as well as material assistance for doing so.

On a personal note, I thank Mary Thompson Hobbs, my wife and professional colleague, who has contributed over the years to Re-ED in ways too varied to record. Most recently, she has greatly improved this manuscript through her insightful and sensitive criticisms. She is a constant source of support and inspiration.

I warmly thank all who have contributed to the book, especially the teacher-counselors who have made Re-ED an enduring source of help for children and their families. I share credit with all contributors for whatever they find felicitous and absolve them of responsibility for error, misapprehension, and an inevitable failure to account fully for a glorious effort, widely shared, that succeeded.

Nashville, Tennessee   Nicholas Hobbs
March 1982

Acknowledgements

Contributing Authors

The following people contributed case studies, biographical sketches, and other observations, which Hobbs used throughout the book (and, especially, Chapter Twelve) to highlight specific aspects of Re-ED:

Donald Alwes	Lee Maxwell
Gus Bell	Lawrence Newton
Eli M. Bower	Rico Pallotta
Mary Lynn Cantrell	William Rhodes
David Friedlein	Sally Robinson
Billie Garrison	Frances Smith Rothman
Ila Gehman	J.P. Sakey
Algund Hermann	H. Kenneth Shaw
Peggy Hester	Kenneth L. Shaw
Frank Hewitt	Robert Slagle
Wayne H. Holtzman	Charles R. Strother
Dante Jackson	Matthew Timm
David Jones	Steve Weinberg
Claudia Lann	Laura Weinstein
Wilbert Lewis	Barbara Wheeley
Paula Litchfield	Jeanie Williams
Reginald S. Lourie	Richard Yell
Clark Luster	

Special thanks to Mary Thompson Hobbs, Nick's wife, professional colleague, and copyright holder of this book, for granting the American Re-Education Association permission to reprint.

Contents

The
Troubled
and Troubling
Child

*Re-Education in Mental Health,
Education, and Human Services Programs
for Children and Youth*

Dedication

To the Teacher-Counselors
of Re-ED

1

Prologue:
Troubled and Troubling
Children and Youth

A National Problem

A friendly critic, having read this book in manuscript, observed that the book offers an interesting solution but that it does not make clear what the problem is. He felt that most readers would respond like the philosopher who, when asked "What is the answer?" replied "What is the question?" This brief prologue attempts to remedy the deficit noted by our critic. In writing the Prologue, we draw heavily on reports of national agencies and commissions in order to avoid shaping the question to conform to our response.

The question may be asked this way: "What is our nation going to do about the large number of emotionally disturbed and mentally ill children and adolescents who desperately need help but are now shamefully neglected?" Further, the question should imply not only that these young people are not getting the help they need, and that a humane society should provide, but also

1

that they are not getting the help the nation needs them to get in the interest of its own secure, tranquil, and productive future. Four subsidiary questions sharpen the issue. What were the problems that led to the establishment of Project Re-ED twenty years ago? How big is the problem today? How, where, and by whom are emotionally disturbed and mentally ill children cared for today? And, finally, why does Re-ED remain an appropriate response to the primary question of what we as a nation should do to help emotionally disturbed children and youth and their families?

What led to the establishment of Project Re-ED? In the early days of the mental hygiene movement, children seemed to fare reasonably well. Lightner Witmer established the first psychological clinic for children in 1896, at the University of Pennsylvania. In 1921, the child guidance movement was initiated by the Commonwealth Fund, when it established eight demonstration clinics for children and youth. The child guidance model was widely emulated, but the noble effort, concentrating on the needs of children, lost its momentum. (It did, however, provide the foundation for the comprehensive community mental health centers that are today largely oriented toward adults in urban areas.)

In the early 1950s, a survey of mental health resources in the South by the Southern Regional Education Board (1954) revealed an almost complete lack of adequate facilities for severely disturbed children in that region. No one knew what to do with them. As a result, many children were incarcerated in large state hospitals, sometimes on wards with psychotic adults, sometimes on special children's units—understaffed, dreary, crowded places without programs. Authorities hoped that the children would somehow get better but knew that many could only get worse.

In 1955, the 84th Congress established the first Joint Commission on Mental Illness and Health; and some fifty national organizations, led by the American Psychiatric Association, spent five years studying the problem. The JCMH, as it was called, came up with recommendations that led to the establishment of the Comprehensive Community Mental Health Center program, which was designed to get the mentally ill out of overcrowded state hospitals and into treatment centers in their home communities. But the Joint Commission, not surprisingly, paid attention primarily to the mental health needs of adults and all but overlooked children and adolescents. It was therefore necessary for the 89th Congress to establish, in 1965, the Joint Commission on Mental Health of Children. This special commission on children got caught up with the social turmoil of the late 1960s, and its excellent report came on the scene at a time of growing disenchantment with government programs for people. The commission's many thoughtful recommendations have gone largely unheeded; however, it had a good grasp of the problem, as is evident in the following passage from its report: "What happens to all our children who receive no help for emotional problems? . . . A vast majority of these children are literally lost. They are bounced around from training schools to reformatories to jails and whipped through all kinds of understaffed welfare agencies. No one is their keeper. No agency is equipped to evaluate either the correctness of their placement or the outcome of the placement" (Joint Commission on Mental Health of Children, 1970, p. 7).

In early 1977, the President's Commission on Mental Health was established "to review the mental health needs of the nation and to make recommendations to the President as to how the nation might best meet these needs." Regarding the mental health of children and youth of the nation, the commission observed:

As the commission traveled throughout America, we saw and heard about too many children and adolescents who suffered from neglect, indifference, and abuse, and for whom appropriate mental health care was inadequate or nonexistent. Too many American children grow up to adulthood with mental disabilities which could have been addressed more effectively earlier in their lives through appropriate prenatal, infant, and early child development care programs.

Troubled children and adolescents, particularly if they are from racial minorities, are too often placed in foster homes, special schools, mental and correctional institutions, without adequate prior evaluation or subsequent follow-up. Good residential facilities specializing in the treatment of special problems are in short supply.

During the past two decades, many adolescents have struggled to adapt to rapid social changes and conflicting, often ambiguous, social values. There has been a dramatic increase in the use and misuse of psychoactive drugs, including alcohol, among young people and nearly a threefold increase in the suicide rate of adolescents.

Services that reflect the unique needs of children and adolescents are frequently unavailable. Our existing mental health services system contains too few mental health professionals and other personnel trained to meet the special needs of children and adolescents. Even when identified, children's needs are too often isolated into distinct categories, each to be addressed separately by a different specialist. Shuttling children from service to service, each with its own label, adds to their confusion, increases their despair, and sets the pattern for adult disability [President's Commission on Mental Health, 1978, vol. 1, pp. 6-7].

Possibly one reason children and youth continue to be neglected after all these years of commission reports and little action is that authorities are not quite sure what should be done even if resources were adequate.

How big is the problem? How many children and adolescents are we talking about? How many emotionally disturbed and mentally ill children are there in the United States? One might think this an easy question to answer, but it is not. The Joint Commission on Mental Health of Children (1970, p. 25) estimated that 2 to 3 percent of children suffer from severe mental disorders and that another 8 to 10 percent suffer from emotional disturbances that require some intervention. The President's Commission on Mental Health (1978, vol. 2, p. 39) estimated that 5 to 15 percent of the child population needs some kind of mental health treatment.

In his annual report of 1977, S. P. Hersh, assistant director for children and youth of the National Institute of Mental Health, describes the dimensions of the problem. Referring to the 65,191,000 individuals 18 years of age and under, he writes:

At least 7 million have a potential need for assistance from mental health professionals because they fall within the sphere of physical and physiological stigmata. Another 1 million . . . fall within the social deviance sphere. And 597,840 children and adolescents were admitted during 1975 . . . to the mental health system as defined by the combination of community mental health centers, free standing out-patient clinics, state and county mental hospitals, and private psychiatric hospitals. (Outpatient private practice data are not available.) Substance abuse problems may add another 2 million children and adolescents to the group of those in need of mental health services. These figures include both the known clients of the mental health system and extrapolations derived from studies of selected vulnerable populations [Hersh, 1977, p. 6].

According to the estimates of Hersh, about 10 million children have a potential need for mental health services, and 600,000 (or .6 percent) were receiving services from the formal mental health system.

Another NIMH official (Silver, 1981, p. 577), extrapolating downward from a study of the adult population by Regier and Goldberg (1978), concludes that between 15 and 20 percent of the population of the United States has a mental disorder during any given year and that "the figures [are] as accurate for children as for adults."

Obviously, much depends on how emotional disturbance and mental illness are defined. We cite these figures to establish the magnitude of the discrepancy between the number of children and youth with mental health problems and the number of children who receive the help they need. For this purpose, we adopt a conservative estimate of 10 percent, or 6.5 million young people needing help, a figure in the middle range of the estimates cited above. The reader should fix this figure in mind to appreciate a later discussion of the number of mental health specialists available to provide services if conventional treatment modes are followed.

Who cares for children? Children with mental health problems are to be found in all the human service systems of the nation, and some of them are in no system at all. In the paragraphs that follow, we try to identify the systems that serve emotionally disturbed children and youth and to estimate how many are in each system and to what extent mental health specialists are involved in their treatment.

The *mental health system* provides assistance to a relatively small proportion of children needing help. One authority (Sowder, 1980), using conservative projections, estimates that 9.4 percent of children needing mental health services actually receive them. Another authority (Kramer, 1976) comes up with a confirming estimate of 10 percent. But there is a problem even with these depressing figures. The National Institute of Mental Health does not keep data on individual children; the data cited above reflect cases, not children. They are based on admissions, not individuals. An indeterminate number of children are admitted to mental health treatment programs twice or even several times a year, thus necessitating a downward adjustment of projections—probably in the neighborhood of 20 percent. When we convert these percentages into children, and use our conservative 10 percent projection, we have to conclude that 6.5 *million* children need help and that 520 *thousand* individual children get help. In other words, the mental health system serves less than 1 percent of the children and youth of the nation.

The centerpiece of the nation's mental health program for the past fifteen years has been the Comprehensive Community Mental Health Centers. These centers have been repeatedly criticized for neglecting children and youth. The United States Commission on Civil Rights (1977, pp. 6-7), analyzing 1975 data from 328 community mental health centers, found that only 16.3 percent of children under fifteen received help, although they comprised 28.8 percent of the population served by the centers. A special panel of the President's Commission on Mental Health (1978, vol. 2, p. 320), charged with studying community mental health centers, reported that children and adolescents are served at approximately one-third the rate of adults in the same service areas.

It appeared for a while that the work of the Joint Commission on Mental Health of Children might pay off in tangible, negotiable terms. In 1972, the Community Mental Health Centers Act was amended to allocate $10 million annually for children's services, the first and only time in United States history that federal funds have been earmarked for mental health services for children. The special allocation was rescinded in 1977. A federal official writes with laconic restraint: "This action posed a threat to children's services" (Silver, 1981, p. 573).

Mental hospitals, of course, play an important role in the nation's mental health system, especially for severely and chronically ill children and youth. In 1975, 83,000 mentally ill children were admitted to inpatient psychiatric facilities, mostly state and county hospitals or other public facilities, with a few in private residential treatment centers (Select Panel for the Promotion of Child Health, 1981, vol. 3, p. 77). No one knows how long children remain in institutions; many may simply graduate to adult wards, and there is apparently no information available on how many children are on wards with psychotic adults. The Children's Defense Fund (1978, p. 6) reports that, of 700 children in California psychiatric hospitals, 50 percent were not mentally ill but had academic and behavioral problems. Arizona and New Jersey officials have reported similar findings. There are many excellent mental hospitals for children and youth, under both public and private sponsorship, but there are also many institutions that are a disgrace to our nation.

Uneven deployment of child mental health specialists compounds the problem of personnel shortages. There are heavy concentrations of psychiatrists, psychologists, psychiatric social workers, and psychiatric nurses in urban centers and, indeed, in a relatively few states. In most states, the supply of specialists is far below minimum requirements for effective programming. A high percentage of psychiatrists and psychologists trained in leading universities and medical schools for work with children go into private practice and consequently have little effect on the bulk of the problem of emotional disturbance and mental disorder in children and youth. Although exact figures are not available, it appears that a number of physicians serving children in state mental hospitals are foreign-born and have language and cultural differences that impair their effectiveness in working with children and families. Finally, several studies indicate that minority-group children and adolescents are less likely to receive mental health services (from private practitioners, community mental health centers, or mental hospitals) than are their white counterparts; that they are more likely to receive an evaluation only; and that, when they are treated, they are more likely to be treated with drugs than with psychotherapy (Sowder, 1980; Jackson, Berkowitz, and Farley, 1974; Lewis, Balla, and Shanok, 1979).

The most frequently recommended solution to the problem of inadequate treatment resources for children and youth is to train more psychiatrists, clinical psychologists, psychiatric social workers, and psychiatric nurses. While we may indeed need more mental health experts, a few minutes with a sharp pencil will show the futility of trying to match numbers with numbers without altering the patterns of deployment of mental health specialists.

The traditional psychiatric disciplines are psychiatry, clinical psychology, psychiatric social work, and psychiatric nursing. Representatives of all these disciplines are in short supply—if used in traditional fashion. There are only 3,000 psychiatrists and possibly 5,000 to 6,000 psychologists who are qualified to provide services to children. There are 20,000 social workers and from 5,000 to 7,000 psychiatric nurses employed in psychiatric mental health facilities, but how many of these work with children is unknown. Let us suppose for the moment that all the psychiatrists and clinical psychologists and one third of the social workers and nurses were trained to provide individual treatment to emotionally disturbed and mentally ill children, and were available to do so. Since, as we have estimated, 6.5 million children and youth need help, each of these specialists would have a case load of 360 children at any one time. Each child could be seen in therapy for fifty minutes every four and a half months. This appears to be an absurd exercise, but it is not. It simply reveals the futility of trying to provide mental health services to children and youth, given the assumptions on which current mental health policy is based. The mental health problems of children and youth cannot be solved on the basis of conventional patterns of organization and treatment.

The *general health system* is extremely important in meeting the mental health needs of children and youth. For the adult population, approximately 60 percent of all persons with emotional disorders are seen in the general medical care system, 22 percent in the human services system, and only 15 percent in the formal mental health system (Regier and Goldberg, 1978). Studies limited to children and youth treated in primary medical care settings suggest that between 5 percent and 30 percent will have mental disorders (Starfield and others, 1980). Thus, a substantial number of children with emotional and mental disorders may receive treatment from pediatricians or other health specialists. An estimated 650,000 children have severe and catastrophic physical illnesses (such as juvenile diabetes, cystic fibrosis, or hemophilia); a high proportion of these children have severe emotional problems as well. But the traditions of pediatric practice, which are usually based on a fee-for-service plan, require visits limited to fifteen or twenty minutes and do not lend themselves to effective engagement with the complex interplay of problems facing the disturbed child or adolescent and her family. One consequence is an overreliance on mood- and behavior-altering drugs, unaccompanied by attention to the causes of the child's difficulties. There are no data on the long-term effects of tranquilizers and energizers on the development of the child.

The *public school* probably is the institution that serves most mildly and moderately disturbed children, simply because that is where most of the children are. The percentages would be low, but the absolute number would be high. Public Law 94-142 requires that the public schools provide free of charge the services needed to enable these children to take advantage of educational opportunities. The opportunities are to be provided in the least restrictive environment possible. At the present time, P.L. 94-142 provides services in the schools for approximately 150,000 disturbed children, ages three to twenty-one. There remains considerable ambiguity about payment for services for children who need residential treatment for mental health problems, presumably as a prerequisite to their returning to regular schools, or for children who require psychotherapy on an outpatient basis in order to continue their education. There is great variability from state to state in how these mental health services will be paid for.

From a mental health perspective, of equal importance to P.L. 94-142 is the training program for special educators that has been in operation under the egis of the Bureau of Education for the Handicapped (now the Office of Special Education and Rehabilitative Services) since 1967. There are in the nation today at least 100,000 qualified special educators who teach over 1,800,000 children with emotional problems, behavior disorders, and learning disabilities. Because of the efforts of these teachers, a substantial number of disturbed children, who would previously have required residential treatment, are being maintained successfully in the public schools. Furthermore, a number of public schools, faced with the lack of adequate mental health facilities in their communities, are developing their own programs for seriously disturbed children. These programs often make effective use of consultants from the mental health disciplines.

For the most part, however, psychiatrists, clinical psychologists, psychiatric social workers, and psychiatric nurses are notably scarce around schools. Psychologists are the single largest group of mental health specialists employed by the schools, but their role has often been limited to that of classification. What is needed, of course, is assistance from mental health specialists to both regular classroom teachers and special educators in dealing with the mental health problems, small and large, of children and families.

The *social services system* is responsible at any one time for the custody and care of approximately 500,000 children. Most of these children are placed in foster homes; only 15 percent are in institutions (Hubbell, 1981, p. 29). While mental health specialists other than social workers have in general paid little attention to the social services system, it is obviously the place where their talents are needed and could be used effectively. Many foster parents and group home leaders are inadequately trained. North Carolina is providing training for these workers through its Re-ED program, which relies heavily on specialists from the traditional mental health disciplines.

The *correctional system* has custody of a number of children who would be recognized as presenting mental health problems. In 1979, more than 500,000 children were admitted to public detention and correctional facilities (Heim and others, 1980). These young people often are frightened, hostile, and defiant, and some are dangerous to themselves or others. Though substantial progress has been made in improving the correctional system, it still is not adequately sensitive to mental health problems of its wards. Moreover, mental health specialists (except for psychiatric social workers) are scarce in the system.

What is the situation today? For a description of the situation today, we quote from the report of a national commission established by the 95th Congress, the Select Panel for the Promotion of Child Health (1981, vol. 1, pp. 300-301):

Emotionally disturbed children come from all socioeconomic classes and can be found in a range of settings, including correctional facilities, programs operated by welfare and social service departments, private and public residential treatment centers, and in the community in their own family homes.

The number of children with mental health problems, and the severity of those problems, seems to be increasing. Adolescents, for example, constitute the fastest-growing admissions category in psychiatric hospitals. Suicide and homicide rates among both children and adolescents are increasing at an alarming pace, and growing numbers of young people display learning disabilities, and problems with drug and alcohol abuse.

The dominant paradigm for treatment of emotional disturbance and mental illness in children and youth is psychotherapy in conjunction with medication, generally in a therapeutic milieu. This treatment mode requires the skills of psychiatrists, clinical psychologists, psychiatric social workers, and psychiatric nurses—highly trained specialists whose services are expensive. Further, this type of treatment tends to be prolonged, which adds to the costs. For families with limited resources, the expense may constitute an insurmountable access barrier—especially because insurance coverage for such treatment is often limited.

Equally troubling is the fact that although traditional treatment approaches are highly effective with some individuals, they do not work very well with (1) children and youth from educationally disadvantaged environments where verbal communication is inefficiently used in problem solving; (2) those whose socialization varies sharply from mainstream expectations; and (3) those from families and neighborhoods so disorganized that the normal sources of affection, support, and discipline needed to sustain therapeutic efforts are lacking. Children in these three categories constitute a substantial proportion of the emotionally disturbed group, but their needs are not being met, and some mental health specialists are actually trying to redefine the problem in a way that will exclude such children. A number of residential treatment centers already refuse to accept them, limiting admission to children who are depressed, suicidal, neurotic, psychotic, or suffering from disorders such as ulcerative colitis or anorexia nervosa, believed to have a high psychosomatic component.

An essential first step toward resolving some of these problems is to recognize that children in need of mental health services are found not only in psychiatric treatment but also in pediatric treatment as well as in the schools, the correctional system, the social service system, and the community. Mental health specialists must be prepared to assist emotionally disturbed children wherever they are, regardless of what service system has primary responsibility for their overall care.

Second, the treatment approach itself must be reconceptualized to include more types of intervention. The mental health problems of children are inextricably bound up with the most basic problems of living, and cannot be "treated" apart from the family, neighborhood, school, and community, which are the normal socializing influences of society. Many emotionally disturbed children need common-sense assistance in relating appropriately to peers and adults, and can be helped by mental health counseling which differs from the traditional approach in that it is relatively nonverbal and does not seek psychodynamic or etiologic roots. The emphasis is on current needs and current function, and upon strengthening both the natural support systems around the child and the youngster's ability to make use of those supports.

In this type of mental health intervention, the role of the psychiatrist or other highly skilled professional is to investigate the child's natural setting and devise a treatment program that takes advantage of the skills of parents, siblings, teachers, friends, case workers, counselors, and others to carry out the bulk of the therapy through day-to-day support, protection, discipline, and guidance. This "ecological" approach emphasizes treatment in as near to normal settings as possible, with an eye to restoring or creating an effectively functioning support network for the child and enabling him or her to respond appropriately to it.

If the full array of young people in need of help is to be reached, new institutional arrangements need to be devised. Psychiatric professionals, for example, should assume major consultant and training functions. They will need to identify and help to train various personnel in the community—social workers, nurses, teachers, counselors, and so forth—who can work effectively with emotionally disturbed children. They will also need to provide backup for such "front-line" workers, especially in handling difficult and complex problems.

What follows in this book is a description of a program for disturbed children and youth that represents one way of addressing the problems defined in this Prologue. It is not the only way to solve the problem, and not necessarily the best. But it is different from conventional programs, it has been tested now for two decades, it solves some of the problems laid out by earlier commissions, and it meets most of the criteria set forth by the Select Panel, quoted above. If nothing else, the account of the program may "loosen our construct systems," to quote George Kelly, and encourage experimentation with new ways of working with emotionally disturbed children and youth, who deserve better treatment than they are now getting.

2

Project Re-ED

From Demonstration Project to Nationwide Program

History and Organization

Origins. Project Re-ED ("a project for the reeducation of emotionally disturbed children") had its beginnings in the early 1960s at George Peabody College for Teachers, now one of the schools of Vanderbilt University, in Nashville, Tennessee. There a small group of psychologists and educators—in collaboration with mental health officials of Tennessee and North Carolina, the Southern Regional Education Board, and the National Institute of Mental Health—joined together to invent a new social institution in the service of troubled and troubling children. The institution that emerged was inspired by ideas and events of the mid-century, but its character has been shaped over the years by new research and theory in child development; by economic, demographic, and social changes affecting families and children; and, most of all, by

13

practical experience in working with thousands of disturbed children and adolescents and their families, schools, and communities.

Two ideas informed early efforts to design a new approach to working with disturbed children, and these ideas have remained central to the evolving institution still known as Project Re-ED. First, the putative role of insight in psychotherapy as a source of behavior change and increased personal integration was questioned; instead, insight was regarded as an epiphenomenon, a possible consequence but not a cause of change in behavior (Hobbs, 1962). This theoretical position made congenial the notion that health or happiness or a sense of self-worth must grow out of life as it is lived, not out of life as it is talked about in the context of some fragile theory of personality. The idea challenged the basic assumptions underlying traditional treatment programs for children.

The second idea brought into question the very nature of emotional disturbance in children. It suggested that emotional disturbance is not something in the person, not something a child or adolescent has, not a neurosis or a behavior disorder or anything else that does not express an ongoing transactional process. Emotional disturbance is a symptom not of individual pathology but of a malfunctioning human ecosystem (Rhodes, 1967, 1971, 1972).

Two events of the 1950s heightened awareness of the seriousness of the problem of providing care for emotionally disturbed children and suggested a possible solution to it.

In 1953, the Southern Regional Education Board (1954) sponsored a study of mental health resources in the South. The study made clear that a national mental health program for children could not be based on traditional psychotherapeutic methods because of their high cost, their uncertain effectiveness, and their demand for highly skilled professional people—then as now in short supply. While some emotionally disturbed children at that time received excellent care, most either received no help at all or were placed in institutions for the mentally ill or mentally retarded, under conditions that were (and in some instances remain) unacceptable. What was needed for children and adolescents, the SREB report concluded, was a program with the following features: demonstrable effectiveness, relatively low cost, access to a pool of talented personnel, and the promise of yielding procedures that could be applied in public schools and elsewhere to reduce the incidence of emotional disturbance and mental illness in children.

In 1956, the Joint Commission on Mental Illness and Health sponsored a study of mental health programs for children in Western Europe, from which came a suggestion of a possible new approach to the problem. After World War II, France found itself with thousands of children in desperate need of care, including children orphaned, homeless, handicapped, and emotionally disturbed. Since there were few psychiatrists, no trained clinical psychologists, only a scattering of social workers, and no special-purpose buildings, people concerned with the well-being of children were free to invent new institutional forms, which they did. The main invention was a new professional role, that of *éducateur* (see Chapter Five), for which there was no counterpart in the United States. In Scotland, children who had been too disturbed to adapt to new homes when evacuated during the bombing of London were sent to a special residential treatment center at Nerston, near Glasgow. The center was staffed by people called educational psychologists, who were comparable in training to the French *éducateur*.

The Joint Commission on Mental Illness and Health found these European models worthy of emulation, with appropriate modifications to American culture, as a promising new approach to helping emotionally disturbed children and adolescents. In its report to the Congress, the commission made the following recommendation: "Pilot studies should be undertaken in the development of centers for the reeducation of emotionally disturbed children, using different types of personnel than are customary. . . . The schools would be operated by carefully selected teachers working with consultants from the mental health disciplines" (Joint Commission on Mental Illness and Health, 1961, p. 259).

In March of 1961, the National Institute of Mental Health granted two million dollars to George Peabody College for Teachers and the states of Tennessee and North Carolina to mount an eight-year pilot project to carry out what came to be known as Project Re-ED. Tennessee established Cumberland House Elementary School in Nashville, North Carolina established Wright

School in Durham, and Peabody College set up programs to train staff for the schools and to evaluate the effectiveness of the project.

The proposal to NIMH defined the problem this way:

> The problem of providing for emotionally disturbed children is a critical one requiring bold measures. Society will not continue to tolerate the assignment of disturbed children to detention homes, to hospitals for adults, or to institutions for the mentally deficient. The social need for imaginative planning is acute.
>
> The United States does not have and will not be able to train a sufficient number of social workers, psychiatrists, psychologists, and nurses to staff residential psychiatric facilities for children along traditional lines. It will not be possible in the foreseeable future, with manpower shortage becoming increasingly acute, to solve the problems of the emotionally disturbed child by adhering to limited patterns. The problem must be redefined if it is to be solved.
>
> For effective work with children, the worker's personal attributes weigh more heavily than his professional knowledge and technical skills. Fully adequate programs for the reeducation of emotionally disturbed children can be developed by (1) emphasizing selection of workers; (2) providing condensed, highly specific, functional training; and (3) backstopping the worker's day-by-day activities with a dependable system of consultation by top-level professional personnel.
>
> The model provided by education—with its emphasis on health rather than on illness, on teaching rather than on treatment, on learning rather than on fundamental personality reorganization, on the present and the future rather than on the past, on the operation of the total social system of which the child is a part rather than on intrapsychic processes exclusively—may provide an effective as well as a feasible approach to the problems of a substantial number of emotionally disturbed children.

The manpower projections cited above were drawn from reports of the Joint Commission on Mental Illness and Health (Albee, 1959). While a substantial number of psychiatrists, psychologists, social workers, and psychiatric nurses have been trained under NIMH auspices in the past twenty years, relatively few are prepared to work with children. Psychotherapy is the method of choice for the treatment of emotionally disturbed and mentally ill children in traditional treatment programs. In planning the Re-ED program in early 1960, we deliberately decided not to incorporate psychotherapy as a means for changing the behavior of students, for reasons reflecting a pragmatism that has generally characterized Re-ED. A primary motivation, as urgent today as it was in the beginning, was to help solve the problem of personnel shortages for children's treatment programs. We wanted to draw on a new and abundant source of talented workers, and we wanted to train them (at that time) at a level below the requirements for training in the traditional mental health disciplines. Two conclusions were inescapable: (1) Because of the limited supply of therapists, a program based on psychotherapy could reach only a small fraction of the disturbed children needing help. (2) Such a program would inevitably be expensive because of the heavy investment necessary for the training of therapists. These two conclusions are as valid today as they were twenty years ago. We therefore sought a new approach to working with troubled and troubling children and youth—an approach based on educational, psychological, and ecological strategies. The need for programs like Re-ED is as acute today as it ever was, and such cost-conscious programs become increasingly attractive as budgets for human services shrink.

The Early Re-ED Program. Just what reeducation meant was not at all clear at the outset. Theory was nonexistent, and techniques of child management were borrowed from as many sources as there were people involved in the project. However, the designers of the project did have some clear preferences: for a vocabulary of everyday life over a vocabulary of pathology; for the idiom of education; for cost-effective solutions; for a staff with natural talents for work with children; for using psychiatrists, psychologists, and other mental health specialists as consultants, thus extending the application of their knowledge; for involving families in programs; for making normal socializing agencies work; and for settings attuned to the needs of children for affection, play, adventure, learning, and a sense of the future as possibility. From these modest beginnings has grown a substantial theoretical structure buttressed by tested operating procedures that are used today with high professional skill in a number of programs throughout the country.

Cumberland House and Wright School, the two original Re-ED programs, provided residential care for moderately to severely disturbed children between six and twelve years old. Both schools were located in pleasant residential neighborhoods, and they were intentionally kept small, serving forty and twenty-four children respectively. The children were divided into groups of eight, with three teacher-counselors in charge of each group: one teacher-counselor for the day, one for the evening, and one for working in liaison with the child's family, school, and community (see Chapter Eight). Each school had a principal, three supervisors (for the day, night, and liaison programs), and a support staff for clerical, food service, housekeeping, and maintenance functions. To prevent the alienation that can come with institutionalization and to give child and family an opportunity to learn to live together constructively, the children went home every weekend (a radical idea then!). The average length of stay of children in the program was from four to eight months, at a cost about half that of traditional treatment programs.

The professional staff of the schools was composed largely of teacher-counselors, carefully selected young men and women with a life history of commitment to children and with specialized training at about the master's degree level. Initially under the NIMH grant, Peabody College trained seventy-two teacher-counselors for Re-ED schools and other programs for emotionally disturbed children. The Peabody training program emphasized child development, remedial instruction, behavior management, group-work skills, the use of mental health and educational consultants, and arts, crafts, and outdoor skills, all in the context of early concepts of reeducation. The first class of trainees had internships in ten different schools in Canada, Denmark, England, and Scotland; subsequent classes gained practical experience at Cumberland House. Today teacher-counselors are drawn from M.A.-level training programs in many universities, most frequently in the field of special education. They are then given on-the-job training in Re-ED concepts and techniques.

Psychologists, social workers, special educators, psychiatrists, pediatricians, and other specialists played essential roles as consultants to teacher-counselors, but the teacher-counselors were fully responsible for the successful operation of the program. Placing such heavy responsibility for a mental health program on people trained at the master's degree level was a novel concept at the time the Re-ED schools were started. Since then, the use of "paraprofessionals" in subordinate roles has become commonplace. But teacher-counselors are not paraprofessionals. They are proven professional people, capable of independent responsibility, whose record of success in working with emotionally disturbed children and adolescents compares favorably with the record of any other professional group.

To understand Re-ED, one must appreciate fully the crucial role that consultants have played in the program. Teacher-counselors deal with very disturbed children and with families that are often ineffectual as a consequence of deep-running pathologies. Re-ED has never suggested that such complex problems can be dealt with on an intuitive basis. In training and on the job, teacher-counselors build up an impressive understanding of the psychodynamics of individual development and family life, but they are not expected to have the depth of knowledge that should be at the command of psychologists, psychiatrists, social workers, educators, and other highly trained specialists. A cardinal principle in Re-ED from its inception has been that the knowledge of specialists should be brought to bear in the day-by-day operation of programs as well as in their general design. Re-ED seeks to use mental health and educational specialists efficiently by having them apply their knowledge and understanding through the teacher-counselors. Thus, they work as true consultants, not only increasing the immediate effectiveness of teacher-counselors but also enhancing the teacher-counselor's professional competence on a long-term basis. Mental health and educational specialists are expensive. We think it extravagant to use them routinely in direct work with children when they can contribute more as knowledge sharers, as advisers, and as enablers of other highly talented but less extensively trained people. (See Chapter Five for further discussion of the role of consultants.)

Camping has from the beginning been an important component of Re-ED programs. Inspired by the work of Campbell Loughmiller (1965) in Texas and by the Outward Bound Schools in England, Cumberland House established a camp early and used it extensively, especially in the summer. All the schools today have activities that include camping, backpacking, rock climbing, canoeing, and other challenging outdoor activities attuned to the young in spirit, students and teacher-counselors alike. The author, in the foreword to Loughmiller's most recent book (1979, p. 15), expresses the essence of camping with disturbed children and adolescents: "Camp can simplify things, remove kids from school and other settings where defeat and despair have become their constant companions. Camp can give these children new opportunities to learn about themselves and others, about skills they will need to manage in this world. The woods simply provide a congenial setting for adults and young people to live together, guided by principles of living that have been worked out over thirty years."

The principles themselves seem—indeed are—simple enough: that young people have a tremendous desire to learn and to do well; that their feelings are intrinsically valid and quite as important as their thinking; that destructive and self-defeating behavior must be faced; that young people can help each other sort things out and arrive at good choices; that the world is rich in things to learn; that life is to be savored at each moment; and that decent, caring adults are absolutely essential in the lives of children if those children are to grow up strong in body, quick of mind, generous in spirit.

In the last decade, the Re-ED program, which initially served only children from six to twelve years old, has been extended upward to adolescents and downward to preschoolers. The early age limitation of the program was deliberate, to favor success. The extension of the program upward to the more difficult years of adolescence was accompanied by the same period of painful discovery that characterized the early, pilot-project years of Re-ED. But today the programs for adolescents are run with the assurance that marks the programs for younger children. Services can be extended downward to children from infancy through five years of age by the addition of an early-intervention component after the model of the Regional Intervention Program (Fields, 1975) developed by John Ora at Peabody College. In this imaginative program, which in 1976 won the American Psychiatric Association's Gold Achievement Award ("Gold Award," 1976), mothers are taught to deal effectively with behavioral and developmental disorders of their children. Then, under the supervision of a relatively small professional staff, the mothers teach other mothers the understanding and skills they have mastered. It is now possible to have an educationally oriented treatment program for troubled and troubling children from early childhood through adolescence.

In addition, the population served by Re-ED schools is increasingly composed of quite seriously disturbed children and youth. The schools have always accepted very difficult children, but in the early years there were from time to time and from school to school some exclusions. Now the schools admit essentially all referrals. Early experimental work at Cumberland House preceded routine programming for autistic children in a number of Re-ED programs today. In Pittsburgh, a juvenile court judge said: "Pressley Ridge takes the really tough kids, the ones no agency will accept." In Tennessee, 200 out of 225 children and adolescents in residential care under the auspices of the Department of Mental Health are served by Re-ED programs; all but two traditional treatment wards in state mental hospitals have been closed.

There are now (in 1981) Re-ED programs throughout the country: seven in Tennessee, three in North Carolina, one in South Carolina, two in Kentucky, three in Virginia, two in Pennsylvania, one in Connecticut, one in Ohio, and three in California. California is launching a major effort based on Re-ED principles. Programs have developed under public and private auspices and within mental health, educational, and social services systems. And Re-ED concepts appear to have had considerable influence on programs for disturbed children and youth that retain many traditional features.

Program Strategies

An early paper on reeducation (Hobbs, 1966) described psychological and ecological strategies in helping emotionally disturbed children. The paper summarized the state of the art of reeducation about five years after Project Re-ED got under way. Psychological strategies referred primarily to ways of working with individual children; ecological strategies referred primarily to ways of working with child, family, neighborhood, school, and community. Although education has from the beginning been implicit, defining the fundamental character of the program, we now underscore education as a central strategy because research and experience have indicated the crucial importance of academic competence in the adjustment of children and youth.

Psychological and Educational Strategies. Psychological and educational strategies, or ways of working with individual children, remain about the same today as they were at the outset, in principle. But they have been extended, refined, elaborated on, and reinterpreted in different contexts (for instance, they must be construed differently for children and adolescents). They are described here briefly, by way of an overview, and are then discussed in detail in Chapter Nine.

The principles stress these ideas:

1. Life is to be lived now, not in the past, and lived in the future only as a present challenge.
2. Trust between child and adult is essential, the foundation on which all other principles rest, the glue that holds teaching and learning together, the beginning point for reeducation.
3. Competence makes a difference; children and adolescents should be helped to be good at something, and especially at schoolwork.
4. Time is an ally, working on the side of growth in a period of development when life has a tremendous forward thrust.
5. Self-control can be taught and children and adolescents helped to manage their behavior without the development of psychodynamic insight; and symptoms can and should be controlled by direct address, not necessarily by an uncovering therapy.
6. The cognitive competence of children and adolescents can be considerably enhanced; they can be taught generic skills in the management of their lives as well as strategies for coping with the complex array of demands placed on them by family, school, community, or job; in other words, intelligence can be taught.
7. Feelings should be nurtured, shared spontaneously, controlled when necessary, expressed when too long repressed, and explored with trusted others.
8. The group is very important to young people; it can be a major source of instruction in growing up.
9. Ceremony and ritual give order, stability, and confidence to troubled children and adolescents, whose lives are often in considerable disarray.
10. The body is the armature of the self, the physical self around which the psychological self is constructed.
11. Communities are important for children and youth, but the uses and benefits of community must be experienced to be learned.

12. In growing up, a child should know some joy in each day
     and look forward to some joyous event for the morrow.

If we were to add to the list of principles today, we would
emphasize the importance of ambient expectancies in Re-ED
schools as a source of affirmative, purposeful, and even zestful living by students and staff alike. When programs are going poorly,
expectations of failure generate failure. But when programs are
going well, the schools are so positive, so alive with learning, that
students and staff are caught up in a deeply fulfilling adventure
every day. And the affirmative expectations are contagious; they
often spread to families, to regular schools, and to cooperating social agencies.

Academic Competence. Research evidence today underscores
the importance of academic competence in a child's achievement
of personal integration and social effectiveness, and it contradicts
the long-held assumption that the seriously disturbed child must be
treated for his illness before he can become an effective learner. All
our experience suggests that the causal direction of the relationship
between emotional disturbance and learning competence may be,
for many children, the reverse of that traditionally posited. The
most probable relationship is interactional, so that early and continuing address to both adjustment and learning problems is indicated.
(For a discussion of this and related issues, see Chapter Ten.)

The children and adolescents in Re-ED programs vary in
age, size, intelligence, and symptomatology. However, with an
occasional exception, they share one specific attribute: they are
retarded in academic development. The amount of retardation
varies. Seldom is it less than a year; two to two and a half years is
typical; and, occasionally, the impairment may be complete, with
an older child or adolescent being unable to read, write, or do
arithmetic.

Weinstein's work in evaluating Project Re-ED (see the section on "Research Studies" in Chapter Three) identifies improvement in academic competence as a crucial element in the general
progress made by children at Cumberland House and Wright
School. Furthermore, children in her matched control group who
made progress in academic achievement overcame their emotional
problems with only such help as happened to come their way.

Clinical observation supports her research finding. Time and again, we have seen children and adolescents learn to read and then become more responsive than before to other experiences leading to increased personal integration and social competence. We have also had children and adolescents whom we were unable to teach to read with passable skill; these were the very few children who could accurately be said to have a true learning disability. With limited success in remedying their reading deficit, we also had limited success in enhancing their general adjustment.

Recently reported work by Feuerstein (1979, 1980) supports the position taken here. Over the past twenty-five years, Feuerstein and his associates have worked with children and youth who migrated to Israel from Europe, Asia, and Africa. As a result of their diverse origins, their disrupted lives, their separation from family by war, many of the children and youth were retarded in cognitive development, and some were moderately to profoundly disturbed. Abandoning traditional intelligence tests as essentially useless in classifying the children for purposes of schooling, Feuerstein developed a method for assessing learning potential. He then developed a formal instructional program designed to repair early cognitive deficits and to teach children and youth the basic skills required for thinking and problem solving. When deficits in cognitive functioning were overcome through formal instruction, Feuerstein observed frequently a radical transformation in general adjustment. Traditional psychotherapies are not used in Feuerstein's remedial program.

*Ecological Strategies.** Perhaps the single most important idea to emerge from Project Re-ED is the conceptualization of the problem of the troubled and troubling child or adolescent in ecological terms. The problem is to be discovered not in the child but in the transactions between the child and the people who play crucial roles in his life. Intervention must involve the ecosystem as a whole and cannot be confined to the functioning of the child alone, or even to the child in the family. Thus, traditional modes of individual or family therapy are replaced by an effort to enable

*This section is a modification of a paper originally published in the *American Psychologist* (Hobbs, 1966) and is used here with the permission of the American Psychological Association, which holds the copyright.

an ecosystem, a system that derives its significance from the troubled child, to function in a reasonably satisfactory fashion. The emphasis is on the way members of the ecosystem behave and the way they expect themselves and other members of the ecosystem to behave. In traditional treatment programs for children and youth, the emphasis is on intrapsychic functioning, and psychotherapy is the treatment of choice. While Re-ED is not opposed to psychotherapy (there are many roads to Rome), we find uncongenial many of its assumptions, not to mention its high cost and uncertain effectiveness.

An overcommitment to individual psychotherapy seems to us to stem from an uncritical acceptance of cure as the goal in working with a child or an adolescent, a consequence of defining the problem initially as one of illness. That some troubled children are ill in the usual sense may be accepted, but to define them all as such leads, we think, to a host of unvalidated and unquestioned assumptions; to a preoccupation with the intrapsychic life of the child, with what goes on inside the head; to an easy use of psychotropic drugs without knowledge of their long-term effects on character development; to the extended isolation of children from their families, the presumed source of contagion; to a limitation of professional roles; to the neglect of schools and of schooling; and so on. The preemptive character of a definition and the semantic sets that ensue are major barriers to innovation in working with troubled children.

Definitions and Their Consequences

Definitions have extraordinary consequences. Once a particular verbal commitment has been made in describing a child or an adolescent, there follows inexorably a chain of actions bent to institutional forms, actions that may be less related to the primary data of behavior than to the social arrangements that have been made to care for generic types of children. Thus, it makes a big difference how one talks about a child or an adolescent and what encompassing rubrics one uses to define his status, especially at crucial points when placement decisions are being made about him. If a child or an adolescent is called sick, the appurtenances of illness become his lot. If he is called delinquent, the strategy of correction is brought into play, with intimations of retribution and expectancies of rectitude in future conduct. And so on.

In each decision, the primary data are the behavior of a child and the interactions of the child with significant people, notably parents and teachers. But the same behavior may lead to diverse arrangements for doing something about it. A ten-year-old boy attacks his father with a kitchen knife. What is it: A sickness? A delinquent act? The expression of bad habits? The breakdown of a social system? Some or all of these? What it is called often seems fortuitous, depending on the agency that gets involved; yet the consequences of the naming are of great moment in determining what then happens to the child. All social institutions have their unique metaphorical imperatives derived from their definition of the problem they deal with. But the irony of treatment institutions is that they often reinforce the aberrations they are designed to cure. Thus, correctional institutions become schools for crime (Morris and Hawkins, 1977); institutions for the mentally retarded provide restricted opportunity for learning (Zigler and Bulla, 1977); and mental hospitals require behavior consonant with being mentally ill (Braginsky, Braginsky, and King, 1969). Re-ED schools are no exception; they, too, respond to their own metaphorical imperative.

Definitions evoke institutional forms, and institutional forms tend to validate the definition by evoking appropriate behaviors on the part of the people they serve. In other words, some hospitals tend to make children sick, some correctional institutions tend to make them delinquent, and some institutions for the mentally retarded tend to make people less bright than they might be. The less adequate the institution, the more it is likely to inhibit the operation of constructive forces. It becomes, in the words of Erving Goffman (1961), a "total institution," requiring the staff and inmates alike to conform meticulously, in matters large and small, to the requirements established by definition.

Although definitions have consequences, the outcomes are not always predictable. There are institutions based on an illness model that look like Re-ED schools and that may indeed be more effective than our schools are. And there doubtlessly will be built somewhere a school that will adopt the Re-ED name, and proclaim its philosophy, yet be a mean and dreary place, without heart or zest, where the forms of Re-ED are preserved but its spirit scorned.

Of course, we have our own ways of talking about the problem, and our metaphors are no less preemptive, so that it is all the more important for us to be explicit about definitions. We prefer to say that the children and adolescents we work with have learned bad habits. They have acquired nonadaptive ways of relating to parents and peers and to members of the larger community. They have learned to perceive themselves in limiting or destructive terms and to construe the world as an uncertain, rejecting, and hurtful place. We also recognize that the child or adolescent lives in a real world that often falls short in giving him the affection, support, and guidance he needs. So we deal directly with social realities as well as with private perceptions.

This kind of thinking has led us gradually to a different way of defining our task, a definition of considerable heuristic merit. For want of a more felicitous phrase, we have been calling it an ecological or a systems approach to the problem of working with a troubled child. We assume that the child is an inseparable part of a small social system, of an ecological unit made up of the child or adolescent, his family, his school, his neighborhood and community, and sometimes, with older adolescents, a work place. A social agency is often a part of the picture when a child has been designated emotionally disturbed, and other people—a physician, a clergyman—may be brought in as needed. The system may become "go" as a result of marked improvement in any component (the father stops drinking and goes back to work, a superb teacher becomes available, the child improves dramatically, an adolescent is successfully placed in a group home), or it may work as a result of modest improvement in all components. The goal is to get each member of the system above the minimum behavioral expectations of the other members of the system. The Re-ED school becomes a part of the ecological unit for as brief a period of time as possible, withdrawing when the probability that the system will function appears to exceed the probability that it will not. We used to speak of putting the child back into the system, but we have come to recognize the erroneous assumptions involved; the child defines the system, and all we can do is withdraw from it at a propitious moment.

Once we abandoned cure as a goal and defined our problem as doing what we could to make a small social system work in a reasonably satisfactory manner, there ensued a number of opera-

tional patterns that contrast sharply with the practices of many
existing residential treatment centers for children and youth.

For one thing, parents are no longer viewed as sources of
contagion but as responsible collaborators in making the system
work. Parents are involved in discussion groups and are helped to
get assistance from mental health centers. They actively participate in the ongoing program of the school, and in many ways they
assume responsibility for reestablishing the child or adolescent in
his own home, school, and community as quickly as possible. As
mentioned earlier, to keep families and children belonging to each
other, to avoid estrangement that can come from prolonged separation, and to give the child and his parents and brothers and sisters an opportunity to learn new and more effective ways of living
together, the children go home on weekends. Visitors ask "Aren't
your Mondays awful?" They are, indeed, but we cherish their disorder as a source of new instruction; we try to keep in mind that
our goal is not to run a tranquil school but to return the child as
quickly as possible to his own home and regular school, or, for
some older adolescents, to independent living and a job.

As a rule, adolescents also go home each weekend, but
sometimes modifications have to be made because a home may
not exist or family ties may have been completely severed. When
this occurs, the adolescent may go to a group home or some other
setting to which he will transfer on graduation. Occasionally, arrangements must be made for the child or adolescent to remain in
the Re-ED program over a weekend, but we regard this as a non-
productive solution to the problem—an easy way out, to be avoided
if at all possible.

The ecological model requires new strategies to involve
home, neighborhood, school, agency, court, employer, and community representatives in a contract with us to help a child or an
adolescent. It requires new patterns for the deployment of a new
kind of mental health worker: the liaison teacher-counselor. The
liaison teacher-counselor is responsible for maintaining communication with the child's home and with his regular school, again to
prevent alienation and to arrange optimum conditions for the
child's early return to a regular classroom. Re-ED programs have
been successful in part because of the heavy investment made in
the functioning of ecosystems; approximately one third of the
professional personnel in a program devote themselves full time to

enabling ecosystems to function sufficiently well to sustain a child or adolescent in his growth to maturity. The topic of ecological strategies in the process of reeducation is examined in detail in Chapter Seven, and the liaison function is discussed in Chapter Eight.

Prevention. By the time a child or an adolescent gets to a Re-ED school, his difficulties have been long in the making, and the disturbance in the ecological system has become profound and persistent. It seems manifest that we must find some way to identify children in trouble early, before things have reached a point where they must be removed from their homes and regular schools. Removal from home and school should truly be a measure of last resort, a step indicated not by the degree of the child's disturbance as usually defined but by the inability of the child's family and his school to sustain him any longer. For all its attractive features, Project Re-ED is a contemporary expression of the clinical tradition. While advances in the treatment of mental health problems after they occur are surely to be appreciated, substantial progress in the elimination or reduction of human afflictions requires the development of adequate preventive measures. It soon became evident that many of the kinds of children who were brought into a Re-ED school could, in fact, be helped very substantially by liaison teacher-counselors without being removed from their homes and regular schools. One of the cardinal principles of the Re-ED idea is that the troubled child should be removed the least possible distance from his home, school, and community—in time, in geographical space, and in the psychological texture of the experience provided. Logically extended, this concept leads to keeping children out of Re-ED schools whenever possible and seeking, instead, to work with the child and significant other people in his life in their natural settings. Special residential placement would thus be indicated only when a child needs intensive, around-the-clock reeducation or when the family is so fragile as to be unable to sustain him. There have been a number of successful applications of this idea (see, for instance, the discussion of the Central Kentucky Program in Chapter Three).

Project Re-ED is most likely to pay off when the concepts developed in it are applied to the public schools. The Ford Foundation has recently published a booklet in which an effort is made to identify principles and procedures in special education that may be applicable to regular classrooms, especially in schools serving children who are difficult to teach. (Hobbs and others, 1979.) Time and time again, perceptive observers of Re-ED schools have remarked: "You know, what you are doing here is nothing more than good education." At first, this observation annoyed us mildly, for we needed to feel that we were developing something quite extraordinary, as, in fact, we were. But, in truth, each of the principles manifested in Re-ED schools is a principle that has been recognized at one time or another as simple, straightforward, effective pedagogy. If a public school system were to embrace these concepts enthusiastically and intelligently, and with sufficient resources to do the job, a model for the transformation of public education could emerge.

We think it important to emphasize that Project Re-ED is a creation of the American mental health system, which, at its best, is a broadly interdisciplinary effort that is secure enough to draw ideas from any source—provided that source can be demonstrated to help troubled people. Re-ED was originally funded by the National Institute of Mental Health as a demonstration project, and the two prototype schools were developed by state departments of mental health. While Re-ED schools may appropriately be developed under other auspices (such as education, corrections, or social services), it is important that Re-ED schools continue to find a hospitable environment in mental health programs and yet not be unduly burdened by requirements and procedures that are antithetical to the Re-ED philosophy. The major benefits from the Re-ED demonstration project will come from the application of the principles of reeducation to a wide array of situations where children and adolescents are having persistent difficulties learning to cope with their worlds: in psychiatric hospitals, in therapeutic camping programs, in day treatment programs, in small group homes, in correctional institutions, in special classes in public schools, in "mainstreamed" classrooms, and in schools serving concentrations of children who do not respond to conventional methods of teaching.

Re-ED, A Becoming Institution

The continuing vitality of the Re-ED program springs, in part at least, from an understanding that every person involved in the program is responsible for inventing what Re-ED should become. The challenge is intellectually and personally demanding; it appeals especially to people who are attracted to the role of teacher-counselor. In a preface to a special issue of the journal *Behavior Disorders,* devoted entirely to the Re-ED School of Kentucky in Louisville (which itself exemplifies inventiveness in its highly imaginative program), the following elaboration of the idea appears:

One of the important early ideas in Project Re-ED was that there should be no orthodoxy, no fixed explanations, no set ways of doing things, no dogma. There are, to be sure, certain pervasive concepts that inform Re-ED programs. They are evident over time in the programs at Cumberland House and Wright School, and they are evident across the programs of the fifteen or twenty schools that proclaim themselves to be in the Re-ED tradition. The concepts are not so much fixed principles as they are working hypotheses about how to help disturbed children and their families. The result is a distinctive character or style in Re-ED schools everywhere. But the concepts have never existed as restraints on discovery, on invention. Should they become so, Re-ED will die or, worse still, will linger on simply because it is hard to do away with organizations, no matter how outmoded they may be. What excites me most about Re-ED is the people who have committed themselves to it, their rational and intuitive grasp of a loosely defined set of principles, and their ingenuity in inventing each day what the Re-ED program should become. A colleagueship of discovery provides the intellectual foundation for what we are doing together, and will do in the future [Hobbs, 1978, p. 65].

3

What Re-ED Programs
Are Like

*Organization, Facilities,
Staffing, Costs, Effectiveness,
and Model Programs*

Frank M. Hewitt, long-time pro-
fessor of special education at the University of California at Los
Angeles, recently visited several Re-ED schools in preparation for
directing a training program for teacher-counselors at UCLA, as a
part of California's commitment to make a substantial investment
in Re-ED programs for troubled and troubling children and youth.
He concluded his report with the following observations:

Two vivid impressions . . . cut across the various settings I
visited. The first was the enthusiasm and commitment of the staff
members. It would be hard to imagine any program which could
fail with such dedication. They were young (mid to late twenties),
articulate, bonded together, curious, creative, opinionated, proud,
and professional. Most importantly, they were believers, they took
everything they did very seriously. I was really impressed by their
attention to detail and their constant efforts to convey to their

charges that everything going on was important and for a purpose. This sense of purpose and meaningfulness is in marked contrast to the confusion, vagueness, and coldness I have often felt in other residential climates. This seriousness and sense of purpose was contagious and readily discernible among the children and adolescents themselves.

One thing that concerned me was whether they were simply extra-special young people who could make any program work or whether or not there was something in the reeducation process itself that activated the many fine qualities which I saw. I believe the reeducation process had a great deal to do with their enthusiasm and dedication. There was an expectancy that their efforts would be effective in helping the children and as this visibly occurred it was self-perpetuating. I believe the special qualities that are needed to make staff effective with disturbed children and youths are much more apt to surface in programs based on a process of reeducation than in programs based on more traditional or dynamic approaches.

Finally, I was impressed by something I have seldom if ever encountered when meeting and visiting with emotionally disturbed individuals in treatment settings—*pride*. Not all but many of the individuals I saw appeared proud of the group to which they belonged, proud of the group's accomplishments and proud of their own accomplishments. In many ways, they were reflecting the pride the staff exuded. I would hope that one of our major concerns in developing and implementing the reeducation process in California would be to create such a sense of pride within all of our children and staff [Hewitt, 1981, pp. 12-13].

In this chapter, we describe the organization and operation of Re-ED programs, including sponsorship, staffing patterns, the grouping of children and adolescents, administrative organization, the role of consultants, physical facilities, costs, and funding. We translate these generalized statements about organization and operation into specific realities by describing several actual programs. All share common characteristics reflecting the Re-ED philosophy, yet each is unique in its particular realization. We have stressed from the beginning the importance of keeping Re-ED a becoming institution, responsive to new ideas from research, scholarship, and practice; to restraints and opportunities always present in particular situations; and, more than anything else, to the creative surmise, the inventive spirit, of teacher-counselors and others who make Re-ED programs work.

Organization and Operation

Sponsorship. The two original Re-ED schools, Cumberland House and Wright School, were established under mental health auspices. The commissioners of mental health of Tennessee and North Carolina took the initiative to get the programs under way, each personally investing much time in the effort. While the NIMH grant paid initial operating costs, each state had to provide a facility as well as numerous services for which there was no federal reimbursement. The states further had to agree to assume the total cost of the schools on an incremental basis during the last three years of the eight-year demonstration period. It is a tribute to the vision and courage of the two commissioners that they were willing to commit themselves and their departments to an experimental project that broke sharply with tradition, especially in giving such heavy responsibility for the treatment of disturbed children to a new and untried professional group not identified with the traditional mental health professions.

While the majority of Re-ED programs today are sponsored by mental health authorities, there is actually quite a wide variety of patterns of sponsorship. Wright School continues its direct connection with the Division of Mental Health and Mental Retardation Services, North Carolina Department of Human Resources. Cumberland House, on the other hand, has become a part of a regional mental health institute, which is under the state mental health commissioner. Other patterns of sponsorship include a philanthropic foundation, a county psychiatric hospital, a consortium of public schools, a university, a mental health authority working under contract to the public schools, and a private for-profit agency.

As mentioned earlier, we think it important for Re-ED schools to continue to find a place in mental health programs. Re-ED has now demonstrated its ability to help seriously disturbed children and youth; it can no longer be regarded as a make-do substitute for a traditional treatment program. However, sponsorship of a Re-ED program by a mental health authority requires a measure of understanding and appreciation of Re-ED principles that has not always been forthcoming. The discrepancy in philosophy between traditional treatment programs and the psychological, educational, and ecological strategies described in this book has led, in some specific instances, to debilitating conflicts between medical program directors and the Re-ED staff. But it has also been demonstrated in a number of settings (including medical settings) over a long period of time that such conflict is not necessary.

Staffing. As Re-ED programs have evolved in different settings to meet varying requirements, a number of staffing patterns have emerged. Nearly all programs, however, are built on the basic three-person Re-ED team, consisting of a day teacher-counselor, a night teacher-counselor, and a liaison teacher-counselor.

Teacher-counselors may be assisted by aides of various kinds; for example, it is a common practice to use an undergraduate or a graduate student to stay with a group of children at night. The work of the teacher-counselor may be supplemented by full- or part-time teachers with specialties in such fields as arts and crafts, outdoor education, physical education, music, and remedial reading. Most programs today have an educational diagnostician, because of the great importance of school learning in the process of reeducation. A common pattern is for an experienced teacher-counselor to move into a supervisory or an administrative position.

It is difficult to prescribe a precise ratio between teacher-counselors (in all roles) and children served, because program requirements vary greatly. However, the ratio used in Tennessee for budget planning for its several programs can serve as a general guide. This ratio is approximately 1 to 2 or 2.5, including supervisors. In addition to teacher-counselors, special teachers, and aides, programs require secretaries, janitors, cooks, maintenance personnel, and others, the types and numbers depending on the circumstances of particular programs. Often these people play important roles in work with children. Some Re-ED programs now have assigned to them physicians and nurses (not as consultants but as staff members) to meet requirements of Medicaid and other third-party payment sources.

Grouping of Children. Most Re-ED programs group children by sex and roughly by age. For example, a program with elementary school children will have a young group, a middle group, and an older group. Generally, older children are divided by sex, but younger boys and girls often are grouped together. One program has adopted family groupings, with groups composed of both boys and girls and a range of ages from six to thirteen. This arrangement is very popular in Europe and works very well in the program that has tried it here. Older children take leadership positions, younger children emulate and learn from them, and the presence of girls changes the quality of group relationships.

In programs for adolescents, various patterns of organization are found. Boys and girls occupy separate quarters at night, often in different wings of a building or at different camp sites. In the day program, boys and girls may be grouped together, or programs can be built around individual schedules, with groups being defined by the requirements of particular activities. In general, programs that stress group process in the management of behavior emphasize the importance of maintaining group integrity; programs that stress individual behavior management naturally put less emphasis on the maintenance of groups. Camping programs, following patterns established by Campbell Loughmiller, normally keep groups intact day and night.

Some programs adhere to the original plan of having eight children or adolescents to a group. Other programs, however, in the interest of economy, have increased group size to nine or ten. There is no research to establish the relative effectiveness of groups of eight or ten. Our clinical judgment continues to support the smaller size, and confidence in that judgment grows rapidly when groups of even larger sizes, eleven or twelve children, are put together.

Other than age and sex and sometimes academic achievement, the composition of groups is almost entirely an intuitive exercise. A group composed entirely of acting-out children is difficult to manage; a group composed entirely of withdrawn children or dull children is not much fun.

Administrative Organization. As would be expected, Re-ED programs are organized in many different ways (see Figure 1). A common pattern consists of a principal or director (we prefer the title "principal" for its educational connotations); three supervisors, one for the day program, one for the night program, and one for the liaison program; and five groups of eight children, each with a day teacher-counselor, a night teacher-counselor, and a liaison teacher-counselor.

Figure 1. Organization of Re-ED Programs *

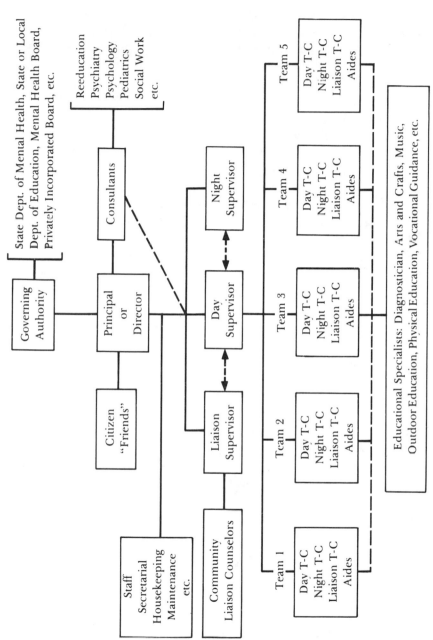

* Hypothetical organizational chart for a Re-ED School serving forty or fifty children or adolescents on a five-day-a-week, residential basis. (T-C stands for "teacher-counselor.")

Some programs have eliminated general supervisory positions and specialty teachers. With saved resources, a senior teacher-counselor is assigned to each group in a supervisory role; thus, there are four teacher-counselors to each group. This arrangement increases group autonomy and decreases the exchange of ideas among groups, an arrangement that obviously has both advantages and disadvantages. Programs that operate only during the day may have a single teacher-counselor in charge of a group, assisted by aides of various kinds and supplementary teachers. Year-round camping programs, which are often in isolated areas, normally have two teacher-counselors on duty throughout the day and night, with blocks of time off duty every couple of weeks.

Two fundamental principles should govern Re-ED programs. First, the administrative structure should be relatively flat, in order to give maximum flexibility and authority to the teacher-counselors working directly with the children; teacher-counselors generally are very competent people and need freedom, with guidance, to exercise their talents to the fullest. Second, all professional positions on the staff of a Re-ED program should be open to any teacher-counselor who has personal qualifications for the job; there should be an open career ladder for teacher-counselors. Especially to be avoided is the absentee directorship held by a person from another discipline.

Consultants. Consultants play a vital role in Re-ED programs; in fact, teacher-counselors cannot do a responsible job without the assistance of experts. The disciplines most frequently represented on consulting staffs are psychiatry, psychology, special education, pediatrics, and social work, but occasional use is made of special consultants from such fields as nutrition, orthopedics, ophthalmology, speech and hearing, research design, recreation, and outdoor life. Consultants seldom work directly with the children, except perhaps for purposes of an examination, but rather work through the teacher-counselors. One of the important concepts in Project Re-ED is that it provides a means of multiplying the effectiveness of highly trained professional people. But the role of consultant is an exacting one, and few professional people are skilled in performing it. Nor does the effective use of consultants come about without a special appreciation of their role on the part of teacher-counselors and with a development of skill in using their counsel. The Re-ED consultant's role is described in detail in Chapter Five.

Physical Facilities. We have an idealized image of setting and facilities for a model Re-ED program. No such facility exists, to the best of our knowledge. The ideal setting for a program for children and adolescents would be five or six acres (or more, if possible) near an urban center where there are residences, schools, churches, and shops. A location five to ten minutes from a university and medical school is desirable, so that staff members can continue their education, students can be employed as aides, and consultants can be readily accessible. Since children go home on weekends and families are engaged in the day-by-day program, access by public transportation, both local and for the geographical area served, is highly desirable. Traditional treatment programs for children and adolescents often are located for the convenience of the professional staff or to conform to patterns of treatment for adults or for people who have physical illnesses; we think this unfortunate and undesirable. Space—to roam in, to run and play and organize games, to pursue a private purpose—is far more important in the lives of children than most adults realize. Cramped quarters and settings almost inevitably mean cramped programs.

As for physical facilities, the ideal design might include the following:

- Five cottages, each with single and double bedrooms; a large living room; a dining area with facilities for light cooking; a conference room for pow-wows and quiet work; a room for athletic equipment, outdoor gear, and heavy clothes; a laundry; and a small efficiency apartment for a night aide.
- A school building, separate from residences, including five or more classrooms; a library; a nature study center; offices; examining rooms for the educational diagnostician; conference rooms; individual instruction cubicles; and areas for various arts and crafts.
- An administrative unit, which may be a part of the school, with offices for principal, supervisors, and liaison teacher-counselors; conference rooms for the whole staff as well as for individual work with consultants and family members; a staff dining room and kitchen (which may supply most meals to children's units); a supply room; and a business office. "Visiting areas" sometimes seen in hospitals and institutions should be avoided; par-

ents and children should be able to visit wherever it is con-
venient to them and others.
•   A small infirmary, with perhaps one or two beds and an office
    for a nurse or consulting physician, with a secure place for
    medications.
•   A gymnasium, a highly valued facility, can stand apart or be
    connected with the school.
•   Play space.

Actually, Re-ED programs have been successfully operated
in a variety of physical settings and facilities, some of which ap-
proximate the ideal and some that miss it by far. Among the patterns are a converted orphanage on spacious grounds; a former
tuberculosis hospital situated in splendid privacy on a mountaintop but near the central city; a former nurses' residence several
stories high but successfully converted to Re-ED purposes; a newly built school adjunct to a psychiatric hospital, but separately
situated and private; a rambling set of old and new buildings that
have been comfortably adapted to multiple purposes in a Re-ED
tradition; and even a program housed in a traditional ward in the
heart of a medical complex in the center of a large city. One arrangement involves a central office and school, with children living in residences scattered over a community. In general, we would
prefer that architecture and settings reflect the spirit of the program, enhancing its purposes; but we know now that Re-ED concepts can thrive under adverse physical circumstances if the program is understood and supported by the people in the organization
within which the Re-ED program functions.

Costs. It is difficult to provide precise information on what
Re-ED programs cost, and comparison of Re-ED programs with
traditional programs treating similar kinds of children must be
made with extreme caution. We are reasonably confident that Re-
ED will cost about a fourth less than conventional programs having an active treatment component, but we advance this estimate
tentatively and would welcome additional systematic studies of
costs of Re-ED schools and other kinds of treatment programs.

A number of circumstances account for this uncertainty in
a matter of crucial importance to program directors as well as to
policy makers.

Costing and accounting procedures vary greatly from state

to state and from program to program. For example, one program may be operating in facilities that have been paid for, another in facilities whose costs are being amortized by an upward adjustment in daily fees. Some programs have new facilities and low maintenance costs; other programs have old buildings requiring constant and expensive repairs.

Overhead costs are handled in many different ways. In some programs, they are absorbed by the sponsoring agency or treated apart from actual operating costs. When overhead is assessed against program budgets, the rates may vary substantially; a range of from 5 percent to 25 percent would not be unusual. In one state, overhead costs (which include, for example, the salary of the mental health commissioner) are divided among all units in the system in amounts proportional to their expenditures, although their actual overhead costs vary greatly.

The Tennessee experience has demonstrated that the use of Medicaid monies to pay for Re-ED programs may be a false economy. Meeting hospital accreditation requirements, many of which are irrelevant to Re-ED programming, substantially increases costs. The scheme has served only to transfer the tax burden from the state to the federal government and has saved the taxpayer no money at all.

There are, of course, great differences between the costs of residential programs and day-treatment programs and mixtures of the two. It is often difficult to unravel these differences from summary financial reports.

Per diem costs are calculated in different ways, often to the disadvantage of Re-ED programs. Re-ED normally requires children to go home every weekend as an integral part of its treatment philosophy and, specifically, as a way of speeding their discharge. The staff remain responsible and on call during weekends. But hospital-derived accounting practices count only "occupied beds" in computing per diem costs. In many Re-ED programs, a week's costs will be divided by five instead of by seven, thus inflating their stated per diem cost by about 28 percent. Programs that keep children seven days a week often have skeleton staffs over weekends and little or no treatment activity, a practice that reduces per diem costs and probably therapeutic effectiveness as well.

But per diem costs are a highly unsatisfactory index of the

meaningful cost of treatment programs. What one needs to know is how much it costs to return a child to her own home, school, and community. Thus, length of stay is a highly important variable. From the outset, Re-ED has insisted that most treatment programs keep children much too long, which may alienate them from their natural settings and may even exacerbate their adjustment difficulties. Re-ED has consistently tried to keep length of stay as short as possible. Not only does this policy cost less but it is therapeutically sound. Mental health officials should be held accountable for every day a child is retained in an institution beyond the time necessary to help her function with reasonable effectiveness in a normal environment.

Finally, there needs to be an observation on kinds of children served. Increasingly, conventional mental health treatment centers are differentiating between children with "mental health problems" and children with "correctional problems," thus relieving the conventional centers of responsibility for youngsters who are extremely difficult to manage. Re-ED programs are committed to accepting essentially all referrals, except a few who require continuing medical treatment or who have to be incarcerated to protect themselves and others.

The cost calculations done by one state provide a direct comparison between projected costs of a conventional residential treatment program and a Re-ED residential program. For planning purposes, the state calculated comparative costs using identical accounting protocols. This was in 1979. The total annual operating cost of treatment for twenty-four children was estimated to be $694,114 for a conventional program and $538,012 for a Re-ED program. The costs of the conventional program were thus estimated to be about 30 percent more than the costs of a Re-ED program to serve the same number and kind of children. It is important to emphasize that these data are based on projections and not on actual operating experience.

Recognizing the central importance of costs in policy decisions, and despairing of being able to provide reliable dollar estimates generalizable to different settings, we decided finally to ask the directors of four well-established Re-ED programs to write a brief letter in which they would attempt to explain to an intelligent layman the costs of their programs. The results are summarized below.

Cumberland House School. During the 1980 fiscal year the residential capacity was forty children. There were thirty-one full-time program staff, four part-time consultant/resource staff, and four clerical staff implementing the program. The total direct costs were $661,260.51. Indirect administrative support services were about 20 percent, including depreciation on buildings and equipment, or $132,252. During that fiscal year the total student days equalled 7,992. The per diem cost (calculated on a five-day-a-week basis) was about $99. The average length of stay was eight calendar months or 176 reeducation days). The total cost of returning a child to home and community was approximately $17,500.

Wright School. The school operates a residential and educational program at its main facility and also a day treatment program in a public school in the Braggtown community. In May 1981, the cost per day (based on five days a week) for the Wright School Campus program was $102 and for the Braggtown program, $34. Because Wright School has maintained a rigorous policy of enrolling children for the shortest time possible in its residential program, the cost of returning a child to home and community averaged approximately $8,160.

Pressley Ridge School. At Pressley Ridge, cost of total operation is contingent upon three variables: overhead, direct cost, and occupancy. Overhead refers to cost charged to operating units for such services as executive and supervisory salaries, insurance, legal fees, and utilities. Direct cost would be teacher-counselor salaries and benefits, plus supplies for a specific operating unit such as a classroom. Percentage of occupancy defines unit cost because overhead and direct cost remain relatively constant regardless of the number of youngsters in attendance in a classroom. The higher the utilization, the lower the unit cost.

For the month of March 1981 at Pressley Ridge, the per diem cost of a day school youngster in a classroom with 100 percent occupancy for the entire year was $23.43; the per diem cost in a classroom with 74 percent occupancy was $41.15. In addition to the cost of the day school program, the residential cost would be added for a youngster needing twenty-four-hour care. The per diem cost of residential service in a living unit with 81 percent utilization would be $44.64. Thus, the total costs for a child would be approximately $85 per day.

At the Wilderness School (camp) the cost reflects both the educational and residential service. In March 1981, the average per diem cost for the total program with 89 percent occupancy was $52.77.

The Positive Education Program (PEP). This public-school-affiliated day program served 354 children in the 1981 fiscal year. The cost per day was $35 per child; the cost per year was $7,630. These figures include the camping program, parent training (group and individual), and liaison services and cover all occupancy and operating costs. In addition to teacher-counselors, the staff includes a full-time psychologist at each of eight centers, supervision and administrative support, training and dissemination activities, and a newly initiated research component.

But in spite of all that has been said above, in spite of all the caveats, we feel compelled to share more than our frustrations and to come up with a dollar figure for the guidance of officials who must make policy decisions regarding Re-ED programs. We believe that a Re-ED program serving forty seriously disturbed children and youth on a residential basis can be operated at approximately $80 to $100 a day (in 1980 dollars), a figure that includes an overhead charge of 20 percent and calculates the rate on a five-day-a-week basis. It should cost approximately $12,000 to $15,000 to return a child to his own home, school, and community functioning at such a level that the probability of continued successful adjustment will exceed by a reasonable amount the probability of further failure. This estimate does not include children brought into a Re-ED program for diagnostic purposes only, nor does it include those few children who may have to spend much of their lives in protective care.

Because of the high per diem costs of residential care, day programs are becoming increasingly popular in providing reeducation services to children and families. Daycare programs following the Re-ED model cost from $35 to $50 a day. However, children tend to stay longer in day programs than in residential programs, and data are not yet available on the relative costs of the two types of programs in returning a child to her regular school. But it is clear that day programs are working effectively with very disturbed and difficult children. It seems likely that, in the future, the decision to admit a child to a residential program will depend more on the adequacy of her family and other support systems than on the severity of her mental health problems as conventionally defined.

Research Studies

It is rare for treatment programs for emotionally disturbed children ever to evaluate their effectiveness or to study systematically the processes involved in the treatment effort. Re-ED grew up in a university setting, and initial program plans stated the expectation that research would be a routine and continuing aspect of the program. Unfortunately, this aspiration has not been fully realized, due variously to lack of funds, to the separation of some programs from university centers, and to the heavy demands of programming for an increasingly severely disturbed population of children and adolescents. In this section, we will briefly describe several studies that focus either on outcomes or on the process of reeducation.

Weinstein (1974, pp. 205-208) evaluated the effectiveness of the program at Cumberland House in a study that has been widely praised as an outstanding example of research on treatment outcomes. Her design called for three groups: a group of emotionally disturbed children who participated in the Cumberland House program, a group of children judged by school principals and others to be equally disturbed who received such assistance as might have been provided by school psychologists and others, and a group of children judged to be "normal." There were approximately 120 children in each group. Only white males were included, and the children in the three groups were quite similar in age, intelligence quotients, socioeconomic status, and other demographic characteristics. Extensive information was gathered on the children prior to the enrollment of the Cumberland House group, immediately after discharge, six months after discharge, and eighteen months after discharge. Similar data were obtained for the two comparison groups. The information was provided by the children themselves, by their parents and regular school teachers, by classroom peers, by teacher-counselors and liaison teacher-counselors at Cumberland House, and, for Cumberland House children, by referring agency staff if the agency had maintained contact with the child and his or her family. The emotionally disturbed children, both at Cumberland House and in regular schools, were further divided into children with and without academic problems and, for those with problems, children who made significant academic progress and those who did not. The data on all three groups are extensive. Below are excerpts from Weinstein's concluding chapter:

The data which have been presented clearly indicate that the Re-ED intervention leads to positive changes in the attitudes, behavior, and learning of disturbed children.

After Re-ED, the Re-ED children, as compared with the untreated children, had more positive self-concepts and greater conviction that they could affect their situations by their behavior. They perceived their parents as more unified in the standards and expectations they held for them. Children initially characterized by Re-ED staff as acting out, for whom impulsivity had been a problem, learned to control their motor behavior when necessary and to spend more time evaluating choices before making them.

After Re-ED, the Re-ED children were seen by their teachers as better adjusted behaviorally than the untreated children. This was true both for children with less severe behavior problems prior to Re-ED and for children with more severe problems. Within the range of children it serves, the effectiveness of a Re-ED school does not seem to be affected by severity of initial behavior problems.

Re-ED children in need of academic remediation prior to Re-ED scored closer to grade norms on standardized achievement tests after Re-ED than did comparable children in the untreated group, and more of the Re-ED than untreated children learned at the normal, expected, month-for-month rate after Re-ED, arresting the increasing retardation in academic achievement over time characteristic of disturbed children.

At discharge, Re-ED staff rated 94 percent of the children as moderately or greatly improved; referring agency workers rated 88 percent of the children about whom they had information at discharge as moderately or greatly improved. Eighteen months after the children returned home from Re-ED, their mothers reported a good deal of improvement or great improvement in comparison with pre-Re-ED adjustment for 73 percent of the Re-ED children; the figure for ratings by fathers was 81 percent. . . .

In contrast to ratings from adults, which indicated that Re-ED helped the children come closer to adults' expectations, sociometric data from classmates indicated no improvement as a result of Re-ED in relationships with peers. This represents an important gap in program effectiveness, one well worth additional effort and experiment. . . .

In all, the data suggest important improvement in the Re-ED children, especially in basic attitudes and in school behavior and learning. Not all of the children improved, however, or became problem-free, and after Re-ED, the Re-ED children, though doing better than the untreated children, continued to differ on most measures from a group of children defined by their schools as not having behavior problems and from a group of randomly selected children. . . .

The literature on "spontaneous improvement" (see, for example, Levitt, 1957) suggests that most disturbed children improve without special intervention. This was not found to be true for the untreated group in this study. . . . Only when the untreated child had no academic deficits associated with his behavior problems was he likely to improve behaviorally over time. . . .

The data which have been presented suggest that there are children for whom present school programs cannot adequately provide, and for whom the Re-ED program is particularly well suited. . . . They also encourage study of the Re-ED program to see what may profitably be adapted for special education programs in the schools themselves—and for education programs for normal children.

At least a half-dozen other Re-ED programs have evaluation studies under way. In general, these studies are impaired by sundry difficulties, including the lack of adequate control or comparison groups, small sample sizes, the use of a variety of measures so that cross-program comparisons are not feasible, loss of contact with students after graduation, and the absence of long-term follow-up for program graduates.

At Wright School, Gregory, Sechinger, and Anderson (1971) compiled extensive information on all children who had attended Wright School since 1964. Questionnaires mailed to parents and teachers provided information regarding children's social and academic behavior following discharge. The children themselves were also interviewed about their current academic and behavioral performances and their impressions of Wright School. Overall findings were consistent with the results of Weinstein's study that Wright School had a positive impact on the lives of these children. Since 1971, data have been gathered on Wright School children prior to their enrollment, immediately after their discharge, and several months after their discharge. These data are awaiting systematic analysis.

At Pressley Ridge, Hawkins and others (1978) have designed a formal evaluation program for both the day school in Pittsburgh and the Wilderness Camping program in the mountains of southern Pennsylvania. Voluminous data are available at Pressley Ridge and will be analyzed in due season. The most important findings to date include the following: (1) Average academic achievement growth, as measured by the Peabody Individual Achievement Test, is almost two months per month in the program. (2) Significant behavioral gains, as measured by the Jesness Behavior Checklist, result from the youth residence in the program. (3) A high level of youth satisfaction with the program is demonstrated. (4) A successful discharge rate of over 65 percent is established for all youth entering the program, regardless of length of stay.

The academic data demonstrate that the program improves the youths' rate of learning over their previous base rate. This represents an average 19 percent increase in their rate of learning. A summary of the annual evaluation reports indicates the following major benefits of the program for the child: learning to function in a community, ego building, developing positive relationships, improving self-concepts, modifying inappropriate behavior, and improving school adjustment. It is interesting to note that at Pressley Ridge, the students attending the Wilderness Camping Program, which does not provide formal academic instruction, made gains on academic achievement tests comparable to those made by children in the day program in Pittsburgh.

At the children's program of Pickens Hospital in Greenville, South Carolina, Short, Kirby, and Wilson (1975) reported that, of the 149 students who had graduated from the program between 1969 and 1974, "82 percent were functioning satisfactorily in their home and school relationships, 18 percent were unable to function satisfactorily in the regular classroom, home, or both" (p. 272). In a subsequent study, Short, Kirby, and Wilson (1977) sent questionnaires to parents of 132 program graduates. The parents reported that their children were attending the program primarily because of disruptive behavior in the classroom and in the home and low academic achievement (p. 695). Although nearly three fourths of the parents reported having some problems with their children after graduation, 92 percent rated the program as having been very much or some help. The children continued to have a number of school-related problems, but about 90 percent were enrolled in school.

The Positive Education Program (PEP) in Cleveland, a day program only, has an internal evaluation program that has focused on four program objectives. The average length of stay for students accepted back in their own school setting is presently under fourteen months. Specific behavior problems were reduced by 50 percent for each successive ninety-day period of treatment. Sixty-five percent of the students improved their problem behaviors by at least 50 percent and maintained this improvement after 90 to 270 days in treatment. After discharge, 80 percent of the students continued to be enrolled in regular schools and attended school at least 80 percent of the time. Of the students accepted back into their home school settings, 12 percent made at least two months' academic gain for each month in treatment; 20 percent made at least 1.5 months' gain; and 41 percent made at least a one-month gain for each month of treatment. The PEP program is in the process of developing an extensive data system that will permit routine analyses, such as the above, to be made in the future.

While outcome studies are as important as they are neglected, it is equally important to do research on the process of reeducation. LaPaglia (1978) has done an extensive analysis of the extent to which the staff at Crockett Academy perform the duties required by their self-defined procedures. Great variability in the achievement of these objectives was evident. Also at Crockett Academy, McGurk (1979) studied the effects of differential knowledge of results on self-monitoring effectiveness of thirteen male and six female adolescents. She concluded that the provision of quantitative knowledge of results, plus graphing of results, may increase self-monitoring effectiveness for clinically relevant target behavior items. Such studies, although extraordinarily difficult to do, are of great value in illuminating the process of reeducation.

As noted, the Regional Intervention Program (RIP) had its origins apart from Re-ED in the work of John Ora at Peabody College. However, its educational orientation and other highly creative features (such as having parents serve as staff) have led to its development as a downward extension of Re-ED, as in the Positive Education Program in Cleveland. Strain and others (in press) report long-term (three to nine years out of treatment) data on forty children who were clients of the Regional Intervention Program between 1969 to 1978:

>   As three-, four-, and five-year-olds, these youngsters exhibited severe and prolonged tantrums, continual opposition to adults' requests and commands, and physical aggression toward parents. The results from school and home-based assessments showed that (1) commands, demands, or requests made by parents were likely to be followed by former clients' compliance; (2) former clients' social interactions in the home were overwhelmingly positive, and their nonsocial behavior was by and large appropriate; (3) parent behavior in the home setting was consistent with the child-management skills taught many years ago; (4) there were no differences between the compliant, on task, social interaction, and appropriate/inappropriate nonsocial behaviors of former clients and randomly selected class peers; (5) there were no differences in teachers' commands, negative feedback, positive social reenforcement, and repeated commands that were directed toward either former clients or randomly selected class peers; (6) both teachers' and parents' ratings of former clients on the Modified Walker Problem Behavior Checklist were highly correlated; (7) there were no differences in teachers' ratings of former clients and class peers; and (8) of all the demographic variables studied, only age treatment began and family intactness were related to current levels of behavior.

Descriptions of Re-ED Programs

Any general description of Re-ED programs inevitably fails to convey the continuities that run through all programs as well as the unique characteristics of particular programs. These can best be appreciated by an examination of descriptions of a number of actual programs. Below are descriptions of about a dozen programs (described as they were in 1980), starting with Cumberland House and Wright School and extending to programs recently established. The descriptions are not intended to be complete but rather to emphasize some distinctive features of the programs described, in order for the reader to get some sense of the range, diversity, and inventiveness represented in Re-ED. Unfortunately, because of space restrictions, a number of excellent programs have had to be omitted entirely. However, they are often represented in vignettes in other chapters of the book.

Cumberland House School
Nashville, Tennessee

Cumberland House Elementary School is the first of the Re-ED schools, the prototype. The first children were admitted in November of 1962. The site, selected after a long search, expressed the character the founders sought for the school. Originally, there were four acres in a residential neighborhood, six minutes from Peabody College. There were two residences on the property: one large, made of brick, and not without a certain elegance; the other more modest, a white frame and clapboard house. Minimum remodeling provided for twenty-four children in a home-like atmosphere. The grounds were perfect for a Re-ED school: spacious, with stately trees, large grassy areas for play, flowering shrubs, and perennial flowers. A low fence and hedge were added to protect children from running into the street. Later, residences for five groups of children were skillfully designed to blend into the setting, and small classroom buildings were added. As the school grew, additional property was bought and modest residences thereon used for special purposes.

In 1977, the program for adolescents at Central State Hospital was moved to new buildings on Cumberland House grounds and named Crockett Academy. The construction required marred the spacious beauty of the setting and reduced somewhat its fitness for children, but the facility nonetheless remains attractive and functional.

For its first six years of operation, Cumberland House had the use of a splendid camp, owned by Peabody College. Only thirty minutes distant, it provided excellent facilities plus a large area for primitive camping and a river just the right size for swimming and canoeing. When this property became unavailable, a friend of the school gave money to purchase another site somewhat farther from the school. The new site is rugged, beautiful, ideal for primitive camping.

Cumberland House from the beginning has been a part of the program of the Tennessee Department of Mental Health and Mental Retardation, which deserves much credit for its early adoption of the Re-ED idea and for its continued strong support of the program over the years. Cumberland House at this writing is an integral part of the Middle Tennessee Mental Health Institute, which provides comprehensive mental health services to twenty-six counties. While most children come from Nashville, the largest city, the most distant family is within two hours by car or bus. Children are referred through mental health agencies.

Cumberland House and Crockett Academy serve essentially all emotionally disturbed children in Middle Tennessee who require residential care. The population could be described as moderately to severely disturbed. The staff of Cumberland House consists of a principal, three supervisors (one for the day program, one for the night program, and one for the liaison program), five liaison teacher-counselors, ten teacher-counselors, three special instructors (in arts and crafts, physical education, and outdoor life), and five night aides (called resident associate teacher-counselors), a registered nurse, three academic resource specialists, two teacher aides, and one liaison teacher-counselor for community work. There are five teams (the Leprechauns, Bobcats, Mustangs, Pathfinders, and Keystones), each composed of a day teacher-counselor, a night teacher-counselor, a liaison teacher-counselor, and a resident associate teacher-counselor. There are four consultants: a pediatrician, a child psychologist, a clinical psychologist, and a psychological examiner.

Cumberland House normally serves forty children, boys and girls, divided into five groups of eight children each. The age range is from about six to thirteen. As is usual, there are four or five times as many boys as girls. The proportion of black children is somewhat higher than in the general population. The children are regarded as normal in intelligence but often have depressed test scores; the average IQ score for one recent year was 85. The average length of stay in 1978 was eight and a half months.

The daily program at Cumberland House exhibits characteristics of Re-ED schools everywhere and may thus be thought of as eclectic, without a dominating theme other than a creative commitment to individual children, their families and schools, and to making ecosystems work reasonably well. Prior to admission, the child and parents visit the school, and the program is explained to them. In nearly all instances, a careful assessment of academic strengths and weaknesses is made to guide the instructional program. The children stay together in their groups most of the time, attending classes, going on excursions, camping, and caring for their quarters—where, incidentally, all meals are served in a family-like arrangement.

The morning hours are devoted to academic work, often remedial in character, and always highly individualized. Intensive classroom work may be relieved by a period in arts and crafts or in vigorous play. Academic progress is carefully charted, since many of the children have severe school deficiencies, and reasonable competence in school is essential to a child's general adjustment and to his acceptance by peers and parents. Children set goals for themselves and monitor their progress in both academic work and conduct.

Toward the afternoon, the program changes to a less structured time and a great variety of activities, limited only by the resourcefulness of the group: sports, a field trip to a science museum, swimming, skating, constructing a greenhouse, rehabilitating a houseboat, working in clay, making a newspaper, buying supplies for a trip, visiting a sick friend, watching television. The evening program is unstructured, too, but tends to be somewhat more serious than the afternoon. Some schoolwork may be done, and there is an occasional evening trip to a movie, a restaurant, or a friend's house. Coming events, such as a camping or canoeing trip, often are planned.

Frequently during the day and evening, a group will come together for a "pow-wow," either to solve some immediate problem faced by the group (behavior that disrupts the group, for example) or to plan for the day or week. Before bedtime, groups meet to review the day, with emphasis usually on the positive events, the things that felt good. The counselors and then the children themselves think up things to do to brighten the day for others. From time to time, an evening will be devoted to a graduation ceremony or to other rituals that get established in the groups.

While the daily work with children proceeds with remarkable inventiveness and variety, the liaison teacher-counselor works with equal imagination and purposefulness with everyone of importance in the life space of the child, with the objective of restoring the ecosystem to a reasonably adequate level of functioning and teaching some person in the system, usually the mother or father, to manage the situation without professional help. The children go home every weekend, and this provides an opportunity for everyone to try out new ways of behaving and to identify problems yet to be worked on. The liaison teacher-counselor is in frequent touch with parents and regular school teachers by phone or visit, and often talks with parents when they pick up their child on Friday or return her on Sunday afternoon. Occasional group meetings with parents provide an opportunity to discuss ways to help a child behave and to make an ecosystem work.

The program at Cumberland House changes with the seasons. When summer comes, outdoor activities—camping, backpacking, rock climbing, spelunking, canoeing, and other adventures—increase. All the Tennessee Re-ED schools are favorably located for children to be able to do the kinds of things children should do to grow strong, bright, competent, and confident, and to acquire respect for self and concern for others.

The rich variety of activities at Cumberland House keeps children's interest and motivation high, contributes to group morale and cohesiveness, and supplies many different sources of practical learning. Not immediately evident, however, is the fact that activities provide an array of settings for carrying out a highly specific and individualized program for each child. The staff at Cumberland House, team members and consultants, develop a comprehensive plan of care, which specifies objectives for all members of the ecosystem, including the child and the Cumberland House staff. The teacher-counselors work out a program plan for each child in the group. The plans incorporate information and suggestions from parents, teachers, community workers, consultants, supervisors, and from the child. Long- and short-range objectives, precisely defined, are agreed on and recorded, and procedures for achieving the objectives are discussed in sufficient detail to guide expected interactions and to support intervention as occasion presents unanticipated opportunity. Consistency among team members and others in the child's ecological system is thereby encouraged. Goals and procedures are reviewed frequently, informally every day and formally at weekly and monthly meetings, and revised to accommodate both experience and a child's growth. Thus, what may appear to a casual visitor to be a lot of interesting but not purposive activity is in fact a varied and engaging context for accomplishing agreed-upon objectives in agreed-upon ways. Re-education is a highly disciplined endeavor that occurs in what often seems to be a casual, venturesome, and even joyous context.

The distinctive characteristics of Cumberland House lie not in comparison with other Re-ED schools, for Cumberland House itself has set the norm, but in contrast to traditional treatment centers for emotionally disturbed children. Knowledgeable visitors find the contrast striking, and visitors acquainted with Cumberland House over the years are invariably impressed by the vitality of its program, the talent and commitment of the staff, the responsiveness of the children, and the engagement in the program of parents, teachers, and community representatives. Perhaps the most remarkable thing about Cumberland House is that it has replicated itself many times and preserved its own distinctive character while serving as the main source of people for leadership positions in other schools. Its continuity of character is all the more remarkable in view of the turnover in staff. Most professional staff members work a few years and move on, after having instructed new staff members. There is a small cadre of people with long service. The principal of the school, a member of the first class of teacher-counselors in 1961, has been on the staff since the beginning. But staff stability clearly cannot account for the essential integrity of the program over the years; the primary source of continuity is the power and effectiveness of concepts that inform the program. Ways of working that succeed in helping children and families while bringing deep satisfaction to the workers are hard to abandon.

The most striking difference between Cumberland House today and in its early years is the professionalism of the staff. In the early days, teacher-counselors were asked to work with emotionally disturbed children in an unorthodox program of unproved effectiveness, guided only by a few concepts, and they were required to invent techniques to make the program work. Naturally, anxiety levels were high; staff conflicts were occasionally intense; and good humor and easy camaraderie, though much in evidence, were hard to maintain. Today, for the most part, the staff work with a quiet assurance springing from confidence in tested methods in a program no longer radical, with quite sufficient challenge provided by the difficult children and families they work with. Each member of the professional staff retains a high sense of responsibility for making the program work, and for inventing what it is to become.

Wright School
Durham, North Carolina*

Wright School is located in suburban Durham, North Carolina, on a twenty-two-acre site of what was originally known as Wright Refuge, a privately operated facility for abandoned and neglected youngsters. Situated near the center of the state and within the Research Triangle with its nearby Duke University, the University of North Carolina at Chapel Hill, and North Carolina Central University, Wright School began operation in January 1963 as the second Re-ED demonstration school.

The Wright Refuge Board, which retains ownership of the campus and buildings, provided a forty-nine-year lease of the facility to the state of North Carolina with the understanding that the Department of Mental Health would operate a short-term residential program for emotionally disturbed children of elementary school age. The board continues to take an active interest in the program, even though the governing body remains the Commission for Mental Health and Mental Retardation Services within the North Carolina Department of Human Resources.

Considerable distress was experienced within the program when, in 1965, an inadequately informed state legislature cut off operating funds. In 1966, however, state appropriations were restored; and the Wright School program rebounded from the crisis

*This description was written by Richard S. Yell, director of Wright School.

with renewed vigor, which was nurtured by its many friends and supporters. Key to that restoration and its credibility through the years has been the unfailing advocacy on the part of both the members of the Wright Refuge Board and the program's clinical consultants from Duke University.

Unlike its sister school, Cumberland House School in Nashville, Tennessee, Wright School was "born and raised" in a geopolitical setting whose approach to child mental health had been shaped and sanctioned by comparatively large numbers of child psychiatrists—something on the order of a 20-to-1 comparison in numbers of practicing child psychiatrists between North Carolina and Tennessee. The first director of Wright School was, himself, a graduate in social work who had been tutored by those from the traditional ranks of mental health and child welfare. Also in the early days, the Wright School teams had consistent weekly access to a consultant group consisting of two child psychiatrists and two clinical psychologists. In retrospect, therefore, it is not surprising that the Wright School, although holding tenaciously to both the original and the emerging principles of Re-ED, began to be seen by some Re-ED behavioral enthusiasts as "different." "Different" may even have been too mild a term, for, not unlike within a religious movement, Wright School was described by those not fully comprehending the process of environmental adaptation as having strayed from the fold to embrace false prophets, such as Freud. Yet, as with many movements that embody a distinct belief system, the kernel of the seed remained intact and unspoiled, even perhaps strengthened through diversity and adversity.

The wedding of more traditional mental health and public health principles with those of education and social welfare is today evident in the several facets of the Wright School program. Still the teacher-counselor team (day, night, liaison) constitutes the heart of the program. The governing principles of short-term intervention, "here and now" programming, competency-based curriculum, liaison work with the child's ecosystem, building on strengths while strengthening weaknesses, and expectations for normalcy remain paramount.

The Wright School program currently includes the original short-term residential units; a community-based, multiagency children's program; and a statewide training operation, which emphasizes Re-ED training, consultation, and program development.

The residential units consist of three groups of nine children each, eight of whom are considered either regular admissions (four-month length of stay) or diagnostic/intervention admissions (four- to six-week length of stay); the ninth youngster in each group is either a day student (eight- to ten-week length of stay) or a respite/emergency admission (four-week length of stay). The children are grouped in family fashion, younger and older, boys and girls, in each group. Other arrangements, such as homogeneous groupings by sex and age, have occurred in the past and seem to matter little to the students or to program effectiveness.

Admission to the residential program has more commonly been through the public school system; however, in recent years, with the coming of child-rights legislation, the referrals have by state policy been mandated to flow through local mental health center programs across the state. Even though at first concerned at the prospect of children and families not having direct access to Wright School, we have found that, by and large, this new process works well and has several advantages. For one, the liaison outreach efforts have the added potential of extension via numerous child workers throughout the state's network of mental health centers. Other advantages include community assessment of the child's needs, the likelihood that existing local resources will be exhausted or at least explored before a referral is made, and the addition of this important "back-home" mental health agency to the support network for the child and the parents during and after the Wright School experience.

Since 1972, Wright School, in collaboration with the Durham County Schools and Durham Community Mental Health Center, has operated a home/school/community program known as the Braggtown Community Project. Located within the Braggtown Sixth Grade Center School, approximately two blocks from the Wright School campus, the project mirrors the residential staffing by use of specially trained classroom, liaison, and neighborhood teacher-counselors. Approximately forty behavior- and learning-disordered youngsters are provided a specialized short-term (six to ten weeks) classroom experience in the setting each year, with accompanying provision of parent work and regular classroom teacher training/consultation services.

In recent years, the project's activities have come to be regarded by the mental health center as part of its day-treatment services, by the school system as an element of its special education services, and by Wright School as part of its training/demonstration services. Each agency contributes staff and resources; each feels a share of ownership. Dissemination efforts of the project were expanded statewide in 1975 with the addition of Title VI-B funds through the North Carolina Department of Public Instruction, Division for Exceptional Children. Since that time, the Braggtown Project has existed as a component of a larger array of local education/mental health services, known as the North Durham County Re-Education Project.

Several years ago, the North Carolina Division of Mental

Health and Mental Retardation Services determined that an effort should be made to capture the uniqueness of the Re-ED philosophy and approach and make it readily available to local mental health and other appropriate child-oriented agencies and schools across the state. Ultimately, this determination made possible the creation of a training and consultation component in the Wright School program.

A small group of training specialists, most of them former teacher-counselors in the program, comprise the training team. These trainers are available on request to provide consultation and in-service training, to conduct mini-courses, and to create other learning experiences for some 1,200 persons each year who work with children and youth in mental health programs, group homes, public schools, and other child-oriented programs across the state. A field-based master's program in collaboration with the University at Chapel Hill provides both preservice and continuing education opportunities for teachers of the emotionally disturbed as well.

Generally, all the training provided relates directly to the Re-ED philosophy and to the skills and technology that Wright School finds effective in its residential and day treatment settings. Specific topics that make up many of the training sessions include Behavior Management, School/Community Liaison, Characteristics of Emotionally Disturbed Youngsters, Life Space Interviewing, Team Building, Affective Education/Values Clarification, and Group Work with Children.

Each of the program elements described above, with the exception of the Braggtown Project, is housed on the Wright School campus. The residential units, classrooms, and administrative offices are located within the one-story brick, ranch-style main building. Training offices, library, and conference rooms are housed in two adjoining modular units. The spacious grounds allow for children's play areas, a roller rink, a basketball court, and a wooded area for outdoor school and camping activities during the warmer seasons.

Pine Breeze Center
Chattanooga, Tennessee

Pine Breeze Center has the distinction of being the first Re-ED program for adolescents. Established in 1969, it is an integral part of Moccasin Bend Mental Health Institute, and it serves teenagers, both boys and girls, from thirty-four counties of southeastern Tennessee. The students, many of whom are seriously disturbed, were formerly treated on psychiatric wards at the Moccasin Bend Hospital.

In many ways, Pine Breeze provides an ideal setting for a

Re-ED program. It occupies a former tuberculosis hospital on a mountaintop about fifteen minutes from downtown Chattanooga. Though old and expensive to maintain, the buildings are attractive and commodious, providing ample space for dormitories, classrooms, recreation rooms, an arts and crafts center, shops of various kinds, and administrative offices. Pine Breeze provides privacy and a sense of identity in a beautiful spot that is immediately accessible to the many opportunities adolescents need to establish themselves in a community. It also provides abundant opportunities for adventure in rugged mountains, white-water rivers, lakes, and caves, and for exploring cultures reaching from pioneer days to the atomic energy era.

Pine Breeze serves about thirty students in a five-day-a-week residential program. A few of the students who have no homes to go to on weekends are cared for at the Moccasin Bend Hospital. The students are organized in groups of ten, and the pattern of staffing is similar to that of other Re-ED programs, except that there is an overlay of essentially nonfunctional mental health personnel required by Title XX funding. Some of the specialists find a consultant's role uncomfortable, and they may attempt to impose traditional treatment methods on a program based on sharply conflicting premises. A number of the mental health specialists, however, have appreciated the opportunity to enhance their effectiveness by sharing their technical knowledge and their rich clinical experience with the teacher-counselors.

In getting its program under way a dozen years ago, the Pine Breeze staff faced the same perplexing problems that had made the first two years at Cumberland House and Wright School so difficult. How can one transform the general concepts of reeducation into day-by-day operations with adolescent boys and girls? Adolescents are more intelligent, larger, stronger, more mobile, more set in nonadaptive ways of coping, more exposed to drugs and alcohol, more mature physiologically, more involved in achieving self-identity, and more in transition from a dependent status at home to an independent status in the community than are younger children, with whom Re-ED ideas were first tested.

After several years of perplexing and painful experimentation with various ways of working with adolescents in the idiom of education, and with the support of sympathetic mental health specialists, the staff worked out routines that maintain orderly and mutually helpful behavior, thus making it possible to get on with the serious tasks of learning. (See the description of the Pine Breeze Motivational System in Chapter Eleven.)

Major objectives of the Pine Breeze Program are to help students get their behavior under control; acquire basic academic skills essential for survival in our complex society; and begin to develop vocational skills—such as finding a job, working effectively with colleagues and supervisors, and acquiring knowledge for advancement. The Pine Breeze staff have been extraordinarily imaginative in teaching basic skills, as well as advanced knowledge, in an array of carefully planned learning enterprises. The arts and crafts center, with youngsters busily at work, is a joy to behold. The staff fully appreciate the importance of the transitional status of adolescents and have developed an imaginative "community re-entry program," which includes skills necessary for return to family or to an independent home as well as a number of different job skills. Numerous other programs have been built around some engaging and adventuresome enterprise designed explicitly to develop knowledge and skill necessary for independent living and self-support. Included among these are an annual canoe trip down Tennessee's Buffalo River; a trip to Washington and to the Gulf Coast; numerous backpacking, rock-climbing, and spelunking expeditions; various shop experiences; and the well-known and continuing project to record old-time mountain music (see the description in Chapter Ten).

A number of students arrive at Pine Breeze on psychotropic medication. As in other Re-ED programs, a steady effort is made to get them off medication, so that they can present themselves without distortion to other people important in their lives and learn to manage their own behavior in constructive ways. For some older students, who have long been on tranquilizers, the new regime is sometimes hard to maintain. They manage extraordinarily well in structured situations, including field trips, but may regress when they have to cope for an extended period with the stress-producing situations at home or in regular schools. Thus, several students at Pine Breeze are repeat admissions and may as adults have to live in sheltered arrangements.

The Pine Breeze staff pioneered in a number of programming inventions that have been adopted by a half-dozen Re-ED schools serving adolescents.

Pressley Ridge School*
Pittsburgh, Pennsylvania

Pressley Ridge School, located in Pittsburgh, Pennsylvania, is the result of the merger in 1969 of two of the city's oldest child-care institutions: the Protestant Home for Children (1832) and the Pittsburgh and Allegheny Home for the Friendless (1861). Pressley Ridge provides an extensive array of services to youngsters classi-

*This description was written by Clark Luster, executive director of Pressley Ridge School.

fied as seriously emotionally disturbed, behavior disordered, status offenders, delinquent, dependent, and autistic. The settings in which services are currently delivered include a day school (130 students), a residential center (48 students), and a year-round Wilderness School (50 residents) in Ohiopyle, Pennsylvania. (The Wilderness School is described in Chapter Eleven.)

The day school and the residential center are located on eighteen acres near downtown Pittsburgh on the site of Fort McKeever, a Civil War fort. Bound on one side by a huge city park and on the other by a cemetery, the location offers a sense of isolation as well as integration within a large urban environment. Four cottages were the first Pressley Ridge buildings on the site. These well-worn but adequate facilities provide shelter for the residential youngsters and staff.

In 1969, construction was completed on the administration and day school facility. This modern two-story brick and glass building houses ten classrooms, as well as observation rooms, offices, conference and dining space, a mini-gym, and adequate facilities for all support services.

The wilderness camp is located in a rugged mountainous area in Pennsylvania, near the West Virginia border. The program is based on the work of Campbell Loughmiller (1965, 1979), who also influenced the design of the early programs at Cumberland House and Wright School. The camp serves boys thirteen to eighteen years old. They are organized in groups of ten, with two teacher-counselors on duty at all times. There is no formal academic work at the camp, but teaching is continuous in relation to such activities as building, extending, and repairing shelters; preparing some meals; developing camp sites; planning and carrying out expeditions; and engaging in nature study. Group process is used with considerable skill to help boys get their behavior under control. The boys, many of whom have no homes or inadequate homes or are ready to establish themselves independently, do not go home on weekends.

The influence of Project Re-ED on Pressley Ridge School is the result of a search by the school's board of trustees during the 1960s for a model of service delivery for disturbed children that was cost-effective, practical, and replicable. After several meetings with consultants from Peabody College, the board decided to adopt Re-ED principles as a foundation for Pressley Ridge programs. The first two directors of the Re-ED model day school program were trained in Project Re-ED, and the current director of Pressley Ridge is a former Re-ED teacher-counselor.

Pressley Ridge School is a nonprofit, private childcare agency licensed by the Pennsylvania Department of Education and Department of Public Welfare as an educational and residential facility. The agency is incorporated under the laws of the common-wealth of Pennsylvania and is directed by a twenty-five member board of trustees. Trustees serve voluntarily and are elected to renewable three-year terms of office. Board members are typically leaders in business, law, the professions, and community service in Pittsburgh.

The chief executive officer and overall program director is the executive director. The executive director is responsible to the board of trustees for the operation of the total agency. Reporting to the executive director is a director of day and residential programs, who is responsible for the staff and youngsters in the school.

The total agency budget for fiscal year 1979-80 was approximately $2 million. There are 110 professional and support personnel. The fiscal philosophy of the agency is that all ongoing programs are self-supporting from public funds. Program deficits, research, and special projects are funded through investment income and fund-raising efforts. Capital expenditures are the responsibility of the board of trustees and are accomplished by general community, corporate, foundation, and board of trustee solicitation.

Many of the principles generated in the early days of Project Re-ED form the foundation on which service is provided today. Critical therapeutic decisions are still the domain of front-line staff. Teacher-counselors are central to change in the lives of troubled children and their troubled families residing in troubled environments. The traditional professions of psychology, psychiatry, pediatrics, nursing, and social work are viewed as key but supportive services to the hands-on interaction of teacher-counselor and youngsters.

Programs are designed to enhance social and academic skills. Although feelings and internal events are important and are nurtured, observable behaviors—both strengths and weaknesses—are the prime targets of address. Remediation of severe academic deficits, to reverse the failure spiral in which most of our youngsters find themselves, is still of prime importance. The teaching of appropriate social skills and coping behaviors completes the framework in which treatment takes place.

Two movements within the field have radically changed the populations of the programs over the last ten years: first, the de-institutionalization of children and the shift of services from large, impersonal, expensive, and questionably successful hospitals to smaller community-based group homes and treatment centers; and, second, the growth of a wide range of special education and mental health services in public schools and community mental health centers. Because of these two phenomena, the problems addressed in the residential setting have become more severe. Representative data of residential youth characteristics show an average age of fifteen years (range of six to eighteen), 57 percent white and 43 percent black and other minorities. Thirty-nine percent of referrals are from juvenile courts, 44 percent from county child welfare agencies, and 17 percent from mental health and other referral agencies. Average IQ is 89.4 (range 64 to 122). The youth are an average of two years (2.06) below grade level. Sixteen percent of the youngsters have no home, 47 percent are from one-parent families, and 37 percent have two parents in the home. All day students are referred by local school districts through the Intermediate Unit and are approved by the State Department of Education. In short, the population of youngsters appears to be getting older, tougher, and larger.

The geographical area served by Pressley Ridge School is primarily the Pittsburgh and Allegheny County area. Approximately 15 percent of the youngsters are referred from outlying counties. On rare occasions, a youngster is accepted from the eastern part of Pennsylvania or out of state.

A treatment planning committee—consisting of the director of day and residential programs, the staff psychologist, a consulting psychiatrist, and other staff, depending on the specific case—decides on the appropriateness of all referrals and on the question of which of the three basic programs (day, residential, or Wilderness School) would be most beneficial. At this juncture, numerous external events (evaluations, releases, approvals) must be completed by a host of bureaucracies in order for the youngster to arrive at school with suitcase in hand.

The youngster is assigned to a group or classroom based on age, sex, level of academic functioning, social maturity, space availability, and such intangibles as how ready a group of youngsters is to accept a new member. The school day starts at 9:00 A.M. Day students are bused in by local districts in taxi or van. Residential students eat breakfast in the central dining hall and move into the classroom at 9:00 A.M.

The typical day for a group of eleven to fourteen youngsters includes a full component of individual and group academic tasks aimed at preparation of the youngsters for return to a public school regular or special class program. Each child must, by law, have an individualized education plan. Pressley Ridge has long been strong in the diagnostic-academic programming arena. Individualized instruction is developed through extensive diagnostic assessment within two weeks of admission. The morning and early afternoon hours are spent in homogeneous groupings with academic tasks. The mid and late afternoon activity is a succession of interest-area mini-courses; youngsters attend two to three of the forty-five-minute sessions. At 2:30, all youngsters return to their classrooms for a wrap-up evaluation and planning session before the end of school. At 3:00 P.M., day students return home by taxi and van while the residential groups return to the cottages for the beginning of the evening program. Spread throughout the daily school schedule are support services in which all youngsters are involved. Art, physical education, speech and language, and prevocational training are an integral part of the total curriculum.

The behavior management systems used in the program vary from group to group, depending on the age of the youngsters, the degree and types of behavior disorders exhibited, and the makeup and experience of the teacher-counselor team. Most management systems are behaviorally oriented group process (see Chapter Nine). The autistic and communication skills classrooms use direct, teacher-imposed behavior management systems, while the adolescent cottages and classrooms are more likely to use a group evaluation, goal-oriented, or level-of-performance system. One of the early strengths of the Re-ED model and certainly one of the precepts of the Pressley Ridge treatment philosophy is an eclectic "If it works, use it" approach. Evaluation is empirically based. Data are an integral part of program decision making and serve as a feedback loop for program change.

Regional Intervention Program
Nashville, Tennessee*

The Regional Intervention Program for Preschoolers and Parents (RIP), in Nashville, Tennessee, provides comprehensive services to parents and their behaviorally disordered and/or developmentally delayed preschool children. The program focuses on teaching parents what to do at home in order to manage their child's behavior in a positive way and to teach their child essential skills. Unlike traditional therapeutic models, in which a clinician works alone with the child, at RIP parents themselves work with the child. In fact, with the exception of five resource staff members, RIP's entire program is run by the parents it serves.

The program, which began in June 1969, was funded initially by a biomedical grant from George Peabody College. From September 1969 through June 1971, the Bureau of Education for the Handicapped provided funding in cooperation with the college and the Junior League of Nashville. Presently RIP is one of three regional children and youth programs administered by the Middle Tennessee Mental Health Institute, State of Tennessee Department

*This description was written by Matthew A. Timm, director, and Peggy Hester, staff member, of the Regional Intervention Program. See also Timm and Rule, 1981.

of Mental Health and Mental Retardation. As noted elsewhere, the Regional Intervention Program did not grow out of Project Re-ED but developed independently at Peabody College under a grant from the Kennedy Center to John Ora and a group of investigators interested in behavior modification. The parallel evolution of Re-ED and of RIP revealed many similarities in philosophy and programming, although RIP retains unique features. Both are educational models, are highly compatible, and have been successfully integrated in several settings.

RIP provides services for families of handicapped preschool children under five years of age. The children served have a variety of presenting problems, ranging from mild behavior disorders to severe developmental delays. There is no charge to the families for services at RIP. Instead, one parent, usually the mother, agrees to participate five mornings or three evenings a week, working with her child and with other families during the active treatment period. In addition, the parent makes a commitment to the program to provide services and training for new families for six months after work with her child is complete. RIP has no waiting list, so families can begin the program as soon as it is convenient for them. The average length of stay for a child is eight months.

The five resource members of the staff are responsible for assessing the status of children, devising individualized programming for remediation, designing data collection systems, and writing and evaluating goals and objectives. They rely on clinical and technological input from consultants in the disciplines of child psychiatry, clinical psychology, special education, pediatrics, and speech pathology.

RIP is organized into several training modules, each with specific responsibilities. The modules include the intake module, the generalization training module, the individual tutoring module, the preschool module, the family module, and the liaison module. Each module is coordinated by a parent and is staffed by additional parents, who provide systematic training for each new parent who enters the program.

Each component of the program runs on a management-by-objectives system. After objectives are established for each child and family, activities and progress toward meeting those objectives are measured daily through data collection on behavioral activity by the parent at home and by other parents at RIP. Child and family objectives are evaluated every six weeks by resource staff. Comprehensive objectives for the program as a whole and for each module are evaluated annually.

When a new family comes to the program, a parent in the intake module familiarizes family members with its format and procedures. If the family members decide to enter the program, they are assigned to a major treatment module or modules—generalization training and/or individual tutoring.

Families in which the parents cannot manage the behavior of their child enter the generalization training module. Many of these children have frequent tantrums and other behaviors that are disruptive enough to cause severe problems for them and for other family members. Through the use of differential reinforcement techniques, parents are taught to manage their child's behavior in this module. The module has a simulated three-room apartment—where RIP staff can observe the interaction of the parent and the child. For twenty minutes each day, the parent and child engage in a highly structured play session and are observed by RIP parents, who systematically record parent and child behaviors. Based on the daily data and feedback after each session, the parent is taught new ways to handle the child's behavior, both in the session and at home.

The individual tutoring module serves children with developmental delays or language disorders. Programming is individualized for each child. Concurrent with the child's programming, the parent is trained in methods designed to develop functional speech and other adaptive behaviors in her child. Parents teach their own children in a one-to-one situation. As soon as a parent learns how to work with her child at RIP, she begins to run sessions at home on a daily basis.

One of RIP's positive qualities is that parents are able to draw strength from each other. One parent said, "I get the strength I need to go home and cope with my child from RIP—from other parents and from helping other children. The most valuable thing that I have gotten is the techniques that I have learned, the behavior controls that I've learned. I feel confident enough about myself doing them that I feel like things will work out. I can then give of myself—pass my strength on to others—so that they can make it through difficult times."

While the training modules concern the child's relation to a parent, the classrooms focus on the ways children behave with each other, and are designed to bring a child's behavior under management while he is in a social setting. Well-trained parents work with children to develop appropriate physical coordination, communication, and social relationships. The objective of this module is to shape a child's social, prelanguage, and language behaviors as quickly as possible in order to prepare him for an appropriate placement in the community.

The liaison module is the last stop for children in RIP. It continues to provide services to a family once all treatment objectives have been met and the parents have completed their six-month commitment to the program. It is staffed by well-trained, experienced parents who have accepted responsibility for finding suitable community placement for children ready to leave RIP. These parents work with community agencies and other parents to secure appropriate educational or daycare placements for children who have completed their stay at the program; conduct systematic follow-up contacts with families following their departure from the program; and assist parents, teachers, and daycare staff in the development and implementation of intervention programs for subsequent problems that former RIP children may experience in the community or at home. Follow-up visits to the home or school are made by RIP parents every six months, so the program is aware of the family's progress or problems.

Traditionally, human service programs have lacked systematic procedures of evaluation and accountability to the clients served. The Regional Intervention Program developed and instituted one system of program evaluation to demonstrate its efficiency and effectiveness. The evaluation provides (1) an economic justification in terms of costs and benefits, (2) an assessment of the degree to which the organization and its clients meet defined objectives, (3) a summary of the progress of children based on objective data, and (4) a judgment of program effectiveness made by a committee of consumers. Collectively, these four components provide a means of continuous and reliable feedback to the funding source and to the clients served.

Since September 1974, the RIP Advisory Committee, Inc., and the Children and Youth Program of Middle Tennessee Mental Health Institute have sponsored training and replication efforts aimed at expanding RIP services to new community sites. To date, the RIP Expansion Project has developed a total of twelve replication sites in Tennessee, Ohio, Connecticut, and Ontario, Canada.

Positive Education Program
*Cleveland, Ohio**

The Positive Education Program (PEP) was created in the early 1970s as a result of the work of a task force formed through a regional special education planning and development project. With the support of the Cuyahoga County Community Mental Health and Retardation Board, two multidisciplinary groups of fourteen professionals were provided the opportunity to attend training institutes sponsored by the Tennessee Reeducation Pro-

*This description was written by Rico Pallotta and Lee Maxwell. Dr. Pallotta is director of the Positive Education Program.

gram. Subsequently, a proposal to establish the Positive Education Program was funded by the Community Mental Health and Retardation Board, and PEP began operation in July 1971 as a teacher training and consultation program aimed at serving children with learning and behavior problems in the schools.

In a short time, teacher training became formalized as a graduate teacher certification program in cooperation with an area university. Direct service then became the focus of PEP, with the beginning of day-treatment programs for severely behavior-disordered children in the spring of 1975. Since that time, PEP has operationalized six day-treatment centers for school-age children, two early intervention centers for preschool children and their parents, and one day-treatment program for adolescents in a psychiatric hospital.

PEP has a $2.5 million annual budget (1980). The Ohio Division of Mental Health provides 20 percent of the funds; the Ohio Division of Special Education provides 20 percent; and thirty-two school systems provide 20 percent. The remaining 40 percent comes from various sources, including mental health centers, county welfare and youth services departments, and federal grants. In its eight-year history, PEP has received substantial grants from several foundations in Cleveland, which provided the start-up funds for program development. PEP has a unique distinction of being a chartered mental health agency, operating under contract to the Cuyahoga County Community Mental Health and Retardation Board, and at the same time a special education program operating under the auspices of the Cuyahoga County Board of Education.

Philosophically, PEP is closely aligned with the basic principles of Re-ED. Carefully selected teacher-counselors develop social and academic competencies in the child, and work to develop more supportive and healthy ecological subsystems within which the child can grow. Behavioral techniques are fundamental, providing predictability and consistency for the child. Emphasis is placed on forming a strong group identity; group process techniques help the child develop a more positive self-concept and learn problem-solving skills.

Certain premises form the basis for PEP programming. In a day-treatment program, children and adolescents can remain with their families; as a result, the PEP staff are involved in the child's home, community, and school setting and can help the schools with early identification of children needing treatment; they can also give the schools assistance in developing mainstreaming programs to serve the children being reintegrated from PEP.

The day-treatment centers serve from forty to sixty children in groups averaging ten; assignment to a group is primarily on the basis of age, although the child's problem, social maturity, and physical size are considered where age groups overlap. Each group is served by a teacher-counselor (with appropriate teacher certification) and an associate teacher-counselor (typically a person with a bachelor's degree and a major in psychology or a related field). As in Re-ED, these "front-line" staff have primary responsibility for implementing the treatment program. Each center has a full-time coordinator (an experienced special educator or psychologist with a master's degree), a full-time psychologist, two or more full-time liaison workers, and a secretary. Central staff—an executive director, an associate director, three assistant directors, and a parent education coordinator—provide administrative and program supervision. One assistant director is responsible for two additional centers (the Early Intervention Centers), which serve preschool children and their families. These centers are replications of the Regional Intervention Program, also developed at Peabody. The staffing for the Early Intervention Centers includes a coordinator, two resource consultants, and a secretary, plus two graduate parents who assist with program responsibilities. In addition, parents in treatment contribute their services on a pay-back basis. Parent implementation of the program is the most important component of these centers.

The day-treatment centers serve school-age youth (six to eighteen years old) from thirty-two school districts in the Greater Cleveland metropolitan area. The population of the centers is 85 percent male. Referrals originate with mental health centers, psychiatric hospitals, private practitioners, and school personnel. Due process laws require that the child's school system process his referral and placement.

The program serves children with a wide range of disturbed or disturbing behaviors, including the withdrawn, phobic child; the child with bizarre behaviors who may hallucinate or engage in obsessive-compulsive rituals; and the hyperaggressive child who may be delinquent or predelinquent. In our experience, the children in day treatment have not been—as might be assumed—less severely disturbed than those in residential placement. In fact, children have been successfully served by PEP in day treatment who have been turned down as too severely disturbed by many residential programs. More children with increasingly severe disturbances are being referred. Average length of treatment is presently under fourteen months.

The PEP treatment program utilizes a wide range of techniques. Although the program is highly individualized, the overall approach is intended to move the child through a structured program where his behavior is initially under external control (token economies, point systems, and the like) to the point where appro-

priate behavior is internally maintained. Whenever operant procedures are used, staff consistently use verbal mediation techniques
to help the child state the relationship between his behavior and
its consequences, both positive and negative.

In each unit, the child moves through four to six levels
wherein he earns more privileges and has more autonomy as behavior becomes more appropriate. The level system is developed by
the group, so that there is a high degree of personal investment in
the system and status associated with upward movement through
the levels. Top levels, interestingly, have few privileges as such.
Behavior at the top level is expected to be age appropriate, and the
child is not only in a high-status leadership position in the group
but is more under the control of naturally available reinforcers in
the environment (approval, recognition)—reinforcers that were
previously not forthcoming because of his unacceptable behavior.
Top-level privileges and responsibilities are designed to approxi-
mate the situation the child will face as he is reintegrated into his
regular school placement. Staff often introduce stressful situations
to top-level students, to enable the students to practice dealing appropriately with them. Students are aware beforehand that such
events may occur, but they will not know when. Experience has
shown that stressful events will frequently be the downfall of a
student after he has completed treatment. Students who deal well
with the stress are highly praised; those who do not receive no
negative consequences. In either event, the situation is reviewed
immediately and provides excellent subject matter for a counseling
session.

Camping, an activity long used in Re-ED, is an integral part
of PEP. Each classroom unit is expected to take six camping trips
per year. Such trips are of varying lengths and range from heated-
cabin camping during the colder months to primitive camping
during warmer months. PEP groups have traveled over much of the
eastern United States. Hiking, canoeing, and other sports are a part
of every trip. Camping provides a richer group experience than the
classroom, and the need for teamwork and cooperation while
camping teaches interpersonal skills. Competence in meeting the
demands of the camping experiences enhances each individual's
sense of achievement. Careful skill sequencing (for both staff and
students) ensures the success of the camping program.

Academic programs are all individualized. It is not uncom-
mon to have an eight- to ten-year difference in skill levels among
students in a unit. Basic skills are often minimal or spotty and
tend, therefore, to be emphasized. For students without basic
skill problems, individualized subject area programs are developed.
A typical day contains five hours of academic work (students are
at the treatment centers from 8:30 to 4:00 daily, eleven months a

year). The social behavior and academic programs are not separable. Point and level systems encompass both. To make academics as meaningful as possible, enterprise teaching units are extensively used (see Chapter Ten).

The treatment program, following the ecological model, goes beyond the child as the center of treatment. Parent education and community involvement are integral parts of the program.

Parent training is accomplished in most cases by weekly two-hour parent group meetings. The psychologist, coordinator, and liaison personnel are involved, and the programs for all centers are monitored by the parent training coordinator. The curriculum emphasizes child management techniques that are consistent with those utilized in the treatment centers. After parents demonstrate skill in these techniques, communication skills are emphasized. For parents who cannot or will not attend the group meetings, or whose own disturbing behavior is interfering with the group's progress, a Parents Training Parents (PTP) program has been instituted in all centers. Exceptionally capable parents are identified and given additional training. They are assigned a parent or family, and they work individually in any setting that is mutually agreed on. PTP parents are paid on an hourly basis for their work. PEP has just concluded a year-long controlled study of the PTP program. The results are very encouraging, and the program will continue as a basic approach in helping the "hard-to-reach" parent.

Each treatment center's liaison personnel are involved in mobilizing community resources to support the child and to work with the school to which the child will return. The work with the school system begins long before the child's projected discharge. Supportive school personnel are identified and given help in developing a program for the child. Liaison personnel are readily available to the child, the family, and the school for crisis intervention when problems do develop. The liaison worker is often involved with juvenile court, the welfare department, and other community agencies in order to resolve a wide range of problems.

Appropriate school facilities for community-based day-treatment programs are an important environmental consideration. PEP has felt that children should be housed in facilities that are similar to their local school. Six of the eight centers are located in school buildings that were recently closed because of drops in enrollment. Two of the centers are located in wings of operating schools.

Program evaluation has been conducted by the Community Mental Health Board. Site visits have been made by the National Institute of Mental Health and the state and local mental health staff.

The PEP day-treatment goal is to return children to their local school in a reasonably short period of time and provide support for their successful reintegration. Follow-up of returning students will require more staff time in the future. Liaison staff are dealing with expanding ecological systems as they work toward solutions to the problems children face.

Future activity will include training and dissemination of the PEP program model, development of transition classes within the schools, and training and consultation to schools for mainstreaming children. Another important future direction is the establishment of group homes for children and youth who are being deinstitutionalized and those whose families are unable to provide adequate support for learning and maintaining new behaviors. Construction grants have been awarded for this new programming.

Two additional service components—a therapeutic camping facility and a program to serve mothers with high-risk pregnancies and possible postnatal problems—are being planned.

Re-ED School of Kentucky
Louisville, Kentucky

The logo of the Re-ED School of Kentucky well expresses its character. A circle is superimposed on a triangle. In the circle is a drawing of a child, who is thus at the center of concern. The three points of the triangle are marked Home, School, and Community, each a focal point for programming in the interest of the child.

The school is located in Louisville and is handsomely housed in the former nurses' quarters of a tuberculosis hospital. A four-story, rectangular brick structure, it inevitably generates expectations of institutional sterility. But, in this instance, cheerful decorations and furnishings, a generous presence of materials used in teaching and working with children, and bulletin boards displaying students' work defeat the expectations and provide, instead, a pleasant place congenial to good teaching and learning.

The building is surrounded by several hundred acres of hilly, wooded terrain, including a wild ravine with a stream—a great place for children to explore. Just in front of the building is a large grassy mound where children can play, and in back is the wild ravine. Nearby public parks are also used for recreation.

The Re-ED School of Kentucky opened in July of 1969, with funds from the United States Office of Education, as a program to demonstrate new approaches to educational problems. Since 1973, the program has been supported by local funds. For some time, the Re-ED program of Kentucky was unique among Re-ED schools in being a residential school that is an integral part of the public school system. It serves thirty-two children, ages six to twelve.

The school is sponsored by the school systems of Anchorage and Eminence Independent Districts; by Bullitt, Henry, Jefferson, Oldham, Shelby, Spencer, and Trimble Counties; and by the Catholic diocese. The Jefferson County Board of Education serves as fiscal agent and employs the staff. There is a board of directors made up of representatives of the sponsoring school systems.

The internal organization of the school is comparable to that of other Re-ED programs. There is a director, three day teacher-counselors, three night teacher-counselors (called "afternoon program specialists" to comply with funding regulations), four liaison teacher-counselors, several associates, and other supporting personnel. There are no day or night supervisors or specialist teachers. There has been remarkably little turnover. The teacher-counselors strongly identify with the program and can afford to stay with it because the salaries are good. The liaison teacher-counselors have been with the program since the beginning and are, as a group, somewhat older than the teacher-counselors, who work with the children directly.

There are no physicians or nurses associated directly with the school. Reliance is placed on family physicians or on selected private physicians when the school must take initiative to get medical care for a child. The school makes relatively little use of consultants. There is a diagnostician on the staff who evaluates children on entrance and prior to discharge. She also works with the teachers in planning remedial programs for individual children.

Since the Re-ED School of Kentucky is a part of the public school system, parents pay nothing for the service. Operating funds are derived from various sources, including the minimal educational support program of the state of Kentucky, plus federal funds administered by the state, such as funds from Title XX of the Social Security Act. Each child is expected to bring to the school each week $2.25, which is used for rewards in a token economy program (described in Chapter Eleven). The school provides the money when a family cannot afford to do so.

The following description of the program appears in a brochure prepared by Donald Alwes, the director, and his staff:

> The typical day in the residence school begins with breakfast at 7:15; classes start at 8:00 with the morning teacher and assistant. Lunch is served family style from 11:30 to 12:00, and at 2:00 the afternoon Children's Program Specialist and assistant assume responsibility for the group of eight. Their program correlates with the academic morning program, but in a more informal manner, which in-

cludes field trips, camping, art classes, yoga, and other social-recreational learning experiences out in the community. From 2:00 to 2:30, there is an overlap period when both morning and afternoon staff are on duty, and this period can be spent in planning coordinated activities, in team teaching, in discussing particular behavior problems and methods for dealing with them, or in meetings with the group's liaison counselor for a three-way dialogue regarding incoming, resident, or graduated students. Dinner is from 6:00 to 6:30 for any group not out on a field trip, followed by planned activities until shower time at 8:30 and lights out at 9:00. Four evening supervisors are on duty until 8:00 A.M., alert to sudden illness, nightmares, wet beds, or spells of homesickness. The unit to which a child is assigned is an integral group that studies, plays, eats, and sleeps together. Group living is effective, through peer pressure, in teaching the child responsibility for his behavior as an individual and as a member of any given group. Some children learn to adjust to life's varying demands and inconsistencies; the emotionally disturbed child has not. It is Re-ED's responsibility to meet each child's above-normal needs by helping him to modify his attitudes and behaviors as a necessary foundation upon which to build his skill-increasing ability.

The school offers various forms of counseling to all parents. There are child management courses, parent group meetings, individual or family counseling at Re-ED as well as at local agencies, and regular in-home conferences. There is also a two-year supportive association with the child who has been graduated, with someone from his team always available for crisis intervention if he gets in trouble, a friendly chat on the phone, a drop-in visit at his school or home just to say hello. A graduate's visits to Re-ED, announced or unannounced, are welcome. Recognizing that change is constant and affects all members of a child's environment, Re-ED continues to work with the schools, churches, and social groups in an effort to more positively involve the child on an acceptable basis.

The program of the Re-ED School of Kentucky is distinctive in several ways. It is a residential program sponsored by the public schools, as already noted. It is operated on a complete and ingeniously devised token economy and is more committed to operant conditioning concepts than any of the other schools for this age group. And, finally, it has a strong and apparently effective program of counseling for parents.

Central Kentucky Re-ED Program
*Lexington, Kentucky**

In 1970, the Advisory Committee for Child Development (an interagency, interdisciplinary group studying the needs of Kentucky's children) initiated efforts to develop a Project Re-ED program for emotionally disturbed children in Kentucky. As had been true in North Carolina and Tennessee, an assessment of the needs of children in Kentucky indicated that many of the 10,000 children in need of services were not receiving help. At that time, traditional mental health services continued to be limited in scope, expensive, scarce, and often ineffective. Kentucky's Re-ED project was begun to serve children who were too disturbed or disturbing to remain in their home communities, but did not require hospitalization, and to expand the scope of services available in the region.

Opened in July 1971, the Central Kentucky Re-ED Program was located on the grounds of Eastern State Hospital in Lexington. In March 1976, the Department of Human Resources assumed full responsibility for the Re-ED program. With a staff of forty, it was serving approximately 500 children in its community program and about 64 in the residential program annually.

An advisory board, comprised of private citizens, meets with the director five or six times each year. Central Kentucky Re-ED Program is the only state program with an incorporated board that is not appointed by the commissioner of human resources. Today, and throughout its history, the advisory board has provided essential citizens' support to the program. Re-ED staff consider the board vital to the program's survival and work in close cooperation with it.

Three types of consultants work with the Re-ED program. A child psychiatric resident from the University of Kentucky Medical Center and a child psychologist from the Comprehensive Care Center work a half day each week with the staff. A special education consultant from the University of Kentucky works two days per month at the Re-ED school. The consultants' primary role is to work with staff members, so they can be more effective with the students. The consultants rarely work directly with the students themselves.

The Central Kentucky Re-ED Program primarily serves children ages six through twelve from the seventeen counties of the Bluegrass Region of Central Kentucky. Although children from

*This description was written by Algund Hermann with the assistance of Lorraine Kroetch, Ronald Ward, Gregory Rayer, and Richard Schenk.

the entire state are eligible, distance remains the primary restriction. Children return home each weekend; therefore, when families live a long distance from the school, it is difficult for parents to participate in the parents' programs or to arrange appropriate transportation.

Children are usually referred by the comprehensive care center in the catchment area where they live or by their local school system. The admissions committee—including the diagnostician, director, community services counseling supervisor, and residential program supervisor—makes the final decisions about the appropriateness of admissions, when a child will be admitted, and which of the four groups the child will join. All admissions are considered temporary for a one-month trial period. Between 1972 and 1977, 219 children attended the Central Kentucky Re-ED Program with an average stay of 7.46 months. In 1977, 38 students were enrolled, with an average stay of 6.92 months. Each year, approximately 500 additional children are served in their communities by the liaison staff (see below). With these services, these children may never require residential treatment. In recent months, a waiting list of children appropriate for the residential program has developed. This, as well as the regional nature of the Central Kentucky Program, suggests the need for Re-ED programs in other parts of the state.

Most staff in the Kentucky program, except dormitory counselors, are required to have a master's degree, preferably in special education, psychology, social work, or a related field. Day teacher-counselors are required to have state certification in special education. Preference is given to those with experience in elementary classrooms or with elementary school children. Initial orientation to the program's philosophy and concepts is provided for all new staff. An active in-service program encourages continuing education for staff development. All Re-ED personnel are paid according to the state scale.

Liaison teacher-counselors and community liaison counselors have primary responsibility for coordination with community agencies, particularly the comprehensive care centers and schools. Liaison teacher-counselors work with the parents, schools, and community agencies of the students in their units. This work begins before students are admitted to the Re-ED Program and continues for two months after students leave the school.

A unique feature of the Kentucky program is the invention of the role of "community liaison counselor," a concept that is highly recommended for adoption by other programs, especially those serving large geographical areas. The ten community liaison counselors work in the seventeen counties served by the Central

Kentucky Re-ED Program. Community liaison counselors work through comprehensive care centers and usually have an office at the center. Their major goal is to provide support services and consultation to parents and teachers, so that children can be successfully maintained within their home communities. Congruent with the liaison role, these counselors attempt to mobilize existing resources by linking children and their families to the agencies already providing services. However, when necessary, they provide the services directly. The services provided include individual, group, and family counseling; academic testing and programming; demonstration teaching; behavior and classroom management; development of communication skills; parent management workshops; and in-service training to public school systems and social service agencies. Other special projects developed by community liaison counselors include summer day programs and camping trips for Re-ED graduates, summer programs for children with special social or academic training needs, and preschool screening.

By working within the communities, community liaison counselors become a part of the link between the Re-ED program and that community. Their initial orientation to the Re-ED program includes working with one of the residential teams for a few days to become acquainted with this phase of the continuum of services. Although based in scattered comprehensive care centers, the community liaison counselors meet at the Re-ED school each Friday to maintain contact and participate in the staff development meetings.

Until recently, community liaison counselors have not been used in any other Re-ED school. Now California is incorporating the idea into its newly developing program, with one community liaison counselor for each county served. These counselors represent an extension of the Re-ED program into the community, with a major commitment to keeping children out of a Re-ED school. Although liaison teacher-counselors and, indeed, all Re-ED staff members work toward this goal, they generally do not enter the picture until the child's system is already too disturbed for the staff to do effective preventive work. Because community liaison counselors work in the community and not with the students at the Re-ED school, they can concentrate on preventive strategies. Over time, these community liaison counselors become trusted members of the community, known by the school, agencies, and comprehensive care center staff. With their knowledge about and emphasis on children, community liaison counselors are valuable members of the community services team. These counselors have greatly expanded the preventive and supportive services and techniques provided by the Re-ED program.

Children's Program, Marshall F. Pickens Hospital
*Greenville, South Carolina**

The Marshall F. Pickens Hospital Children's Program is located within the Greenville Hospital System, in Greenville County,
South Carolina. Before 1969, the only adult psychiatric unit was
located on a floor of Greenville General Hospital, and no children's facilities were available. The decision was made to buy 128
acres outside Greenville on which a new psychiatric unit and other
hospital facilities would be built. Monies from the National Institute of Mental Health, the Comprehensive Mental Health Centers
Act, and private sources were combined to finance the building of
the fifty-bed adult unit. Originally, there was no provision for a
children's unit, but during the planning and development phase
the decision was made to add a children's program. A group of
psychiatrists and administrators interested in a children's program
had become acquainted with Project Re-ED, visited Cumberland
House in Nashville, and designed the children's program according
to this model. Opened in April 1969, the Children's Program is
housed in two free-standing buildings near the adult unit. Initially,
it served eight day students and eight residential students. Demand
was such that only boys ages six to thirteen were admitted. In
1972, the day program was phased out, primarily because the public school system opened self-contained classrooms appropriate for
emotionally disturbed children, and the program was expanded to
twenty residential students.

The internal administrative organization of the Children's
Program is comparable to that of other Re-ED programs, but with
a change in vocabulary to adapt the program to a medical setting
and to ease problems of third-party payment for services. The day
teacher-counselor has become a "day therapist," the night teacher-
counselor an "afternoon therapist," and the liaison teacher-counselor a "liaison therapist." A diagnostician and two liaison therapists work cooperatively with both teams. In general, staff duties
have remained essentially the same as those of teacher-counselors
in other Re-ED programs. The diagnostician is primarily responsible for educational evaluation and assisting the treatment teams
with curriculum planning for each student. The two liaison therapists have extensive responsibility for performing the liaison
functions of the Children's Program as well as psychological evaluations and individual or group counseling. The liaison therapists'
responsibilities begin at intake, when psychological evaluations,
parent interviews, and community contacts are made. Before a stu-

*This description was written by Algund Hermann with the assistance
of Claude Wilson, director of the Children's Program.

dent is fully admitted to the program, parents must participate in the Child Management Program, which is led by the liaison therapists. The liaison therapists also meet with parents about once a week while children are enrolled in the program. These meetings often take the form of couple or family therapy, counseling about the child's progress and relationships within the family, and discussions about behavior management techniques. Finally, the liaison therapists are responsible for coordination of discharge planning, placement, and follow-up.

Each of the two treatment teams is responsible for planning and executing the students' programs. The day therapists, with the assistance of the therapist aides, have major responsibility for the students' academic programs, while the afternoon therapists concentrate on implementation of activities designed to foster development of social skills. The residence counselors supervise the children from 6 P.M. to 8 A.M. and are responsible for that portion of the treatment teams' plans.

The Children's Program primarily serves the children of Greenville County, which has a population of about 275,000. Children from outside the county are also eligible. None of the children at the program has been placed as a result of a court order or commitment procedure. The family initiates contact with the program, usually on the advice of school or mental health personnel. The program is designed for children ages six to twelve and has traditionally served only boys. Presently, students stay an average of seven months. As has been true for other Re-ED programs, however, the Children's Program has found that more severely disturbed children and families are being served now than were served ten years ago. Apparently, less severely disturbed children and families are served in the community or by agencies outside the mental health system. Consequently, admissions criteria have become more flexible, so that a broader range of children can be served.

The director and two liaison therapists have focused particular attention on working with principals and teachers in the public schools. Besides working directly with the schools their students have come from or will return to, the Children's Program's director and liaison therapists conduct workshops and orientation programs at the schools in the county. These programs have helped orient educators to the services available and to inform them about Project Re-ED philosophy, concepts, and techniques.

As a prerequisite to a child's final admission to the program, parents must agree to participate in and, if at all possible, complete the Child Management Workshop. This workshop meets for six sessions, each lasting one and a half hours, and is led by a liaison therapist. The sessions provide an introduction for parents to the hows and whys of the Children's Program, information about behavior management and problem-solving techniques, and a supportive group setting for parents to discuss problems, feelings, and attitudes. Parents are encouraged to complete the workshop before their children begin the Children's Program, so that they can better understand what program staff are doing and can improve their own skills in rearing their children.

While the children are in the program, parents meet regularly, at least twice a month, with one of the liaison therapists. These sessions may focus on individual, couple, or family therapy, on management counseling, or on the child's progress.

In addition to these parental commitments to involvement with the program, parents are included in periodic treatment-team conferences to discuss the child's progress. Brief discussions with team members also occur when parents pick up and return children to the program on Friday and Sunday. The Children's Program policy is firm on the necessity for parental participation. The general rule is that children will not be accepted if parents do not complete the Child Management Workshop, and children's stay will be terminated if parents do not attend counseling sessions.

One of the most interesting features of the Children's Program of the Marshall I. Pickens Hospital is that it is an authentic Re-ED program that operates with minimum strain as an integral part of a psychiatric hospital. The psychiatrists who established the program a dozen years ago first searched the country for a children's program model that made sense to them and then settled on the Re-ED idea. To this day, the program operates in a congenial setting under the general direction of psychiatrists who understand Re-ED principles as well as their own Children's Program, and they give them both unfailing support.

The next two Re-ED programs have distinctive features not represented in the schools thus far described. These programs are either newly established or have not been visited.

Centennial School
Bethlehem, Pennsylvania

Centennial School was established in 1972 and converted to the Re-ED plan in 1980. A descriptive brochure describes the school this way:

Centennial School is a private, state-supported day school for socially and emotionally disturbed students. The program is nongraded and individualized and serves elementary- and secondary-age students whose problems include psychotic disorders, aggressive reactions, and other types of nonadaptive behavior. The educational program is designed to remediate the learning defects that often accompany emotional and social difficulties. The goal of the comprehensive program is to return the student to the educational mainstream as soon as possible.

The school is unique among Re-ED programs in that it is an integral part of the graduate-level School of Education of Lehigh University. Graduate students who are certified special education teachers with master's degrees staff the classrooms, assisted by aides who are first-year graduate students, under the supervision of master teachers of the Centennial School staff.

Tuition, which is now $3,300 for the academic year, is completely paid by the county and state. Currently, an effort is being made to extend the program to a full year.

Southeastern Co-op Education Program (SECEP)
Norfolk, Virginia

This program is sponsored by eight public school systems in southeastern Virginia. The SECEP Day Re-ED Program serves about sixty children and adolescents during the school year in two attractive settings. The children are described as having histories of hyperaggression, disruptive and delinquent behavior, and school truancy. They may have difficulty relating to peers and adults and may demonstrate inappropriate or immature behavior. Some may be depressed or withdrawn, and others tend to develop somatic complaints and fears associated with personal or school problems.

The school is operated very much like other Re-ED programs though its services are currently limited to the school day and school year. There is a sophisticated behavioral management system, a highly individualized academic program, a parent training component, and a liaison unit that works with the child's family, regular school, neighborhood, and other social agencies involved, including the courts. A camping program is being initiated this year. Efforts are being made to extend the program from an academic year to a full calendar year.

4

The Teacher-Counselor

A New Professional Role
in Mental Health, Education,
and Human Services Programs

But most of all, a teacher-counselor is a decent adult; educated, well trained; able to give and receive affection, to live relaxed, and to be firm; a person with private resources for the nourishment and refreshment of his own life; not an itinerant worker but a professional through and through; a person with a sense of the significance of time, of the usefulness of today and the promise of tomorrow; a person of hope, quiet confidence, and joy; one who has committed himself to children and to the proposition that children who are disturbed can be helped by the process of reeducation [Hobbs, 1966].

These words define our level of aspiration for the teacher-counselor, the professional person who has been called many times "the heart of Re-ED." In this chapter, we will review the roles that teacher-counselors play in a Re-ED school; how they are selected and trained; how they function; and, as shown in several autobiographical sketches, what they are like as people.

Background

Origins and Development of the Role. The title "teacher-counselor" is clearly no idle choice. It is an invention, strongly shaped by expectations of the role it serves to identify. The person would be a teacher, with education a central motif in her work. But she would do more than teach. Her relationship with a child or an adolescent would be more personal than that of instructor; thus, "counselor" seemed fitting. Put together in "teacher-counselor," the term seemed at first ungainly; now it seems altogether right and even pleasing. It rolls off the tongue quite easily. It is a durable term. What else indeed could the people of this new profession be called? Anything else would seem awkward now. In conversation, it gets compressed to "T.C." and this is useful.

The role of the teacher-counselor had its origins in a study of programs for retarded and disturbed children in several Western European countries, undertaken by the author in 1956 under the auspices of the Joint Commission on Mental Illness and Health. Observations in Scotland and in France were particularly helpful.

In 1956 in Glasgow, Scotland, there was an extensive, public school-based program of mental health services for children, including a residential treatment center in a suburb called Nerston. The teachers who staffed the program received three years of in-service training, leading to certification as an educational psychologist—not in the American research tradition but in a mode highly relevant to the practical problems facing a community where only one psychiatrist was available for consultation. The residential treatment center had been established during World War II, when air attacks on London led to the evacuation of large numbers of children to the country, where they were placed with families. Some children were too disturbed to be sustained in the foster family arrangement. The exigencies of war led to a solution that might not have survived professional disapproval in more settled times. These very disturbed children were sent to Nerston to be cared for by teachers who did not have the formal credentials widely regarded, at that time, as necessary to work effectively with disturbed children. But obviously they were doing a first-rate job. The center is still going strong and now has new facilities in which to continue a long record of successful operation. The program in Scotland provided not so much a model to be emulated as a demonstration that patterns of care other than those sanctioned by professional groups in the United States could do effective work with seriously disturbed children.

Following World War II, France developed a large number of residential programs for orphaned, handicapped, emotionally disturbed, and delinquent children and youth. The schools or treatment centers had the following characteristics: a small number of children, often around forty and seldom more than sixty; a pleasant, homelike setting, often a converted chateau with spacious grounds; close community ties; a staff variously composed with a preponderance of people with educational rather than psychiatric orientations, including the *éducateur*. The centers were directed by an educator, a social worker, a psychiatrist, or a psychologist, the talents of the person carrying more weight than professional affiliation in his appointment. Though all institutions had to meet national accreditation standards, many of them took on a particular character, reflecting the personality or theoretical persuasion of their directors. A return visit to French programs in 1975 revealed that the programs had been expanded, modern facilities provided, and staff trained in an array of special educational programs. France has emphasized institutional care for children, and done it very well; today there is a new emphasis on work with children and youth in the community.

The *éducateur spécialisé*, a new profession, emerged in France in 1942 and quickly spread throughout Western Europe.*

*The concepts that informed early French programs for disturbed children and youth are explicated in a remarkable book by French psychiatrist Robert Lafon (1953), *Psychopédagogie Médico-Sociale*. Lafon was the long-time president of the French association concerned with the welfare and protection of children and youth and until recently was president of the Union Mondiale des Organisations Nationales pour la Sauvegarde de l'Enfance et de l'Adolescence. He is also the author of an important encyclopedia, *Vocabulaire de Psychopédagogie* (Lafon, 1973). For a brief history of the *éducateur* movement, see Ginger (1979). Progress in the development of the idea can be followed in the *Bulletin de l'Association pour la Sauvegarde de l'Enfance et de l'Adolescence*. For an interpretation of the idea in English, see Linton (1973). The development of Project Re-ED in the United States has been paralleled in Canada by the emergence of a new professional group known as the *psychoéducateur*, inspired by the work of Jeannine Guindon (1973). Teacher-counselors in the United States have recently formed a na-

At present, there are about 25,000 government-certified *éduca-teurs* in France. They are trained in a three-year program in fifty institutes sponsored by the Ministries of Public Health, Justice, and Education, and they work with maladjusted children and youth, as well as with handicapped children, in a variety of set-tings. The *éducateurs* enter the special institutes on completion of the equivalent of our sophomore year in college. The first two years of the program are devoted to didactic study and the last on the job as an apprentice or intern in a reeducation center. Instruc-tion in group work provides the core of the training program. In addition, the *éducateur* is taught mental health principles and some psychodynamics, the characteristics of the kinds of children he expects to work with, some skills in psychological testing and educational evaluation, and games, crafts, and other skills useful in working with children and youth during out-of-school hours. The *éducateur* carries heavy responsibilities in the program of a center, he attends professional meetings to upgrade his competence, and he may be a member of an international association with a large and growing membership.

Observations of these European programs served essentially to loosen the conceptual situation for the founders of Project Re-ED, to unbind us from commitment to the approved American model, to invite invention, and to expand our sense of the possi-ble. At no time did we think it wise to try to transplant a Euro-pean institution to American soil. Institutional arrangements are and should be an expression of indigenous traditions, require-ments, and resources. Our task was to take such ideas from Euro-pean experiments as seemed most useful in the United States and then freely adapt and transform them to local service. Even this description of what happened in the invention of Re-ED is not completely accurate. What we did was to prepare the roughest sketch of a new social institution, with the full expectation that its living character would be determined over a period of time by people engaged in attempting to translate general conceptions into day-by-day operating procedures, and to generate, in the process,

---

tional organization, the American Re-Education Association (A.R.E.A.). For information about A.R.E.A., write Clark Luster, Pressley Ridge School (see Appendix A for address).

new and more precise formulations of general principles. Doubtlessly, the most important general conception borrowed from Europe was that of the *éducateur,* but the extent to which this notion
has been transformed in the evolution of the teacher-counselor,
whose role is quite different from the French model, suggests the
process of transformation and creation involved generally in the
development of Re-ED schools.

We entertained the notion for a while of borrowing the
French term *éducateur* but refrained for two reasons: in English,
educator already has preemptive meanings; and in French, *éducateur* designates a professional person different from the kind of
professional person we aspired to see at work. The French *éducateur* is a skilled childcare worker and not a teacher. Schooling is
not his responsibility. Classroom teaching in French programs is
the responsibility of yet another kind of professional person (*le
professeur, l'instituteur,* or *le mâitre*), who comes into a residential center and takes charge of the children during school hours.
He is a person properly called a teacher or a special educator, such
as can be found in most residential treatment centers for emotionally disturbed children in the United States. With his fellow teachers, he sits apart in the dining room at lunch and is seldom an integral part of the institutional community. Although the children
are entrusted to the teacher's care for five or six hours a day, he
has been a low-prestige person, far down the professional pecking
order; what he does often is not seen as therapeutic.

No existing professional role, not that of the psychiatrist or
psychologist or social worker or nurse or *éducateur* or teacher or
counselor, met the requirements for staffing the kind of social institution for children we wanted to create. Following are some of
the specifications we had in mind as we tried to imagine a special
institutional arrangement designed to give maximum help to a
child or an adolescent when the normal socializing institutions of
society—the family, the school, the neighborhood, and the community—had failed him.

We wanted the Re-ED effort to be informed by the vocabulary, and thus the expectancies, of normal development. We believed the vocabulary of therapy often to be untherapeutic and the
vocabulary of psychopathology often to be pathogenic. Our biases
led to semantic preferences: for *school* instead of *hospital,* for
teaching instead of *treatment,* for *pupils* instead of *patients,* for

habits instead of *symptoms,* for *learning* instead of *therapy.* We wanted a vocabulary that set no one apart from the normal course of living, that could be used comfortably by everyone involved in helping a child, by his parents, by the staff, by the child.

We wanted teacher-counselors to be competent. Re-ED is sometimes referred to as a "competence model." The achievement of competence, step by step, in matters small then large, is an attractive challenge not only to children and adolescents but to teacher-counselors as well. The competence of teacher-counselors today is perhaps best evidenced in their skillful management of individual children and adolescents, groups, and ecosystems, as facilitators of change. What they do might best be called precision programming. Precision programming involves (1) shared identification and definition of a problem; (2) agreement on means to effect desired changes; (3) specification of outcomes sought, preferably in behaviors that can be counted, measured, or consensually validated; (4) assignment and acceptance of responsibilities for carrying out the plan by specified target dates; and (5) periodic evaluation of progress and redefinition of the problem—in a continuing cycle. Everyone (students, parents, teacher-counselors, consultants, aides, caseworkers, regular classroom teachers) is kept ever aware of goals, means to ends, and outcomes. Thus, a measure of treatment consistency is achieved that would otherwise be impossible.

We wanted to build a social institution with a relatively flat administrative structure. Finding uncongenial the sharply pyramidal character of most residential treatment centers, with their elaborate professional hierarchies, we aspired to an arrangement permitting the fullest possible exercise of authority and responsibility as near to the action as possible. We wanted the people who worked with the children, hour after hour, day after day, night after night, to have the freedom, the authority, the responsibility to use all the resources at their command, spontaneously, to their fullest effectiveness.

We wanted an institution with an open-opportunity structure, with minimum restraints to advancement for the staff. The person responsible for working with the children—the central responsibility, after all—should be able to move into any position in the system of care for the disturbed child, without encumbrance based on professional prerogatives.

We wanted an arrangement with minimum barriers to com-

munication among those responsible for the children; this suggested having one professional group, rather than two or more,
centrally responsible for the Re-ED program.

We wanted to be able to use staff with maximum flexibility; thus, day teacher-counselors, night teacher-counselors, liaison
teacher-counselors, and administrators should be interchangeable,
having had the same professional preparation.

We wanted to avoid the dichotomy between "therapy" and
other putatively less consequential activities; we sought a unity of
programming day and night, in class and out, with the expectation
of gain for the child from varied and often unpredictable sources.

We wanted to encourage, in the emerging professional role,
initiative, creativity, spontaneity, self-criticism, and pride in
achievement at the point of contact between the teacher-counsel-
or, or teacher-counselor team, and the child or adolescent and the
important people in her life. Industrial organizations probably require for efficient production a precise differentiation of roles and
a vertical line of command. But the production model is not appropriate to the objectives of reeducation. The teacher-counselor
is a participant in an emergent situation, not the producer of a designed product. The teacher-counselor must be able to deal freely
and confidently with complex transactions among people who are
trying to discover satisfactory and satisfying ways to live. A child,
his parents, a teacher, and the teacher-counselors themselves are
experimenting with the possible in a dynamic system of interpersonal negotiations, some of which succeed and some fail. The balance between success and failure often depends on a teacher-counselor's perceptiveness and ability to act immediately, guided both
by an agreed-upon strategy and a private surmise about what should
be done. It is a difficult job and takes a special kind of person.

A Day Sufficient Unto Itself. Apart from the emphasis on
working with the total ecological system, perhaps the one thing
that most sharply differentiates a Re-ED school from many other
residential programs for children is the fullness and purposefulness
of each day in the life of a child. The constant challenge to the
staff, and especially to the three teacher-counselors responsible
for a group of children, is to design a daily program so engaging, so
varied and new yet orderly and stable, so exuberant, so filled with
mystery, exploration, and discovery, so physical, so meshed with

the growth of the child's mind, so rich in human interchange, so responsive to mood, so tranquil and safe as occasion demands, so filled with success in matters small and large, so unconcerned with failure, so appreciative of individuality and of common purpose, so evocative of a sense of community, so finely modulated to the needs of a particular child and a particular moment, so joyous, so aware, so filled with good talk, so fatiguing, so rewarding to children and teacher-counselors alike—in sum, so resonantly normal—that the disturbed child finds himself immediately committed to a new way of living at once more satisfying to himself and more satisfactory to the people in his life. Indeed, when a day's program is well planned and executed, when things are going well with the group, it is exceedingly difficult for a disturbed child to behave in a manner that earlier caused him to be so described. Such a day is by no means easy to make happen. It takes good people, extensive resources, and careful planning.

Obviously, the teacher-counselor is the pivotal person in making such a day possible. The teacher-counselor has to be a person of considerable resources. She must have qualities of personality that make such a day rewarding to her, and she must have the resilience to keep at it week after week. She has to have technical skills of a wide-ranging character. She must be able to work effectively with her teammates. She has to be able to do things with competence and assurance, so that she can have heart and mind to respond personally to children. The level of technical skill required is quite high, yet much cannot be acquired completely in professional training. The teacher-counselor makes professional use of experiences acquired over a lifetime, and, for this very reason, such people are available for professional work of high caliber without extensive professional training. Furthermore, teacher-counselors are not burdened with the trained incapacities so evident in, say, the Doctor of Philosophy in psychology. And, being young, they have the energy to do what would not even be considered important by the aging mental health specialist, so filled with study and so far from childhood. Teacher-counselors have climbed mountains, of all kinds, and recently, and are ready to do so again.

To make such a day come to pass also requires material resources. It is the falsest of economies to bring children and teacher-counselors together without adequate facilities and materials to work with. Needed are space of many kinds and buildings for many purposes, vehicles for transportation, books, classroom supplies, shop and crafts equipment, access to facilities in the community, diagnostic educational tests, sports equipment, musical instruments, backpacking gear, television sets and movie projectors, and so on—an array of material resources not ordinarily considered important in many residential centers for children. The cost of adequate equipment and supplies is actually not great; the barrier may most often be a lack of appreciation of their importance. Most things can be planned for in an orderly way with plenty of lead time. But provision must also be made for an orderly and easy handling of unanticipated needs, since these are so often tied with exciting possibilities for some immediate learning by the students. If a teacher-counselor needs a tape recorder or a ham to cook in a pit or some fishhooks or a set of Shakespeare's plays or a special vocational guidance program, these should be easily acquired.

Finally, a tremendous amount of careful and creative planning is required to make such a day possible. One thing is certain: it cannot happen otherwise. Planning needs to be at all levels, at the highest echelon to provide resources in advance, at the administrative level to assure coordination among elements in the school, between the teacher-counselor team members especially, and then, finally but far from least in importance, with the students themselves.

To come as close as possible to making each day sufficient unto itself, with each child or adolescent coming as close as possible to a mastery of it, is what lies at the heart of the concept of reeducation.

Descriptive Statistics. The original NIMH grant funding Re-ED as a pilot project provided training stipends for seventy-five prospective teacher-counselors. Peabody College provided the training program for six classes, between 1961-62 and 1966-67. The first class of trainees had internships in ten different schools in Canada, Denmark, England, and Scotland; subsequent classes gained practical experience at Cumberland House. Today teacher-counselors are drawn from diverse training programs and then given on-the-job training in Re-Ed concepts and techniques. Data are available on the characteristics of the seventy-five early trainees and on a nonrandom sample of approximately a hundred staff members of Re-ED schools in 1978. These are summarized below.

Teacher-counselor trainees in the six training classes at Peabody consisted of forty-four women and thirty-one men. Forty-four were single and thirty-one married. The average age was twenty-six years, and the age ranged from twenty-one to forty. All but nineteen had had prior teaching experience; thirty-three had had three or more years of experience. The students came from all over the United States and two foreign countries, with a somewhat heavier concentration from the southern region than elsewhere in the country. All the trainees had a bachelor's degree or its equivalent; a few had master's degrees, most often in elementary education. A great diversity of backgrounds was reflected in undergraduate majors. A majority of the students had degrees in education, but others had emphasized psychology, political science, philosophy, French, German, religion, nursing, and physiology in undergraduate training. Prior teaching and other work experiences were also quite different among the seventy-five trainees. Most had had formal teaching experience in public or private schools in regular classrooms and in special education. Others had been involved in recreation work, nursing, behavioral research, camp counseling, college teaching, arts and crafts instruction, kindergarten teaching, and juvenile delinquency work. A number had been Peace Corps volunteers. Nonprofessional interests of the students included Civil War history, model airplane building, Sunday school teaching, sports, music, nature study, dramatics, modern dancing, gardening, scouting, scuba diving, Little League baseball, ceramics, and auto mechanics.

In 1978, 121 staff members from eleven Re-ED schools responded to a questionnaire, providing information similar to that available for the early trainees. Among the respondents were seventy-two women and forty-nine men. Most Re-ED programs try to maintain an even ratio of men and women. Since there are more women than men teachers in the population, there is in most schools a slight tendency to have more women teacher-counselors than men. However, in programs closely affiliated with the public schools, women may substantially outnumber men. Most of the imbalance in the sample of 121 is contributed by two schools. The average age of respondents was 31.6 years, with a range from 22 to 61. The respondents had an average of three years' experience in Re-ED programs. There are employed today in Re-ED programs a few teacher-counselors (now mostly administrators) who were members of the early training cadres. Not unexpectedly, the educational level of current Re-ED staff members is considerably higher than that of entering trainees in the early program. Of the 121 respondents, 4 had less than a bachelor's degree, 28 had a bachelor's degree, 82 a master's degree, 1 an educational specialist degree, and 6 a doctoral degree. Current employees represent an even wider range of undergraduate majors than the trainees in the early classes, and the area of specialization for graduate degrees is naturally much greater. The most frequent graduate specialization was special education, followed by psychology and social work. Other specializations ranged from religious studies to Slavic languages. The array of special skills for working with disturbed children exhibited by the currently employed Re-ED staff members is even greater than that of the early trainees: camping, arts and crafts, music, sports, backpacking, canoeing, swimming, dramatics, nature study, dance, photography, carpentry, astronomy, sewing, cooking, sign language, aquarium maintenance, and magic tricks.

Roles and Functions

That the teacher-counselor is "the heart of Re-ED" bears several meanings. One meaning emphasizes the crucial importance of direct work with children, through the day and night, with the full talents of the professional worker available to the children at all times. Another meaning emphasizes the fact that most if not all the full-time professional workers in a Re-ED school are teacher-counselors. They may perform special functions, as that of school principal, but they are teacher-counselors by profession.

The *day teacher-counselor* is responsible for a group of eight or ten children or adolescents during what is essentially the school part of the day. Although teaching goes on during all waking hours, the mornings (for school-age children and youth) are devoted to formal academic work.

The day teacher-counselor working with elementary-level children must have skills in teaching reading, writing, spelling, and arithmetic in contexts that expand the child's understanding of his world. She must understand psychoeducational appraisal and have at her command many special instructional procedures of a remedial character. While helping the child begin to catch on to the mysteries and joys of language and number, to develop the cognitive skills essential to adequacy in his world, the day teacher-counselor is equally concerned with the child's growth in all areas. She is concerned with the specific learnings required by a particular child to regain access to normal opportunities for learning in home, school, and community, from which he has been excluded because of his unacceptable behavior. Thus, helping a child to like school, to stop fighting, to quit bothering other children, to control his temper, to clean up his vocabulary, even to sit still in class are crucial role requirements for the day teacher-counselor. And she is concerned with more elusive learnings, of integrity and self-respect, of giving and receiving affection, of play and fantasy and celebration, of private delight and shared joy, of loyalty and community—all those qualities of humanness essential to fullest realization of the person. No small task.

In working with adolescents, the day teacher-counselor has essentially the same responsibility as the teacher-counselor working with younger children. But methods of work must be adapted to older, and in many ways more complex, individuals. Although many adolescents may still require rudimentary instruction in basic academic skills, in reading, writing, and arithmetic, they must also be instructed in the traditional subjects of the curriculum of an approved secondary school: language arts and literature, science and mathematics, social studies and history, and health and physical education. In some programs for adolescents, day teacher-counselors specialize in an academic subject, with children rotating classes individually or in small groups. In other programs, groups are kept intact, and the day teacher-counselor teaches the whole curriculum, a seemingly impossible assignment but a not unreasonable arrangement considering the amount of remedial instruction usually required. Whatever the formal arrangement, most children in Re-ED schools are on individually designed instructional programs. Day teacher-counelors with adolescents frequently develop long-term enterprises that bring diverse components of work together in a situation designed to heighten motivation. Of course, the day teacher-counselor is frequently called on to do the kind of informal personal counseling that becomes more and more important as children move through adolescence and into matur-

ity. The behavior of adolescents in the classroom is more difficult
to manage than that of younger children in general, if for no other
reason than that the adolescent is larger and stronger and is often
better schooled in the art of defiance. Also, the adolescent has had
a longer exposure to failure in school than has the younger child;
thus, both teaching and counseling present a substantial challenge.

The *night teacher-counselor* has precisely the same goals as
the day teacher-counselor. Only setting, style, and means to ends
are changed. She works perhaps with a somewhat wider range of
opportunity and with less structure than is required to help a child
learn to profit from a regular school. The world is her classroom,
and her interests and the children's are the curriculum. She arranges with a museum for her children to work as guides and ani-
mal caretakers. She learns model rocketry as she shares her skills
with the children in a project that is pursued with high enthusiasm
and much incidental learning for months. She extracts from the
television set such instruction as is to be had from that misman-
aged medium. She arranges field trips to a planetarium, a Civil War
battlefield, a state capitol building, a fossil field, a shipyard, a
hydroelectric project. She builds identification with the community by involving her children in a community center, a boys' club,
a YMCA, a church. She nurtures responsible friendship by arranging for the children to visit a group member hospitalized with a
broken leg. She fosters creativity by projects in painting, singing,
acting, story writing, and story telling. She engenders group identification, loyalty, and security. Finally, she continues in the
afternoon and evening in sundry ways, including a formal study
period, the learning set in motion in the morning by the day
teacher-counselor.

In work with adolescents, the kinds of experiences planned
and learnings sought change, but the role of the night teacher-
counselor remains essentially the same. Evening activities in a Re-
ED program are integrated with daytime activities, so that learnings in the classroom can be consolidated and preparations made
for the next day's work. Adolescents are members of ecosystems
that differ in characteristic ways from those of young children,
and these changes naturally affect the work of all teacher-counselors. Emphasis in programming may shift from family to the larger
community, with the night teacher-counselor frequently playing a

crucial role in creating opportunities in the community for students, and monitoring their execution. Relationships between boys and girls become more urgent and more intricate, with these developments marking both day and night programs. Because the lives and worlds of adolescents are increasingly complex and the individual increasingly able to make differentiations, to talk to himself about himself, the importance of counseling increases. The less structured nature of the afternoon and evening program means that the night teacher-counselor is frequently involved in informal counseling.

Not only are the roles of the day and the night teacher-counselors interchangeable but they also merge occasionally, as when the group goes on a trip for several days or is at camp, where there is somewhat less emphasis on formal academic work and more emphasis on learning from natural and contrived events of the day. Teacher-counselors, day or night, teach, teach, teach—all the time.

The *liaison teacher-counselor* is the third member of the team responsible for a Re-ED group. She is a teacher-counselor with a special and important assignment: to translate into daily operations the concept of ecological planning and intervention so central to the Re-ED idea. A period of service as a day or night teacher-counselor is the usual route to the post of liaison teacher-counselor. This is an experience of great value in building understanding within the team and in preparation for interpreting the program to mental health centers, schools, and various agencies as well as to parents and other individuals in the community. The liaison teacher-counselor must have a deep understanding of how communities are organized in their people-serving functions and must be able to marshal resources in the interest of a child and the child's family. Skills in consultation, in planning, in assessing the adequacy of family or school for a child, in designing intervention procedures to reduce discord in the ecological system—these are some of the requirements of this exacting function.

The *training supervisor* or *curriculum consultant* is another specialized role for the teacher-counselor. It has proved desirable in some schools, especially those with heavy training commitments, to select an experienced teacher-counselor and give her responsibility for assisting in program planning for the several groups in a school and providing equipment and materials required for the execution of the plans. She may also provide special supervision for teacher-counselors in training or for other personnel—pediatricians, teachers, psychologists, social workers, and others—who are assigned to a Re-ED school as a part of their practicum training. The role is an important one but is not as well defined as other roles described here. This teacher-counselor with a special responsibility often serves essentially as an assistant principal.

The *principal* of a Re-ED school is usually a highly experienced teacher-counselor who understands the functions of all involved in making a program go, and who has demonstrated the administrative skill necessary to coordinate their efforts. She is an educator, a manager, an interpreter of the program. Her exacting task requires her to arrange circumstances for other people to work to their utmost capacity. She sets the tone of a school and helps define the expectations of all those associated with it. Hers is a demanding assignment indeed and one rich in opportunity for personal growth and for contributing to the growth of others, of children, staff, parents, consultants, and members of the larger community alike.

Selection

One notion runs through the early planning papers for Project Re-ED, the idea of the natural worker with children. We have all known adults to whom children respond readily, with enthusiasm and trust, and these are sometimes people with little or no professional training. It seemed a reasonable strategy, considering the short training period, to try to identify these natural workers and to bring them into the training program and thereby gain a valuable head start. We would thus capitalize on individual differences in readiness to work with children. We would try to find people whose life experiences in their own families and in relationship with other significant people had already prepared them in substantial measure for the professional role of teacher-counselor. Professional training is important, but we have come to doubt that it can ever make up for the kinds of subtle learnings that our best teacher-counselors seem to have acquired in their years of living before entering the program. For these reasons, the selection of prospective teacher-counselors has from the beginning seemed to us to be enormously important.

The application to the National Institute of Mental Health for a pilot-project grant to demonstrate and evaluate the Re-ED idea contained further specifications regarding personal attributes thought to be desirable in teacher-counselors. Though the list formulation is now twenty years old, it seems as reasonable and as demanding today as it did before the first trainees were accepted for the program. The grant proposal specified nine attributes desired in teacher-counselors:

1. *Ability to experience, accept, and handle feelings with minimum distortion.* The teacher-counselor must be able to hold an accepting and predictable relationship with a child who expresses and demands intense affection, intense hostility, intense indifference—or a welter of these in unpredictable sequences. He must be as aware of his own feelings and as responsive to them as he is to the feelings of a child.

2. *Ability to tolerate anxiety without dulling.* The teacher-counselor will live intimately with children who will be intensely anxious. He must be able to live with anxiety without blunting his perceptiveness. His own anxieties will be aroused—both sympathetically, by ambient anxiety, and realistically, by the responsibilities of his position. He must be able to handle his own anxiety.

3. *Ability to exercise authority.* While acceptance and permissiveness are frequent themes in the work of the teacher-counselor, he must also know how and when to exercise authority, to define limits, to dramatize the reality principle in living.

4. *Ability to refresh himself independently of his work.* The teacher-counselor should have dependable personal sources for self-renewal. It seems likely that the teacher-counselor cannot do a good job if he is heavily dependent on work as the only source of self-definition. He should also have resources for personal refreshment in nonprofessional interests, and he should be able to withdraw from his work without feeling guilty.

5. *Commitment to children.* There are doubtless many quite mature people who are not the least bit interested in children. Thus, in addition to the attributes of personal maturity mentioned above, the teacher-counselor should like children, care about them, and want to work with them. In selection, one would look for evidence of a long-standing commitment to children, as in early interest in teaching, church work, scouting, and camping.

6. *Effective interpersonal relationships with adults.* There are teachers who are comfortable with children but strained with

other adults. Since heavy emphasis will be placed on team relationships and on professional consultation as a means of ensuring adequate attention to psychiatric, educational, and other problems,
the teacher-counselor must have a history of amicable and productive relationships with other adults and with adults in various role
relationships.

7. *Skills in general teaching.* The teacher-counselor must
know what to do in a classroom on Monday morning. He must
have had training and experience that will enable him to plan a
school day and, more important in the new setting in which he
would be working, to improvise, to make adjustments in routine
to help the group or a class through a stressful period.

8. *Skills in special teaching.* Educational disabilities go with
emotional disturbance. The teacher-counselor would most desir-
ably have had some familiarity with remedial education procedures in reading, arithmetic, and other subjects. He will be given
some training in these skills, but prior acquaintance with them
would be a distinct advantage.

9. *General culture.* A child in school has a right of access to
an adult who is intellectually alert and engaged with his world.
Thus, one criterion for selection would be a manifestation of continuing involvement with intellectual, artistic, social, and political
concerns.

It is worth asking whether we would change these statements were we defining selection criteria today, after some twenty
years of experience in training teacher-counselors and observing
them at work. We would not particularly disagree with the list today, but we would certainly write it differently. The statements
are dreadfully clinical. They were obviously written before we
reached a full appreciation of the educational idiom, of the normal
language of living, in the helping of disturbed children. Our statement today would be much more affirmative and much more appreciative of the range of people who are good with children. We
would seek somehow to describe a real person who is living his
own life with reasonable success but always with a problematic
edge. We would continue to stress commitment to children, beyond doubt; but we would be disposed to add such words as *sensitive, resolute, creative* or *inventive, exuberant* or *zestful* or *quietly
purposeful, serious* and *joyous* altogether, *inquisitive, enthusiastic,
warm* and *affectionate, stern* even, *professional* in the demanding
sense of that word, *playful* perhaps, *resourceful* surely, *responsi-*

ble, and *aware*—aware of themselves, of their world, of children in all their marvelous simplicity and complexity.

And there are other considerations. We would certainly include physical stamina as a necessary attribute; the work of the teacher-counselor is physically demanding. We might add patience as a desirable characteristic, for it takes time to help restore a human ecosystem to a reasonably adequate level of effectiveness. Some good ideas work and some do not, and human frailties as well as strengths abound in the enterprise. Tolerance for sustained intimacy with other people, with adults as well as children and adolescents, is clearly required; indeed, the program draws sustenance from intimate relationships in the context of planned objectives. The most successful teacher-counselors seem to us to have a bit of the antic spirit, a gentle sense of the absurd in life, a real appreciation of fun.

One can make too much of it, but Re-ED does appeal to some kinds of people more than others. Teacher-counselors have been referred to as "Peace Corps" types, and this description is probably as accurate for Re-ED teacher-counselors as it is for Peace Corps volunteers; that is, not very. There are in Re-ED schools more beards and less makeup than in an insurance broker's office or a law firm, more vans than sport cars, more sweaters than vests, more boots and running shoes than ballroom slippers, more books on nature and philosophy than on computers and cost-benefit analysis, more arrowhead collections, guitars, Kelty packs, compasses, carbide lamps, ropes, dogs, aquariums, macramé pots, and personal paintings. One could call teacher-counselors practical idealists. They want to do good well. But such stereotyping is bound to fail; there are more exceptions to any typology than there are pure representations of it. One of the best teacher-counselors of all times dresses primly, wears skirts, hose, high heels, and is manicured, made up, and coiffured; she might wear slacks in a blizzard. So it goes. On the other hand, self-selection does seem to operate, and wherever there are Re-ED schools, there are men and women who find each other congenial and who would fit comfortably into any other Re-ED school. Perhaps the overriding common bond is a deep caring for children.

The problem today is that criteria for the teacher-counselor have been made to seem anemic or academic by people who have been teacher-counselors, real people all, each defying classification, each elusive to measurement: Nelle, Fran, Bill, Jay, Ken, Laura, Larry, Judy, Tom. Who could be left out? Probably no one who has seriously tried to be a teacher-counselor.

In any event, we now have rather clear notions about how teacher-counselors should be selected. At the outset, years ago, we gave applicants for training a battery of psychological tests. We probably would not bother to do so today. We would look for evidence of a long commitment to children in the life histories of people interested in becoming teacher-counselors. The evidence is often there in abundance: camp counselor, Sunday school teacher, teacher's aide, Scout leader, tutor of handicapped children, music teacher, recreation worker, elementary or secondary school teacher, vocational counselor, and so on. People tend to become more of what they already are. Being a teacher-counselor is often a natural next step for someone who is good at working with young people, who believes in them, whose own self-realization is linked to their full development.

We would certainly add special interests and skills. Far more than hospitals and public schools, Re-ED programs give full range for staff members to exercise their unique talents. Today we would give pluses to applicants for teacher-counselor positions who are good at and enthusiastic about African violets, cross-country skiing, darts, finger painting, carpentry, glass making, recording, wild flowers, Cherokee history, bird watching, cooking, weaving, chess, jewelry making, tumbling, drums, square dancing, scuba diving, poetry, jazz, classical music, meteorology. The key words are competence and enthusiasm. The teacher-counselor should never be guilty of trying to teach something that bores her. All she will succeed in doing is to make the student dislike the stuff.

We would stick to graduation from college as a requirement for entry into teacher-counselor training. This eliminates the need for an intelligence test, and teacher-counselors do need to be reasonably bright, since many children they work with will be bright or very bright. A college degree asserts, usually, that the person is motivated to get a job done, and it is something of a measure of character. We also believe that children and adolescents have a right to grow up with the help of reasonably well-educated adults, and college graduation may give some assurance of this.

We would rely heavily on self-selection as perhaps the most reliable indicator of serious purpose, of qualification for working as a teacher-counselor. Whenever possible, people who aspire to be teacher-counselors should be given an opportunity to work with disturbed children or adolescents, perhaps as an aide or a teaching assistant. Electing to withdraw from a training program should be made a perfectly honorable alternative, an intelligent decision for the person who finds troubled and troubling kids not her cup of tea.

And that would be about it.

Training

A governing requirement for training a teacher-counselor was this: the program had to be substantially shorter, and thus less expensive, than the training programs of the other mental health specialists. It was the chronic short supply of these professionals, who were essentially the only people regarded at that time as qualified to work with disturbed children, that led to the effort to develop a new profession and to the evolution of the role of the teacher-counselor. We first decided to limit the training period for the teacher-counselor to six months, then extended it to nine months to make it possible for the candidate to get a Master of Arts degree. The economic advantage of a short training program is clear. But there are tradeoffs. Staff turnover may be higher than it would be with more thoroughly trained people. Job advancement and civil service status may be compromised. And, finally, the complexities of the job of the teacher-counselor are better appreciated today than they were at the beginning of the program. These considerations argue for at least a full calendar year of graduate study, including an internship.

An advantage of the teacher-counselor role with reference to the personnel problem is that Re-ED taps a major new source of talent for working with troubled children, a large group of young people who would ordinarily not be attracted to the established mental health professions. They see themselves as teachers, and they are attracted by an opportunity to work *as teachers* with troubled children and adolescents. Although Re-ED has developed and is now prospering under mental health auspices, its character as an educational enterprise is well established.

The training program for teacher-counselors assumes considerable competence in candidates on entry. It builds on skills already acquired and practiced as an elementary or secondary school teacher, as an arts and crafts specialist, as a recreational leader, as an athletic coach, as a person in some way committed to and experienced in working with children. The teacher-counselor must start with some dependable skills that she adapts for work with disturbed youngsters. She must know how to teach reading, for example, at a level of competence permitting her to do so with ease, in order that she may have mind and heart for the disturbed child whose problems are much greater than being unable to read.

As we have gained in experience in Re-ED, new avenues for becoming a teacher-counselor have opened up. For example, several excellent teacher-counselors now in the program started out as night aides during college, gained rich experience in working with disturbed children, and then entered the training program. Some experienced elementary school teachers have gone directly into a Re-ED school, obtaining their orientation and special skills on the job as full-time staff members.

We are not inclined to prescribe a curriculum for the training of teacher-counselors but rather to set down certain general goals that could be met by various patterns of instruction. In fact, the Re-ED training program at Peabody has varied considerably from time to time, and one would expect new training programs in other universities to take advantage of special local resources and to be free to create new and more effective arrangements for the professional preparation of teacher-counselors.

As we see it now, we would specify nine areas to be covered in teacher-counselor training programs:

1. *Introduction to Re-ED Concepts.* We believe the most important function of a training program should be to give the student a substantial sense of what Re-ED is about, its purpose, its underlying assumptions, its differences from other programs, its limitations. Re-ED is a becoming institution and must always be so if it is to be adequate to the enormous challenge facing all agencies aspiring to help troubled and troubling young people. So little is

known; so much is yet to be discovered. Re-ED has supplied one set of assumptions about disturbed children and adolescents and their worlds and one evolving set of operations for helping them. That the assumptions and operations will change is not just assumed but is advanced as a requirement for continued healthy development of the program. Teacher-counselors have invented Re-ED as it is today, and teacher-counselors will be responsible for its redefinition in the future. The first goal of a training program, then, is to provide an orientation to philosophy and to procedures in order that the teacher-counselor may not only work in harmony with her colleagues today but also help shape the course of Re-ED tomorrow.

2. *Normal Child Development.* The teacher-counselor should have a thorough introduction to what is known about children and adolescents and their normal patterns of development from birth through the early adult years. She should be familiar with patterns of development: of physical characteristics, speech and language skills, cognitive competence, affective expression, interests and values, and concepts of self and others. She should be acquainted with patterns of family life of various socioeconomic groups, and she should know something about what might be called the social psychology of childhood, about the institutions that sustain or thwart child development (the family, the school, the community), so that she can understand the ecological concepts that inform Re-ED and that provide a basis for many aspects of its operation. Emphasis on normal development is stressed here, since the reestablishment of normal developmental patterns in appropriately responsive settings defines the major aim of the Re-ED effort.

3. *Psychopathology of Childhood.* The teacher-counselor should have some acquaintance with current concepts of maladjustment in childhood and adolescence, including concepts of illness and the psychodynamic explanations thereof. Partly this is a vocabulary and communication problem. Much that has been written about disturbed children is in a psychodynamic idiom. The teacher-counselor will use consultants and have contacts with the staffs of community agencies; all are likely to use the language of psychopathology. We suggest familiarity with the concepts of psychopathology and psychodynamics but purposely avoid using

them. There is some evidence that the more sophisticated we have
been in vocabulary and concept, the less successful we have been
in working with particular children. Thus, knowledge of psychopathology is an accommodation to the culture in which we work,
not a commitment to its metaphor.

4. *Psychological, Educational, and Ecological Assessment.*
The teacher-counselor needs to have sufficient knowledge of the
assessment of performance in order to design programs of maximum value for particular children. We do not suggest a thorough
knowledge of psychometrics but simply useful skills in identifying
strengths and weaknesses in a child's behavior repertory, always
with reference to the expectations others have about his performance. This means the ability to detect, through tests when appropriate, the sources of difficulty in doing arithmetic or algebra
or in reading or reasoning. It also means identifying specific behaviors that get the child or adolescent in trouble in school or
community—behaviors that cause him to be regarded as unacceptable. It further suggests skills in identifying patterns of behavior
on the part of parents or teachers that sustain the behavior regarded by them as unacceptable or nonadaptive. It may mean the
development of skill in counting the occurrence of particular responses in order to provide a baseline for assessing the effectiveness of some intervention. Finally, it may involve skill in assessing
the adequacy of operation of a total ecological system defined by
a particular child, to guide a decision about his admission to a Re-
ED school or the readiness of the total system to accept responsibility for the child without further assistance by Re-ED.

5. *Teaching Skills.* The teacher-counselor should be accomplished in the skills of the elementary or secondary school teacher,
whether she is to work as a day teacher-counselor, a night teacher-
counselor, a liaison teacher-counselor, or in other posts in a Re-ED
school. In working with preschool children, the teacher-counselor
must understand thoroughly the principles of behavior modification, including the identification of critical behaviors, the plotting
of behavior frequencies, the selection of reinforcers, the scheduling of contingencies, and the evaluation of outcomes. She must
have special skills as a teacher of adults, since mothers and fathers
are taught to manage the behavior of their own children, as well as
to teach techniques to other parents. In working with children of

elementary school age, she must know how to teach reading, writing, spelling, and arithmetic as basic skills, and she should be able to use these in the context of music and art, history, science, social problems, and literature in a way that will enrich and expand the life of the child. In working with adolescents, the teacher-counselor must command a fairly wide range of knowledge and be able to teach secondary school subjects. The use of subject matter specialists in Re-ED programs (with students moving from specialist to specialist) is not encouraged because it attenuates the relationship between the teacher-counselor and the student, and it may decrease the effectiveness of the group in encouraging constructive behavior. The teacher-counselor also should be well acquainted with the strategies of remedial instruction in basic skills and be thoroughly familiar with the range of resources available to supplement the normal instructional program for the child or adolescent who has a particular learning problem.

6. *Consultation.* A basic premise of the Re-ED program is that a person of limited training (one or two years of graduate study instead of four or more years) can perform effectively on the job considerably beyond ordinary expectation, provided she is backed up by consultants with the specialized understandings and skills required to solve technical problems. The teacher-counselor thus must be able to communicate with and get assistance from a pediatrician, a curriculum specialist, a psychiatrist, a social worker, a sociologist, or a community development worker. Acquiring an appropriate vocabulary is a part, but a minor one, of this requirement. Of more importance is the confidence on the part of the teacher-counselor that she can get help from others with specialized competencies, and a set toward her work that leads her readily and comfortably to turn to consultants for assistance. Unfortunately, however, many "consultants" do not know how to consult. The teacher-counselor may often have to teach the consultant how to provide needed help, not didactically, of course, but by framing problems in ways that elicit from the consultant the kind of help the teacher-counselor needs. In this two-way process of communication, the teacher-counselor will gain some humility as well as skill for her own service as a consultant. The teacher-counselor is essentially a consultant for the parents of the children with whom she works, and she frequently serves as con-

sultant to a school, agency, or employer in helping them use the special knowledge developed about a child or an adolescent during his Re-ED experience.

7. *Special skills.* The effective teacher-counselor has to have an incredibly wide range of specialized skills: how to teach reading, arithmetic, or algebra, how to calm an enraged child or encourage a defeated adolescent, how to pack a canoe, how to produce a play, how to identify a fossil, how to help a group plan, how to use a psychiatric consultant, how to write a case history, how to design and carry out an operant conditioning program, how to play a guitar or build a rocket or mold a pot or use a map and compass, how to handle an epileptic seizure, how to build a model airplane, and (for adolescents) how to apply for and get a job, how to write a computer program, how to record a folk song and press a record, how to edit a serious newspaper, how to keep books for a commercial enterprise. Most teacher-counselors bring to their jobs a fairly wide range of skills at the outset, but all find deficiencies, things they would like to know about or be able to do. Some of these special skills are taught in the training program; others have to be acquired on the teacher-counselor's own initiative, on the job. In the first class of teacher-counselors, for example, all trainees were required to learn to play the guitar. This requirement, later abandoned, was instituted not just for the virtues of guitar playing but to demonstrate that a person can learn almost anything and to generate this kind of positive self-expectation among teacher-counselors.

8. *Personal Development.* The training program for the teacher-counselor should allow time to nourish personal interests not directly related to performance on the job with children. The teacher-counselor should be a person of range and depth, and she should have access to sources of intellectual and affective refreshment. These will be highly idiosyncratic, of course, a source of private enrichment for a particular person. The importance of this general requirement should not be minimized. Personal development can be neglected only at the price of diminished professional competence.

9. *Learning to Learn.* The training of the teacher-counselor is far from complete at the end of the formal training program. Indeed, it has just begun. The original Re-ED proposal explicitly

identified the need for in-service training programs, for attendance at conferences, for a conscious and purposeful continuation of the teacher-counselor's education. We now put greater emphasis on the responsibility of the teacher-counselor herself to plan for her own educational development, both formally and informally. The training program should set a teacher-counselor on a trajectory that would involve continuing commitment to being a learner. Thus, learning to learn is a major goal of the teacher-counselor training program.

In this discussion, we have avoided reference to credit hours, to kinds and numbers of courses. We have explicitly not talked about formal classroom instruction and practicum or internship training. We assume that many and varied patterns will emerge for the training of teacher-counselors, just as we have observed in our own work a shifting of arrangements from year to year. In all this, we would have only one rather formal expectation, the importance of which we have come to believe in deeply. The teacher-counselor in training should have some kind of continuing involvement with children or adolescents and with an ongoing, educationally oriented treatment program. Some of us have come to believe that the involvement should start the first week in graduate school and should continue throughout the total program. Others of us believe, however, that a concentrated internship experience for a solid block of several months is to be preferred to a spread-out experience paralleling daily the work done in the classroom. We simply argue here for continuing involvement, in some way, with the activities that will at some point become all-consuming.

Stresses

Competence, and confidence in one's competence, are essential to effective living, to doing a good job, to feeling good about oneself. The biggest single change that has come about since the beginning days of Re-ED at Cumberland House and Wright School is in the achievement by teacher-counselors of a high level of professional competence. Teacher-counselors *know* that they can work effectively with children, parents, family members, teachers, and other professional people, as well as with each other, and they *know* that they can communicate these skills to new staff members. They go about their work—most of the time—with assurance and good humor. They know what to do when a child explodes, a group deteriorates, a family defaults on its responsibilities—and they know that they know what to do. It has not always been thus. In the early days at Cumberland House and Wright School, teacher-counselors were often not sure of what to do, and we were often unable to instruct them. At that time, there was neither a theory nor a technique of reeducation, such as are available today. In consequence, anxiety ran high, contagious depression swept through the schools from time to time, interpersonal conflicts occasionally mushroomed, and staff turnover was high.

Currently popular among people who work on the front line in programs for difficult children is the concept of "burnout." The term is catchy; programs of professional meetings are filled with papers on it. Indeed, burnout has become a profession-generated expectancy, so that the teacher-counselor might well wonder if she is not (through insufficient zeal or sensitivity) somehow lacking if she does not "burn out." We do not doubt that the phenomenon is genuine, and it seems important to sort out sources of the difficulty, so that steps can be taken to reduce the toll on people and on programs.

A first source of difficulty: any institution for disturbed children, especially one that tries to avoid locks and drugs, will operate normally with a fairly high tension level. One can expect a good bit of "noise" in the system all the time. And Re-ED schools will be subject to more tension than most institutional arrangements for disturbed children, for several reasons also related to their effectiveness. For one thing, many teacher-counselors are young and open to disappointment; they are idealistic, deeply committed to children, and impatient with their own bungling as well as that of others. This is great for the children but hard on the teacher-counselors. Furthermore, many teacher-counselors are still discovering themselves. The urgency of self-discovery has not yet been blunted, but it makes them vulnerable to criticism from within and without. The work of the teacher-counselor is physically and emotionally demanding, even exhausting. Disturbed children are often skillful at detecting and exploiting the weaknesses of adults; indeed, this is one reason adults reject them and call them disturbed. Add to these strains the sustained intimacy among staff and students and the absence of a strong authority structure characteristic of traditional residential treatment programs, and there results a situation of high psychological lability. Under the most favorable circumstances, difficulties can be expected.

A second source of tension that sometimes disrupts the professional life of a teacher-counselor is his private, personal life, apart from Re-ED. Private stress can lead to public inadequacy and discouragement. While the mutual support systems among a Re-ED staff may sometimes be helpful in alleviating this source of stress, there is little that can be done officially to reduce it. Sometimes a consultant may be of help.

A third source of excess tension, however, is clearly the responsibility of the administrators of Re-ED programs as well as of teacher-counselors themselves, and that is the deep discouragement that can emanate from the work situation itself. With regard to this source of burnout, we have the same attitude that we have toward the growth of children and adolescents in the program. If a child fails to thrive in a Re-ED program, we regard it as the program's fault, not the child's. If a teacher-counselor, having been carefully selected and thoughtfully trained, is unable to find a fulfilling engagement with Re-ED over time, it is the fault of the program, not of the teacher-counselor. While there may be circumstances in which the unbending application of this rule is unrealistic, it is, pragmatically, by far the best rule to operate on.

A common pattern in Re-ED is for teacher-counselors to work in various roles and then move on to other opportunities, most frequently in graduate or professional school but in other settings as well. This kind of change in careers is normal and healthy, and teacher-counselors who move on under these circumstances do so not out of defeat but with a sense of accomplishment and a zest for future developmental adventures. Of course, a number of teacher-counselors have stayed with Re-ED programs over the years, finding deep satisfaction and fulfillment in various kinds of leadership roles. It is exceedingly important that there be built into Re-ED programs avenues for staff advancement, to encourage the full utilization by the teacher-counselor of his growing capacities.

The discouragement, the demoralization, the incapacitation suggested by the term *burnout* are caused by excessive fatigue, by a sense of incompetence on the job (whether truly sensed or not), by a feeling of powerlessness in the face of higher authority, by private anxieties generated by relationships with particular children, and by guilt at the feelings of hostility generated by any or all of the foregoing sources of distress. The important thing is that all these sources of distress are usually remediable by informed and intelligent administrative action, either on the part of immediate superiors or on the part of people responsible for the general design of a Re-ED program. Excessive fatigue may require a readjustment of schedules, including leaves when rest is required. Apart from planned rest and recreation, the most important antiburnout measure is understanding, appreciation, and support of the work of individual teacher-counselors. More than anything else, it is important for teacher-counselors (and Re-ED supervisors and administrators as well) to feel that they have some control over what happens to them. Staff conferences where problems can be aired in an atmosphere of respect, gentleness, and good humor are extraordinarily important, provided, of course, they do lead to constructive action. Finally, sponsors of Re-ED programs, administrators, and supervisors should not impose discordant expectations on the staff. For example, a current major source of demoralization in some Re-ED programs is the imposition on them of alien expectations generated by medically oriented third-party payment arrangements. Program administrators and supervisors have to spend much of their time fending off medically appropriate but Re-ED-inappropriate directives that would destroy the program if honored, and they have sharply reduced time to perform their normal functions of supporting and guiding teacher-counselors in their work.

Autobiographical Sketches

Writing about teacher-counselors, listing criteria for their selection, even describing how they work, as we shall do later on—none of these constitutes a satisfactory representation of the professional person who makes Re-ED successful. As a partial and admittedly insufficent solution to the problem of making teacher-counselors seem real persons, which they must be above all else, we present here four brief autobiographical sketches. We would need hundreds of such sketches to suggest the range of people who are teacher-counselors. But even this would be inadequate, for the next person to assume the role would be different still, the same only in his commitment to children and to the discovery of effective ways of working with them.

Kenneth L. Shaw
Cumberland House*

The invitation to submit an autobiography comes at a time in my life when I am feeling the warmth of a degree of both personal and professional success which has been recently preceded by a period significantly lacking in this feeling. Thus, the prospect of this writing is both entertaining and forbidding. I would much prefer to talk with the reader.

I am presently a night teacher-counselor at Cumberland House Elementary School, sharing responsibilities for eight boys (called Pathfinders) with a day teacher-counselor, a liaison teacher-counselor, and a night aide. I have come to thoroughly enjoy the children, the school and its meanings, and the people with whom I work. To have mutually supportive co-workers and an administrative atmosphere encouraging both individual and team autonomy has been most meaningful. Gratifications in my work have come concomitantly and inseparably with those of a new marriage.

I am thirty-three years old, six feet tall, and stocky in build. Texas is my home state. I lived mostly in Dallas, but was fondest of the East Texas countryside where my parents grew up. East Texas is sandy land with rolling hills, mixed pine and hardwood forests, cotton, peas, tomatoes, watermelons, and enough rabbits, squirrels, quail, sunfish, bass, swimming holes, water moccasins, and copperheads to occupy a boy's time during summers and weekends during the school year. Fishing, hunting, camping, and such skills and accoutrements as are primary to these pursuits are to this day my favorite pastimes. I also enjoy playing guitar, singing, folk music, tinkering in my workshop, working on our home and yard, reading a good book (preferably on outdoor topics), and being with good company around the table.

My dad is a successful CPA-lawyer in Dallas and has taught for a number of years in the School of Business of Southern Methodist University. He is third youngest in a family of two girls and

*This autobiographical sketch was written in 1967. The supplementary paragraphs were written in 1981.

five boys. Mom keeps house, does a little church work, and accompanies Dad on weekend and vacation fishing and sightseeing outings. She also comes from a large family. My younger brother, Les, is an accountant and lives with his wife and baby son in Dallas.

Although my parents' respective families have what might be termed a normal cohesiveness in that they reunite as often as possible and are mutually supportive, our own family is not addicted to outward expressions of closeness. Communication, until recently, was largely functional and left me looking for warmth in relationships outside the family while growing up. Dad did serve as an adequate model in limit setting. He was a hard worker and firm disciplinarian, and he wanted what he saw as best for us. I had never realized the depth of his feelings for me until my separation from my first wife and son three years ago. His support emerged during that difficult period and meant much to me, in spite of his awkwardness of expression. At that time, I learned something of what one man can mean to another, and I am grateful. Mom is a motherly, forgiving, and naturally sympathetic woman. She was both father and mother while Les and I were growing up (Dad worked long hours and served in the Navy during World War II), and she imbued us with a sturdy set of middle-class values from which I have never been able comfortably to depart.

I hold a B.S. degree in Elementary Education from Southern Methodist University and a Master of Arts degree in Special Education for Emotionally Disturbed Children from Peabody College. While my grades in an overall sense have been adequate, I could not be described accurately as a scholar. Except for a handful of very special teachers and courses, formal education has been for me, so far, a matter of fulfilling some sort of vague obligation. I am, however, looking forward with considerable enthusiasm to work on the Education Specialist degree next year at Peabody.

In addition to formal schooling, I am pleased to have had some variety in work background. As a boy, my work experience included delivering newspapers during elementary school years, house painting, automobile painting and repair, construction welding, and, during high school summers, carpentry. Since graduation from college, I have been engaged in public school teaching (sixth grade, three years), YMCA after-school athletics instruction (three years), summer camp counseling (three years), day camp supervision, and my current work at Cumberland House, where I have been for two years.

I have attempted to extract in the following section those experiences that have been most relevant to my role as a night teacher-counselor.

In public school teaching, I gained a working knowledge of

classroom materials and procedures and a good feeling for the age group with which I worked. Because I did not organize well, I developed an ability to "play by ear," which has served me well in the relatively unstructured role of night teacher-counselor, a role that suits me better than being a public school teacher.

The aversive routines of lunch money collection, daily lesson plans, computing A.D.A.s, grading papers, etc., etc., convinced me that, although I could fulfill the basic requirements of the teacher's job, my bent was not for the conventional classroom.

The YMCA program and philosophy in children's athletics demonstrated to me the values of fun and fair play over those of highly regimented skill development and adult-like competition.

I spent several pleasant summers as a camp counselor. I learned more about my own as well as the boys' atavistic responses to the adventures of primitive living. The director of the camp, a long-time sportsman and conservationist, provided many lessons in the healthful relationships between woods, waters, wildlife, and growing boys.

I served for three years as administrative assistant to Campbell Loughmiller, who runs a camp for disturbed and antisocial boys, sponsored by the Salesmanship Club of Dallas. Under his expert guidance, I acquired knowledge about working with maladjusted boys in small groups under very primitive outdoor conditions. I also gained valuable experience in parent-child conferences centered on the development of problem-solving processes within the family.

In order to complete this writing, I must refer to some personal situations and influences in my life. Only recently have I come to feel comfortable with problem boys and their troubled parents. I value this feeling for myself and for whatever it may mean to the children and families with whom I have had professional contact over the past two years. It has evolved mainly during the period that began when my first marriage ended. During this time, I came to realize, largely through the impact of the separation from my son, and aided by the previously mentioned new ties with my own father, how vital and meaningful a relationship can be between a man and a boy. These events were accompanied by a brief period of professional counseling, which helped me to collect my wits, and were followed by the beginning of my new marriage, which included the role of stepfather to my bride's three-year-old son. Had not this peculiar, but fortunate, sequence of circumstances occurred, I doubt that I could have ever reached a really effective level of communication with the students and parents who come to Cumberland House.

My experience has been extended further by the influence of a theoretical frame of reference in behavior modification. I do not refer strictly to the laboratory use of learning theory but rather to a concerted effort to identify and utilize effectively those reinforcers—both positive and aversive—that are present and available in our regular daily activities. I hope to do a systematic study of the use of social reinforcements that exist within small-group settings.

I shall close with an anecdote which explains clearly my pleasure as a night teacher-counselor. Several months ago, the Pathfinders took a rather sparsely planned one-day trip by canoe down a scenic stretch of the Harpeth River. Rain drizzled down on us for the first hour as we navigated "deep waters" (4 feet) and "white-water rapids" (12 inches deep). We stopped for lunch at a gravel bar at the foot of a "mountain" (200 feet), which we climbed, and disrupted a "flock of eagles" (buzzards). Later, armed only with slingshots, we were "almost attacked by wild boars" (domestic pigs pasturing in the woods). We then located a tunnel through solid rock (a local historic landmark) and threw rocks into the waterfall below it. We spotted a deep cave (10 feet) and climbed up to explore it with gopher matches. At the bottom, we found a "huge snake" (large stick). Crawling out of the cave, Barry, whose dull appearance and mannerisms often disguised his above-average intellect and subtle wit, said with a sly grin, "Boy! I feel like Cuckeberry Finn!" The experiences of that afternoon are the kind of thing that makes me glad I am a teacher-counselor.

[*Supplement: March 1981.*]

Following my work at Re-ED, I have fulfilled an apparent destiny to live near the mountains in Colorado. In October of 1969, I was employed as a Special Ed teacher for the newly forming Adolescent Treatment Team at Fort Logan Mental Health Center in Denver. I became clinical team leader and served in that capacity for nearly six years. The team did innovative work in both outpatient and inpatient services, focusing heavily on total family involvement in the treatment process, and including school, church, and other available community resources. I must say that the hospital setting and its inherent medical model for treatment was quite a switch for me, and I found it a difficult adjustment. Many other problems arose—some financial, some administrative, some interpersonal—but mostly related to the intermixture of adolescents with the full range of adult mental patients.

In 1975, somewhat burned out on the public mental health scene, I resigned from Fort Logan and took some time off for reassessment of personal and professional goals. Under supervision, I maintained a small private practice in psychotherapy for a year or so. During this interim, an old interest rekindled itself—fixing houses. Since the fall of 1976, I have entered the business of renovating older homes, plus remodeling and some new construction. I have found this second profession rewarding and personally satisfying. My partners have come from business management and university teaching backgrounds, so we have many areas of mutual interest.

I have maintained some activity and interest in mental health in several ways. Currently, I am serving as a consultant for two adolescent shelter care programs (in addition to remodeling and maintaining their homes). I also see myself in a sort of "Johnny Appleseed" role, spreading a few seeds here and there amongst friends, clients, and co-workers that encourage healthful parenting practices and adult relationships. My wife is a social worker in active practice, so we have plenty to talk about in the human services area.

It would not be fitting to close this short sketch without saying that I feel very fortunate to have trained and worked in the Re-ED project. Those experiences and the high-quality relationships developed there remain sharp for me. My life—and, I hope, the lives of others—has been greatly enriched from that time.

Frances Smith
*Wright School**

When I was a child, I had a lot of orthopedic work done, which necessitated my spending much of my time from ages two to four in bed. I remember two things. I choked on the ether and struggled with the anesthetist. The next time, the doctor made a deal: if I would be very quiet and still, no ether. I was fascinated and can still remember the green tile room, a lady getting a cast put on, the bright lights. The other thing I remember was my feeling about adults—how lovely some were and how fake others were, bearing gifts to the poor little child when I only remember being happy.

My father was an aircraft designer and a dreamer of dreams. In the 40s, he used to tell how men would fly to the moon, how men were capable of so much. He didn't talk about his feelings much, just went about his business. But he usually had projects. A lady greeted my mother, "How nice what Smitty did for Al." For the past year, Daddy had been helping a guy who had lost his job, his wife, and his self-respect. During the year, Daddy had gone to work early to clean his apartment, cook his meals, do his laun-

*This autobiographical sketch was written in 1967. The supplementary paragraphs were written in 1981.

dry, be his friend, and help him find a new job. "He needed a little help, that's all" or "I liked him." A mechanic called him long distance once to say "I made foreman, just like you said I could." And he had become the first Negro foreman in the company. Dad also could slam doors when he was mad, wander through a city for hours, and swear he didn't really care about helping people.

Both Momma and Daddy were always doing things, pounding copper, sewing, refinishing furniture. The kids were included and came to expect to be able to do anything, including fixing toilets and leaky faucets. The most fun times with Momma were helping fix dinner and running errands. Just working side by side was satisfying.

We moved to Atlanta in 1951. We might as well have moved to another country. My first spelling test the teacher pronounced "dawg" and "tin" and I wrote *dawg* and *tin* only to be loudly told that I must be dumb since the words were *dog* and *ten*. Our favorite seat on the bus was the last one—and did people stare as my sister and I raced gleefully to the empty back seat. And the ugliness in the trolley driver's voice as he yelled "This bus won't move until all colert moved to the back" was appalling, so I didn't get on. I went to a largely middle-class school. One girl's father drove a trolley, and many wouldn't so much as smile at her.

My dream as a Girl Scout was to participate in the Mobile Camps of the Southwest. The year I was eligible, I only applied at the urging of an adult who said it wouldn't hurt to apply. What a lesson learned when I opened the letter saying I was accepted!

I was always catching bugs and caterpillars. Once I noticed the chrysalis beginning to move back and forth as if in a struggle with some unknown force. As I watched, I saw the chrysalis break, a butterfly emerge, pump its wings, and spread them to dry. I've never seen a more beautiful butterfly.

We were taught to look at the consequences of actions and if we could take them to go ahead and act.

I had a tree that overlooked the train tracks way in the back of our yard where I went when I wanted to shout for joy, or throw angry rocks, or sit and think. No one ever commented on my goings and comings from the tree. When I came home from college one year, the tree was gone. I was sad but OK because I didn't need the tree anymore.

In the Fulton Bag and Paper Mill section of Atlanta was Sister Keil, who was something on the order of Jane Addams. I helped her on Saturdays at her playground. She showed me beaten children, hard and ancient four-year-olds, two-room houses for fifteen people, Christmas bicycles reclaimed by the loan man. But she also showed me a child's response to warmth and respect, a poor mother's real caring for her kids, and that being paid a penny was better than a dole even if you had to be given the job to earn that penny. I also watched slum landlords, the most interesting of whom was an officer in the Council of Christian Church Women. I eventually had to tell her what I thought of her brand of Christianity as I had watched her extract $40-$60 per month for two-room shacks. I also saw things change on Sister Keil's block—a lowering crime rate, improved health and sanitary conditions, an effort to get out. The church women began putting in more and more money—built a new building—taught piano—gave away food and clothes. Pickets Alley was never the same again—it was middle-class nice and no longer belonged to the neighborhood. The people quit learning from Pickets Alley and began taking. I quit going. Sister Keil died of cancer.

I went to Duke glad at least to begin living more on my own. My aspirations were to be a scientist, but the liberal arts program soon caught me up, and I couldn't get enough of anything. I worked as an attendant on the adult psychiatric ward of the university hospital. For the first time, I had begun to feel effective and comfortable. The most impressive observation was from many adults' account of their childhood and how desperately they had needed some help then. I soon began to feel restricted by the school's idea of freedom. I began testing their rules and got expelled in a, to me, Kafkaish sequence of events. Many letters were sent home reporting how irresponsible, indiscriminate, etc., I was. And the next day, I went to work at Re-ED.

I don't remember when I first realized it, but I found that understanding and helping kids grow was a job I could do well and one that I enjoyed. I felt like I wasn't really working. In the beginning, when I was unsure of my own abilities, I did what others did and suggested. But gradually I began to try my own ideas and found that I could be innovative and effective on my own. And at this point, my own needs to explore and grow ran headlong into a then-adolescent agency. Like most adolescents, we have both grown up and benefited from a confrontation with each other.

I was the night teacher-counselor for the younger boys' group. I viewed this as the at-home time. We played games, collected bugs, explored the countryside, went shopping, talked events and our feelings over, made things. The kids may have received some help, but me—wow. First I learned that taking care of children was a huge job—and I didn't have to prepare meals, clean, wash clothes, nor have them on weekends. I wasn't ready to be a mother. I also found that fairness, self-respect, and recognition of one's individuality went a long way toward helping a kid. Changing specific things about a kid eluded me at the time but was filled in at Peabody later in my work in behavior modification. I gained a healthy distrust of professionals and their bag of cans and cannots. One of the consultants saw making me self-reliant as part of his job. He goaded and picked until I screamed "I live with the kid and I think I know better than you." And his response: "I thought you would never realize that." In a frightening way, I learned to listen to kids. I learned, too, that flexible programs are essential. One morning Johnny woke me to say "There is a fire in my bed and I can't get it out."All I could see in his room were smoke and flames. No one even got a scratch, but each held a memory of a terrifying sight. The kid who lit the fire said "I just wanted to light a little fire so you would let me go home for a little while." His plan for helping himself had been far superior to ours. We refused his plan because it involved tailoring our program to him. Thus, we forced him into setting a fire, and he was allowed to go home for good.

The worst part was my adolescent clashes with the administrators. I felt there should be more room in the program for my own development, thinking, and experimentation. I thought and experimented anyway because without it the sameness was deadening. I kept thinking I could do their job at least as well as they did.

I joined the Re-ED training program after working as a teacher-counselor. This gave me a chance to review the year in the role and to do a lot of reading. At the end, I was ready to move on and happily found the Re-ED people agreed.

I found a perfect job in Kansas City, the teacher-director of a small school for severely disturbed children, and my chance to be administrator. My, but things looked different from that perch. Gradually the light dawned that it was up to me to change things. I saw a job could allow for staff development—in fact, that the kids benefited from this, too. My distrust of professionals came in handy, since we had children in our school that they said you "couldn't help." My recently found behavior modification skills took away many of my former frustrations with changing behaviors. But I found I was a lousy administrator in the area of details, and as a fund raiser I was a zero.

Now I am director of a daycare facility on Chicago's South Side. We handle disturbed, retarded, and educationally deprived children who are excluded from school.

As a teacher-counselor, I began a pattern of testing educational and psychiatric traditions that excluded many from the learning process. Most importantly, I found that, for me, seeing children and staff grow is like watching the butterfly hatch.

[*Supplement: July 3, 1981.*]

What have I been doing? Well, for one thing, I changed my name. I am now Frances Smith Rothman. My husband and I moved about the country from Chicago to Baltimore to San Francisco and back to Chicago again. My stints as administrator of children's programs helped me decide that, for me, running things my way wasn't worth the grief. And I found I didn't have to run things to be able to influence what happens. And besides—I really liked direct work with children and their families better than I liked budgets, buildings, and meetings.

So through the moves, I worked as a teacher with mentally retarded elementary kids, as a reading teacher, and finally as a teacher with disturbed adolescents. As I became more and more interested in their emotional and social development and their families and less and less interested in teaching reading and algebra, I decided to go to social work school so I would have the precious credential to change jobs. But where did I end up in social work school? With a field placement on an inpatient unit for delinquent adolescents, arguing for field trips and more family contact. And remembering again the Re-ED principles and people—and contacting Nick—and getting trapped into writing this.

"A child should know joy." I think if anything from Re-ED kept leaping out at me through the years, it was this. How neglected is this aspect of human experience, and how important and healing joyful experiences can be not only for children but for families—and for staff. And yet how hard one has to argue to provide pleasurable experiences in programs.

I've also become interested in working with families and have been struck with the similarities between some of the family literature and Re-ED ideas.

Anyway, I find myself going back over and over again to that first major Re-ED paper (Hobbs, 1966) and remembering, and feeling good about a solid and productive beginning to my professional work in social services. Thanks.

Me? Now I'm job hunting. And of course I look to continue working with children, adolescents, and their families—and their schools—and their communities.

Claudia Lann
*Positive Education Program**

Throughout the difficult process of attempting to begin the task of writing an autobiography, one thought continuously returned. I believe my childhood was typical of that of most children born to suburban working-class families after World War II. I guess there were times when we were in trouble financially, but I never knew it. My early years were characterized by sibling rivalry, neighborhood antics, swimming in the summer, skating in the win-

*This autobiographical sketch was written in 1981.

ter, dancing and piano lessons, and summer camp when it could be afforded.

I am the youngest of four children born to two people whom I greatly respect. I am also the only girl, consequently rather pampered and admittedly a little spoiled—especially by my dad. Now that I'm older, I've enjoyed switching those roles. Although initially difficult, I now take great pleasure in openly expressing my love, gratitude, and respect.

For the most part, I always liked school. I can still remember thinking how silly my crying peers were in kindergarten on the first day of school. Having gone to preschool for two years while my mother completed her PTA business, I knew that school was fun. By the time I reached the first grade, my vocational plans were set. I was going to be a teacher.

It was a decision that was supported and encouraged by my parents. Having been denied an education past the twelfth grade, my parents' goal was to send each of their children to college. My first brother went off to college when I was six years old. Every four years after that, another one went. In June of 1976, their dream was realized. Every one of their children had at least a bachelor's degree. Those of us who didn't have a master's started getting hints about doing so.

Following the footsteps of two of my brothers, I chose to go to Kent State University. My parents impressed upon me that getting an education was important, but so was utilizing the experience to grow up. Consequently, I maintained a B average and had a lot of fun. My earliest experiences in counseling came at Kent. Trying to help with the financial burdens of maintaining two kids in college, I became a resident adviser in the dorm during my junior and senior years. We were trained to counsel students, maintain order, and to do what I now know is called "develop group process."

My declared major at KSU was elementary education. By my sophomore year, I'd heard enough stories about the surplus of teachers that I decided I had better specialize to increase my chances on the job market. I had heard something about behavior disorders, which caught my attention. One of my brothers was always special. Although incredibly talented, intelligent, handsome, and popular, he never seemed totally happy. Things got to him. He was too emotional and tried too hard to be perfect. I thought I might like working with children like him. But I wasn't sure, so I began doing volunteer work with different kinds of exceptional children. I found much of it personally depressing and for the most part decided that I didn't have what it took to be a special educator. Then I arranged a field placement in KSU's lab school. I had found my niche! The work was hard and the students challenging, but the emotions that accompanied the task were right for me. I found myself caring but not pitying. I came to believe that the prognosis for these children was good. For the most part, there were no physical or intellectual barriers to becoming a happy, competent person. To use an old cliché, the sky was the limit. So with this thought, I transferred into the special education department at KSU and pursued a major in learning disabilities and behavior disorders.

When I graduated, my fears were realized. Unable to find a teaching position, I took a job as an educational aide. By December of that year, I'd heard of a need for special education teachers in Texas. On the first of January, I packed my car and left Cleveland for Brownsville, Texas. The next six months were spent in culture shock. Being immersed in a Mexican-American culture, I learned what it meant to be a member of a minority. As many of my students either refused or didn't know how to speak English, I learned to communicate with children in crude, nonverbal ways. Then we started teaching each other our languages. It was an exciting and worthwhile experience.

I may have stayed in Texas longer, but at the school year's end, family problems brought me home. My time that summer was divided between counseling my brother and looking for a teaching job in the area. As luck would have it, I was hired by the Positive Education Program (PEP) as a teacher-counselor in one of their Re-ED day-treatment centers.

The first six months of my career at PEP could be characterized as traumatic. Surrounded by unbelievably competent coworkers, I feared I could never meet the expectations of the position. Many hours were spent planning, reading, experiencing successes and failures, and replanning. I believe now that academic planning and behavior management techniques can be learned. It is the personality of the teacher-counselor and his or her commitment to the reeducation of children that really count. An ability to recognize and enjoy small successes and learn from mistakes is essential.

About midyear, I realized that things were going pretty well, and my confidence began to build. The support and training of my fellow staff members had been effective. I began to feel competent and confident in my ability to treat emotionally disturbed children and thoroughly enjoyed my work. I spent a little over two very satisfying years in the classroom.

In November of my third year at PEP, I was offered an opportunity to transfer centers and become a liaison teacher-counselor. The prospects of doing so were both exciting and frightening. Leaving a staff with whom I'd grown terribly close seemed too difficult a thing to do. Leaving my class, the Samurai, was even harder. Even so, the decision was made to transfer, and after a brief adjustment period, I grew to enjoy my new position just as much and have become just as fond of my new co-workers.

At the time of this writing, I'm in my fourth year at PEP, still in day treatment, and still committed to the belief that emotionally disturbed or disturbing children can become capable, happy persons through the process of reeducation. At the risk of sounding a bit corny, I still believe that the sky is the limit.

I'd like to close this autobiography by sharing one of my memorable experiences of day treatment. I had one student whose treatment had taken considerably longer than the average length of stay. From my experience, I would say he was considerably more disturbed than many. About a week before his graduation was to occur, we were sitting around after school "rapping." In the course of the conversation, he asked me if I made a lot of money. My reply was that it was enough but not a great deal, that teachers really didn't get paid as much as some of the other professions. I'll never forget his reply. He told me that I should be satisfied with my job because I was helping to "straighten out" a lot of kids like him, and that should make me feel good. It does, and I suppose that that explains what Re-ED is all about.

Dante Jackson
*Positive Education Program**

Being selected or asked to write this autobiographical sketch represents another milestone in my growth here at the Positive Education Program (PEP). I certainly wouldn't have thought it possible two and a half years ago, when I arrived as an associate teacher-counselor at the Eastwood Day-Treatment Center.

My initial reaction to the hands-on experience of working with severely brain-damaged children was a shocker indeed. I remember vividly attempting to explain to my parents and family (to say nothing of friends) just what I was doing and have them say "Oh, that can't be true" or "You must be crazy" as I related the events of my early days.

Thankfully, there was Gretchen, my first partner, who single-handedly (almost) convinced me to stick around and let it fall into perspective. "Take it easy," she'd say, "and let yourself get involved; it's the only way to learn." So I did, and I learned, and I grew to appreciate the tremendous responsibility of the teacher-counselor.

Life began for me in the inner city of Cleveland's east side. I was born second of five children to a steelworker father and

*This autobiographical sketch was written in 1981.

laundry worker mother. I remember my childhood as particularly happy (nobody told me we were poor, so how was I to know!). Many a warm summer day was spent on the local sandlots, playing baseball, basketball, or football. Many a warm summer evening was spent at the downtown mall or the lake, hanging out with the brothers. It occurs to me that growing up in the ghetto allows a kid of lot of experiences you can't get anywhere else; for instance, the opportunity for getting into trouble was always available, and I took my share of spills. In a lot of ways, that's why I've found success with my kids. I understand the pressure they live with. I've been there and I'm OK, so I know they can make it too.

During my early life (seven to fourteen), three things kept me out of the penitentiary or morgue. They were my mother, sports, and my girlfriend. My mother, the high-strung, emotional leader of my early life, was always pushing us kids for a little more. The funny thing was that with each goal met, her expectations rose, and we knew she'd never ease up. She always wanted more for us, and often it came at her personal expense. You see, money was an alien creature in our house; therefore, we were budgeting long before it became fashionable. It was through my mother's direction that I got involved in scouting. She wanted me off the street and doing something positive. So I got involved and really enjoyed the experience, particularly being a member of the Order of the Arrow. Without my mother's direction, I doubt seriously if I would have made it through high school. I never really liked school in an academic sense. School for me was the center of my social connection and the place which allowed me access to sports, particularly football.

Though it was Mom's direction which kept me in school, it was football that made higher education a reality. I quickly learned that if I transferred my enthusiasm and dedication for sports toward my academic pursuits, I would enjoy the best of several worlds. Besides, I'd enjoyed enough success in high school sports (all-conference football) to indicate I might go pro.

In the summer of 1973, I applied for and received a combination grant-scholarship and off I went. College represented for me the ultimate distraction from authority. ("What, I can do all of this and nobody knows but me! Great!") Needless to say, my euphoric state lasted only until grades went home. I was issued a stern warning, and my allowance ($25 per month) was cut.

At this point, I needed some stabilization. I found it in my high school sweetheart, who spent a lot of time talking and guiding me in commonsense directions. It was through her direction that I initially got involved in education. She suggested that I seek a teaching certificate as insurance. Once introduced to the field, I became very involved and truly enjoyed the work. I completed my studies in sociology/communications and took a position as a co-ordinator for Project Integrate.

One year later, I interviewed for and received the position of associate teacher-counselor at Eastwood.

As indicated earlier, the first weeks represented much turmoil and indecision, but something compelled me to go on, to continue. As the associate teacher-counselor, I was entirely responsible for the behavioral aspects of the classroom. It was through this experience that I began to find some tangible grips on the feeling that compelled me to go on. What I later discovered was that the blue book, the data collection instrument, began to reflect increased behavioral control on the part of some of the students. This, coupled with my own observation, told me that the behavioral strategies we were employing were working. I suddenly remembered friends who were teachers, who had for so long wondered if their presence had any real effect on the students. Well, I now had the instrument, a data-based collection system which reflected my impact on the children. I could see and measure their growth. The kids who I felt were hopeless started to change. I found a reason, a purpose to go through it all. I had finally begun.

About this time, the second phase of the PEP experience came into play. The comradeship brought about by the uniqueness of the working conditions began to take hold. I found myself caught up in the successes and failures of other teacher-counselors. We saw ourselves as mutual extensions of each other's efforts. The entire staff was striving to facilitate the needs of the kids. The year began to pass quickly, and the successes became more frequent. Then suddenly (it seems that way) I was asked to be a teacher-counselor in another PEP classroom. I was overwhelmed to be recognized thusly.

The issue now became to disenfranchise myself from these children (something I had longed to do on several occasions after a rough day). Yet, now that it was a reality, I wanted to cry foul. I'd worked hard and long with these kids. How could I give them up? With the assistance of Gretchen and our coordinator, Jim Jones, I was able to make the break successfully. Thinking back on the occasion, I now realize how unprepared I was to meet my new challenge.

My transfer to Northeast Day-Treatment Center thrust me into a completely alien situation. At Eastwood, organization, structure, and implementation of behavioral strategies were well into operation. At Northeast (a new center), these were dreams not yet realized. My early days at Northeast were filled with students acting out all day, and late evening strategy sessions among staff members. In between, many hours were spent developing the level system and sequencing academic materials, a job further complicated by the fact that my partner had not yet been selected.

The Northeast support staff (particularly the coordinator and staff psychologist) spent a lot of time helping me adjust and plan for the upcoming school year. My first year at Northeast was filled with ups and downs, ranging from partner difficulties to my delight in having the first student in a new center to graduate. Toward the middle of the second half of the school year, the hard work and planning began to show results. The group process, so carefully nurtured, had taken hold. I finally was in a position to allow the level system to be the heavy and enforce the classroom rules. The children were finally investing in the system, which allowed the behavioral strategies to take effect. Again, the blue book began to document what my eyes were seeing. At this point, we (my partner and I) noticed the development of a nucleus of students who began to reinforce class rituals and pressure other students to do the same. Acting out was no longer viewed as the cool or smart thing to do by the children. Serious efforts toward succeeding and graduation became the classroom theme.

The current academic year, 1980-81, found the classroom prepared to go far beyond the behavioral constraints of the past years. This year we devote about 90 percent of our day to academic difficulties. I've found a lot more time for planning and group instruction is now a reality.

Life is a funny thing. It often hides the answers to a great many mysteries. Yet, if given ample time, and study, life, like a flower, will blossom and expose itself to you. Being a teacher-counselor at PEP has allowed a portion of life to blossom and expose itself to me. I've had the hands-on experience of helping a child, considered by many to be unreachable, to regain his life's balance, to set foot on the road to normalcy and consistency. I've been part of a process which has given a broken child a second chance. I've seen parents in tears after finally receiving some positive feedback during a parent conference. I've had the opportunity to grow professionally as well as personally. I've had the chance to expand my conception of human development and involvement.

5

How Consultants Contribute
to the Reeducation Process

The application to the National
Institute of Mental Health requesting funds for Project Re-ED contained the following paragraph:

The effective use of consultation is a cornerstone in the structure being developed. The basic idea is that good but less extensively trained people can work effectively with disturbed children, *provided* they are backed up by excellent consultants who know how to extend their usefulness by working through other people. The challenge is to achieve a double gain in the manpower crisis. The first gain is to recruit workers for disturbed children from a broader population base, thus solving the problem of numbers, and the second is to multiply the impact of extensively (and expensively) trained personnel by using their knowledge and skill while reducing the demands on their time. Psychiatrists, educators, pediatricians, social workers, psychologists, and other specialists will have to be helped to learn a new role. Teachers will have to be helped to learn to use the help of consultants. The success of the program will depend on the level of skill that can be developed in giving and using consultation services.

An early account* assesses the role of consultants in Re-ED as follows:

As with most good intentions, this one has been only incompletely implemented, but we are continuing to learn how mental health consultation can enhance an educational program. The dialogue between teacher-counselors and consultants began when the demonstration schools opened and has continued in spite of occasional frustrations, perplexities, and role confusions. It has not always been easy, but on the whole the engagement has been rewarding, not only in the development of meaningful professional relationships between mental health specialists and teachers but in the development of a climate that encourages earnest debate about the relevance of techniques to goals and of practice to theory. It is our conviction, although it is difficult to document, that consultation has been an important factor in the evolution of a stable and effective program in the schools. A well-trained and enthusiastic staff, capable administrative leadership, and access to educational and group-work methodology are obvious requirements for a good residential program, but mental health consultation has added depth and directions that would otherwise not have been present in its development.

Roles of Consultants. In general, consultants are of two types: those who have a regular, ongoing relationship with a teacher-counselor team and those who are brought in to assist in the solution of particular problems. The regular consultants are usually from one of the traditional mental health disciplines, but they are valued by teacher-counselor teams not as representatives of particular disciplines but as professional people who can use their understanding and wisdom to help a team deal effectively with individual children. In other words, a psychiatrist might be assigned to one group, a social worker to another, and the relationship might last for a number of years. Regular consultants normally meet with the teacher-counselor team once a week and at other

*This description of the evolution of the concept of consultant was written by Wilbert Lewis.

times when needed. Special consultants come in for brief periods in response to particular programming needs, such as in the design of a token economy for a school, the development of a unit on nutrition, or the assessment of learning potential.

Ordinarily, consultants do not work with individual children except for specific purposes, such as giving a medical examination. They work through teacher-counselors. But to do their jobs, they often become well acquainted with individual children, their problems, their histories, their ecosystems, their responses to efforts to help them. Consultants also become thoroughly acquainted with the teacher-counselor teams and the groups of children they work with. Such knowledge is necessary for consultants to perform their role of enabling teacher-counselors to do their work well.

The role of the consultant demands understandings, sensitivities, and skills not normally included in professional training programs. Thus, professional people in the role of Re-ED consultant often have a good bit of learning to do if they are to be successful. Furthermore, teacher-counselors have to learn to use consultants. Neither skill is easily acquired. Role relationships have to be worked out. The consultant often has a superior understanding of some particular problem, but the teacher-counselor has a primary and continuing responsibility for its solution. An especially important skill of a consultant is to teach another professional person how to use his skills.

Some consultants have found it difficult to adjust to the consulting role and to the democratic and collegial workings of a Re-ED program. Occasionally, consultants (actually few in number) have persisted in acting out the authoritarian roles often assumed by professional people of many disciplines. Their concept of "professional responsibility" conflicted with a fundamental Re-ED principle: that the teacher-counselors who work directly with children must have the freedom and authority to act in accordance with their own judgment of what needs to be done in any situation, subject to the guidance of other teacher-counselors and supervisors. Other consultants (again few) have attempted to impose on the program theoretical notions or operational procedures that are not harmonious with the traditions and evolving character of Re-ED programs. But, on the whole, these failures in role realization have been infrequent.

In some Re-ED programs, regulations associated with third-party payment for services have also generated conflicting expectations with regard to the role of consultants. For example, regulations may require that a psychiatrist approve a formal diagnosis in accordance with an established classification system (such as the American Psychiatric Association's *Diagnostic and Statistical Manual*) and, further, that the psychiatrist approve a formal "treatment plan." These arrangements are derived from hospital practices, where they make sense. In a Re-ED school, however, they work at cross-purposes with roles and procedures derived from an altogether different formulation of the problem. In most instances, an accommodation has been worked out between the two sets of conflicting expectations. Psychiatric approval of diagnoses and treatment plans can be considered to be a *pro forma* matter, and teacher-counselors may then proceed in accustomed ways, their responsibility for programming undiminished. In a few instances, however, an effort has been made to impose roles and procedures derived from medical settings, with predictably unhappy outcomes for all, the children especially. Re-ED administrators and supervisors in these few unfortunate situations have to spend much of their time reconciling differences and protecting teacher-counselors as much as possible from discordant expectations.

Because Re-ED programs have been proven effective and because they are considerably less costly than traditional programs, it is understandable that adherents of traditional treatment philosophies would like to take over Re-ED operations, but they do so at the risk of losing the strengths of conventional treatment programs and destroying the Re-ED effort as well. Conventional treatment programs clearly have their place, as do Re-ED schools. But it is most unwise and unproductive to attempt to combine the two. The highest authorities in agencies sponsoring Re-ED programs should insist that teacher-counselors not be crippled by intrusive discordant "consultation." It would be better to abandon the program entirely than to create conditions that will undermine its effectiveness.

A problem occasionally encountered by consultants is how to translate their specialized competencies into the idiom and process of reeducation. Most consultants are well versed in psychodynamic theory and know how to apply their rich understandings to traditional treatment modes, such as psychotherapy. Insights derived from psychodynamic theory are often exceedingly valuable, but they first must be translated into procedures that can be used by teacher-counselors. For example, the psychodynamic concepts of transference and countertransference obviously have implications for the relationship between teacher-counselors and students. The usual strategy in psychotherapy when transference phenomena become evident is "to interpret the transference," a tactic completely inappropriate in the Re-ED setting. Neither the teacher-counselor nor the student could benefit from such an interpretation. In such a situation, the consultant needs to suggest what might be going on in the relationship between teacher-counselor and student and to help the teacher-counselor work out Re-ED-appropriate steps to manage the situation so that it is a constructive experience for all. Many mental health experts have become remarkably adept in utilizing their rich understanding of human behavior to expand the repertoire of teacher-counselors in managing specific situations.

Without a strong commitment to consultation, Project Re-ED could not have succeeded. And the future of Re-ED may well depend on the extent to which individual programs can draw nourishment from consultants who are aware of the continuing flow of new ideas from education, from biology and medicine, from the behavioral and social sciences, and from the humanities. Re-ED is a continuing vital force in current conceptualizations of how to work with troubled and troubling children and youth, largely because it has remained open to emerging thought in universities and in professional practice. Re-ED provides a splendid model of the transfer of knowledge from laboratory and library to a practical program to help young people. This work of transferring knowledge from research and theory in many disciplines had to be done initially by highly trained people, and the work must continue today. The knowledge base needed to help disturbed children and their families is constantly evolving, becoming each year richer, more precise, and more encompassing than before. As emphasized earlier, Re-ED is not a fixed set of ideas; if it is to retain its early and essential character, it must continue to be responsive to new learnings about human development, education, and mental health. Consultants are crucial in this process.

What Consultants Do. A number of consultants have worked in the program for many years and have contributed substantially to its development. They have done an extraordinarily good job, with wisdom, high technical competence, sensitivity to the difficult roles of teacher-counselors, and appreciation of the unique character of the Re-ED endeavor. Individual consultants inevitably shape the consulting role, but it is possible to identify nine ways that consultants have contributed to Re-ED programs. Choice among the functions is often a matter of personal styles, professional backgrounds, adventitious circumstance requiring particular kinds of assistance, and so on, with the personal preference of the consultant making a major difference. Below are some of the ways consultants have worked to make Re-ED programs effective:

1. *Program Design.* Consultants often contribute to the design and realization of a Re-ED program. As has been emphasized before, we have deliberately tried to avoid creating an orthodoxy, an approved way of carrying out the general principles that inform Re-ED programs everywhere. A major strength of the Re-ED idea is that it is highly adaptable to local opportunities and constraints, to a variety of settings and organizational structures, and even to kinds of children and youth served. While all Re-ED programs have attributes in common, each program is distinctive—the expression of the initiative and the inventiveness of the staff and of mental health authorities as well. There are numerous examples past and present of consultants making a major contribution to the building of a new and unique Re-ED program.

2. *Program Management.* Consultants have been especially valuable in helping principals and program directors work through a wide range of issues. Running a Re-ED program can present formidable problems of management, such as the following: Should a well-functioning school be moved to inadequate quarters on state hospital grounds in order to "help consolidate programs"? How can broad citizen support be mobilized to get the state legislature to reverse itself on a decision to cut off funds to a Re-ED school? What are the best strategies for getting understanding and cooperation for a statewide program in a state that has strong county mental health programs? What should be done about a psychiatric consultant (actually an assigned staff member) who insists on using his time in individual psychotherapy with psychotic adoles-

cents in a school program? What can be done about a group of boys (the "Confederate Aviators") who have, over a period of time, consolidated a tradition of being tough and antisocial and are unresponsive to all efforts of teacher-counselors to turn the group around? What is the best way to help a supervisor who, though skilled as a teacher-counselor, gets repeatedly into unproductive conflict with teacher-counselor teams? What can be done to decrease staff turnover? What is the best way to deal with a mood of discouragement and depression that has permeated a school?

3. *Support to Teacher-Counselors.* Consultants support teacher-counselors in the realization of their difficult professional roles. Because teacher-counselors are less extensively trained than consultants generally are, the consultant's store of knowledge and understanding can greatly extend the professional competence of the teacher-counselor, who, on the other hand, has a unique role that must be thoroughly understood and appreciated by a consultant. The relationship between the two is not a therapeutic one, although consultants may frequently help a teacher-counselor sort out her feelings about herself or a child or a fellow worker. A teacher-counselor's job is very demanding, and it is not always possible for her to achieve a desirable combination of objectivity and commitment. A good consultant can help a teacher-counselor in specific circumstances as well as in the construction of a professional career.

4. *Admissions.* Consultants routinely serve on admissions committees and in some instances are required to do so by agency policy. They can often be of great value in making an ecological assessment and designing an enablement plan (see Chapter Seven). The insights of a thoughtful and well-trained consultant can greatly increase the sophistication of this vital process in reeducation programs. Because of their more extensive training and experience, they should be aware of both difficulties and opportunities that a teacher-counselor may not be sensitive to or aware of. But they must also respect the teacher-counselor's final responsibility for ecological assessment and enablement planning.

5. *Group Composition.* Consultants may advise on the formation and evolution of groups of students. Putting together a group of students for Re-ED purposes is a complex matter in

which professional judgment is the determining factor. The process has a high intuitive component; it is far more art than science. But it is extremely important. A group with too many aggressive, acting-out youngsters may be impossible to manage. A group of children with limited intellectual ability may be boring to all. A group of withdrawn or fearful children may be difficult to stimulate. Having observed many different groups, the good consultant may bring a valuable perspective to the probable effects of adding a particular child to an established group. But, again, the teacher-counselors are responsible for the final decision.

6. *Behavior Management.* Consultants routinely advise on techniques of management of individual students and of groups as well. From his rich experience, a consultant essentially offers an array of alternative strategies attuned to particular situations, with the teacher-counselors remaining responsible for selecting particular procedures to be used. The process is in fact a transactional one, with consultants, teacher-counselors, and others—including supervisors, regular classroom teachers, and parents—making suggestions about what might be most effective. Subsequently, the consultant can often be useful in looking back on how the procedure worked, thus enabling teacher-counselors to generalize about what works and what does not work and to sharpen their skills in managing children and groups.

7. *Ecological Perspective.* Consultants who have a firm grasp of Re-ED concepts can often help teacher-counselors maintain an ecological perspective. The responsibilities of the day and night teacher-counselors can be so absorbing as occasionally to limit their perspective. In staff conferences, the liaison teacher-counselor will represent the counterplay of forces that will determine the overall effectiveness of the Re-ED effort. The consultant will often be closer to day-by-day interactions between teacher-counselors and students and can help sustain and enhance an ecological perspective, so vital to the total effort.

8. *Training.* Consultants contribute to the in-service training of staff members of Re-ED programs. This function is one of great importance, for two reasons. First, teacher-counselors are drawn from many different kinds of training programs. Ordinarily, they have a master's degree but in such diverse fields as psychology, health and recreation, and the teaching of emotionally dis-

turbed, mentally retarded, and learning disabled children. And
they come from many universities. It has been reassuring to discover that concepts of reeducation can be taught to teacher-counselors on the job. Much of the learning comes from guidance provided by team members and supervisors, but consultants also play
an important role in formal instruction during frequent in-service
training periods. Second, consultants bring to teacher-counselors
an appreciation of new theoretical and applied developments relevant to their work with children. For example, behavior modification was not prominent in the early Re-ED programs. As Skinner-
ean theory and practice influenced university programs, consultants
helped translate the new ideas into Re-ED practices. Ideas like engineered classrooms, criterion-referenced testing, and prescriptive
teaching were introduced by university-based consultants. In the
past several years, concepts from Piaget and his associates have infused Re-ED programs by way of consultants. Currently, there is
growing interest in the work of Feuerstein (1979, 1980) on the
assessment of learning potential and the remedying of cognitive
deficits through instrumental enrichment—again, an idea brought
into the orbit of Re-ED thought by consultants. Re-ED is constantly being revitalized by emergent theory and practice, and consultants play a crucial role in transferring knowledge from library
and laboratory to the practical, day-by-day operations of Re-ED
schools.

9. *Research and Evaluation.* Consultants may advise on assessing the process and outcomes of reeducation. Teacher-counselors are not ordinarily trained in methods of research and evaluation; yet they often have high interest in the outcomes of their
work. Several Re-ED programs have made effective use of consultants in the design of evaluation studies, ranging from the quantitative assessment of changes in behavior of an individual child to
the assessment of academic gains accompanying participation in a
wilderness camping program.

Observations by Consultants

To clarify the role of consultants as well as to illustrate the
variability in their ways of working, we asked four consultants
with many years of experience in Re-ED programs to describe

their professional backgrounds, to tell what they actually do as consultants, and then to comment on the process of consultation. The consultants represent four disciplines: psychology, special education, psychiatry, and pediatrics. Three of the consultants worked in school programs; one first worked for many years as a teacher-counselor and then became a consultant in reeducation to help a number of new programs get established.

Gus Bell
Psychologist and Consultant, Cumberland House*

A Ph.D. degree in clinical psychology and licensure by the Board of Healing Arts of the State of Tennessee were the required credentials for employment as psychological consultant to Cumberland House School of Project Re-ED in 1964. However, it was my broad experience in the community that best prepared me to be effective in the consultant role within the Re-ED model. I am in private practice of clinical and consulting psychology and formerly served as chief clinical psychologist and coordinator of training at Nashville's major mental health center.

While psychological consultation at Cumberland House has taken many forms, the teacher-counselor most often initiates a request for consultation. Occasionally a supervisor will recommend consultation, with the concurrence of a teacher-counselor or a teacher-counselor team. My visits to the school have been on a weekly basis, from two to four hours a week, and I have provided emergency consultation at other times when requested. Consultation has covered a variety of topics, such as a teacher-counselor's concern about an individual child or about effective group process, as well as personal or interpersonal issues that can affect teacher-counselor effectiveness. Sometimes administrative matters, which may ultimately affect staff morale, have been discussed, either with supervisors or with team members. I have done little didactic teaching at Cumberland House but have concentrated instead on staff development around particular children and specific issues.

The most frequent goal of consultation has been to provide an opportunity for teacher-counselors to conceptualize their difficulties in programming for the problem child and to assist them in making the most appropriate choices in developing new ways of approaching a problem. As psychological consultant, I have frequently reviewed and interpreted evaluations of children referred to or enrolled in Cumberland House and have assisted the staff in

*These observations were written in 1981.

planning therapeutic goals for individual children and in utilizing appropriate techniques to achieve those goals. I have also related diagnostic information to planning classroom and group living activities to increase the effectiveness of the group in shaping individual children's behavior.

I have found it a continuing challenge to provide sympathetic support of a teacher-counselor in his or her efforts to understand and relate to a child. Sometimes this calls for concentration on an individual teacher-counselor; other times, for emphasis on staff relationships and team skills. I always encourage teacher-counselors to explore their own feelings and to consider how their working with the disturbed child and the child's family is creating stress for the teacher-counselor. Enabling staff members to mobilize their own resources and resolve their own tensions has sometimes been necessary to restore confidence and, in turn, to stabilize feelings or behavior within a group of children.

The introduction of behavior modification concepts into Re-ED led to a more precise definition of treatment goals than had previously been attempted. Later, with the addition of Medicaid requirements, even more guidelines, followed by professional scrutiny of treatment plans, were imposed on the system. Important as these guidelines may be, I have tried consistently to encourage teacher-counselors to define their treatment plans on the basis of their own experience and within the context of their personal relationship with a particular child.

Before this level of consultation is reached, I have ordinarily spent time with the liaison teacher-counselor developing an understanding of the child's ecological system. In doing so, I have assisted the staff in assessing family dynamics and how they affect the child's behavior and school performance.

I have found that I can get most valuable information for consultation on an informal basis, by having lunch with a group of children, by visiting a classroom, by being with a group during story time or during games on the playing field. After thoroughly reading records, talking with the liaison teacher-counselor and getting to know the child about whom consultation has been requested, I have felt better prepared to enter into a discussion with teacher-counselors regarding their special concerns.

As the Re-ED model of Cumberland House has become incorporated into the Children and Youth Services of Middle Tennessee Mental Health Institute (a psychiatric hospital), new staffing patterns and procedures have become necessary to meet hospital accreditation standards and requirements for governmental third-party payments. Regularly scheduled meetings of teacher-counselors with the staff psychologist, staff psychiatrist, pediatrician, and nurse partially replace the role of the psychological consultant. Nevertheless, the role of the psychological consultant, with a thorough knowledge of the program's history and philosophy and a broad community perspective rather than one of the institution, becomes even more vital to the perpetuation of the original spirit of Re-ED. The carefully selected teacher, with full professional decision-making status to affect the ecosystem of the disturbed child, must not be lost in the maze of new diagnostic nomenclature, institutional guidelines, or funding requirements.

Ila Gehman
Clinical Psychologist and Consultant, Wright School*

It has been my great pleasure to have been a consultant to Wright School since its inception in 1963. Probably I was invited into this happy affiliation because of previous training and experience and because of the position I was then holding as a clinical child psychologist.

I started my professional career as an elementary teacher in Pennsylvania. After graduate work, I became a teacher and guidance counselor in junior high school and later a school psychologist. The completion of a doctorate with a major in psychology led to six years of teaching and assisting in directing the psychological clinic at Pennsylvania State University. In 1954, I moved with my husband to Durham, North Carolina, where I gained two more years of experience, the time being divided between psychological services at the Veterans Administration Hospital and a state mental hospital. In the latter institution I had an opportunity to help establish a children's treatment unit. I then began my affiliation with the Durham Child Guidance Clinic and with Duke University, which continued for twenty years until my retirement in 1978.

These various experiences have been very useful to me in the past and as I continue my work as a consultant to the Wright School Re-ED program. I have always had confidence in the tenets and structure of Re-ED and felt sure that teacher-counselors could learn to perform their difficult tasks very well. They have proved themselves more than equal to this expectation.

When Wright School was starting, there were three consultants—one child psychiatrist and two clinical psychologists, each of whom spent four hours per week at the school. Originally all three consultants attended the same meetings with the majority of the staff. As mutual confidence grew and working principles became established, the meetings were divided, with one consultant to each unit for any given hour. This pattern gradually evolved into the present system with two consultants instead of three—one

*These observations were written in 1981.

child psychiatrist and one child psychologist. The consultants work at the school on Friday afternoons where they rotate individually by prearranged scheduling among the three units, one hour for each meeting.

A case conference, called the admissions planning conference, is held for newly admitted children with the purpose of developing mutual understanding of needs and central issues, setting goals, and charting the course in general. Typically, the liaison teacher-counselor serves as chair and all persons present are potential discussants. Those in attendance usually include the child about whom the conference is being held, the parents or parent surrogates, principal and/or other personnel from the child's regular school, the parents' counselor, and any appropriate representatives from other involved agencies, such as social services or juvenile court. Wright School staff present are the day and night teacher-counselors from the child's unit and any aides or trainees who have contact with the child.

A discharge planning conference is held with the same group near the end of the child's stay to evaluate progress and to assess possible needs and resources for further professional or other help within the home community, the most appropriate and available school placement, and other individual factors which will have relevance to the child's return home.

Sometimes a midpoint planning conference of similar nature is held for a child when puzzling elements or new data arise in a given case. Another frequently scheduled type of meeting is the central issues conference, which is held prior to or early after the child's admission. This conference is attended by a consultant and the staff of the unit to which the child has been assigned. Salient points of the child's history are delineated, integration of materials considered, goals discussed, possible remedial approaches proposed, and often a tentative working diagnosis agreed upon.

Prior to these conferences, extensive case materials have been placed in the hands of the consultant. The consultant thus has background to become an active participant and as such may be involved in any of several functions, depending on circumstances: support (of the child, parents, agencies, teacher-counselors), interpretations, speculation on dynamics (at the conference, if appropriate, or with the staff later), interviewing of the parents or child or both to clarify feelings and/or dynamics, encouragement of dialogue relative to significant issues, and sometimes giving information or making suggestions for handling problems.

These conferences are helpful to the consultant in that the child and his family become real instead of just "paper" people. They are helpful to the teacher-counselors in enabling them to observe small samples of work from experienced consultants. Teacher-counselors often privately express surprise and gratitude for information and feelings expressed, for these can be used constructively in their work with the child and family. Actually, the teacher-counselor and especially the liaison teacher-counselor are themselves consultants. They represent viewpoints in mental health that they articulate in the child's home, regular school, and community agencies as they go about their daily work. Like other consultants, they learn to collaborate and to elicit collaboration from others.

Although the greatest investment of consultation time has been focused on case conference meetings, the Wright School teacher-counselors freely request discussion sessions of didactic type designed to increase their knowledge in particular problem areas. Samples of these topics that come to mind are:

- What are the special problems of adopted children and how can we deal with their concerns?
- What is the meaning of "basic trust"? How is it developed and what can be done when it is notably lacking?
- There is too much concern in our unit with sexual matters. How do we approach and handle this problem constructively?
- What are the underlying causes of encopresis and how should we handle this problem?

From this sampling it can be seen that in-service training is expected of the Wright School consultants. It has become a viable part of the program, and the topics are always selected by the consultees out of the concerns of teacher-counselors. This creates lively discussion and high interest levels.

The consultant's role is perceived as that of a resource person, a collaborator, and not as a group leader, supervisor, or direct service individual. By virtue of not being present in the hour-by-hour work of the school, the consultant is free to call attention to gains that have been made by the child and his family and thus lend encouragement. Sometimes these gains fall so short of "normal" progress that it is easy for staff to overlook their significance. The ten-year-old absolute nonreader who hates reading but who learns to read at first-grade level in four months' time has made commendable progress. He has caught onto what reading is and has some belief that he can do it. This is progress. When the child who enters the school with unsocialized, almost feral behaviors and learns to act in more acceptable ways, he begins to feel that he too can earn friendship. That is progress. Teacher-counselors and other staff members are less likely to burn out in their work when they are energized by recognized success.

The ideas of the founders of Re-ED have been proved to be

sound, viable, and exportable. Classes based on Re-ED principles have been started in regular schools and in various mental health organizations. The establishment of training facilities for teacher-counselors in colleges and universities has helped in the availability of staff recruits. It feels good to have some part in such developments.

David Jones
*Psychiatric Consultant, Wright School**

When Wright School opened in 1963, John Fowler was the child psychiatry consultant, and I was the combined pediatric and child psychiatry consultant. I had obtained full training in both medical specialities. For the past eighteen years I have pursued my primary career goal of bringing child psychiatry into the Duke University Medical Center, a large general hospital with teaching, service, and research activities. I am director of the adolescent psychiatry ward. During these years, I have also provided weekly child psychiatry and pediatric consultation at Wright School.

I collaborate with many different professionals of varied disciplines about troubled children each day. One of my enjoyable teaching activities is to take a group of pediatric residents and medical students with me every Friday afternoon when I go to Wright School. These visits provide a demonstration of how much teachers know about emotionally disturbed children and how effective they are in helping them make a better adaptation. All too often, young physicians have the idea that only the pediatrician knows how to help children. The Wright School experience enhances my pediatric teaching activities.

I perform a number of functions at Wright School. My pediatric consultative activities have been curtailed over the past ten years, and I now serve primarily as consultant in psychiatry. However, I am available as a pediatrician to phone call consultations, and I go over every child's physical examination and medical history as part of admission procedures. In addition, I provide information and instructions for the staff about coping with and caring for children with such problems as asthma, seizure disorders, diabetes, allergies, and insect stings.

Many children are admitted who have been prescribed stimulant drugs for hyperactivity and tranquilizers for anxieties. I assist the staff in gaining a perspective on the benefits of these medications. Most of the time, these medicines are discontinued and are no longer needed during the child's stay at Wright School. However, on rare occasions a child is given medication on my recom-

*These observations were written in 1981.

mendation, and the psychopharmacological agent proves to be a helpful adjunct to the total Wright School effort. Many of the children entering Wright School are overmedicated. It is helpful to parents and referring agencies to demonstrate that they often rely too much on these types of medications.

At the admission planning conference and the discharge planning conference the child, parents, local mental health workers, and school teachers participate with the Wright School staff and consultants. I might be asked to discuss a child with the staff in advance in order to arrive at a clearly defined set of central issues pertaining to goals and the methods and techniques of implementing those goals. My presence at the conferences is useful to the staff as a resource and support, especially when more qualified and experienced professionals from mental health clinics express conflicting views at these meetings. For example, physicians can be intimidating to parents and to teacher-counselors, as well. I can relieve some of this pressure.

Because I see the child at infrequent intervals, I am able to provide a perspective on the process of profound and subtle changes that take place, and these are often difficult for the staff to appreciate when seeing the child every day. These observations provide the basis of a diagnostic assessment and treatment recommendation or planning after discharge. The state of North Carolina requires a psychiatric diagnosis; also, insurance diagnostic forms require a physician's signature. Through in-service training, I instruct the staff to understand diagnostic classifications from an adaptive, developmental, and dynamic viewpoint. In addition, I help them have a prognostic perspective of the meaning of various diagnostic classifications.

Other in-service training functions I provide are didactic discussions of clinical issues. For example, I have spoken to the entire staff on the use of medications, hyperactivity, minimal brain dysfunction and seizure disorders, borderline psychosis, sadomasochism, encopresis and enuresis, sexual behaviors, personality development, and defense mechanisms. These discussions are quite lively and enjoyable as they provide the Wright School staff with the needed depth and breadth to evaluate clinical reports from referring mental health workers.

Occasionally, a child is very difficult for the staff to understand and I am asked to interview him or her alone. By providing consultation of this nature, I am able to help formulate a program for the child. This request for a psychiatric interview is needed, at times, when there has not been adequate evaluation of the child by the referring mental health agency.

In thinking about my eighteen years of consultation at Wright School, it has been a very enjoyable experience. I have, I

am sure, gained a great deal. I have had a first-hand opportunity
to observe profound and, at times, dramatic changes in many disturbed children—changes that have been quite remarkable in such
a short period of time. I have referred many of these children to
Wright School myself, and I have had benefit of follow-up that
comes from being involved in the same settings for many years.
I have gained a perspective of short-term residential treatment that
helps the child develop better coping skills and, at the same time,
draws on ecological resources to continue the process in the community. I am continually amazed at the enthusiasm and dedication
and the effectiveness of the young teacher-counselors. They enjoy
their work and utilize psychiatric consultation to gain an understanding of what they can realistically achieve. Mutually shared
success by the child, parents, staff, and consultant brings about a
close working alliance. It is difficult for the child to tell the staff
good-bye and vice versa. The same applies for the consultant as he
sees new teacher-counselors grow and develop and move on to
other jobs. During the past eighteen years, I have seen many talented and dedicated teacher-counselors embrace new challenges. I
am gratified that I may have had a small part in their development
and in their understanding of troubled children.

Robert Slagle
Special Educator and Consultant, Re-ED Programs*

In 1966, four years after the first children had enrolled in
Cumberland House, the State of Tennessee decided to establish Re-
ED programs in Memphis and Chattanooga. This was a vote of
confidence in Cumberland House and in the concepts of reeducation. I joined the Cumberland House staff as a teacher-counselor
shortly after the first children were enrolled. When Sequoyah Center in Memphis and Smallwood Center in Chattanooga opened in
1967, I became director of training for the State Re-Education
Program.

The consultation approach that developed during the following decade emerged largely from trial and error during our first
efforts at "replication." Other replications (Pine Breeze in Chattanooga, the first Re-ED school for adolescents; the Positive Education Program in Cleveland, Ohio; Pressley Ridge school and camp
in Pittsburgh; and Centennial School at Lehigh University) all provided opportunities to refine the special and somewhat unorthodox consultation style begun in the late 1960s.

As a consultant, I usually visit a Re-ED school only two or
three times a year, spending four or five days on each visit. This is

*These observations were written in 1981.

frequent enough to become well acquainted with each program, with individual staff members, and even with some children. It is also infrequent enough that changes in the program, the staff, and the children are more apparent than if I were to visit weekly or monthly.

A typical consultation visit begins with observation of ongoing activities, preferably by spending several hours with each group of children, sitting in a classroom (being as unobtrusive as possible, a skill that can be developed but that is not easily described), jotting down notes to myself as I watch teacher-counselors and children—reminders of things to share during the feedback sessions with staff later that day. I try to observe the groups in as many settings as possible during the limited time available. The children are accustomed to observers in the classroom and have been told that there will be a visitor observing their group. These observation periods provide me with the background information needed to sit down with a team and share ideas. For me, it is a necessary ingredient in consultation.

During the feedback time with staff (what most would consider the "consultation time") I find myself playing several roles. A consultant is an invited guest in a program—without any authority or decision-making power in the program. Staff should feel free to accept or reject the consultant's advice and suggestions. Consultation sessions provide an opportunity to give positive feedback as well as to criticize things that need improvement, such as an inappropriate seating arrangement, too many negative rules, not enough praise or reinforcement for particular students, and the format of a group meeting. Again, it is obvious that this level of specificity requires direct observation of the program.

A good consultant asks questions more often than she makes suggestions. In some instances, the staff might deliberately ignore a child's misbehavior or consciously set a goal very high for a child who needs a challenge; both might be misinterpreted in a brief observation period. In such instances, a question can prevent a possible misinterpretation. At other times, the right question might help the teacher-counselor plan a more appropriate strategy or encourage her to persevere with an approach that has promise.

Often, while I am observing a group, I am reminded of a particular technique or strategy being used in another program that would fit in ideally in the group I am visiting. I find myself spreading gimmicks, games, and ideas from one Re-ED program to another and regularly updating my mental catalogue as I continue to visit and observe. Since its inception, one of the richest qualities of Re-ED has been the creativity and inventiveness of the front-line teacher-counselors. With so little communication between programs, sometimes separated by hundreds of miles, a consultant who visits regularly can play a crucial role in the exchange of ideas.

Re-ED teacher-counselors have one of the most demanding jobs in the helping professions. Listening with a sympathetic ear and encouraging a frustrated teacher-counselor to keep on trying is sometimes part of the role of a consultant; it is even more effective if the listening and encouraging can be followed with some specific suggestions or strategies that the teacher-counselor might not have thought of. A good consultant is constantly aware of the importance of watching for things that are going well; for group processes that deserve a compliment, for that one time that morning when Johnny did control his temper and his teacher-counselor told him how proud she was of him. When a consultant is invited into the intimacy and privacy of a Re-ED cottage or classroom, he accepts an obligation: to observe carefully, to share both the positive and the negative as honestly as possible, to make constructive suggestions and to contribute in some small part to the quality of the reeducation process. After spending the past fifteen years as a consultant in Re-ED programs in several states, I find it difficult to differentiate between good consultation and good in-service training.

The reeducation process is a dynamic, highly personal phenomenon. There are many differences among Re-ED programs, but all have some basic common characteristics. The Re-ED philosophy, with its emphasis on joy, success, learning, growing, and competence, is an integral part of all Re-ED programs. Programmatic emphasis on the ecology, group process, academic competence, and interpersonal skills must be incorporated into the daily goals and objectives for each child. Effective consultation in a Re-ED setting requires an awareness and commitment to these basic elements.

As Re-ED continues to grow and adapt to new settings and challenges, the value of consultants will increase. It is imperative that reeducation programs not become isolated entities. Each generation of teacher-counselors has a wealth of front-line experience —an ever growing reservoir of ideas that can be shared. The use of experienced teacher-counselors as consultants has proven to be both an effective and efficient response to the need for ideas, stimulation, and *esprit de corps* so vital to the reeducation process.

6

Problems and Profiles
of Children and Youth Served

To evoke for the reader a sense of the kinds of children and adolescents served in Re-ED programs, we here discuss criteria for admission and exclusion; present sundry classification and epidemiological statistics; and, in an effort to make the statistics come alive, conclude with eight case histories. We are trying here to answer the often-asked and altogether appropriate question: "Just what kinds of kids does Re-ED serve?" But to answer this question, we must temporarily suspend a fundamental theoretical principle: in Re-ED, we work not with individual children but with ecosystems, of which a particular child is the defining member. Unfortunately, there is not yet available, as there should be, a standardized procedure for the classification of ecosystems. Thus, the statistics reported are alien to our thinking; the case studies reported permit an appropriate emphasis on contexts and relationships that comprise the ecosystems of the children whose fictitious names identify each account. Each account, of course, is altered to prevent identification of the child.

Admission and Exclusion Criteria

At the beginning of the Re-ED program in the early 1960s, the project designers at Peabody laid out certain criteria for admission. The age range from six to twelve was initially agreed on to increase the probability of success in what was then a pioneering effort. But there were exclusion criteria as well, at least on paper: the child should not be mentally retarded; he should be in sufficient contact to be incorporated into a group of same-age children (that is, he should not be psychotic); he should be able to be contained in an open setting (that is, he should not be a habitual runaway); and he should not need continuing nursing care. Just about all these criteria have gone by the board.

For a number of reasons, Re-ED programs are now working with more seriously disturbed children than at the outset. In the beginning, Wright School needed children and thus accepted essentially all referrals. The Cumberland House staff found itself working successfully with children more disturbed than the original rules would have permitted. In more recent years, the movement toward deinstitutionalization in mental health and correctional programs and the growing capability of public schools for handling disturbed children have resulted in a heavy requirement for the kinds of services Re-ED programs can offer. Furthermore, some psychiatric treatment centers are differentiating between children who are "mental health problems" and those who are "correctional" problems, and excluding the latter. The former include children with neuroses, psychoses, and affective disorders, while the latter are the mean, aggressive, highly unsocialized youngsters. Re-ED schools continue to work with both groups.

A small group of older children and adolescents—especially adolescents who are persistently and violently assaultive and homicidal; who are having acute reactions to drugs or drug deprivation; or who habitually run away, often stealing a car to do so—are difficult to serve in a Re-ED setting. Such students may require a different type of special service than can be provided in the relatively open, group structure of a Re-ED program. Some may require medical treatment in a hospital. Some Re-ED programs for adolescents exclude extremely violent youngsters, who tend, as a consequence, to end up in the correction system. But most Re-ED programs, of which Pressley Ridge with its wilderness camping program (described in Chapter Eleven) is an example, take students regarded as unmanageable by other agencies, and two states are developing Re-ED programs especially for this group. Fortunately, the number of truly unmanageable young people is relatively small; they do, however, attract attention by the disturbances they cause, and they exert steady pressure on the community to build special facilities for them.

Re-ED schools are ordinarily not set up to handle multiply handicapped children, especially those who are mentally retarded or who suffer from severe cerebral palsy, epilepsy, or a crippling condition requiring a wheel chair, a special bed, or other elaborate equipment. And Re-ED schools ordinarily do not take children requiring continuing medical and nursing care, such as children with severe ulcerative colitis, anorexia nervosa, uncontrolled juvenile-onset diabetes, or other severe chronic illnesses requiring constant medical supervision.

Finally, two new policies have emerged that affect admissions. The programs now offer service to children from eighteen months to eighteen years of age, with varying patterns in different localities. And a new criterion has emerged: children and youth served should ordinarily live within a couple of hours at most from the program, since liaison work with the child's family, school, and community is essential to the success of the effort.

Referral sources vary widely from program to program. A common pattern in programs sponsored by mental health authorities is to have students referred through a mental health center. But patterns vary from program to program and from time to time within any one program. As Re-ED programs have been extended upward into the adolescent years, an increasing number of students are admitted on the order of a juvenile court, either as delinquents or, in some states, as status offenders. Some programs accept a direct referral from psychiatrists, pediatricians, psychologists, and public schools or by parents themselves. In recent years, several Re-ED programs have been developed under the auspices of public schools. In these, the child's assignment may result from decisions embodied in an individual educational plan. Whatever are the sources of referral, Re-ED schools across the country are admitting more and more seriously disturbed youngsters.

A treatment program can, of course, improve its success rate by carefully selecting the most promising referrals, a process appropriately referred to as "creaming." In Re-ED, this practice is regarded unfavorably, since it would limit the social usefulness of the program and would eventually undermine public confidence and support. We have come in time to talk about "an optimum failure rate" rather than a maximum success rate. We do not know what that rate should be, exactly, but we do know that a program with a *very* high success rate is probably creaming and not doing the job it should be doing.

Statistical Summaries

For a number of reasons, it is difficult to present a precise statistical picture of children and youth in Re-ED programs. The children served vary somewhat from program to program, depending on the program's history and the constellation of other services available in its community. Since programs are variously sponsored, there is no uniform record system. However, people in charge of Re-ED programs would be in accord with several general statements about the children. Various programs serve children from ages eighteen months to eighteen years. In programs serving preadolescent children, the ratio of boys to girls is about four to one; in programs for adolescents, the ratio begins to even out somewhat but with a continuing greater frequency of boys. In general, racial and ethnic composition of children served reflects the composition of the community or region where the program is located, adjusted for the fact that minority families tend to underuse mental health resources and minority children and youth tend to be overrepresented in the correctional system. Mentally retarded children are not ordinarily served in Re-ED programs, though a number of children perform poorly on intelligence tests. The children tend to be from two to three years behind grade in academic development, and deficiencies in reading, writing, spelling, and arithmetic are the rule, with an occasional exception. Nearly all the children come from disrupted or fragile families, and most of the children have a history of difficulty in school or in the community. By the time a child enrolls in a Re-ED program, there will usually be a history of several years of maladjustment.

The programs in Tennessee are under one office, the Office of Children and Youth of the Department of Mental Health and Mental Retardation; thus, there is a central source of information. We thought at first that children served in Tennessee could be classified according to categories in the *Diagnostic and Statistical Manual,* since those categories are standardized and understood by mental health professionals. This source of specific data proved to be disappointing because of the understandable reluctance of psychiatrists (who must approve diagnoses under Tennessee regulations) to use the full array of diagnostic categories. Because of concerns for possible stigmatization, the psychiatrists have a strong preference for the category "Behavior Disorders of Childhood" or "Behavior Disorders of Adolescence." For example, in one annual report from Cumberland House, thirty-one out of fifty children were so categorized. Nineteen children were given sundry diagnoses, including anxiety neurosis, depressive neurosis, antisocial personality disorder, inadequate personality disorder, drug dependence, epilepsy, simple schizophrenia, childhood schizophrenia, and paranoid schizophrenia. Since Tennessee Re-ED programs are in fact "the end of the line" for seriously disturbed children and youth, one would expect the same array of *Diagnostic and Statistical Manual* categories to be found as in the population at large, but, for reasons noted above, this does not happen. Except for meeting requirements of third-party payers, the diagnostic categories have little utility either in programming or in describing the kinds of children and youth served.

Data are also available on 975 children served in the children and youth program of the state of Tennessee in 1979-80. Although installations vary in their commitment to Re-ED principles, they serve total populations by regions; therefore, there is no basis for believing that installations vary in types of children and youth served. Within the limitations described previously, the data are useful in depicting the character of the population served. Children ranged from one year of age to seventeen years of age, with a median age of fifteen. Programs served twice as many boys as girls. The ratio of whites to blacks was roughly proportional to the racial composition of the population, with a modest overrepresentation of blacks. Approximately 80 percent of the children lived with one or both natural parents, 10 percent with relatives, and 10 percent with others. As to psychiatric diagnoses, the following assignments were made: 23 percent behavioral disorders of childhood or adolescence, 18 percent transient emotional disturbance, 6.5 percent alcohol or drug abuse, 5.5 percent schizophrenia, 3 percent personality disorders, and 2.5 percent neurosis. Two hundred and forty-eight were undiagnosed. Approximately 10 percent of the children and youth were transferred from the corrections system, and another 12 percent were admitted directly on order of a juvenile court.

Systematic data are available on children and youth served by Pressley Ridge (Ziegler and others, 1980). During the 1977-78 year (July to June), eighty-seven youth in the camping program were evaluated. About half of these were new admissions. The median age at entry was fifteen years, and the length of stay was approximately sixteen months. Racial composition of the group indicates an overrepresentation of black students: 73 percent were white, and 27 percent were black. The major sources of referral were the juvenile court (38 percent) and child welfare (54 percent). The mean IQ was 86.52, with a range from 66 to 117; the mean grade deficiency was −2.83 years. As in other Re-ED programs, children and youth admitted to Pressley Ridge School usually have a long history of adjustment difficulties. More than half of the students first became involved with the mental health–mental retardation system, then moved on to the courts and finally to Pressley Ridge. Fifty-eight had had contact with the mental health system at an average age of 9.7 (range 2-16); 39 had a first court appearance at 12.3 (range 5-16). Six percent of children had no parents; 52 percent came from homes with a single parent; and 42 percent came from homes with two parents. The residential program in the city yielded comparable data, except that the proportion of blacks was higher than for the camp program and the mean level of grade deficiency was one full year greater.

Case Studies

The best way to appreciate the kinds of children served in Re-ED programs is to know the children themselves. Case studies of "representative" children and youth would thus be one way to help the reader know some of the students—imperfectly, to be sure, but with more a sense of personage than the *Diagnostic and Statistical Manual* categories can ever convey. But there are problems. What student is "representative"? None, of course; each of the several thousands of young people who have been in Re-ED programs represented a unique combination of individual characteristics and ecosytem constellations, a singular mixture of inadequacy and competence, of meanness and good spirit, of despair and hope—and, for the Re-ED staff, of failure and success. Anything short of several thousand case studies would therefore be inadequate. But we must settle here for eight accounts of the children themselves. Throughout the book, there are vignettes of others, and the reader is urged to think of those other accounts too as clues to the kinds of children and youth served in Re-ED programs.

The case studies that follow are more or less typical of the young people served, of the Re-ED experience, and of outcomes. Eight children and youth are described, six boys and two girls, ages four to sixteen. As to outcomes, four may be thought of as rather typical; favorable results were achieved, but problems clearly remain. One, Cissy J., was a stunning success. At age eleven, her future promised violence, defeat, despair, but she is now a splendid young woman with a master's degree in social work. Such success does not happen every day, but it happens often enough to encourage teacher-counselors to keep going in the face of seemingly insurmountable odds. And failures occur as well. We thought it useful to report on two: one the consequence of our own ineptitude in the early days, for others will have the same experience; and the other because we did our best and still failed, as others will as well.

Six Successful Experiences. Below are six more or less successful engagements with children, ages four to sixteen, and their families and schools. Ages indicate age at admission.

*Zach, Age 6**

Three years after Zach left Cumberland House, I made a follow-up visit to his new school and saw a tall, handsome ten-

---

*This case study was written by Sally Robinson.

year-old boy on his way to lunch. His teacher described him with
obvious warmth and affection. "He's learning well—reading is his
best subject, but he prefers working with numbers, probably because they're impersonal. . . . Having his routine change and not
being able to do his work upsets him. . . . He learns in a weird way,
but he's definitely not retarded . . . loves to listen to music when
his work is finished . . . can be stubborn . . . repeats sentences only
when he's upset . . . usually keeps to himself and has no problems
with the other kids. He's doing at least second-grade work in all
subjects."

    That account was not what I had expected after reading rec-
ords of Zach's early life. His mother, Elsie Douglas, is reported to
have had a "nervous breakdown" when Zach was one-and-a-half
years old. She later came to the attention of a social service agency
when she made a call pleading for help in managing her son. The
social worker who went to the Douglas home found a healthy, attractive, strong four-year-old boy who was totally out of control.
During a fifteen-minute period, Zach broke a dial on the television
set, pulled magazines off the tables, emptied tissues in handfuls
from a Kleenex box, jumped on the furniture, hit his mother, and
pulled her hair. He appeared to try to talk but only called out
words or phrases in a repetitive, chanting way. His mother alternately yelled at him and attempted to hit him, becoming visibly
nervous and agitated herself. When corrected, Zach would scream
out "no, no," slapping his ears and head or falling to the floor and
kicking wildly. After an investigation, the worker arranged for foster care, which Zach's parents readily accepted.

    Zach's behavior deteriorated steadily in his foster home. He
refused to eat or play, picked at his dry skin until he developed
bleeding and infected impetigo sores, pulled out his hair, and severely burned his legs and feet by turning over a pan of boiling
water. He was hospitalized for treatment but was not discharged
until four months later because his foster mother refused to take
him back. Transferred to a home for mentally retarded children,
Zach lasted only two months before he was thrown out for attempting to drown three younger children by holding their heads
in the toilet. The evaluation done at that time referred to Zach as
a "severely damaged human being with a lack of control of psychotic proportion, severely delayed language development, and
moderate mental retardation." Antipsychotic medication was prescribed, and Zach was placed in a long-term residential program
for autistic children.

    Fortunately, Zach began to make gains in self-control under
consistent expectations. Staff members noticed that he seemed
quick to learn and responded well to social reinforcement. Recog-

nizing that he had more potential than other children in the program, they contacted Cumberland House.

The liaison teacher-counselor from Cumberland House had two serious reservations about accepting Zach: his parents' ambivalence about being involved and his severe delay in language and speech development. He had a vocabulary of only ten to twelve intelligible words and used language in a repetitive or meaningless way. What if he could not understand what was expected at Cumberland House?

Zach may have made his own luck. His need for affection was so evident that Mrs. Watson, a woman who worked at the residential treatment center, volunteered to provide weekend care as his foster parent until his home situation was resolved. The Cumberland House staff decided to risk accepting him. He was enrolled in the Leprechaun group shortly after his sixth birthday.

The first month was trying for both Zach and his teacher-counselors. He did not comply with directions of any sort and responded to every correction with screams of "no, no" and a tantrum. He had to be physically restrained for as much as half an hour many times a day. There wasn't a day when he didn't bite at least one child. Sitting through a pow-wow was especially difficult for him. The teacher-counselors were worn out, but they persisted with clear, one-step directions and a combination of ignoring, time-outs, and restraint to teach Zach the basic procedures of group living.

A breakthrough came when Zach began to develop a close attachment to Phil, his night teacher-counselor. He responded to the special routines that Phil created, such as his saying "I'm watching who's following directions." Zach observed Phil carefully and imitated his behavior.

Mrs. Watson turned out to be an exceptional foster parent. She both loved Zach and had the necessary skills to manage him. She and her husband were encouraged to observe at Cumberland House and to attend parent meetings to discuss problems they had with Zach. Zach tested the limits at home as fully as he did at Cumberland House, but after the second month the Watsons were feeling competent and not reporting any serious problems on weekends. The family included two daughters who were playmates for Zach—more gentle and more able to teach him than the Leprechauns. After a few weeks, Zach seemed genuinely sad to leave the family when weekends were over.

Zach was assigned a tutor who worked with him half an hour a day on basic reading and math skills, initially using food, then praise and physical affection, as reinforcers for attention and correct responses. A hearing and speech evaluation was scheduled but was impossible to complete because Zach refused to cooperate. Consultants were invited to Cumberland House to help staff members develop a plan for increasing Zach's functional speech; that plan worked well.

On the recommendation of the psychological consultant, a small room was converted to a preschool, where Zach spent some time each day in play activities appropriate for his developmental level. Less structured than usual routines, these activities provided remedial experiences for those Zach seemed to have missed.

After the initial adjustment period, Zach appeared to be learning from every aspect of his day at Cumberland House. Gradually he began to express genuine pleasure and to laugh. He developed an interest in music and was fascinated by playing records. He continued to work with his tutor, but he also joined the group to do classwork for twenty minutes a day.

About six months after Zach started at Cumberland House, Phil left. Zach was noticeably upset. In one of his first meaningful contributions to a pow-wow, he expressed in a few phrases what he would miss about Phil.

During this period Mr. and Mrs. Watson were divorced, and Mrs. Watson was uncertain whether she would be financially able to care for Zach as his foster mother. The liaison teacher-counselor contacted the Department of Human Services and made the strongest possible case in support of Mrs. Watson; his interest and participation were critical in ensuring that the additional allowance for Zach as an exceptional child would not be cut—which in turn allowed Mrs. Watson to continue as foster parent.

When planning for Zach's transition to public schools began, the liaison teacher-counselor explored possible school placements and selected a small class for behavior-disordered children as the most appropriate for Zach. He scheduled a conference with Cumberland House staff and Zach's new teacher to plan Zach's school program. Having assisted in establishing an excellent foster home and school setting, Cumberland House was ready to relinquish a primary role in Zach's life. Staff members were amazed and pleased at the progress the boy had made in one year.

All was not smooth sailing, however. Zach was overwhelmed by the change. In the first weeks of the transition, he turned "wild" again, talked incoherently, and required physical restraint both at home and at school. The liaison teacher-counselor talked with the teacher and with Mrs. Watson daily to reassure them and coordinate management. Within weeks, Zach responded to the consistent rules and expectations and settled down to a routine and made steady progress. When Mrs. Watson was notified that Zach's parents planned to put their son up for adoption, she applied and received approval to adopt him.

At ten, Zach can look forward to a future with people who genuinely love him, who will help him maintain the stability he needs, and who will provide a home environment in which he can continue to learn. That's quite a change from his prospects at age four.

Mark W., Age Four*

"It was either me or him," Mrs. W. told the parent intake worker at the Regional Intervention Program (RIP) in Nashville. "I have been going crazy. I have to keep an eye on him all the time. I'm always yelling. I'm so tense. I lose control and scream. And the more I scream, the worse Mark gets. Then when my husband comes home, I am so keyed up that we get into an argument. The whole family is in an uproar."

The family pediatrician had suggested RIP as a way to deal with Mark's behavior problems. At first, Mr. W. had been against getting outside help. He felt that four-year-old Mark would outgrow his problems and that his wife needed to manage the child better. However, on the occasions that he tried to care for Mark, Mr. W. soon found that he was not able to manage the child either.

Mrs. W. felt that she had somehow failed with Mark. "All my friends have such nice, well-behaved children. I'm embarrassed to take Mark anywhere. Sometimes I think that there is something wrong with Mark. Maybe he is retarded or hyperactive. But our doctor can't find anything wrong with him, and there are no signs from his medical history to indicate problems. So I guess it's me."

The parents described to the interviewer how Mark's behavior disrupted the whole family. "Mark does what he wants," said Mrs. W. "He rules the house. He throws tantrums and hits and throws things at his sister, my husband, me, and the cat. He runs away all the time. I never know what he is going to do next. The other day, I was on the telephone for five minutes, and I found that Mark had emptied out the contents of the refrigerator onto the kitchen floor. I just went wild. He is unmanageable."

As a parent of a child who had gone through the Regional Intervention Program, the intake worker understood these parents' plight. She told them about some of the problems she had had with her preschooler. She explained how RIP worked, asked more about the specifics of Mark's behavior, and asked about which behaviors the parents felt were the most troublesome. She then gave Mr. and Mrs. W. and Mark a tour of the facility. When Mr. W.

*This case study was written by Paula Litchfield.

asked how soon they could begin the program, the intake worker told him that they could begin the next day because there was no waiting list.

In order to enroll Mark in RIP, the parent worker told the parents, one of them would need to work with Mark at the center. Mark and one of his parents would be required to attend the center every weekday morning from 9 A.M. to 12 P.M. The intake worker explained that she and her child had attended for three months before beginning "payback." She noted that while there were no fees for services, the family needed to make a commitment of a "payback" of service to the center for seventy-eight mornings after Mark completed the program.

The parents agreed that they wanted to try the program. Since Mrs. W. did not work outside of the home, it was agreed that she would return the next day to begin the program with Mark. Her two-year-old daughter would also be able to attend.

When Mrs. W. and Mark arrived on the first morning, Mark was placed in the intake preschool. It had been explained to Mrs. W. that the preschool was a class which all the children attend initially. Here Mark's behavior would be assessed, and Mark would learn behaviors like paying attention, sitting in a group, and playing alone or with other children. His behavior would have to meet a particular criterion before he would be moved to another class. While Mark was in class, Mrs. W. was assigned to work in the language preschool with language-delayed children.

Also during that first morning, Mrs. W. met her case manager, a mother who had been through the program and was there to lend support and knowledge. The case manager explained to Mrs. W. that she and Mark would be starting in the generalization training module that day. She told Mrs. W. that the module was a simulated home living area where staff could observe a parent and child interacting from behind one-way mirrors and could help the parent develop effective ways of dealing with the child's behavior. The program entailed a special procedure to elicit oppositional behavior, so that parents could immediately learn to handle it.

In her first generalization training session, Mrs. W. was asked to play with Mark as she would at home, with one difference. Her case manager told her that she was to change the toy her child was playing with every two minutes. The case manager and a resource person (one of the professional staff involved in the program) watched from behind the window and tapped to signal toy changes. Since Mark wanted to keep the toys longer than two minutes, the procedure allowed the staff to see parent-child behavior in frustrating situations. Mark began to cry and yell when Mrs. W. changed the first toy, and he refused to play with the new one. He quickly became frustrated and, at one point, threw a toy at his mother. The more aggressive he became, the more negative attention he received from his mother. Both parent and child left the play session angry and frustrated.

In the meeting right after the session, the case manager went over what happened. She explained that the session was a "baseline" session to find out what happens between a child and parent. She showed Mrs. W. a graph of the behaviors which Mark had exhibited during the session. He had yelled for fifteen minutes of the twenty-minute session, hit himself five times, threw a toy one time, and hit his mother two times. The case manager and resource person then talked to Mrs. W. about how to change Mark's behavior. They explained, "When you like what Mark is doing and would like him to do more of it, give him a lot of attention. When he does things you don't like, ignore him and don't respond. You need to 'turn on' when he does what you want. Talk to him, hug him, praise him. You need to 'turn off' when he does not listen or obey. This means you ignore him. Don't look at him or talk to him. Just stand with your back to him and play quietly with the toy."

"In the next session, tell Mark, 'It's time to play with the blocks.' He has to know what you expect. If he does what you say, give him a lot of attention and praise. If he doesn't do as you ask, ignore him and turn your back on him. If Mark comes up to you to play correctly with the toy, then it's time to turn on."

For the next two weeks, Mrs. W. worked with Mark in the generalization training sessions. She encouraged her son when he played with the toys correctly and ignored him when he did not. She found that Mark did not like the turning off. Sometimes he begged her to play and sometimes he kicked her, but usually he went back to the toy quickly. She told her case manager, "I can't believe that this is all it took. Rather than begging him to do things, nagging, and just getting mad, all I have to do is just turn my back on him, and it works. It is such a relief. Yesterday I went home and showed my husband. He couldn't believe it either. I'm so thrilled because for the first time in my life Mark is responding positively to something I have done, rather than me reacting to something he has done. This is terrific. I'm going to be the mother for a change."

The graphs of Mark's behavior in the play sessions proved what Mrs. W. already felt. Mark's behavior was under her control in the sessions. Now she had to be able to control Mark's behavior without rewarding him or ignoring him all the time. "You can't always pay attention to your child when you are at home trying to fix dinner and do the laundry," the case manager told Mrs. W. "Now you need to begin giving intermittent attention to Mark's good behavior in the play modules. I want you to read a book in the next session while Mark plays." Thus, Mrs. W. began the final phase of the generalization training module—teaching Mark to learn to play and follow instructions without constant attention and supervision from his mother.

After a month and a half, Mark progressed from the intake classroom to the community classroom, which was designed to prepare the preschooler for attending a regular nursery school or kindergarten after completing RIP. Mark was in that class for another two months.

During the time that Mark and his mother were progressing through the program at the center, a home program was begun to deal with the problems that his parents had initially reported as serious concerns. Mrs. W. wanted to work first with Mark's aggression, which included throwing toys and hitting his little sister and the cat. After home baseline data were obtained, Mrs. W. and her case manager worked out a plan such that whenever Mark threw a toy, he was told, "No, Mark, don't throw the toy." His toy was then put away for twenty-four hours. When he hit his sister or others, he was to be put in his room and told that he could come out when he could play nicely. There was to be no nagging or scolding during these times.

Mrs. W. was warned that it might be hard to stick to the plan because Mark's behavior would probably get worse before it got better. The case manager was right. Mark's hitting and tantrums increased for the first week until he learned that tantrums did not get him attention. During that week, Mrs. W. made several phone calls to her case manager and another mother in the program to get help and support. The mothers kept reassuring her that it would work if she could just stick it out for a few more days. In the end, they were right.

As Mrs. W. learned the RIP techniques and taught them to her husband, Mark's behavior began to improve at home, and the arguments between his parents were fewer. For the first time, the parents were able to hire a baby sitter and go out together. Mrs. W. became obviously more relaxed. She laughed about even trying the RIP techniques on her husband: "You know, I've stopped nagging and reminding him, and it's made a difference."

While family life seemed easier, there were some ups and downs. The two-year-old daughter began some "junky" behaviors when Mark's behavior at home improved. As Mark got more positive attention and fewer spankings and as Mrs. W. began using RIP techniques with two-year-old Nancy, the toddler began to become whiny and demanding. It took a while for Nancy to learn that these behaviors would not get her the attention she wanted.

There were also problems with Mrs. W.'s own mother, who was very suspicious of the RIP techniques. She felt that places like RIP should be for handicapped or disturbed children and that Mark was just a normal child with a few problems, which he would certainly outgrow if his parents were just more patient.

For a while, Mrs. W. did not let Mark stay with his grandmother because she was catering to all his demands and undoing the system that Mrs. W. had begun. Then one day, when Mrs. W.'s mother was visiting, Mark would not eat his lunch. His grandmother began following Mark around the kitchen and spoon-feeding him. Mrs. W. told her mother, "Just wait till he sits nicely before giving him any more food." Her mother waited and was surprised that Mark came and sat down and began to eat quietly. From that day on, Mrs. W.'s mother asked questions about the RIP techniques and began trying them herself.

Mrs. W. commented that neither her parents nor her husband's parents raised them to know how to handle a child like Mark. "When we were kids, we got three square meals on the table, clean clothes, and a bed to sleep in. The only time we got attention was when we did something wrong. No one ever gave us much attention for being good. Most parents don't have a child like Mark. Mark didn't respond to the techniques I learned from my mother. Nancy did. That was what was so puzzling and why my own mother had such a difficult time accepting a new way of disciplining Mark. We all needed to learn, and I had to reeducate several of our friends and relatives."

As Mark and his family finished the program at RIP, Mrs. W. began thinking about a nursery school placement for Mark. The liaison staff person at RIP helped Mrs. W. select an appropriate school for him. She also agreed to visit the school and talk with the teacher in order to make the transition a smooth one.

When Mark's work at RIP ended, Mrs. W. began her seventy-eight days of payback time. She was going to work in the toddler preschool and as a behavior rater in the generalization training module. Both of her children would be able to come with her during the summer while she worked on payback. Mrs. W. told the staff at the center that she was interested in continuing as a parent staff person after payback, since she had gained so much from the program. "I finally feel competent. I haven't felt that way in a long time. There are still problems at home, but my perceptions of them have changed. I'm not letting the kids run the household— my husband and I set the rules. Mark still does his thing. The staff at RIP told me he will always do those things. It's just him. He still does it, but I don't react. So he has stopped, and I don't go crazy. I don't think he has changed that much. Things just flash through his brain, and he does them. But now when he empties out the refrigerator, I stay calm, and I always make sure he picks up the mess. He'll get tired of it. It is great to feel that I can handle it. When I came to RIP, it was the first time I met other parents who had problems with their children like we did. You can talk to the professional resource people, and they really back us up; but the other parents really understood. They have been there. They gave me the support and confidence I needed to get through this. Now I want to continue working here so I can help other families."

Cissy J., Age Eleven

Cissy, a tall, slender, eleven-year-old girl, was brought into a hospital emergency room in a state of hysteria, alternately screaming and crying, her eyes bulging, her extremities shaking, her body covered with perspiration. She was accompanied by her twenty-nine-year-old mother, a sanitarium laundry room worker, who insisted to hospital personnel: "Somebody's got to do something with that girl." Doing something with "that girl" spanned five years. It required help from many community resources to support her along the road to what we hope will be a future of productive participation in the community.

During the first eleven years of her life, home for Cissy was a variety of houses in slum neighborhoods, peopled by a variety of relatives, four younger siblings, her mother's assorted men friends, and a drunken, paranoid stepfather. Presiding over the household was a maternal grandmother, always at war with any and all of its occupants. On the fringe, an aunt provided the only source of warmth and encouragement Cissy knew. A severe beating with a belt followed Cissy's slightest deviation from what her mother considered proper behavior. Proper behavior in the mother's view included washing and ironing, cooking and cleaning, minding the "kids," and steering clear of mother's new husband.

In school, soft spoken and affable, Cissy was generally accepted by her fifth-grade peers, but she had no sustained relationships with them. On the playground, she stayed on the fringe of a group, preferring to ingratiate herself with the teacher in charge. Academically, Cissy never functioned at a satisfactory level. She was retained in second grade, and psychological testing was recommended. Poor reading skills interfered with comprehension in all content subjects. She complained frequently that words disappeared from the page she was reading. Always restless, she could never satisfactorily complete assignments. Any confrontation over schoolwork produced headaches and withdrawal. Cissy's mother was never available for school conferences.

Cissy was two when her father deserted the family. She clung to the fantasy that someday an all-loving, perfect father would return to her. It was a letter from her father, Cissy's perception of which was that he totally and finally rejected her, that had precipitated the hysterical outburst that brought her to the hospital and ultimately to Cumberland House.

Testing by the hospital showed that Cissy had intelligence in the superior range, with much of her potential lying dormant as a result of deprivation. In addition to being academically retarded, Cissy had identity problems related to her feelings of rejection at home and her role as a black.

Cissy made an easy adjustment at Cumberland House and repeatedly begged to be allowed to live there "forever." She was sure that her mother would not care if she left home permanently. Cissy was openly hostile toward all males at Cumberland House. Attractive and mature in stature, she had often been the victim of overtures from neighborhood males. Her mother had repeatedly warned her about men.

Cissy was ambivalent about her mother. She said that she loved her mother but feared that she might kill her in anger. Cissy's mother had worked in a mental hospital and had raised fears in Cissy regarding her loss of control. Cissy needed reassurance that she was not mentally ill. Her rebellion at home was not supported by the Re-ED staff, but her feeling that she was treated unfairly *was* supported, because it was based on reality. She was encouraged to try role playing at home and passive withdrawal through reading and crafts to reduce the stress she experienced there.

Cissy was also ambivalent about being black. During the early part of her stay, she was the only black child in residence at Cumberland House. She reacted with hostility toward her day teacher-counselor (who was black), identifying her verbally as "mother." She did not show any hostility, however, toward her night teacher-counselor (who was white), even though the night teacher-counselor more normally would be seen as the mother figure. Planning for Cissy's group activities was deliberately centered around experiences in black community recreation centers. Cissy learned that she was accepted by and could accept non-whites.

Through art, music, and handicraft experiences, Cissy came to see herself as one who could achieve and give. She did not need to compare her work to that of other children. She could appreciate making something and gave value to it because she had made it. She began piano lessons, and her music teacher felt that she was a gifted student.

After nine months, Cissy had become more certain of her own worth, her rights as an individual, and her academic ability (brought to near grade level), so she asked to be discharged. While this period had produced significant changes in Cissy, her home situation had not altered appreciably. Her mother's gains in therapy were limited. Drunken brawls with the stepfather had intensified. Her mother was expecting another child. Clearly, Cissy would require constant support to facilitate her readjustment, both to public school and the home environment.

School and community support were mobilized before Cissy was discharged. In a meeting with Cumberland House staff, personnel from Cissy's public school (her principal, her teacher, a guidance counselor, and a social worker) charted her future academic course. Also meeting with this group were directors from two neighborhood community centers near Cissy's home. They agreed to find a place for Cissy in their afternoon and weekend programs to help her sustain adult and peer relationships and to provide an outlet for her creative talents in music and crafts.

With such support, Cissy successfully completed the tenth grade as an honor student. Cissy called frequently on Cumberland House staff to help her get through a bad time at home. In one drunken rage, Cissy's mother beat her and kicked her out the front door, telling her to "get lost." Aided by a school social worker, Cissy filed a negligence complaint with the juvenile court against her mother. (The mother always promises to stop drinking and to return to therapy, but has yet to do so.)

Encouraged by her school guidance counselor, Cissy secured a job as a clerk-typist in the Neighborhood Youth Corps office, afternoons and Saturday, during the school term. This past summer, Cissy lived on a university campus as a participant in OEO's "Upward Bound" program for disadvantaged youth. Plans are being made now to obtain a full working scholarship for her to a state college when she graduates from high school next year. She will major in sociology. "I want to help other young people as I have been helped," she says.

[*Follow-up: 1981.*]

Cissy keeps in touch with Cumberland House staff members who worked with her. She graduated from college and went on to earn a master's degree in social work. She is employed as a social worker in the health department of a large southern city, specializing in work with children and families.

Deric P., Age Fourteen*

Deric, a fourteen-year-old male, was referred to a Positive Education Program day-treatment center after receiving no educational or treatment services for nearly two years. Deric had been excluded from school for physical aggressiveness toward teachers and peers; frequent use of weapons, such as pipes and belts; abusive language when confronted by authority figures; refusal to stay in his seat or to complete work, even when given one-to-one tutoring; and destruction of school property. In addition to school problems, Deric was frequently brought home by police for curfew and trespassing violations. During the period when Deric was excluded from school, his mother reported severe physical fighting with his older sister, as well as with neighborhood children.

After Deric was excluded from school, the school's psychological services made several attempts determine what type of placement would be appropriate for him. Because of the mother's hostile response to school professionals, including verbal abuse and refusal to keep appointments, an assessment was not completed until nearly one year later. Because of the mother's response, the school filed dependency charges against the mother in juvenile court. Temporary custody was awarded to the county welfare department; custody was to be returned pending the mother's cooperation and interest in Deric's education and treatment.

At the court hearing, the court psychologist recommended residential treatment because of the severity of Deric's problems, as well as the anticipated lack of cooperation from the mother. Deric was later rejected by all ten residential programs to which he was referred, two for lack of space, eight because of his extreme physical aggressiveness. The court psychologist's interim recommendation was for family counseling at the community mental health center; however, the mother missed most appointments.

Nearly a year later, after the applications to residential centers were rejected, the school and court referred Deric to a recently established PEP day-treatment center.

When Deric entered the program at twelve years of age, he demonstrated ability to sit in his seat for only five to ten minutes at a time, could sit quietly for only three or four minutes, would attempt work only with one-to-one assistance, frequently destroyed materials when frustrated, was physically aggressive toward peers on an average of five times per hour, engaged in

*This case study was written by the staff of the Positive Education Program, Cleveland, Ohio.

verbal abuse of peers and teachers, and refused to follow directions fifty times per day.

Academically, Deric was working at a second-grade level in reading and third-grade level in mathematics. Psychological testing indicated Deric's abilities to be within the low-average range, with significant perceptual-motor developmental lags. Predictably, Deric's emotions were dominated by intense anger and hostility. He tended to perceive the world as attacking him personally, and typically used physical aggression as his major defense against this hostile world.

Before Deric's admission, his mother was interviewed in her home by a day-treatment staff member. She described much frustration with Deric's behavior at home, as well as great concern regarding communication problems with Deric's father, who lived three miles away. Deric frequently left her house when angry and stayed with his father for a number of days. Deric's mother expressed interest in the day-treatment program and agreed to attend weekly parent meetings.

Mrs. P.'s attendance proved to be a problem because she had no phone, and therefore could not be reminded to attend, and no transportation. On the other hand, Mrs. P. would infrequently drop by the center, angry about Deric's father or about Deric's behavior at home. A meeting was arranged that included Deric, his mother and father, their county worker, and the day-treatment staff to discuss how communication problems were contributing to Deric's problems, and a strategy was agreed on regarding Deric's visiting between his mother and father. Transportation was offered to parent meetings in the evenings.

Deric's behavior during the first month of treatment was violent. He began to respond to group pressure to follow class rules while on a four-day camping trip. Following the trip, he began to show interest in the level system, which defined privileges and responsibilities. His academic skills began to improve slowly. Growth was uneven, but Deric showed more interest in learning. Episodes of physical aggression continued for nearly seven months but showed a steady decrease in frequency. He became able to review his behavior in verbal mediation sessions. He developed a strong relationship with a male teacher-counselor after the episodes of physical aggression had nearly disappeared. Interestingly, this was the same teacher-counselor who had done nearly all restraining of Deric when he was out of control. After a year and a half, Deric's behavioral and academic gains were sufficient for him to be reintegrated into his home school in a learning disabilities classroom.

A few months later, Deric's mother was in a car accident, resulting in a back injury. At this point, Mrs. P. was assigned to another parent who had been trained by the day-treatment staff in a Parents Training Parents (PTP) program. This specially trained parent met with Mrs. P. in her home on a weekly basis. Mrs. P. responded very favorably to this parent.

Follow-up plans were made through the community mental health center to provide Mrs. P. with an outreach worker, while Deric continued the Scouting activities he had begun at the center with his neighborhood troop. A continued source of concern is the significant lack of an appropriate male model in Deric's life. Efforts to provide one have not been fruitful to this point. The PEP liaison teacher-counselor continues to work with Deric and the staff of his school. Behavior remains controlled, but academic progress is very uneven. Deric works to earn the privilege of returning to the center for visits and of going camping with his former class.

John S., Age Fourteen

John S. was admitted to a Re-ED program when he was fourteen years old. John was quite small for his age and was just entering puberty. He came from a family with many problems. The family lived in extreme poverty. Although their home was quite small, it housed ten people: John, his parents, three younger siblings, the mother's retarded daughter (from a former marriage), and the daughter's three children. The father had been diagnosed as a schizophrenic and periodically needed hospitalization. The family income was derived from Social Security and a pension. John had been manifesting severe emotional problems for several years: extreme nervousness and hyperactivity, vivid imagination with feelings of being powerful, distrust of others, need for constant attention, violent temper tantrums, and harming other children for no apparent reason.

John had been excluded from school twice, and a foster home placement had been tried when he was eleven. He could not adjust to the foster home and was returned to his own home. At the time of admission to Re-ED, John was in the eighth grade, having received social promotions. He had been in therapy at a local mental health center.

At the time of referral, the liaison teacher-counselor began to gather information and formulate plans. His report included the following comments:

> When we first became involved with John S. and had received the social history and other data, we questioned the parents' ability to provide other than a disruptive existence for him. Was change possible in the family situation?

John's mother obviously had some strength, or she would not have been able to hold the family together, but was this strength waning under the prolonged pressures? Was the father a source of potential strength, or was he too sick? Did the father need to get out of the home into a long-term treatment center such as the VA offers? Did long-range plans need to be made for John in a children's home or a group home for adolescents? The family caseworker from the welfare department, who had known and worked with the family for some time, thought that John should stay with his family. Foster home placement had not worked, and she felt that the parents did care for their children and that there was hope for change in the family situation.

Each parent came for separate interviews three times to determine what they wanted and how willing they were to work toward a better understanding of each other and their children. After the interviews, they were to talk things over together. They recognized that their relationship was intolerable, not only to themselves but to their children, and they agreed on an effort to try to change. Arrangements were made for them to get individual counseling at the local mental health center.

The liaison teacher-counselor had visited John's public school and prepared the following school history:

This child has a notorious school history. He was expelled from school after attending only a few months of the second grade. He missed most of the next year. In the following year, he was reenrolled in the third grade, but was expelled for the last three months of that year. John has been quite disruptive of the whole school. He has temper tantrums that have become worse toward the end of the past year. He is also a problem on the school bus, where he hits children and calls them bad names. On the playground, he picks fights with boys for no apparent reason. He has also spit on a teacher when she tried to stop his fighting. He smokes on the school grounds in violation of rules. John stole two books of a set that a parent had donated to the class. He denied taking the books until his sister brought one of them back; then he said he did not put them in his bookcase but that they jumped in by themselves. A softball from school also disappeared; John said he took it because he wanted to paint it and was going to return it right away. The principal and staff have tried to keep him at school. However, one incident finally led to his being expelled. It was necessary for John to start traveling on a new school bus. When he was told this, he threw a temper tantrum. He said he did not want to go on the new bus, that he did not know the kids on the new bus and was afraid of them. He said these kids would beat him up. He refused to get on the bus. At this point, the principal told John that if he did not want to get on the bus he would take him home and that everything would be okay. At this, John started another tantrum and said that he was afraid of the principal, also. Finally, he did go home with the principal.

John also seems to have periods of depression, where he becomes quite sullen and moody, and he participates in a great deal of fantasy. He is continually telling stories about himself riding off on a big white horse.

At the time this history was prepared, the principal would not consider John's ever returning to his school. Thus, a new school placement was explored with the director of guidance for the school system. The principal at the new school assured us that he would take the child if he first came to Re-ED.

We began seeing John's disruptive behavior from the very beginning. Here is a note from a teacher-counselor:

> The first day John was here, he seemed to be on the defensive about his small size, since the first topic of conversation with everyone involved was guessing his real age. He was quick to show the others he could take up for himself with his fists when any of the boys in the group happened to cross him. He was very warm to me, flattering me, defending me, chattering to me. The "honeymoon" period was brief, since the temper outbursts began the second day and have continued daily. The slightest disagreement or name calling from anyone in the group can initiate a violent outburst of tears, screams, and blows from John. In one incident, he asked Berry to stop doing something but then hit him over the head with a mop handle before the words were out of his mouth. Another time, Gary asked him to stop saying other boys' parts in a skit practice, and that precipitated a tantrum. Still another tantrum was produced when someone spilled pickle juice on John's plate in passing.

In spite of the fact that John was hard to manage, his teacher-counselors felt that some progress was being made and wished to continue with him. They felt that he was responding to firm, consistent limits, and they were beginning to see his tantrums not so

much as lack of control but as controlling devices to get his own
way and to get attention.

Three months later, the teacher-counselors reported that
John was making progress on his temper problem. He had made
positive responses—sometimes bizarre, at other times really comi-
cal—to efforts to help him develop a sense of humor. He and his
teacher-counselors worked out a special message to use when the
other boys were baiting him. The teacher-counselor asked John
whether "the fuse is wet." His response would let the teacher-
counselors know how he felt about his own ability to control
himself.

By the following month, John had settled down considerably in the classroom, although he was still using negative atten-
tion-seeking devices. He was reading a great deal and choosing his
books with some care. His self-concept had improved, and he
could take teasing better. Except for occasional blowups, John
was relating well to the rest of the group, playing well with them
much of the time. Following temper flareups, John was usually
able to discuss his part in the problem and to suggest how he could
act to avoid trouble in the future.

While John was in Re-ED, his parents did make an honest
effort to use the help the caseworker offered them. The liaison
teacher-counselor had this to say about their progress:

> The father's drinking abated for a time; the parents
> were more consistent with John on weekends and worked
> cooperatively on trying to find better housing, as well as a
> place for the mother's other three children.

Eventually, in spite of their efforts, it was necessary for the
father to be hospitalized. At about this time, a new director was
appointed to the family agency and a new caseworker for the family. The new director of the welfare department was under orders
to cut costs. As a result, he formulated plans to have John put in a
custodial mental institution. His feeling was that too much had
already been spent on this family and too little change had been
noticed. After much persuasion by the liaison teacher-counselor,
the director of the welfare department agreed to try to maintain
the family together in the community. At this point, a community
plan was organized, since the Re-ED staff were convinced that
only with community support could this child and family succeed.
Representatives of several community organizations—the housing
administration, Alcoholics Anonymous, the Veterans Administration, two churches, the public schools, the welfare department,
and a homemaker service—were invited to a planning conference.

At this time (seven months after John's admission to Re-

ED), the liaison teacher-counselor completed a school placement for John. The principal who had originally agreed to take John was now having second thoughts. After discussion with the liaison teacher-counselor and the director of guidance from the school system, the principal agreed to take John on a trial placement. A week or so before John was to be discharged, his father left the hospital without permission. Since he had voluntarily admitted himself, he could not be made to return. However, by this time, the community was getting organized and began to incorporate plans for the whole family, including the father.

At the first meeting of the community representatives, there was optimism about the plans and agreement to do whatever they could. Within a few weeks, new low-cost housing was made available for the family, as well as separate housing for the mother's daughter and the daughter's children. The representative from Alcoholics Anonymous called on the father to take him hunting. The move to a new neighborhood necessitated another change of schools for John. This was carefully planned and worked out well. The liaison teacher-counselor visited the new school after John was enrolled, and, except for one minor incident, the principal and teacher were quite pleased with his progress.

An eighteen-month follow-up showed things to be going reasonably well. Two factors seemed to be making the most difference. At home, John's father, with the help of Alcoholics Anonymous, was coping well with his drinking problem and providing some stability that had been lacking in the home for a number of years. At school, Johnny's own behavior made a difference. At Re-ED, he had made up academic deficiencies, and he had learned to control his behavior reasonably well. These two changes brought positive responses from the two important worlds of John's life, home and school, thus reinforcing and extending the gains made at Re-ED. The situation is far from ideal, and the prognosis must be guarded; but the Re-ED effort, with its emphasis on community mobilization and enhanced coping skills for the child, has clearly gotten child and family above threshold and in the company of a large number of families of marginal personal resources who can make it if general circumstances remain reasonably supportive.

Pat B., Age Sixteen*

Pat was sixteen when she was referred to Crockett Academy (a Re-ED program for teenagers) by a local community mental

*This case study was written by Barbara Wheeley.

health center. The liaison teacher-counselor arranged a joint meeting of the referring staff who had worked with Pat and the Crockett "Searchers" staff for the purpose of gathering preadmissions data and determining the suitability of Crockett's program.

Pat was presented as an intelligent, affectionate girl, talented in cooking and dancing, and helpful with small children. She had had an extremely unstable childhood: at different times, both parents had been in psychiatric hospitals for treatment and were separated when Pat was five. Pat lived with her mother, who had remarried and divorced two more times. Pat's father was also remarried and divorced. At the time of referral, both parents seemed relatively stable and were able to cooperate with each other and to assume some responsibility for Pat. They were supportive of her enrollment at Crockett. The Department of Human Services had custody of Pat's brother, who was at that time enrolled at Cumberland House (Re-ED program for younger children) and was in foster care on weekends.

The community mental health center staff thought that Pat needed a structured therapeutic environment that would provide some stability for at least a year. In recent months, Pat had threatened suicide, become hostile and destructive of property on several occasions, and withdrawn from normal peer and adult relationships. She appeared to be frightened by the intensity of her mood swings and her lack of control of her own impulsiveness. Usually, Pat was able to tell her counselor if she felt she could not handle a situation. The community mental health center staff recommended working toward Pat's eventual future placement with her father.

Crockett Academy agreed to Pat's enrollment, which legally was of voluntary status. The liaison teacher-counselor arranged for her to have routine medical examinations and outlined the following plan, which emerged from the ecological assessment:

1. Further medical and dental examinations, initiated by the Crockett Academy nurse.
2. Academic and psychological testing, conducted by appropriate staff during the first few weeks.
3. Twice-weekly counseling sessions for Pat at the community mental health center with a view toward terminating these in favor of increased involvement of Crockett Academy staff. (Pat's parents wished to pay for this and to provide her transportation.)
4. Therapy for the parents to continue at the community mental health center.
5. Visiting opportunities for Pat and her brother, arranged by

liaison teacher-counselor at Crockett Academy and Cumberland House.

An early interview with Pat's parents raised the possibility of her eventual placement at a children's home if she was not able to function well at either of her parents' homes on weekend visits. Pat's own special objectives during her stay at Crockett included attending seminars on smoking, drugs and alcohol, and Planned Parenthood. She worked to meet the weekly goals of using appropriate language, controlling her temper, solving problems in a calm manner, and achieving continued academic progress. Her improvement was gradual and steady, yet not without its difficult moments.

After several months at Crockett, while at home for a weekend with her mother, Pat was allowed to go with her friends to the local skating rink. Her friends brought her home early—quite sick from smoking pot. Pat's mother felt guilty and upset about letting her go in the first place, but she was reassured by the liaison teacher-counselor that Pat needed opportunities to develop her sense of responsibility. In this case, Pat had made a poor choice. Later, Pat claimed that she had been raped by one of the boys with whom she was smoking, and a subsequent investigation ensued through the Metro Youth Guidance office. Pat's mother hired an attorney for her, and both sets of grandparents became more active in expressing their concern for her well-being. Pat did not seem to suffer an extreme setback from this incident and was able to cope fairly well with the police investigation.

Pat continued meeting her weekly goals until shortly after Thanksgiving, when she was involved in a fight with another student. She and several others then took a window out of a bedroom and ran away. When found, Pat and her comrades spent one week in juvenile court detention. Upon return to Crockett, Pat and her parents were asked to sign a contract in which the parents agreed to file run-away petitions through the appropriate juvenile authorities should that be necessary in the future. Pat agreed not to use physically abusive force in handling interpersonal problems and not to run away from Crockett Academy. It was made clear again that, with a voluntary admission, the student is free to sign out of the program if she does not wish to adhere to contracted agreements.

During her stay in detention, Pat stated to the Youth Guidance officers who were prosecuting her rape case that she had not been raped. She had been angry at the boy because he had lied to her. In general, Pat seemed to respond inappropriately to males, often in an obviously flirtatious manner. She got along better with female staff members at first, but was gradually able to improve her relationships with both male and female adults.

Several days after returning to Crockett, Pat decided to sign out during an angry outburst. Her letter was processed promptly, but she changed her mind the next day. During this period, Pat's parents were concerned about where she would go and wanted to explore a civil commitment.

At the time of her sixth-month review, Pat, her parents, and the Crockett Academy staff agreed that she could profit from continued enrollment in the program. The liaison teacher-counselor arranged a more formal contractual agreement regarding the sequencing of Pat's visits with relatives and eventual discharge to the children's home. Her specific objectives were to be able to maintain positive interactions and appropriate language for a continuous period of three weeks prior to leaving Crockett.

Pat's positive qualities became more obvious as her life took on greater stability. She was able to profit from feedback and responded well to consistent discipline. Pat is a friendly person and seemed to enjoy being with older girls and participating in all activities. She was creative, had definite leadership ability, and enjoyed challenges. While at Crockett during the week, Pat was able to maximize her strengths and often assisted other students to do the same.

However, Pat's weekend visits with her mother, and alternately with her father, were only moderately successful. She was reluctant to visit her mother and reported that she and her mother had frequent arguments. Most arguments centered on Pat's desire to have greater freedom to do things on her own; Pat's mother had become more restrictive because of past abuses of free time. The liaison teacher-counselor suggested that Pat and her mother schedule more joint activities on weekends, an approach that met with greater success. Pat eventually reported more enjoyable experiences with her mother, and the serious difficulties subsided. Pat's mother was cooperative in implementing staff suggestions for managing both her own and Pat's behavior.

With her father, Pat was more responsive, but he seemed unable to manage a full weekend stay. Therefore, day visits were scheduled for Pat and her father on some weekends, with the objective of enhancing their positive relationship. Both seemed to enjoy and profit from their activities together.

By the end of seven months, Pat had met her goal of three continuous weeks of calm appropriate behavior. The "Searchers" staff met with Pat and her parents to decide where she would live after leaving the program. All concurred that regular weekend visits had not been successful enough to warrant her placement in either home. Pat's parents agreed to initiate a referral to the children's home within the next two weeks.

Following the referral, the liaison teacher-counselor met with the director of the children's home to facilitate the transfer. Pat was accepted there and given an enrollment date a month later. During this month, Pat and her parents visited the new home and went with the liaison teacher-counselor to make arrangements for her to attend the local high school. The liaison teacher-counselor also met with Pat's teachers to offer support during the transition period. Because Pat was now seventeen, it was understood that she would work toward independent living by the time she left the children's home a year later. The staff at the children's home offered to provide counseling for Pat and her parents, so the community mental health center was no longer to be involved. The liaison teacher-counselor would be available as needed to facilitate the transition.

Pat left Crockett Academy a stronger young woman, still with struggles to face but with a system of support that made success seem likely.

Two Failures to Help. It is easier to remember and to write about successes than it is to report failures. But schools have failed and do fail to help some children, and it is instructive to examine, when one can, what went wrong.

The first account to follow is presented with some pain, for it describes the breakdown of the system within a Re-ED school in the early days of its development. The staff were just learning, and consultants and supervisors were still uncertain about how best to proceed. These shared incompetences resulted in the program's inability to help a child, even when he was manifesting a great deal of competence himself. The account was prepared by one of the teacher-counselors in the group to which the child was assigned. The account is undoubtedly biased, as it would be no matter which participant recorded the story. Its absolute truth is less important than its credibility. Yet it is written with compassion and with about as much objectivity as could be expected. There is no recrimination but a sense of shared responsibility for an effort that went wrong. One cautionary note. It is not enough to say that the child was too disturbed to be admitted to a Re-ED school; children who were much more troubled have been worked with successfully, before and since. It is fair to say that he was too much for the staff (and for the consultants and supervisors as well) at this particular juncture, and that they were willing honestly to admit their limitations.

The second account is different. It records the story of a boy who was recently enrolled in a Re-ED school. The significant thing here is that the staff did appear, on review, to have done their job well. While some actions might be called errors retrospectively, these were minor events and probably of no consequence in determining the negative outcome. Actually, the staff devoted a lot of intelligence, affection, time, patience, and determination to working with the adolescent as well as with his family, school, companions, and a prospective employer. But the best the staff could do was not good enough, and failure had finally to be recognized.

Timmy K., Age Eleven*

This is probably the most notable example of a failure that I was a part of. Timmy was eleven years old. He had many problems. His vision was poor—probably, according to the psychiatric clinic that had referred him to us, as a result of neurological damage. He engaged in many rituals. He would take two steps at a time when walking, would not step on shadows, would sometimes touch and sometimes not touch people, and would dress in a certain invariable order. If these things were not done, "Something bad will happen to Mommie." His gross motor coordination was very bad. He would have nothing to do with other children. He was extremely involved emotionally with his mother (almost ESP-like) and generally seductive toward females. He would play the role of the helpless child to gain control over adults, but he was also violently explosive when angry. He made good grades in public school and was not seen by his teachers as a disturbed child. His parents saw him as "a pain."

What happened in the next six weeks is still not completely clear to me. But from going over my notes, thoughts, and feelings, and from talking with others, I can conclude the following.

Timmy was probably more aware of himself, of what he needed, and perhaps of how he might get there than any of us were. I believe I failed to meet him on these terms. As early as his third day in my group, he was asking to slow down the speed of the adjustment away from mother that we were requiring. He

*This case study was written by Frances Smith.

desperately wanted to make a break from her and had been working toward it for quite some time. My colleagues and I chose to treat him like the rest of the children—come on Sunday and leave on Friday, no phone calls in between. I think by this I blocked communication between Timmy and his home and thereby prevented his getting the assurance that while he was trying to change, those at home were safe—that is, his changing was not destroying or "causing bad things to happen to his family."

During his stay, he repeatedly told me in every way how much he needed to keep in touch with his family while he was trying to change. On one level, I felt these requests to call home were legitimate, and on another level I faced school precedents. I chose the latter and received staff support in doing so, thus blocking a more realistic and creative way of handling the situation. Subsequent weeks were like acting out a Greek tragedy.

Another facet was staff communication. A child as noticeable as Timmy can easily become everyone's property, and our team allowed this to happen. People watched and moved in to help whenever they saw fit. Inconsistency reigned. And soon all were aligned for keeping Timmy or against keeping him. The "fors" said if we would relax certain usual expectations, he would fit in; and besides, Timmy is likable. The "againsts" said he took too much teacher-counselor time; expectations and routine could not be relaxed for him; he was disturbing the whole school.

Timmy responded best to men. W. P. was especially able to help him move through his rituals and get things done. Again, we did not build on this in a constructive way.

Timmy began using old tricks—not getting dressed, breaking his glasses, creating confusion, running away. He commented each time that these were old behaviors. At one point, he told me, "Miss Smith, I'm so confused I don't know who you are. I don't know where I am. Why do I have to go to the group?" The last week of Timmy's stay was full of messages sent and not received.

Sunday: He tried to open the car door while I was driving. When another child asked why he didn't go ahead and kill himself, he responded, "I can't do that. Miss Smith doesn't want me to." In a group meeting, he commented freely about himself: "It's like I got stuck somewhere and can't go on." "What if I get to like it here. Maybe I won't want to go home."

Monday: "Will people still like me if I change?"

Tuesday: Timmy left school very early in the morning and began walking home. A friend found the pajama-clad, barefoot boy, picked him up, and took him home. Timmy's father promptly returned him to school. During the day, his conversation centered on "I will get my own way. I'll do anything to get my way."

Wednesday: Timmy talked about doing things only once (he usually did things twice). Would his parents still love him since he was only doing things once?

Thursday: Timmy refused to get dressed. He urinated repeatedly on the floor and smeared his feces on himself.

Friday: Timmy set the mattresses on fire during the night. His comment was "Now can I go home?"

Timmy was sent home after a brief and rather unintelligible (to me, at least) staff meeting that morning. Would that one of us had had the presence of mind to waive this hearing until the horror of that early morning had calmed. Two months later, at a full staff meeting, this case was again discussed. Although still veiled by much feeling, some interesting comments were made.

We did not structure appropriately. The extent of Timmy's problems was not clearly understood by anyone but Timmy, and we did not listen to him or respond appropriately. We did not allow the teacher-counselors to respond spontaneously in their work with this child. There was too much interference on one level and not enough support and direct consultation when asked for. I chose a path which blocked my own creativity in handling a child. I think now that we (the teacher-counselor team) could have stood firmer for our right to plan for a child's stay and to prevent interference and ask for help when needed.

And yet Timmy himself reported gains in understanding the ways he related to his environment and people. His speech cleared and remained clear after his discharge.

I can't help thinking we might have helped Timmy. I am sure that increased maturity of the school operation and of those dealing with the child will make it possible for the school to serve such a child. Blame seems an inappropriate question, yet we all shared responsibility for the failure.

Jonathan Y., Age Eleven*

Jonathan Y. lives at a state psychiatric hospital now, ready for independent living but with no place to go that can provide him adequate support. His social worker is seeking a placement for him—again—for this has been Jonathan's life story. Apparently capable of managing his own behavior, Jonathan shows definite progress in highly structured situations, then is unable to cope when he leaves. He has received the best efforts of numerous agencies, including three Re-ED programs and has made some progress but also has become somewhat immune to most behavior-shaping techniques. Jonathan's workers remain hopeful, for he is a hand-

*This case study was written by Barbara Wheeley.

some, orderly young man who at twenty-three is often charming in conversation and quite insightful about his own difficulties. Re-ED remains hopeful, too, for we continue to see in Jonathan the same potential for positive growth that led us to accept him at Cumberland House over ten years ago. Here is his story.

Having participated in intense family therapy with a private psychiatric social worker, Mr. and Mrs. Y. applied to Cumberland House in the spring when Jonathan was eleven years old. Six months before, they had moved to Nashville from another state, where Jonathan had been asked to withdraw from the public schools because there was no program for him. Already Jonathan had been to five schools in four years, including a special diagnostic center and a residential program for special students. He was a "severe behavior problem" and at the time of application had been out of school for over a year. His parents reported that in his early childhood he had contracted a high fever, which left him with some brain damage and mild epilepsy. Jonathan had made a good adjustment in the first grade and was doing well academically; however, when his family moved so that his father could take a better job, his behavior deteriorated. Three moves and three schools later, the parents came to Cumberland House because they were worn out and had exhausted their resources in trying to cope with Jonathan's inappropriate behavior.

Their social worker had referred them to Cumberland House and continued to coordinate the application process. She believed that Jonathan's behavior could be brought under control and sustained once his parents had the necessary skills. Information was obtained from Jonathan's two previous schools and from the diagnostic center.

During the initial ecological assessment, the liaison teacher-counselor visited the home and found the parents to be a happily married, middle-class couple, deeply concerned for Jonathan's welfare and willing to cooperate in any way they could. They were convinced that brain damage was Jonathan's major problem, and they had difficulty accepting the fact that he might also be experiencing emotional difficulties. An older brother and sister were both doing well in school and had adjusted well to their life situations. Jonathan's mother indicated that she was beginning to be frightened because she could no longer physically manage Jonathan's outbursts due to his size.

Jonathan's numerous academic assessments over the years showed him to be functioning in an average range of intelligence, but with considerable variability in his scores. One evaluator pointed out that his lack of integrative ability and response to the concrete and obvious were typical of a brain-damaged person, but that his acting-out behavior had been reinforced by the frequent moves and changes of approach in his earlier years. Jonathan's behavior had been extreme and unpredictable, and he demonstrated abrupt mood changes. He was often silly and giddy, going from hugging, clinging behavior to angry, explosive attacks on staff and other children. His posture was very poor and his appearance sloppy, for he took very little care of himself.

Cumberland House enrolled Jonathan in the fall and, together with him, his family, and a social worker, developed the following goals for him:

1. Gain control of himself and his actions.
2. Demand less attention from adults and peers.
3. Discriminate properly regarding physical contact.
4. Accept and admit faults and mistakes.
5. Handle social situations appropriately.
6. Increase attention to task.
7. Function within a classroom without disrupting.

Jonathan's parents would continue in intensive therapy to develop their abilities to work with him on weekends at home.

Jonathan made "slow, steady progress" at Cumberland House. He was good in art and very conscientious about his schoolwork. In his second month there, he was recognized as "outstanding group member of the month" and at Christmas was chosen to be Santa, a task he handled quite appropriately. Jonathan showed great stick-to-itiveness when given a task, and his relationships with his peers gradually improved. His parents reported after three months that "he was a pleasure to have at home" on weekends.

As Jonathan settled into the Cumberland House program, his attempts to gain attention became more subtle, and staff began to question an apparent increase in his seizures. Since Jonathan was on medication, they decided to ignore the seizures, which took the form of Jonathan's stumbling around and biting his tongue. The seizures decreased in frequency, and Jonathan eventually admitted some faking. By his eighth month at Cumberland House, Jonathan was showing more interest in his appearance, was doing well in arithmetic, but was still having difficulties in reading. Jonathan had met with success in overcoming a number of problems, but usually new ones would arise that required a new approach.

As Jonathan met most of his goals, the teacher-counselors began to plan for his graduation three months hence—at which point his behavior began to deteriorate. Jonathan acknowledged that he did not wish to leave Cumberland House, but with support gradually began to look forward to his return home and to the public schools. (The social worker incorporated Jonathan into regular family therapy sessions to assist the transition.) The liaison teacher-counselor and Jonathan's parents arranged for him to be enrolled in the fifth grade at the public school near his home; the liaison teacher-counselor visited the school and planned with the teacher the best approaches to working with Jonathan. The Cumberland House staff were optimistic, and so was Jonathan.

Within three months, Jonathan was suspended from two different public schools for deliberately disruptive behavior. He frightened both his teachers and other children by exposing himself, cursing, and throwing severe temper tantrums. The liaison teacher-counselor and the social worker attempted to provide assistance but found that neither his parents nor the schools were able to provide the necessary structure for him. Without a consistent environment, Jonathan's behavior regressed rapidly.

Jonathan returned to Cumberland House with the understanding that his stay would be brief, a transition period to a new Re-ED program for adolescents. His reentry was difficult, viewed negatively by both peers and staff because he was again so disruptive. Since he was older than the other boys in his group, the Cumberland House staff decided to build a special one-to-one program for him. The program was to have the following features: (1) It would be consistent at all costs. (2) It would be kept as simple as possible. (3) It would maintain high expectations. (Jonathan had shown himself quite capable of immediate cooperation with negative expectations!) Social interaction, such as evenings out with a counselor, was the primary reinforcer.

Again Jonathan was successful and began to work consistently on his own. New staff saw immediate limit testing, regression in behavior, and some running away; but, with reinforced consistency, Jonathan improved. Jonathan left Cumberland House "on top" for his new residence at Pine Breeze, the only adolescent Re-ED program in the state at that time. People were proud of him, expressed their high expectations for him, and thought he seemed friendlier and happier.

Pine Breeze maintained a more open atmosphere for the older students, which Jonathan found difficult. He was in frequent conflict with other guys, and after two months he ran away. His parents picked him up after he had broken into an unlocked house to call them. By now Mrs. Y. was in poor physical health, so Mr. and Mrs. Y. filed a delinquent petition against Jonathan with the courts. The judge ruled "guilty as charged" and committed Jonathan, now thirteen, to the state school for boys. There he "made progress due to firm discipline" and was released when the school closed, even though the staff recognized that his behavior and mood deteriorated when he was home.

Again it became necessary for the judge to intervene, and

again Jonathan was committed to a state school for delinquents in another city. On his first day there, he was described as "troublesome, demanding, no patience, upset all supervisors . . . a regular nuisance." By now, Jonathan's sexuality became manifest in adolescent behavior. He often made homosexual advances to both staff and other students, immediately alienating them and provoking fights. He dug at himself until he bled and frequently required nursing attention. While no one liked Jonathan, and staff reported that all they could do was "provide custodial care," they did record that he was improving slowly and learning to earn privileges. Jonathan was placed in security whenever he got into fights or became physically abusive of staff. After six months, Jonathan was released and enrolled in the junior high near his home.

Within four months, Mr. and Mrs. Y. admitted Jonathan to Crockett Academy, a newly opened Re-ED adolescent program in the state mental health system. It was clear that they did not want him at home. Jonathan remained in this program for two years, until he was eighteen and not making any clear progress. His academic and social progress had been erratic; reports indicated that he "does well when he chooses, but is often disruptive." The following is a list of the interventions tried: (1) positive reinforcement and ignoring inappropriate behavior, (2) point and level systems involving positive and negative reinforcement, (3) numerous individually designed programs, (4) individual programs designed specifically for Jonathan to achieve success with minimal effort, (5) routing questions through one individual, (6) day-to-day contingencies for privileges such as refreshments and off-grounds activities. The Crockett Academy staff felt that these methods, along with family therapy and appropriate medication, had met with success, but then Jonathan stopped trying. His peer relations were at low ebb, and his verbal and physical abuse of staff had increased when he was discharged from Crockett.

Shortly thereafter, Jonathan reported that he was at home and happy but in need of daytime structure. The liaison teacher-counselor from Crockett assisted him in applying to a vocational rehabilitation program, but he was not successful in following through with training. Several months later, he was admitted to the Middle Tennessee Mental Health Institute (because of his disruptive behavior and his mother's poor health, his father had refused to have him at home). He was discharged a year later with his "behavior well under control" and readmitted within one month.

Since that time four years ago, Jonathan has made definite progress and, with the assistance of his social worker, has left the institute three times to live in a boarding house or with friends; each time, he has experienced difficulties and returned. Jonathan now assumes more responsibility for himself, has learned to keep out of fights, and acts appropriately toward other patients and staff. He has participated in the Work Adjustment Program and acquired maintenance skills which build on his natural tendencies for neatness and order. He is still viewed as weak in self-control, discipline, and impulsiveness. Mr. Y. continues to visit Jonathan regularly, and he spends occasional weekends at home when his mother is feeling better. Jonathan is living in the predischarge unit of the institute, cooperating with efforts to try vocational rehabilitation again, and meeting regularly with his counselor to facilitate a future transition.

7

Working with Children in Settings

The Applied Ecology of Child Development

The way one defines a problem will determine in substantial measure the strategies that can be used to solve it. In Project Re-ED, we have moved away from the traditional definition of emotional disturbance, which emphasizes intrapsychic conflict as the source of the child's difficulty, to a definition that stresses difficulties arising from interactions of the child with significant people in his world. We refer to this view as an ecological perspective. We believe we were among the first to use ecological principles in an effort to understand emotional disturbance in childhood and adolescence and to improve procedures for working with children and youth and with the people who are the normal sources of affection, discipline, inspiration, and instruction.

From an ecological perspective, emotional disturbance is not something in the person. Instead, a child or an adolescent is considered emotionally disturbed when some consequential member of the ecosystem can no longer tolerate the discord in the system. A parent, a teacher, a juvenile judge declares publicly: "I cannot put up with this child any longer. Something must be done!" They mean, of course, that something must be done about or to the child; we, in contrast, define the task as helping the significant members of the ecosystem, including the child or adolescent, take the steps necessary to enable the system to work reasonably well—that is, within tolerable levels of discord.

How did we arrive at this unconventional view? We asked William C. Rhodes, who led us in developing it, to reconstruct the debates that occurred in the early days of Project Re-ED. He writes as follows:

The way the thinking got started was through a great deal of talk among the early conceptualizers regarding an alternative to the then current psychodynamic paradigm as employed in emotional disturbance, delinquency, and so forth.

As I recall it from this distance, we were very concerned with the environmental relativity of the condition called emotional disturbance. We felt that environmental contributions had been totally ignored in traditional psychiatric treatment of children. We felt that "disturbance" was a relative term, that different settings saw different kinds of behavior as "disturbed" depending on the cultural values and expectations of that setting, as well as the particular predilections of the child's own parents and teachers.

Also, we were aware of the problem of institutionalization and its contribution to the states and behaviors observed in child hospital units. We felt that, to avoid the negative influence of institutions, treatment had to be in a setting as nearly like the child's natural habitat as possible. Therefore, residential treatment had to be radically modified to overcome the pathology created by the residential setting itself.

We particularly felt that the then current practice of removing the child from school, "curing" him or her in isolation, and then returning the child to a peer group which had been moving on in development and learning, was nonsense. It was this idea, incidentally, which caused our first (NIMH) review committee to suggest a liaison person who would keep the child abreast of his or her own school and peer group.

Since there was then no current term for this environmental inclusion, we borrowed "ecology." We did not really know much about what Roger Barker was doing with respect to that term until much later; when we did begin to look at Barker, it seemed to be related, but quite different conceptually. It was the same genus but not the same species.

As part of "ecological treatment," we felt we had to go into the child's own environment and alter it in just noticeable ways, so that, matched with the just noticeable changes in his or her behavior which we focused on in the child's brief stay in residence, we could bring about greater tolerance in the environment which was being disturbed by particular aspects of the child's behavior and performance. This, also, we saw as the role of the liaison teacher-counselor.

This, as nearly as I can reconstruct it, was the way we moved into ecological conceptions [Rhodes, Personal Communication, April 19, 1979].

Ecological Constructs in Emotional Disturbance

Effects of Settings on Behavior. To say that a child is emotionally disturbed is to employ both a euphemism and a catchall phrase with few operational referents. Some children called emotionally disturbed are remarkably serene when removed from a noxious environment and placed in a benign one. Other children not called emotionally disturbed live turbulent lives in environments that accept their turbulence as natural; they come to no one's attention. In the age group from six to twelve, there are four times as many boys called disturbed as there are girls, a ratio not plausibly explained by assuming a greater affective vulnerability among boys. A more probable explanation is that boys are more likely than girls to behave in ways that upset people and invite rejection; schools and communities are not organized to meet the developmental needs of boys. In the adolescent years, the ratio of boys to girls called disturbed begins to balance, but the social definition of the problem is evident in disparities between sexes as to what kinds of behaviors are regarded as evidence of emotional disturbance. For adolescent boys, the most frequent complaint is antisocial behavior; for adolescent girls, it is sexual promiscuity.

Surveys of school-age children (Bower, 1960) show that a substantial proportion of them have conventional characteristics of "emotional disturbance," yet only a relatively small number are referred for mental health or special education services. An ecological view would suggest that a child's behavior, however disturbed by conventional criteria, is only one side of the coin. The other side of that coin is the evaluation of his behavior by other members of his ecological system within that particular context. The identification of a child as disturbed tells us only that his behavior, at that time, is not meeting the expectations held for him by those who are responsible for his socialization. Fighting, truancy, and stealing, for example, may be evaluated quite differently by a middle-class mother in the suburbs and by a lower-class mother in the inner city. For one, it signals "emotional disturbance"; for the other, "That's the way kids are."

Effects of Time. We actually know little about the long-term course or natural history of the condition called emotional disturbance in children and adolescents. We are not at all sure that the child we call disturbed at age seven will still be so identified at age ten, even with no treatment, or that the child who is a disturbed child in school will be a disturbed child at camp a month later. Some kinds of behavior that invite the label of emotional disturbance—notably, withdrawn behavior—may be relatively transient, while antisocial behavior may be more persistent (Robins, 1966). For a class of children moving through the grades of elementary school, successive teachers will identify as emotionally disturbed approximately the same percentage of children; however, the particular children so identified change from year to year.

Follow-up studies of children who have been identified as emotionally disturbed lend support to this relativistic view of children's problems. A high proportion of children who have been on clinic waiting lists without receiving any treatment and public school students identified by classroom screening methods are, on later follow-up, not judged to have serious problems of personal adjustment. If emotional disturbance were a relatively stable characteristic of a child, it seems unlikely that "spontaneous remission" would occur in two thirds to three fourths of the cases so studied. What seems more likely is that a child and the other members of his ecological system are often able to make mutual accommodations, including some combination of increased competence in the child, improved parent skills, modified expectations of the child's performance, and greater opportunity for mutually rewarding transactions among the participants. Whatever a child's

behavior, it is our view that the judgments made about that behavior by the natural evaluators in his life are highly important
and demand attention in planning ecological strategies.

Effects of Treatments. Treatment methods may perpetu-
ate some kinds of disturbance more than others. Antisocial behavior patterns may persist not because they are intrinsically more
refractory to treatment than withdrawal patterns, for instance, but
because they evoke punishment, which may, in turn, provoke
more antisocial behavior. To put a retarded child into a typical institution for the retarded may guarantee that he will remain dull
or grow duller. Such reflections as these make it seem unwise to
regard emotional disturbance as being "in" a child, or as something a child "has." Analogies with conditions like measles or a
common cold may deflect us from a productive description and
analysis of the situation and suggest by analogy inappropriate
helping strategies. There is a tremendous difference in the implications of "getting over a condition" and of learning to live in a real
world of real people here and now and for the future.

A child gets identified as emotionally disturbed when normal support systems falter, when the ecosystem of which he is the
defining member reaches a low point in functional effectiveness.
Ecosystems tend to be self-repairing. Often wisdom lies simply in
not doing something that may impede the restoration of the ecosystem, such as institutionalizing the child or prescribing tranquilizing drugs. Both of these acts create abnormal situations; they cut
off or distort feedback of information needed to modify or re-
direct behavior, and thereby impair an essential component of the
regulatory process in all living systems. From an ecological perspective, the widespread practice of sending disturbed children out
of a state for treatment elsewhere makes no sense at all. This convenient but expensive practice makes it impossible to build a sustaining ecosystem for the child and thus impedes a return to normal patterns of development.

Effects of Psychotropic Medication. Generally speaking, the
use of tranquilizers, energizers, and other psychotropic medication
does not harmonize well with the assumptions and objectives of
reeducation. Administration of a drug may indeed restore an ecosystem to a measure of tranquility, but only at the expense of denying the system, and the young person, an opportunity to deal in

forthright fashion with the discord-producing behavior. All living systems require accurate, cybernetic feedback in order to make internal adjustments necessary for the healthy operation of the system. Without accurate information about its internal state, the ecosystem cannot operate effectively. One can induce the illusion of smooth operation by administering psychotropic drugs to the child, but sooner or later the behavior masked by the drug must be dealt with.

The general policy of Re-ED programs is to get children off psychotropic medication as rapidly as possible and to substitute new transactional strategies designed to restore the system to effective functioning on a realistic basis, undisguised by drugs. Often discord is generated by other actors in the ecosystem, and not by the child alone, so that putting the child on medication makes little sense at all. It would make equal sense to administer drugs to the mother or father, a classroom teacher, a juvenile court judge, or anyone else of consequence who happened to be dissatisfied with the way a child is behaving—even a physician. Since it is easier to hold the child at fault than to recognize the participatory contribution of adults in transaction with the child, it is more acceptable, if not more sensible, to prescribe drugs for the child.

As we have worked with increasing numbers of adolescents for whom the diagnosis of psychosis is at least temporarily appropriate, we have come to recognize the benefits that various psychotropic drugs can introduce into the ecosystem. Sometimes a student's behavior is so bizarre, so distressing, and so self-defeating that a temporary distortion in the ecosystem is well worth the disadvantages that ensue. Drugs can modulate the behavior of the child so that the ecosystem of which he is the defining member can mobilize its resources to give the child the kind of understanding, support, encouragement, and renewed competence that are required for him not to continue his radical, or psychotic, solution to living. But the general principle holds: children and adolescents are removed from medication as rapidly as is feasible. We are not willing to settle for a tranquilized life as the outcome of the reeducation effort.

It seems to us deplorable that these drugs are widely dispensed to children and adolescents without any sustained effort to understand either the antecedents or the consequences of drugs in the ecosystem of the individual. No one knows the long-term effects of tranquilizers on the ability of a child to learn, on the benefits to be derived from dealing with anxiety, on the ability of the young person to form enduring and sustaining relationships, and on the proclivity of the child to turn outward for solutions to inward problems through other drugs, such as alcohol and other privately prescribed substances.

In this discussion, we are not referring to drugs used to control seizures, diabetes, or other conditions springing largely from neurological or metabolic difficulties. We are even prepared to believe that the bizarre and antisocial behavior of some children and youth springs from comparable organic impairments or insufficiencies. But we are not willing to join in a rush to that judgment. The potential consequences for the young person are entirely too grave to make this easy and popular solution attractive. We prefer the more arduous and the more parsimonious solution even if it increases enormously the demands made on the child, his parents and siblings, his teachers, his physician or social worker, and his teacher-counselors. To reduce ecosystem discord by blunting a child's cognitive and affective processes should be a last resort, a step taken only after an honest investment by all concerned to make the ecosystem work without subjecting the child to hazards the scope of which are as yet unknown.

Role of Child in Ecosystem. We recognize that some children place a heavier burden on ecosystems than do other children. An autistic child, a hyperactive child, an obese child, a retarded child, a constantly misbehaving child—all place severe stresses on the systems of which they are a part. So, too, does an adolescent who steals automobiles, abuses drugs, threatens suicide, hallucinates, lies compulsively, bullies children, engages in destructive sexual activity, or rejects all authority. We do not subscribe to the simplistic theory that society defines deviance for purposes of social control and then blames its victim for his outcast status. We emphasize that the child or adolescent is the central participant in the transactions that make up the ecosystem; modification in his behavior may be imperative for the system to work well over time. We simply think it a dead end to single out the child or adolescent as the only person expected to change.

Implications for Intervention. We define a disturbed child or adolescent as a person whose behavior is such that he has been rejected by one or more of the normal socializing agencies of our society: by the family, the school, or the community. Or, to be more precise, he has been rejected by a specific family and a specific class and school and community at a particular time in their common history with the child. The identification of a child or an adolescent as disturbed is regarded as a signal of the breakdown of a small social system, as a symptom of ecological imbalance that has reached a crisis stage.

The method of intervention appropriate to this definition of the problem requires that we work with the ecological system of which the child or adolescent is an integral part—with the young person, yes, but also with his family, school, church, neighborhood, work place, and community. In working with this system, we will pay special attention to the specific circumstances that caused its breakdown, and we will take such practical steps as may be indicated to make it function reasonably well.

The goal implied by this formulation is not to cure the child but to make the system work, to reestablish ecological balance, to get each component of the system (child, family, school, neighborhood, work place, community) either to modify expectations or to meet the requirements of the other components. The Re-ED school becomes a part of the ecological system of a troubled and troubling young person for as brief a period of time as possible, withdrawing when the probability that the system will function appears to exceed the probability that it will not.

Ecosystems of Children and Adolescents

Ecology means the study of the complex interaction of energies in natural systems. It seemed an apt term to express our concerns for children in settings and for mobilizing the natural resources of a system in the service of a child or an adolescent who is its central member. We began to draw ecological diagrams, to gain skill in assessing the sources of discord in ecosystems, to learn to help significant members of the system (and the young person especially) behave in ways to make the ecosystem work effectively. A diagram best conveys the idea of an ecological system (see Figures 2, 3, and 4). At the center of the diagram is a circle to rep-

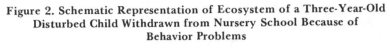

Figure 2. Schematic Representation of Ecosystem of a Three-Year-Old
Disturbed Child Withdrawn from Nursery School Because of
Behavior Problems

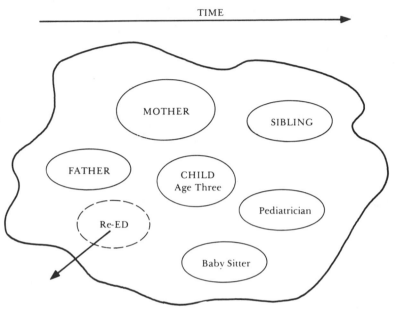

resent the child or adolescent who is the defining member of the
ecosystem. The other circles represent people or agencies that are
or might be functionally important in the life of the child. They,
along with the child, are the sources of the changes required to
make the ecosystem work reasonably well in the interest of the
child's healthy development. Re-ED enters the scheme for a period
of time (usually four to eight months) sufficient to enable the ecosystem to function reasonably well; that is, to function above the
threshold of expectancies on the part of the principal members of
the system, including the child.

From the outset, we have been sensitive to the importance
of time in the life of a child. So we put a bold arrow in graphic
representations of ecosystems to emphasize the passage of time.
Development is the central feature of childhood and adolescence,
distinguishing these ages from all others later on. And as the child
grows in stature, strength, intelligence, and character, people in his

Figure 3. Schematic Representation of Ecocostem of an Emotionally
Disturbed Elementary School Child

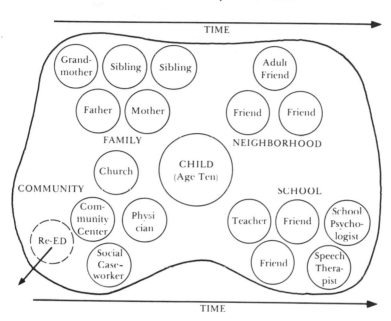

or her world change as well. The father is injured in an accident at work, a new baby arrives, the mother goes to work, school teachers change, parents get divorced, someone dies, or staff changes occur in the Re-ED school.

The ecosystem of the preschool child (Figure 2) is most notable for its simplicity. For the first two or three years, the mother looms large in traditional families, but fathers are becoming increasingly important. In some families, of course, there is only one parent. Then there may be other family members who play important roles in the transactions that help define the behavior of the child: siblings, a grandparent, possibly a neighbor. In the years from three to six, the ecosystem of the child who is developing normally becomes somewhat more complex; staff and children in a daycare center or a kindergarten may contribute to the variance in ecosystem events. But when a child is not develop-

Figure 4. Schematic Representation of Ecosystem of a Male Adolescent
at Age Eighteen

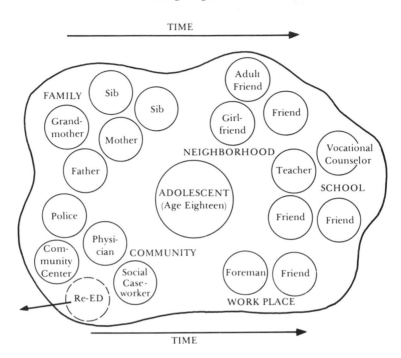

ing normally, the ecosystem may again become quite constricted. Temper tantrums, soiling, a prolonged illness may result in withdrawal of the child from preschool experiences, thus "shrinking" the ecosystem.

Going to school greatly broadens horizons and engages the child in important relationships with a number of new people: teachers especially, other children, parents in the neighborhood, playground directors, pediatricians, camp counselors, and so on (Figure 3). Again, if a child has a health or developmental problem, professional people may move into roles of central importance: a speech therapist, an orthopedic surgeon, a remedial reading specialist. Furthermore, the child herself will be changing rapidly in size, strength, physical competence, and intellectual abilities. For children of direct concern to us, Re-ED may become for a time a vital part of the ecosystem while efforts are being made to reduce discord in the system and mobilize resources necessary to ensure its effective functioning in the future.

As the child moves into adolescence, the fundamental structure of the ecosystem changes (Figure 4). Consider some of the special challenges presented by adolescents: they have lived longer and had time to overlearn personal styles of adaptive—or maladaptive—behavior; they have grown in intelligence, so that the world is more ambiguous than it was; language has become both an enmeshing and a potentially liberating instrument for making sense of experience; the self-concept is increasingly elaborated but still fragile, sometimes mercurial; identity is the elusive issue; to achieve independence and build new interdependencies can be a source of victory and defeat; the body has become exquisitely pleasurable and at the same time a source of confusion and guilt; automobiles, alcohol, and drugs complicate everything; the ecosystem alters radically, with new actors taking crucial roles—a boyfriend or girlfriend, a foreman, a valued teacher; and the future often seems completely compressed into right now. Advanced education, a job, military service, the responsibilities of adult status, and the prospect of having a family begin to emerge as problem or challenge and alter the Gestalt of life.

The most profound change in the ecosystem of the adolescent is brought about by changes that have occurred in the adolescent himself:

Piaget posits a qualitative shift in the nature of intelligence in the adolescent years, from the concrete operational stage of childhood to the formal operational stage of adolescence. The adolescent becomes capable of formal thought; that is, the ability to treat events abstractly, to subordinate the real to the possible, to use metaphor in construing the world, to engage in hypothetico-deductive thought, to manipulate combinatorial systems, to use internalized speech, to think about thinking, to use nameable strategies for problem solving, and to monitor his own thought. The changes that begin to occur around eleven to twelve years of age "constitute a major revolution in the individual's way of thinking about the world, and these changes continue to occur throughout the period of adolescence" (Day, 1979, p. 1). Adolescent thought appears to be more like adult thought than like the thought of the child, thus making adolescence a period of crucial importance for the nurturance of general cognitive competence. Not all adolescents achieve the ability to distance themselves from a problem and address it with formal problem-solving strategies; indeed, some people never achieve an adequate level of formal operational ability [Hobbs, 1981, pp. 16-17].

With young children, one or both parents or a parent substitute have to be helped to become effective managers of the ecosystem; with older adolescents, the person himself must be helped to become the system manager.

Misconceptions Regarding Ecological Concepts

Ecology has now become a popular concept in working with emotionally disturbed children and youth, yet it seems to us that many who use it do not understand its meaning and thus lose the advantage of its full theoretical force. These days, one hears or reads frequently of "the child and his ecology" or some similar construction. Obviously, what is meant by the phrase is "the child and his environment," which is not exactly a novel idea. What is powerful in the concept of ecology is the idea that the child or adolescent cannot be juxtaposed with the environment, that she is an inextricable part of an ecological system. The only way we know how to talk about it precisely requires a circumlocution: our concern is with the ecological system of which, for our purposes, the child or adolescent is the defining member.

The child, family, school, agency, neighborhood, work place, and community, with their dynamic interrelationships, make up a nonfractionable whole. We work with any and all aspects of the system—with child or adolescent, mother, father, teacher, foreman, juvenile judge—and we guide our work with one component of the system by specifications drawn from the system as a whole. We judge the effectiveness of our work by the increased functional adequacy of the total system. A Re-ED school becomes a part of the ecosystem for the explicit purpose of increasing the adequacy of the system with respect to the development of a particular child or adolescent. This is an important point. We are not concerned with the general adequacy of a family, or with the goodness of a school for all the children it serves, or with the community in general, but with goodness of fit of family, school, and community with the needs of a particular child. And we are quite as much concerned with the ability of the child or adolescent to meet the requirements of her family, her school, her neighborhood, her work place, her community. We are not concerned with her adequacy to meet the demands of all possible roles—of all tasks that a school might produce, of all the possible expectations of a family, or of the competences for all job settings—but simply with unmet expectations that keep a particular system from working reasonably well.

To cast the problem of emotional disturbance in ecological terms is to invite a further misconception: that the child or adolescent is relieved of responsibility for her own behavior, that other people, past and present, are responsible for an unsatisfactory state of affairs. This formulation comes from thinking of the person as being shaped by the environment, thus continuing the person-environment dichotomy, which we regard as an error. The child is a contributing and receiving member of a system made up of contributors and receivers, and the totality of their significant transactions is what is meant by a system. The child is the defining member of the ecosystem that concerns us; and we, in turn, become a contributing and receiving member of the system for as long as the child is affiliated with the Re-ED program. Just as we expect to do our part to make the system work reasonably well, so do we expect the student to do her part. We try in the daily program at Re-ED to help the child or adolescent accept responsibility for what happens in her life and to acquire skills needed to make things happen better.

Ecological Assessment and Enablement Planning

From the earliest days to the present in Project Re-ED, staff members have had to struggle with issues involved in the diagnosis, classification, and labeling of children. It became apparent quite early in the project that traditional psychiatric diagnoses were of little use in planning the kinds of programs we had in mind for children. In fact, the problems generated by traditional methods of classifying children were dramatically revealed when we discovered that North Carolina children appeared to be sicker than Tennessee children! The children referred to the Re-ED school in

North Carolina had diagnoses like "incipient schizophrenia," "childhood autism," "brain damage," and "psychopathic personality," while the children referred to the Tennessee school were *all* classified as having an "adjustment problem of childhood." The difference derived, of course, from different policies in the two states regarding the labeling of children. While we preferred the Tennessee policy to that of North Carolina, both were equally useless, equally irrelevant to the task of deciding exactly what should be done to help the child. As indicated earlier, we simply ignored the ritualistic and nonfunctional tradition of diagnosis and classification of children before treatment and sought a way of describing in simple terms (1) the problems faced by the child and the people important in her life and (2) the specific steps that could be taken to solve these problems or render them less severe. What started as an informal, commonsense way of getting on with the helping of children and families has gradually developed into a formal system for classifying children and planning programs to help them. We now call the system an ecologically oriented, service-based system for the classification of children, the central feature of which is the ecological assessment and enablement plan.

Actually, ecological assessment and enablement planning grew out of two projects, Project Re-ED and the Project on the Classification of Exceptional Children (Hobbs, 1975a, 1975b). The latter project was undertaken in 1972 at the request of Elliot L. Richardson, then secretary of the Department of Health, Education, and Welfare (HEW). In announcing the project in an HEW internal memorandum, Richardson called attention to a serious national problem: "The inappropriate labeling of children as *delinquent, retarded, hyperkinetic, mentally ill, emotionally disturbed,* and other classifications has serious consequences for the child. Although experts in the various disciplines concerned with exceptional children have undertaken useful studies on appropriate diagnostic procedures and practices, there is lacking sufficient dissemination of their findings to professionals and the public and nationwide standardization and enforcement of appropriate diagnostic procedures."

The study resulted in a summary volume, *The Futures of Children,* that reports the outcomes of the inquiry and summarizes policy recommendations, and two volumes, *Issues in the Classifica-*

tion of Children, that consist of technical papers related to the problem. According to *Futures* (p. ix), "Secretary Richardson called for a systematic review of the classification and labeling of children, an assessment of the consequences that ensue from current policies and procedures, and recommendations for improving practices." In the course of the Project on the Classification of Exceptional Children, it became clear that the procedures for describing children's problems and for planning remedial programs could provide the basis for a national system for improving classification procedures, called for by the secretary.

Experts in classification advise that a first and crucial step in the development of a classification system is to define clearly what purposes are to be served, to specify what the classification system is supposed to do. The current system for classifying children exemplifies well the failure to observe this fundamental principle. Existing classification schemes are supposed to provide a basis for service delivery, for etiological and epidemiological studies, for research in general, for the organization of public and private agencies, for planning and accounting, and for ease in communication among professional people. It is not surprising that, in attempting to do all these things, they do none of them well. The ecologically oriented, service-based classification system we are proposing is designed primarily for the purpose of improving the delivery of services to handicapped children and their families.

The system is ecologically oriented in order to recognize that the functioning effectiveness of a handicapped child (as is, in fact, true of all individuals, handicapped or not) may be substantially affected by environmental influences, logistical arrangements, and individual-environment transactions. Traditional classification systems make no provision for this important fact. The system here proposed embraces environmental determinants of effective functioning, as well as environmental responses evoked by the behavior of the individual. Environmental determinants might range from the removal of access barriers and the provision of prosthetic devices to having a hot meal provided or putting the child with a teacher or a pediatrician who understands the coping problems of handicapped children. The unit of classification, therefore, is not the individual child but the individual child-in-setting. The system is referred to as ecological to take into account the situational, developmental, and transactional character of the demands on a service delivery system.

The system is service-based in order to maximize its utility in planning, delivering, and accounting for services to handicapped children. Individual children are classified, to be sure, but not on the basis of clinical nosologies; they are classified on the basis of services required to achieve specified goals at a particular period in the life of the individual. The classical categories of handicapping conditions are not employed and can be allowed, at least for the purposes of service delivery, to wither away.

The system makes appropriate use of traditional assessment procedures but is not limited to them. In order to work out a service plan for a particular child or adolescent, it may be necessary to have the results of an intelligence test, an electroencephalogram, a test of educational achievement, an evaluation of motor functioning, and so on. However, the results of all tests are used not to arrive at a diagnosis but to contribute to an ecological assessment and, subsequently, to a specific service delivery plan.

The ecologically oriented, service-based plan for the classification of children consists of two inseparable components: the ecological assessment and the enablement plan, both of which are expected to change with time. The plan thus avoids two severe limitations on current classification schemes: (1) the fixed diagnosis, with diagnosis being an end in itself; and (2) the separation of diagnosis and treatment, often to the neglect of treatment.

While the classical categories of handicapping conditions would not be used in the proposed system, it is not proposed that the classification of children and adolescents be abandoned, an impractical recommendation heard occasionally these days. The proposal here advanced is, in fact, a classification scheme. It simply classifies many variables for the purposes of improving service delivery.

To classify a child in accordance with the plan here proposed, the first step is to develop an "ecological assessment and enablement plan." This is a systematic audit of assets and deficits in the child's ecosystem, again with respect to requirements for service. The assessment involves (1) identifying sources of discord in the ecosystem, as well as sources of strength that can be used to improve the goodness of fit between the individual and important people and places in his life, and (2) specifying what services are required to assure that the child will be able to make reasonable progress toward achievable developmental goals. The ecosystem of which the child is the defining member should be brought sufficiently into balance to function without undue stress, and to nurture the child's development in an adequate fashion. The goal is not to make the child perfect but to make the ecosystem work reasonably well. The goal might be achieved by effecting changes in the child but also by effecting changes in settings in which he is expected to grow and learn, especially in the expectations and conduct of people (such as mother, father, teachers, siblings, and friends) who are important in the child's life.

An ecologically oriented, service-based classification system requires some arrangement to determine the service requirements of the child, in a setting, at a particular period of time. This is done by means of an assessment conference. In a hypothetical optimum situation, there would be a conference participated in by all the people who have something of substance to contribute to the shaping of a service plan for the child: usually the parents or guardian, the child when old enough, a psychologist, a teacher, a special therapist perhaps, a physician, a social caseworker, a supervisor at the prospective place for after-school care, a probation officer, and so on. Pragmatically, such a comprehensive conference might seldom occur, but information from and about crucial people must be available at a planning session. The purpose of the conference is to arrive at a plan for providing services to the child in a particular setting at a particular time, and to define responsibilities for accomplishing the plan. The record of the conference will specify what must be done in order to achieve agreed-upon objectives. Below is an ecological assessment and enablement plan for a very troubled and troubling boy.

Ecological Assessment and Enablement Plan for a Ten-Year-Old Boy

Client: Robert Washington
Liaison: Margaret Smith, Cumberland House Elementary School
Date: May 15, 1978

Robert Washington, called "Bobby," is a ten-year-old boy with a long history of involvement with social agencies and hospitals. Large for his age and powerfully built, Bobby is highly aggressive and combative, and it is largely his assaults on other people, children and adults alike, that keep him in constant trouble. He is described in several public school records as "unmanageable." At the time of referral, he had been out of school for a full year.

Bobby has spent six months during the previous year at the state institution for the mentally retarded. Although his test scores are quite low, he showed evidence of intelligence that made the placement appear inappropriate. He was therefore transferred to the psychiatric ward of a medical school, where he stayed for approximately two months. During this period, he was kept under heavy sedation to control his often violent behavior. He had been discharged and was living at home with his mother and several siblings when referred to Cumberland House. He was continuing on the medication under supervision of a nurse-practitioner with an office in the housing project where the Washington family lived.

Bobby presented a puzzling psychometric picture. He had been evaluated a number of times in various centers. Intelligence tests yielded IQ scores in the 50s or lower, but the response pattern was erratic, with Bobby showing some signs of considerably higher intelligence. Bobby could not read or cipher. Indeed, he could not consistently identify digits or letters of the alphabet. Efforts to teach him to read had frequently been occasions for violent outbursts. Although mental retardation was a functionally accurate diagnosis, there was much evidence, especially in social negotiations, of a higher level of intelligence. For example, Bobby could readily learn unschoolish tasks, such as sculling a canoe or lashing a table in the woods. He remembered people's names remarkably well, and was ordinarily friendly and interested in other people. It was difficult not to like him in spite of violent attacks which were hard to control and not easy to accept.

Bobby lived with his mother and three siblings plus the infant child of his eighteen-year-old, unmarried sister. His mother is of borderline intelligence and can neither read nor write. But she does provide a stable home for the children. She has a steady relationship with a man, not Bobby's father, who is ordinarily kind to the children, except when drinking, which is not infrequent. Bobby has an uncle (the brother of his father) who lives in the same housing project and who is a competent and dependable person and the major potential source of adult strength in Bobby's ecosystem.

Bobby's teeth are in bad condition, and, although he is of robust constitution, he is not properly nourished. His diet consists mainly of carbohydrates. Soft drinks and packaged pies are a staple in his diet.

At the conference to work out an ecological assessment and enablement plan, the nurse-practitioner suggested that Bobby's episodic violence might be related to epilepsy and asked if this possibility had been considered. A review of available records, including those from the psychiatric hospital, showed no record of an evaluation for epilepsy. At the time the ecological assessment was made, Bobby was on 300 mg of Thorazine a day.

If the Cumberland House staff were to succeed with Bobby, neighborhood and community resources would have to be mobilized to help him on weekends and in transition back to regular school. Among assets in the system are Bobby's mother (who, though limited, is always present and always accepting of him), his uncle (perhaps the pivotal person), the nurse-practitioner in the housing project, several staff people at a community center about six blocks away, and, eventually, the special education staff of the elementary school in the neighborhood. The community center agreed to be the pivotal cooperating agency with the Cumberland House staff.

Margaret Smith, liaison teacher-counselor at Cumberland House, was assigned the liaison role. She personally visited all the people mentioned above plus some others and held a planning conference to work out an enablement plan. Present for the conference were the uncle, the nurse-practitioner, and a representative of the community center, plus involved members of Cumberland House.

Bobby could have been diagnosed as mentally retarded or emotionally disturbed. His confinement to a psychiatric ward suggests that the label "mentally ill" would find ready acceptance. The actual case records carry these terms: "character disorder, antisocial type, violent." But such information says nothing about the social context in which unacceptable behaviors occurred and is actually of little use in planning a program for Bobby. The assignment of Bobby to a diagnostic category is not only a useless step but it also diverts attention from the crucial task, which is to work out a detailed plan of things to be done and objectives to be achieved.

The ecological assessment and enablement plan conference identified the following specific steps to be taken in an effort to restore Bobby's ecosystem to an acceptable level of functioning. With respect to each step identified, the plan also specified (1) the person responsible for seeing that the task is done, (2) the person who would do the work, (3) the date by which the task should be accomplished, (4) the estimated cost of the service, (5) the source of funds to pay for the service, (6) the criteria to be used to establish a successful outcome, and (7) an identification of required follow-ups (see Table 1).

     '   In the conference, the following agreements were reached and a simple record made:

     Bobby needs:

1. Admission to Cumberland House and assignment to the Bobcat group, following a preliminary orientation visit by Bobby, his mother, and his uncle.
2. Dental work to repair a number of caries.
3. An adequate nutrition program, to be provided by Cumberland House during the week, by the community center on weekends, and by efforts to get Bobby himself to be responsible for choosing good foods.
4. A complete assessment for the possibility of epilepsy.
5. A regime for removing Bobby from tranquilizing drugs, to be supervised by the consulting pediatrician and the nurse-practitioner.
6. An arrangement with the community center and possibly with a local branch of the YMCA for Bobby to have an activity program on weekends.
7. An agreement with the uncle to see Bobby at least three times every weekend, at least for a few minutes each time.
8. A program at Cumberland House that would initially focus primarily on socialization with a gradual introduction of academic tasks. Reading instruction would be avoided at first, but a major goal of the Cumberland House effort would be to teach Bobby to read, write, and do arithmetic.
9. Bobby's main responsibility would be to learn to control his temper, and all initial plans at Cumberland House would be arranged to support him in this effort.

At the case conference, it was agreed that a second conference would be held at the end of sixty days and that necessary interim adjustments in the program could be made by Cumberland House staff.

For each of the steps identified, a detailed plan of action was worked out. For example, with respect to the agreement that Bobby should have a thorough assessment for possible epilepsy, the record looked something like this:

Table 1. Ecological Assessment and Enablement Plan

Child: Robert Washington
Date of Birth: August 18, 1967
Liaison: Margaret Smith

Date of Assessment: May 15, 1978
Date for Review: June 15, 1978

Service Required	Who's Responsible?	By Whom?	By What Date?	At What Cost?	Source of Funds?	Criterion?	Follow-up?
1. Admission to Cumberland House	Margaret Smith	Mother	June 1	$1,500 month	DMH	Return to special education classroom	None
2. Dental work	Nurse-Practitioner	Meharry Dental Clinic	July 15 (plan)	$125?	Medicaid	Work done satisfactorily	None
3. Nutrition program	Pediatrician and VU Nutritionist	C-H, Mother, Comm. Ctr.	June 15 (plan)	Routine	DMH	Off junk foods	Monthly
4. Assessment for epilepsy	Nurse-Practitioner	VU Neurological Clinic	July 15, 1978	$350	Medicaid	Freedom from seizures	If epileptic, provide medication and periodic checks
5. Removal from medication	Smith and Nurse-Practitioner	Pediatrician	June 15 (plan)	Routine	DMH	Off medication	Monthly by Margaret Smith
6. Activity program on weekends	Uncle	Howard Community Center	June 15 (plan)	Routine	Metro Govt.	Regular program	Monthly by Margaret Smith
7. Uncle to see Bobby	Smith and Uncle	Uncle	Immediately	$3/week	DMH	Regular reported contacts	Monthly by Smith
8. Program at Cumberland House	T-C team	T-C team	June 1	Routine	DMH	Progress prescribed by plan	T-C team
9. Control of temper	Bobby and T-C team	Bobby	August 1	Routine	DMH	Progress as plotted by T-C team	T-C team

Key to abbreviations: C-H = Cumberland House, VU = Vanderbilt University, T-C = teacher-counselor, DMH = Department of Mental Health.

Service required: *Assessment for Possible Epilepsy*

1. *Person responsible.* Some one person must assume responsibility for seeing that Bobby gets a thorough assessment for possible epilepsy. In some instances, it might be the child's parent or guardian, sometimes even the child himself. In Bobby's case, it was decided that the nurse-practitioner would be responsible for getting the examination accomplished and reporting back to the group. The nurse-practitioner signs to indicate acceptance of the responsibility.

2. *Service provider.* Arrangements are made by telephone for the assessment to be made by the Neurological Clinic of the University Hospital. The contact person at the clinic is Dr. Ronald Bates. His telephone number is 477-3257.

3. *Target date.* The assessment should be completed within a period of two months, giving a target date of July 15, 1978, by which time it is expected that the needed information will be available.

4. *Cost of service.* Inquiry of the clinic indicated that the service would probably cost $350 but that additional costs might be incurred if repeated assessments are required.

5. *Source of payment.* Here it is specified where the money is coming from. Sometimes it might be from the child's parents, but Bobby's mother is unable to pay. Arrangements are made with the State Department of Health to pay for the service out of funds of the Crippled Children's Program, with reimbursement from Medicaid.

6. *Criterion check.* Here is specified what standard is to be met by the service provided. All of the above (items 1-5) are "inputs" or "processes"; here, in item 6, is registered the expected output or product. An ultimate goal, for example, might be to have Bobby reading at a grade level one year below his expected level. The objective of the assessment for epilepsy is to determine whether or not he has epilepsy. If he does have seizures, the objective would be to get the seizures under control by appropriate medication.

7. *Follow-up.* At the time of the initial planning, it may be desirable to arrange for future services when these can be anticipated. For example, if the assessment showed that Bobby needs anticonvulsant drugs, plans would need to be made to have periodic assessment of the effects of the drugs on his blood and on his behavior. It may be anticipated, in addition, that Bobby might be helped sufficiently to return to the special education program in the neighborhood elementary school. If so, contact with the school would be made at the outset, with arrangements made for Bobby to visit the school

from time to time, to identify himself with it, and to get acquainted with some staff and children.

8. *Conversion to the classical categories.* If for any reason there is a need to report on services rendered in terms of specific handicapping conditions, as is required by Public Law 94-142, Education for All Handicapped Children, it is possible by a conversion formula (based on service requirements) to arrive at a conventional classification category, without having to use resources for a conventional diagnosis. Thus, a child receiving a particular pattern of services may be designated, if necessary, as mentally retarded, orthopedically handicapped, visually impaired, emotionally disturbed, or some other appropriate category.

The enablement plan calls for checks on progress on specific dates set for the delivery of particular services. In addition, the conference will agree on a date by which the total service plan must be reviewed, say in six months, or nine months, or one year, after which a new enablement plan must be worked out. In Bobby's case, a review at the end of nine months indicated that he had made no progress in learning to read. While there had been considerable improvement in his behavior and a decline in frequency of violent outbursts, outbursts still occurred and were frequently associated with incidents involving his inability to read. The prospects of his returning to a regular school were not promising, and a particularly violent series of episodes led to a proposal that he be committed to the state mental hospital. Recognizing the damage that such a commitment would do to Bobby's life, as well as the long-term costs of a custodial placement, the staff decided to expend a substantial amount of money on a short-term, individually designed program to teach Bobby to read. He was removed from formal instruction with his group and placed in an individually designed tutorial program, with an expert teacher and two graduate students to prepare daily schedules of instruction following an operant conditioning paradigm. Though the costs were heavy, they were considerably less than the cost of long-term hospitalization. Bobby responded remarkably well to the operant program. It began at the level of making simple differentiations among letters of the alphabet and among digits, and, with Bobby's notable success, proceeded rapidly to word recognition, simple sentence reading, and simple arithmetic processes. Bobby's at least average intelligence could be brought into play, and he learned to read and to cipher within a six-month period. Another formal review led to placement of Bobby in a special education class in the elementary school. The staff prepared a new ecological assessment and enablement plan that drew upon the natural resources of his life setting and permitted the gradual retirement of Cumberland House from an active role in the ecosystem.

These notes, with appropriate alterations to conceal individual identities, are a reconstruction of a situation of a child who entered Cumberland House in 1967. Bobby continued in special classes in the public school until he was sixteen. He left school and got a job, which he has held for five years. He has been married for three years and has a two-year-old child. He occasionally visits Cumberland House to keep up old friendships.

Thus far, what has been described is a local service management scheme. Bobby has been classified with respect to the services required to help him return to a reasonably normal pattern of development, according to the best judgment of people important in his life, including the professional people who have been mobilized to help. But the classification system has advantages beyond that of providing assistance to an individual child. It is also an instrument for planning and for assessing accountability.

To assess accountability, each service requirement is reviewed and a record made of what actually happened. Have Bobby's teeth been filled? Were they filled at Meharry or somewhere else? Did the person responsible for having the teeth filled actually fulfill his responsibility? What was the actual cost? Where did the money come from, in fact? Were the agreed-upon criteria successfully met? Were appropriate plans made for follow-up? The system provides a powerful means of assuring that Bobby gets the help he needs and that the service delivery system is working well.

Although the concepts and techniques described here were worked out in a residential setting, the ideas also can be applied in situations that do not involve residential care. A Re-ED school in Kentucky has, in addition to its regular liaison staff, an adjunct group of liaison workers who operate in ten counties served by the school. When a child or an adolescent gets into serious trouble with family, school, or community, the liaison worker studies the situation, engages the help of essential people, and works out with them an ecological assessment and enablement plan. Their goal is to make it unnecessary for the child or adolescent to be removed from his natural setting and placed in residential care. The program is working very well and at cost considerably less than residential placement.

The idea of an ecologically oriented, service-based classification system has developed independently in several other programs in the United States. One of the most interesting of these is the Eleanor Roosevelt Developmental Services in New York State, which began operating in 1970 as a prototype for a community-based service program for mentally retarded children, adolescents, and adults. The program, which served all of the retarded people in a large community in a strategy emphasizing prevention, collaboration, advocacy, and direct service, was remarkably effective in sustaining mentally retarded individuals in the community and making institutionalization unnecessary. An interesting feature of the Eleanor Roosevelt program was its reliance on a computer to facilitate case management. We believe that this is the first extensive effort to use the remarkable capabilities of computers to operate what was essentially an ecologically oriented, service-based classification and service system.

There are two other examples of large-scale, computer-managed, child and adolescent service programs. One is in Massachusetts and the other in Connecticut. In Massachusetts, the state's public school program for handicapped children and youth has abandoned the classical categories of handicapping conditions in favor of a planning, management, and accountability system based on the services actually provided to individuals. The system works very well, but it is confined to the public schools of the state. In Connecticut, a further advance in the application of ecological concepts and computer management technologies is being worked out. All state services involving children and youth, including education, health, corrections, and welfare, are committed to developing a common classification and service system that will have the characteristics described in this chapter: an emphasis on the child or adolescent in his normal setting, the preparation of an ecological assessment and service delivery plan, the development of procedures for tracking service delivery, and the provision of information required for local case management, long-term planning, and accountability recording. A computer capability essential for operating such a large program is now midway in development. The Connecticut experience will clearly provide the single best model for the development of an ecologically oriented, service-based system for the classification of handicapped children.

The Prevention-Intervention Project involving several counties in Middle Tennessee is another example of the successful application of ecological strategies. This program, based in the public schools, sought to identify at an early stage children and youth who were beginning to manifest adjustment difficulties. In each instance, an ecological assessment was made, an enablement plan worked out, and resources mobilized to bring the child and his ecosystem up to an acceptable level of functioning.

Prevention-Intervention Project, Tennessee*

The primary purpose of the Prevention-Intervention Project (PIP) was to field-test in public schools the effectiveness of Re-ED principles in the prevention and remediation of children's behavioral, academic, and other ecological problems. The adaptation of teacher-counselor roles to regular school settings was seen as necessary because of the inability of residential schools to serve the great numbers of children with problems and the desirability of programming for them on their own home grounds.

The Prevention-Intervention Project was a cooperative endeavor of the Tennessee departments of mental health and education and five Tennessee school systems, funded by several federal and state agencies. Objectives of the project were (1) to train teachers recruited by school systems to serve as "support teachers"; (2) to provide supportive services to parents and classroom

*This account was written by Mary Lynn Cantrell. The similarity between the names of the Prevention-Intervention Project (PIP) and the Regional Intervention Program (RIP) (see Chapter Three) is a coincidence. They were both developed at Peabody College but by different groups with different theoretical positions. PIP applied Re-ED principles in public schools to *prevent* serious maladjustment of children. RIP applied behavior modification principles to *treat* serious maladjustment of preschool children in a region served by the program.

teachers in order to solve children's problems within their own home and school settings; (3) to assess the effectiveness of the program in changing the knowledge, attitudes, and behavior of support teachers and classroom teachers and the achievement, classroom behavior, and specific problem resolution of the children.

Support teachers served as members of a team that included the regular classroom teacher, the parents of the target child, and any other home or community agents involved. Target children were identified solely on the basis of someone's concern, without formal labeling; problems and strengths were stated in concrete terms; a program was planned to modify the discordant ecology; and the program was evaluated continually to determine its effectiveness and need for revision. Team members functioned interdependently in two roles: (1) as a school-community liaison teacher and (2) as a learning resource teacher. The liaison teacher mobilized community resources and served as the problem-solving link between the child, the child's parents, teachers, peers, and others in the community. The learning resource teacher made use of educational and behavioral programming skills, principally through working as a consultant to the regular classroom teacher. The learning resource teacher might see the target child individually for diagnostic work or special tutoring or to try a new program with the child that might later be used in the child's regular classroom. Ordinarily, the roles of learning resource teacher and liaison teacher overlapped, each complementing the other.

The program was based on an ecological model, with emphasis on skill building that required an analysis of the child's skills, of the demands made on those skills by the environment, and of the capability of environmental agents to teach needed skills. In this view, emotional or maladaptive behavior is a function of the child's lacking the skills demanded by his world (Bricker, 1967; Hobbs, 1975a). The same analyses were used in assisting other members of the ecosystem to acquire the skills they needed. The basic tenet is that behavior is learned in lawful ways and can be relearned through skilled use of Re-ED principles.

The Prevention-Intervention Project training program for support teachers evolved into six weeks of intensive training with subsequent year-long consultative assistance for trainees in their work with children, teachers, and parents. Training staff were recruited from teacher-counselors experienced in the Tennessee reeducation programs.

The initial training period consisted of a progression through eight "modules": Behavioral Principles, Basic Evaluation Techniques, Contingency Management, Program-Relevant Assessment, Academic Programming, Communication Skills, Dealing with Other Problems, and Coordinated Ecological Planning. Each module included a list of specified concepts for training, which were keyed to behaviorally stated training objectives and activities. The central commitment of PIP to a continuing training model through consultation and continued follow-up from training staff was critical. This continuing service was designed on the assumption that, for adults as well as children, learning must be reinforced for newly acquired behaviors to be maintained. Consultation was provided through workshops, site visits, phone calls, and written feedback.

The primary aim of the training program was to provide support teachers with the skills to analyze problem situations and to coordinate resources needed for intervention. The support teachers had to know which organizations in the community provide help to children and families. The value of home visits or contacts with individuals was impossible to overemphasize. Once helping resources had been identified, the support teacher had to tell helpers what they needed to do and then inform them of their progress with a child. If communication lines were not kept open, potential sources of help tended eventually to "dry up." On the other hand, when such resources were given recognition for their contributions, they tended to continue their support. This strategy helped support teachers create new community resources where none existed to fill a specific need. For example, nearby university students were recruited to tutor and serve as educational models for inner-city children; an after-school daycare center was established in a church near the school; and a parent volunteer group provided language training for first graders from deprived environments.

After four years of operation, the Prevention-Intervention Project was presented for the validation process used by Title III of the Elementary and Secondary Education Act prior to approval for dissemination. In May 1975, the project was validated, with the highest score possible, and recommended for state, regional, and national dissemination. Evaluation of objectives and other relevant research findings are summarized below.

Comparisons were made between experimental schools that used Re-ED principles and control schools that did not. Support teachers trained in the project made statistically significant gains on measures of knowledge of behavioral principles and of teacher attitudes. Classroom teachers with whom support teachers had contact also made significant gains in knowledge. One independent measure of the effectiveness of the teamwork of the support teacher and the classroom teacher was the number of students referred to psychological services units. Teachers in the control schools referred significantly more students than did teachers in the experimental schools, where support teachers worked (Cantrell and Cantrell, 1976).

To investigate impact on behavior problems, data collectors were trained to observe teacher-pupil interactions in both experimental and control school classrooms. Thirty-minute classroom observations took place, on the average, twice per month for each classroom in the forty elementary and junior high schools involved. Students who were referred to support teachers because of behavior problems became significantly less disruptive and nonattentive across the intervention time period, while control school students increased somewhat in disruptive and nonattentive behavior across the year's span. Other results obtained from PIP data have relevance to this result. Cantrell, Wood, and Nichols (1974) reported that classroom teachers who had made significant gains in knowledge, as a result of their contact with support teachers, used more praise than criticism, whereas teachers who did not manifest such gains used more criticism than praise.

Impact on academic problems was also of concern. Achievement tests were used to indicate the difference between year-end achievement and predicted achievement scores for each first grader in both experimental and control schools. Significant achievement gains were obtained in favor of experimental compared with control group students in listening achievement and reading achievement, but not in numbers achievement.

Project data also demonstrated significant differences in classroom teaching style. Three distinct profile groups were obtained: (1) a low-knowledge, authoritarian-attitude group; (2) a high-knowledge, positive-attitude group; and (3) a low-knowledge, positive-attitude group. The achievement levels of students in each of these teacher groups showed significant differences. The high-knowledge, positive-attitude teachers produced significantly higher achievement from their low-IQ pupils and middle-IQ pupils than did the other two teacher knowledge-attitude groups, without significantly hindering achievement of the high-IQ pupils (Cantrell, Stenner, and Katzenmeyer, 1977).

Additional research (Cantrell and Cantrell, 1977) indicates that when the appropriate sequence was followed behavioral objectives for children were met in significantly less time than in cases where information and/or planning was incomplete or out of sequence.

Experience in the Prevention-Intervention Project confirmed the belief that an ecological problem-solving process involving the regular classroom teacher and other natural agents via trained support personnel can successfully mainstream many youngsters who previously were not "making it," and this process can be sufficiently flexible to succeed in a wide variety of school settings.

8

The Liaison Function

*Developing Support Systems
for Children and Families*

If emotional disturbance is de-
fined as a signal of an inadequately functioning human ecosystem,
then new and different intervention strategies are called for, and
new professional roles as well. The gradual development of the
ecological systems idea was paralleled by the development of the
concept of liaison services in Re-ED schools. Perhaps in no other
operation do the schools differ more in their current realization
from their original conception. Early staffing plans for a model
Re-ED school made provisions for a single social worker, an arrangement in keeping with the clinical tradition of mental health
agencies. Role expectations for the social worker were limited:
there would be need for intake interviews and for contacts with
agencies and families. But the fact that we were setting out to
build a residential school and not a treatment center introduced
some creative dissonance. Should there not be someone who would

213

maintain liaison with the child's regular school? Of course. And thus was conceived the idea of the liaison teacher-counselor. So we planned to have one social worker and one liaison teacher-coun-selor on the staff of each school. As we got the schools going and gained experience, two things became clear: (1) there was too much work for two people to do, and (2) the roles of social work-er and liaison teacher-counselor were not discrete; they both worked with families, schools, agencies, and communities, as well as with children and teacher-counselors. So we merged the roles and increased the number of staff assigned to what has come to be known as the liaison unit.

We describe the process of enabling an ecosystem to work as "the liaison function." The liaison teacher-counselors in the early Re-ED schools invented the role, and it has in recent years been generalized into the liaison specialist, for whom there is now a for-mal, professional training program and a growing national identifi-cation (Dokecki, 1977; Newbrough, 1977; Williams, 1977). Ac-tually, any person concerned with facilitating human development can perform the liaison function, provided he appreciates the rich-ness of the ecological perspective and acquires the new skills re-quired by the role. In fact, an important strategy in liaison work is to teach the liaison function to one or more adults who are impor-tant in the life of a child, and to the adolescent when old enough and competent, so that the ecosystem can function effectively and meet new crises without external assistance.

The President's Commission on Mental Health (1978) rec-ommended the development of the role of "case manager" as a means of integrating now highly fragmented mental health serv-ices. We think the recommendation is a movement in the right di-rection, but it has avoidable shortcomings. The term *case manager* is semantically infelicitous. No one wants to be a "case," and no one wants to be "managed." And agencies are unlikely to turn over their prized autonomy to an external manager; mental health agencies are notoriously resistant to coordination. The liaison per-son is effective in part because he does not presume to have any managerial authority. His effectiveness derives from the authority of a simple but powerful idea, an idea that gains in potency when shared. Indeed, the liaison concept may be an idea immune from the professional tendency to keep knowledge arcane; if not openly shared (so that others can take over the liaison function), the idea destroys itself.

The function of the liaison person is to help members of an ecosystem conceptualize what keeps the system from working, identify sources of discord, modify behaviors, mobilize resources required to achieve shared goals, and acquire the capacity to deal with excessive discord in the future. As a tool for accomplishing these goals, the liaison teacher-counselor helps devise an "ecological assessment and enablement plan" (see Chapter Seven). This is a procedure to facilitate the definition of shared objectives, to specify what behaviors should be changed and what resources mobilized, to assign responsibility for accomplishing particular objectives, to track the progress of the system's reorganization, and to assess the outcome of the effort.

The ecological assessment and enablement plan is usually worked out in a conference for which the liaison teacher-counselor has made careful preparation by talking with major participants, reviewing records, and perhaps visiting in the home, school, or clinic. The participants in the conference will vary, of course, but might include the mother and father, a teacher, a school psychologist, a pediatrician, a caseworker, an adult friend of the family, and often the child or adolescent whose problems initially signaled the breakdown of the ecosystem. The conference produces an assessment and a plan of action and also initiates the feedback process essential to course correction in any complex, goal-directed system.

The ecological assessment leads to an enablement plan. We prefer the term *enablement* to such terms as *treatment* or *intervention,* for it suggests both a goal (enabling an ecosystem to function on its own) and a role for the liaison teacher-counselor (as temporary facilitator or consultant to those who are and must remain responsible for making the ecosystem work). The enablement plan is highly specific. It records the steps that must be taken to restore the system to an acceptable level of functioning, as judged by the participants in the system, and it is oriented to sources of strength as well as of weakness, to assets in the ecosystem as well as to liabilities.

The enablement plan is updated as goals are accomplished and as changes in the ecosystem occur, and it is periodically reviewed to check on progress; in some programs, there is a required formal review every thirty days. When the participants in the liaison conference judge that the ecosystem is likely to function at a reasonably adequate level, that the probability of continued success exceeds the probability of a new breakdown, the Re-ED staff withdraw, but they remain ready to assist in the transition or if new crises occur. An important consideration in this judgment is the extent to which a member of the ecosystem (the older adolescent or the mother or father of a younger child) is prepared to take over the function of problem identification, behavior management, and resource mobilization. Ordinarily, schools follow up each student eighteen months after discharge to be sure that the ecosystem continues to function satisfactorily.

Liaison Teacher-Counselor as Facilitator. The liaison teacher-counselor should acquire early a clear conception of her role as facilitator. She should reflect constantly on her experiences in order to avoid the temptation to become a manager. The locus of responsibility for effecting changes in the ecosystem should remain, insofar as is possible, with the people who are ultimately responsible for making the ecosystem work. With preschool children, parents or surrogate parents normally play the central role. Their behavior accounts for a substantial portion of the variance in the child's behavior, within genetic and constitutional limitations. Increasingly, with more and more women working outside the home, childcare workers and preschool teachers come into the picture, but the responsibility of the parents remains central. With the elementary school child, the ecosystem becomes increasingly more elaborate, with teachers playing a very important role, and other adults entering the picture: neighbors, playground supervisors, coaches, counselors, and professional people providing services to the child or the family. With the adolescent, the locus of responsibility for the effective functioning of the ecosystem shifts more and more to the young person; parents often recede in importance and teachers, job trainers, and job supervisors play increasingly important roles. A Re-ED program may become a part of the ecosystem, sometimes becoming for a short period the dominant experience in the life of the child or adolescent. However, the constant challenge to the liaison teacher-counselor is to keep managerial responsibilities where they belong, in the eco-

system without Re-ED. She avoids assuming "professional responsibility" for others, knowing that the true experts on particular
ecosystems are the natural clusters of people who make up the system over time. She is effective precisely because she has no authority: no office, no badge, no check to give out, no cachet. She is
armed simply with a powerful theoretical construction and with
information.

Discord and Harmony in Ecosystems. The liaison teacher-
counselor is interested in what it is that keeps ecosystems from
working; she is not interested in what is wrong with people—not
the child, or the parents, or teachers, or any others. The question
is: What needs to be changed in order for the system to work reasonably well? Suggestions for needed changes nearly always come
from the people who make up the ecosystem, including the Re-ED
staff members, but the final authority for any particular choice is
not the liaison teacher-counselor but the people who will have continuing responsibility for the child, including the child himself
when old enough.

In the assessment of ecosystems, the liaison teacher-counselor looks for sources of discord, to be sure, but she also looks
for sources of strength, for assets, for pivotal people. Most professional people providing services to others are well trained in the
identification of pathology and can become preoccupied with that
pursuit. The liaison teacher-counselor, however, though sensitive
to what might be called ecosystem pathology, is oriented toward
the normal, the healthy, even the exceptional in resources. Of
great importance, of course, is to find positive assets in the child in
order that these can be enhanced in an emerging satisfactory and
satisfying ecosystem.

A Present and Future Orientation. The liaison teacher-counselor is concerned largely with present realities and future possibilities, not with the origins of difficulties in the past. Social histories
of particular children and families are useful only to the extent
that they illuminate the contemporaneous operation of the ecosystem and that they generate hypotheses about what might be
done to enable the system to operate effectively in the future.
Thus, the liaison teacher-counselor departs from the traditions of
psychodynamic psychology, with its assumptions that past hurts
have to be dealt with before new learnings are possible. From an

ecological perspective, every day is a new day, and the challenge is to make each day lived as resonantly successful as possible.

Objective-Subjective Balance. The liaison teacher-counselor works with both objective and subjective data, with events that can be measured and with events as perceived, often quite differently, by ecosystem members. Both objective and subjective data are important. The fact that a child is three years retarded in ability to read may be a crucial objective factor in the development of an enablement plan; the fact that father, mother, and child perceive differently the nature and sources of their stress is also important and to be expected. Behavior of members of ecosystems is based not on reality but on perceptions of reality; thus, the perceptions themselves must be dealt with with the same concern as so-called objective facts.

Limited Objectives. The liaison teacher-counselor, along with her colleagues in a Re-ED program and with the principal members of the ecosystem, strives to achieve limited goals. There are no perfect systems in life; all are flawed. Efforts to make systems perfect are doomed to failure, not only because the goal is unachievable but because a prolongation of intervention itself can produce a pathological situation.

The Enablement of Parents

Keeping in mind that our goal is to help restore a small social system to a functioning balance as quickly as possible, we strive to strengthen family ties while giving the family and the child or adolescent enough relief from each other to enable them to come back together again on a workable basis. The primary agents in this process are the child's parents. The enablement of parents is a critical concept in Re-ED strategies.

We try to prevent the rupture in family life that occurs when a child or an adolescent is sent away to an institution for an indeterminate period of time. When a child is completely removed from her home for long periods, the family tends to close ranks against the ejected member, so that reinstatement of the child in the family becomes in itself a major and sometimes impossible undertaking. We avoid this familiar problem by keeping the child and her family involved with each other, thus preventing needless alienation.

In Re-ED residential programs, children go home every weekend, often traveling many miles to do so. The student and her family continue to belong to each other and to work together toward the child's early return. Weekends provide a time for testing new ideas about how to get along, on the part of both parents and child as well as of other siblings and family members. Weekends raise problems and stir up feelings that can be worked on during the subsequent week, by the child at her Re-ED school and by the parents in discussions at a mental health center or with the Re-ED staff. Living is never put aside to be taken up later.

Keeping the child and her family belonging to each other makes for turbulence and confusion, especially on Fridays and Mondays. But we cherish the chaos as a source of instruction for everyone: the child, her family, our staff. It is easy to reduce confusion around weekends simply by keeping child and family apart. Many residential treatment centers elect this option, but they do so at the loss of a larger opportunity. The parents (or surrogate parents) of a disturbed child are and must be the central agents in efforts to help the child and the younger adolescent. However, to accept parents as the true experts on their children is a difficult concept for most professional people to learn.

To blame parents for the difficulties of their children and to reject them for their inadequacies is widely prevalent in mental health and educational efforts, manifested in daily practice as well as in theoretical works. The tendency to blame parents must be guarded against, especially by young staff members who have not themselves experienced the humbling complexities of a parent's role. Furthermore, the conventional schema for conceptualizing emotional disturbance makes it seem reasonable to isolate disturbed children from their parents, who are seen as the source of contagion. The illness idiom commends separation as a solution. Yet another way of avoiding entanglement with parents—a method too readily countenanced because it seems so professionally respectable—is to require parents, or at least the mother, to be in therapy at another agency and then to avoid engagement with them on the grounds of a possible confusion of therapeutic roles.

Parents are encouraged to be as much a part of the Re-ED program as possible. Mothers sew for the children, help in the classroom, assist at special functions, put out a handbook for parents. Fathers help on field trips, in construction projects, in backpacking and canoeing. One father and mother sponsored a Cub Scout program and continued it after their child had gone back to his regular school. There are frequent conferences between parents and both the liaison staff and the day and night teacher-counselors, often on Fridays or Sundays, when parents are at the school, and sometimes by telephone during the week. Parents keep a diary of significant events over each weekend, providing both a record of progress and a source of information useful to the child's teacher-counselors. The diaries often give focus to conversations between parents and staff.

In a Re-ED program, parents should be able to visit their child at any time. There should be no visiting hours and no formal visiting rooms. The liaison teacher-counselor should be able to say to parents: "Look, this child right now is your most important responsibility. Ordinarily, parents visit on Fridays and Sundays, on special occasions, and by appointment at other times. However, if you feel it will help you or your child for you to see him at any time, day or night, come. You will be welcome." Of course, such an invitation may mean that a mother or a father will occasionally interfere with the program, but such interruptions are better handled on an ad hoc basis than by a formal rule that limits visiting. There are several advantages to this open policy. It affirms our commitment to the principle that parents must remain responsible for their children; it thus has high symbolic value even if the privilege is seldom used. It creates a good feeling, a feeling of partnership, between parents and staff. It may demonstrate to a child that her parents care about her. And, finally, it may bring parents and staff together at moments of heightened concern and sensitivity, when parents are most communicative and most receptive to assistance.

Commitment to the goal of making a small social system work suggests a strategy of identifying specifically what it is about a child's behavior that leads a family to reject her and, when reasonable, to proceed to modify that behavior to increase her acceptability to her family. Of course, this is done only when the changed behavior would be generally regarded as desirable rather than undesirable and in a context of work with the parents that seeks both to modify their expectations in appropriate ways and to help them play their parental roles more adequately.

A ten-year-old girl, whose parents were both professional people, began to soil herself, precipitating her referral to a Re-ED school. The staff were able to alter the child's behavior in a relatively short period of time, thus relieving one strain on the family unit. In the meantime, the agency worked with the parents, trying to alter the parental behavior that may have caused the child to start soiling.

A ten-year old boy was fearful and somewhat effeminate, a "sissy." This bothered his father immensely, probably because he was doubtful of his own masculinity. While the agency worked with the father, we were quite successful in helping the boy overcome his fears, become more assertive, and develop a number of masculine interests and skills. Such achievements seemed to us to be generally constructive for the child and to have the further virtue of making him more acceptable to his father, who might not be as available to change as the child.

Parents are nearly always much more concerned, much more highly motivated to help their children, than professional people ordinarily recognize. We have been surprised at the number of times that a father has been willing, even pleased, to spend more time with his son simply on the basis of our suggestion that it might be a good thing to do. In a special project for autistic children at Cumberland House, the intelligent and highly motivated mother of a mute child was taught how to use operant procedures to supplement our efforts to teach her child to speak. She observed the procedures, then assisted a skilled teacher, then practiced at school under supervision, and finally started a program at home. The child, who had been in individual psychotherapy for four years without apparent profit, acquired in six months a vocabulary of fifty words, to the delight of all, himself especially.

In putting into practice ecological concepts, and in seeking to return a child home as quickly as possible, we have to face the hard fact that some families are too disorganized, too destructive, too lacking in social purpose to give a child what he must have in order to grow up well. Of course, such families are represented in high proportion in programs for disturbed children. Sometimes a family can be brought above the threshold of adequacy through some kind of long-term assistance, as by a visiting nurse, a homemaker service, or a community center program. Sometimes, however, we have to seek some solution for a child outside his own family, through a foster home arrangement or a special placement in a group home. In such instances, the liaison teacher-counselor usually arranges an appropriate placement through a local agency. Removing the child from a deteriorated family is simply one of the strategies that must be employed occasionally to make the ecological system work.

Adolescents present a special challenge in working out relationships between parent and child. One of the developmental tasks of adolescence is to establish independence from parents, usually a gradual process that, when successfully negotiated, ends in a new and mature relationship between caring adults. But even in the best of circumstances, it is a difficult process, and children who are referred to a Re-ED program are likely to have grown up in far from ideal relationships with their parents. The younger adolescent has a particularly difficult situation because he is usually dependent on parents for support. The older adolescent, on the other hand, can move into the community, get a job (if fortunate), and become independent of parental obligations. But even the older adolescent in a Re-ED program is likely to be deficient in academic achievement and in readiness to take a job and live independently. Increasingly, Re-ED programs are sponsoring small group homes to ease the adolescent's transition to independence. Although the adolescent's parents may be inadequate or unavailable, the adolescent still needs responsible and sensitive guidance from an adult, as well as good adult models to emulate.

The ecological concept involves not only the reeducation of children but also the reeducation of parents, regular teachers, relatives, professional people, our own staff. For the most part, it is an informal process attendant on the working out of some problem. Some of the schools, however, have formal parent education programs. A good example is the parent counseling program at the Kentucky Re-ED school in Louisville. Here is the description from the school's brochure for parents thinking of entering a child:

The parent counseling program is unique in its nature and extensiveness. Before children are placed into the Re-ED program, the parents sign a contract to participate in scheduled counseling sessions with the staff or to continue in the counseling program in which they are already enrolled. Parent training sessions run throughout the school year, occurring continuously on Wednesday evenings or Friday mornings. Input for the areas to be covered in these programs was compiled from questions and suggestions offered by parents, teachers, counselors, and contact agencies. In addition to the child management training or other counseling with a community agency, the parents have weekly sessions with both the morning teacher and the afternoon teacher working with their child. When the parents pick up their child on Friday, they are informed by the morning teacher of the child's behavior and progress during the week. On Sunday, the parents meet with the afternoon program specialist and discuss the home behavior during the weekend visit, and return the weekend behavior checklist. The weekend behavior diary is unique in that it involves parents in the evaluation of their child from initial contact with Re-ED on the referral form throughout the two-year follow-up program. Parents use this evaluation list in relation to their concepts of the problems in the home and neighborhood when they give permission for possible placement in the Re-ED program. They check the same list weekly on the behavior and periodically throughout the follow-up period. With the advent of Public Law 94-142 and the requirement of parent involvement, we are pleased that we have utilized parents this way for many years. In the two weekly sessions, the teachers counsel the parents in what to expect during the child's home visit, how to manage behavior problems at home, how to reinforce the behavior modification program being used at school, and how to conduct a "pow-wow" session and talk through family problems in the home. These sessions provide parents with an opportunity biweekly to receive information and counseling with two professionals working directly with the child. Liaison counselors assigned to the family are available to the parent for counseling at any time, and make periodic checks with the parent and work directly with the family to secure suitable school placement for the child upon graduation. Upon graduation from Re-ED, the family and school personnel receive counseling from the liaison counselor in frequently scheduled home and school visits.

All these processes keep the parents in constant touch with the child and his daily progress, even though he may be in a residential program, and provide parents with the support needed to produce change in the child's behavior and environment.

Improving School Relationships

It would be hard to overstate the importance of the school in causing as well as in remedying emotional disturbance in children. Psychodynamic theory puts the locus of the problem inside the child and its etiology in the family—or, more accurately, in parent-child relationships, with the mother generally regarded as more important than the father. Conventional intervention strategies deal mostly with phenomenological data, with the stuff of the minds of children and parents, to the neglect of the real world of family structures, living arrangements, neighborhoods, schools, and communities. The school, relative to its importance in the life of the child, is often the most neglected.

The one most frequently observed and shared characteristic of children and adolescents called emotionally disturbed is academic retardation. Children in Re-ED schools, though generally normal in intelligence, are retarded from two to four years in academic development. From four to five times as many boys as girls (ages six to twelve) are called emotionally disturbed; there are fewer disturbed children in the summer than in the winter; and referrals of children to agencies follow cycles of stress in school. Such observations lead one to expect the school to be regarded as a possible major source of the child's trouble and thus worthy of much attention in efforts to help a particular child. But conventional concepts imply that school failure is a result rather than a cause of emotional disturbance—a backward construction in our view; so school and schooling get neglected in many mental health programs for children and adolescents. In Re-ED, academic competence is a central concern.

Schools do not ordinarily expel children for academic failure but for academic deficiency plus misbehavior. Often the misbehavior is highly specific: the child runs away from school, he fights too much, he won't sit still in class, he uses bad language, he passes vulgar notes, he is rebellious against teachers. Again, the system's approach to the problem of the disturbed child leads us to be greatly concerned with the child's school situation, to identify specific problems, and to seek remedies for the child, for the school, and for the family, in order to put into more favorable balance the odds for success in this crucial enterprise.

Our goals are highly pragmatic. We go to work directly on school skills, on reading, writing, and arithmetic. We favor an interaction hypothesis regarding the relationship between school failure and emotional disturbance, but we elect to attack academic deficiencies directly because of their central importance in the child's development and because of their part in creating emotional disturbance. We regard repeated failure as destructive and success as beneficial, and we strive to reverse the ratio of the two. When schooling is neglected in residential programs for disturbed children, a child often will return to his regular school with an educational handicap more severe than he had before being removed from school, an extra strain on the system that is often unnecessary. The liaison teacher-counselor visits the child's school to get information to determine what is expected of him in specific curricula or even in particular books. The liaison teacher-counselor also tries to identify specific behaviors that the school has found objectionable, so that we can go to work on these as well. The information is conveyed to the teacher-counselor team and is used for program planning and for assessing when a child is ready to return to his own school.

The liaison teacher-counselor arranges school visits to achieve for the child in relation to his school what weekend visits achieve for the child in relation to his family. It is important for the school to continue to feel responsible for a child and for the child to retain his identification with a particular school. To these ends, liaison teacher-counselors in one program have arranged for monthly visits of most children to their own schools. These visits are scheduled at a time when the Re-ED staff is occupied with an in-service training day, usually a Monday. Careful preparation is made for a child's visit, every effort being bent to make it successful and pleasant. School principals and teachers are usually willing, even eager, to make the extra effort required to arrange a single day for a child and to make it a good experience.

Informal Support Systems

In mapping the ecosystem and mobilizing resources to sustain the child or adolescent after graduation from Re-ED, the liaison teacher-counselor is especially attentive to and appreciative of opportunities provided outside the formal mental health or social service system, referred to sometimes as "informal supports." Of special importance are members of the extended family, individuals in the community, child- and family-serving institutions, and self-help groups.

The extended family is often neglected in treatment programs, reflecting the widespread assumption that the extended family is no longer a functioning reality in American life. This is far from true. Though extended family members seldom live together in the same residence, as they once did, they often share a sense of family obligation, remain in communication, assist in the minor routines of life (baby sitting, car pooling, giving advice, lending money or goods), and respond effectively in times of crisis. Minority-group families have been extolled for the responsiveness of members beyond the nuclear family, yet there is much evidence that mainstream families also deserve recognition for mutual support. Liaison teacher-counselors have had repeated successes in arranging for a relative to become a contributing member to a child's ecosystem, sometimes assuming the continuing liaison role.

Individuals in the community can frequently be enlisted to help a child in some particular. Limitations on these sources of help derive less from their lack of willingness to help than from our lack of imagination in arranging it. We have made such arrangements with a neighbor, a clergyman, a teacher, a public health nurse, a bus driver, a playground supervisor, a museum director, an apartment house superintendent, a policeman, a graduate student, a corner store owner, a Girl Scout leader, and so on.

Institutions outside the mental health or social service system are extraordinarily important and often neglected. They are the main supports for normal family life and thus are extremely important to all family members, including the child or adolescent. We think readily of schools, churches, synagogues, community centers, social clubs, service organizations, advocacy groups, sports leagues for children and adults, hobby groups, relief organizations, the YMCA and YWCA, fraternal organizations. Their number is legion.

Self-help groups are emerging as a major source of support for individuals and families. We have used Alcoholics Anonymous, Parents Without Partners, Weight Watchers, nonsmoking clinics, Buddies, Inc., New Neighbors, and so on.

The work place is an exceedingly important part of the separate ecologies of adult members of the family, and thus influential on the ecological system defined by the child when that adult is included. For adolescents, the work place may be the determining factor in helping sustain the ecosystem. We thus often work with personnel people, job trainers, and job supervisors. Enlightened business people often recognize the mutual benefits to be gained by their contribution to the successful entry of an adolescent into the labor market or in keeping an employee productive.

When arrangements are made for a mental health or social service agency to take over responsibility for the liaison function after Re-ED has withdrawn, the liaison teacher-counselor gives preference to agencies that have an ecological orientation in their programs. Sometimes the liaision teacher-counselor has taught, by precept, example, and participation, the liaison perspective to caseworkers or other representatives of agencies. We are ordinarily reluctant to work out a continuing relationship between a child or adolescent and a mental health or social service agency that defines problems strictly in intrapsychic terms.

On what basis does the reeducation team and the liaison conference decide that sufficient progress has been made for the ecosystem to operate on its own without special assistance from Re-ED? Again, it is the judgment of the principal members of the ecosystem that provides the answers for this question. Here are some notes from a liaison conference near the end of the stay of a child at Cumberland House. At this particular conference, only professional people were present; the liaison teacher-counselor checked the observations with the child's mother and father and with school personnel as well. The final decision was to arrange a two-week period when the boy would stay at Cumberland House but attend the school where he would be enrolled on graduation. The transition worked well, and the child continued to progress satisfactorily, sustained by a reordered ecosystem.

"Well, Billy seems generally happier than he was five months ago.

"He is still a year behind in general educational development but his school was especially concerned about his poor reading ability which is substantially improved now.

"Of course, the reason the school expelled Billy was that he kept annoying other children, getting in frequent fights, etc.; we have worked on this hard and it is no longer much of a problem.

"For one thing, Billy's improvement in sports seems to make it unnecessary for him to show off so much.

"When he goes back to school we have arranged for him to have a new teacher, a man who seems interested.

"Billy's mother has a fragile hold on her own life but can help some.

"But his older brother who is his favorite will be back from the Army and will be living at home; he's a real plus in the system.

"Billy has been getting a lot out of the YMCA and we have arranged a membership for him.

"Maybe we could bring him back this summer for a couple of weeks at camp, as sort of a booster.

"You know Billy's father used to punish Billy an awful lot; he has gone back to work now and seems more understanding.

"Looking down the road a bit, after next year Billy goes to X Junior High, a really good school that will work with us closely.

"Billy's mother will continue in therapy at the Guidance Center and the social worker there has agreed to keep us posted on how things go at home.

"Incidentally, his mother has been introduced to his school principal and to his new teacher; my guess is they will now keep in touch.

"Billy is still pretty fearful of going back to his old school; his visit last month helped; maybe there is enough going for him now so he can make it at school.

"Well, let's see how we stand: does it look like the system will go if we pull out now?"

Steps in the Liaison Process

Liaison is a dynamic process not readily reducible to steps, but for didactic purposes it is useful to try to do so. The reader should bear in mind that, when we speak of steps, we are imposing on events a hypothetical structure into which real-life happenings will seldom if ever fit. The liaison process is not linear and sequential; there is inevitably much looping back and leaping forward. And the flow of events adheres to no clock; time is sometimes highly compressed and turbulent, with distressing setbacks or exhilarating progress; sometimes it is as limp as a Dali watch, with no perceptible change in the ecosystem. We propose to describe the liaison process in five steps. The steps are illustrated here by an interspersed narrative account of a child whom we shall call Mike.*

*This study is adapted from a paper by Jeanie S. Williams titled "Liaison Function as Reflected in a Case Study," *Journal of Community Psychology*, 1977, *5*, 18-23, and is reprinted here with permission.

Mike was a seven-year-old boy with average physical and mental development. He came from a deprived socioeconomic background. He had never been to school. Mike had been abandoned by his parents at approximately age five and left with his maternal grandmother, who lived on a farm near a large metropolitan city. Several other grandchildren of various ages had been left with the grandmother as well.

A few months after Mike had been left with her, the grandmother had called the county welfare worker and insisted that she come to get Mike. She refused to keep him any longer because of his uncontrollable and destructive behavior. She said that the other children "hated" him and she was afraid he would be pushed into an old, abandoned well located on the farm. The grandmother had no knowledge of his parents' whereabouts. Eventually Mike was removed from his grandmother's home and was placed in a series of foster homes. He exhausted them all and was, as a last resort, placed in a state mental hospital on a ward with adult males.

Mike had been in the state hospital for about seven months when he was called to the attention of the principal of the Re-ED school by a social worker at the state hospital. The principal asked the liaison teacher-counselor to do an initial ecological assessment to determine whether enrollment in the Re-ED school was appropriate for Mike.

Step 1: Making an Ecological Assessment. When a child or adolescent is referred to a Re-ED program, the liaison teacher-counselor initiates the liaison process by working with the family and community agencies to assess the ecological sytem identified by and with the referred child. This process is sometimes referred to as "mapping" the ecosystem. It involves the following activities:

The liaison teacher-counselor first reads all available records of the child and his family. The records will usually have been prepared with the conventional assumption that the child is singularly the problem. The liaison teacher-counselor will have read the record with an intuitive appreciation of its transactional implications —implications not likely to have been appreciated by others.

Next, the liaison teacher-counselor discusses the situation with the principal members of the ecosystem: parents, the child or adolescent, teachers, social agency caseworkers, friends occasionally, employers or prospective employers of older youth, relatives, members of the larger community. The objective of the discussions is partly to obtain information necessary for developing an enablement plan, partly to begin the process of helping all involved own the problem and begin to do something about it.

The liaison teacher-counselor then prepares an inventory of community resources that might be mobilized to meet the developmental and ecological requirements of the referred child. The assessment should be future oriented, guided by the principle that the goal of Re-ED is to enable normal social systems to work reasonably well in the interest of the child. Children and families often get into serious difficulties in the first place because of inadequate support services in the community. Thus, at the outset the liaison teacher-counselor tries to identify the configuration of services that will be needed for the ecological system to function reasonably well when Re-ED is no longer in the picture. Usually agreement is reached with a particular social agency to be responsible, along with Re-ED, for planning and monitoring the transition from an ecosystem supported by Re-ED to an ecosystem that makes effective use of normal community support systems. The child's family can often be an important source of information about community supports and must be fully involved in the process.

Either before or soon after enrollment in a Re-ED program, the liaison teacher-counselor arranges for a complete psychoeducational evaluation of the child. The evaluation provides information essential to the development of the enablement plan. Re-ED programs stress the importance of helping a child or an adolescent overcome academic deficits, for reasons discussed in detail elsewhere (see Chapter Ten). Assisted by an educational diagnostician, teacher-counselors meticulously design a remedial program for each child, with precise objectives and agreed-upon methods for accomplishing goals.

The liaison teacher-counselor obtains such health records as may be needed to ensure that the enablement plan will attend to the health needs of the child. Of particular importance is information about health problems, medications used, dietary requirements, prosthetic devices, limitations of activity, and, with adolescents especially, drug and alcohol abuse. If a child has not had a recent physical examination, it is imperative that arrangements be made for him to have one and steps taken to remedy any physical problems that may be found. It is especially important to be attentive to the child's nutritional status.

Finally, during the period of making the ecological assessment, the liaison teacher-counselor obtains required permissions and clearances for the enrollment of the child and for the exchange of information about him.

The liaison teacher-counselor observed Mike on the ward, interviewed him, read the records about him, and interviewed the social worker at the state hospital. The ecological assessment included mapping the key systems in Mike's world. Figure 5 shows

**Figure 5. Mike's Ecological System at the Point of Entry
by the Liaison Specialist**

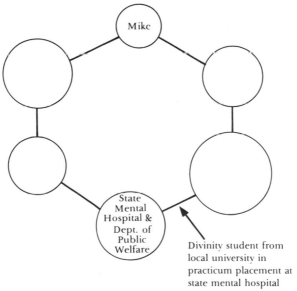

the map of the key systems at the time of entry by the liaison teacher-counselor. Typically, the ecological system would include the child, the family, the school, the community and neighborhood, and the social agency, plus a doctor, minister, Boy Scout leader, and so on. Mike's ecological system included himself, the ward of the state mental hospital, the patients and workers on the ward, the hospital social worker, and the county and state Departments of Public Welfare. There was no family, no school, and no community and neighborhood in the usual sense.

The ecological assessment did yield, however, a surprising and important piece of information: a divinity student from a local university doing a practicum at the state hospital had shown an interest in Mike. The student had on two or three occasions taken Mike home for weekend visits with him and his wife. The assessment confirmed as fairly accurate the previous descriptions, in the records and by the social worker, of Mike's behavior. The descriptions named such behavior as hyperactivity, manipulation of adults (playing "catch me if you can" with the social worker), little if any eye contact, ignoring directions and commands, living in his own world, showing no impulse control, and wetting his pants to get attention when he, Mike, wanted it. He would use "needing to go to the bathroom" to get out of situations that were threatening to him. However, Mike was able to sit down with the liaison teacher-counselor for an interview when he was shown some crayons and asked to draw a picture.

The next step for the liaison teacher-counselor was to share the gathered information with her team at the Re-ED school (day teacher-counselor, night teacher-counselor, and night aide who worked directly with the eight children in their group) and with the administrative staff. A review of all the information gathered led to a decision that the Re-ED program could serve Mike, *provided* he could be placed in an appropriate foster home. The foster parents would need to agree to work in collaboration with the Re-ED school, keep Mike on weekends, and continue to keep him after he left the Re-ED school.

Step 2: Developing an Enablement Plan. The liaison teacher-counselor is responsible for seeing that an enablement plan is developed. The enablement plan is normally worked out in an initial planning conference held at the Re-ED school. As noted above, before the conference is convened, the liaison teacher-counselor would ordinarily have visited the referring agency, the child's home, and the child's school. Participants in the liaison conference might include parents or surrogate parents of the child or adolescent, agency representatives, a school psychologist perhaps, the child's teacher or the adolescent's vocational counselor or job supervisor, a representative of the juvenile court, a Re-ED consultant (pediatrician, psychologist, special educator, psychiatrist), and the psychodiagnostician. Presence of the reeducation team—the day teacher-counselor, the night teacher-counselor, the liaison teacher-counselor, and sometimes a team supervisor—is essential. Sometimes the child or adolescent joins the group for part of the discussion. It is not always possible or even desirable to get all the principal members of the ecosystem in the same room, but the liaison teacher-counselor is responsible for interpreting for the group the perceptions and expectations of those not present.

The purpose of the enablement plan is to lay out the specific steps that need to be taken to restore the ecosystem to a level of functioning that is satisfactory to its principal members (including, now, the Re-ED team). After agreeing on what needs to be done, the conference specifies for each item (1) who will be responsible for getting the task done; (2) who will actually provide the service, if a service is required; (3) by what date the service will be completed or the goal achieved; (4) what the service will cost; (5) where the money will come from; (6) what criterion will be used to determine whether objectives have been met; and (7) what follow-up steps may be required.

The liaison teacher-counselor then met with the hospital social worker and explained the Re-ED school decision to her. Together they planned the next steps in the proces: (1) They would meet with the divinity student and his wife to explore their interest in taking Mike as a foster child. (2) They would contact the public welfare worker in Mike's home county, the state public welfare worker, and the local county welfare worker for the purpose of setting up a meeting to discuss Mike's situation, his possible enrollment in the Re-ED school, and possible foster home placements for him. Both meetings were held at the Re-ED school.

The results were gratifying: (1) The divinity student and his wife agreed to provide foster care, work with the Re-ED school, and keep Mike as a foster child after the Re-ED experience. (2) The three welfare workers and their supervisors, meeting with the hospital social worker and the liaison teacher-counselor and her team, agreed with some reluctance to speed up the usual process for investigating a home and designating it an approved foster home. They would investigate the divinity student's home within two weeks. In one week's time, the divinity student's home was declared officially a foster home. In addition, the department offered the services of the welfare worker in providing counseling to the foster parents.

In two weeks' time, Mike was scheduled to enroll in the Re-ED school. Three weeks after the liaison teacher-counselor entered the situation, Mike's ecological system included, besides himself, the key systems of a home and family, the social agencies (Department of Public Welfare and state hospital), a neighborhood and community on weekends, and the Re-ED school (Figure 6).

The enablement plan includes changes in the behavior or competence of the child or adolescent that appear to be required

**Figure 6. Mike's Ecological System at Three Weeks After the Point of Entry
by the Liaison Specialist**

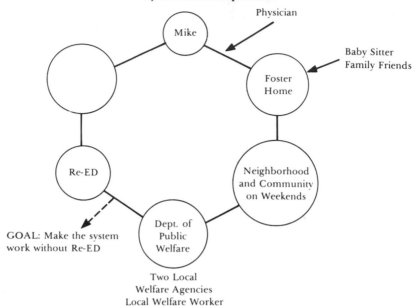

to enable the ecosystem to work. The conference therefore systematically reviews the sources of discord and of potential harmony related directly to the child or adolescent. Thus, plans may
be necessary to modify or enhance the child's behavior, his health
and physical development, his academic competences, his vocational skills, and his social development.

The enablement plan rests on the judgment of participants
or potential participants in the ecosystem of the referred child or
adolescent. It is thus distinctly different from a prescription provided by an external expert. Conference participants should be
able to endorse the plan, identify personally with it, and accept
individual responsibility for carrying it out. It is expected that the
enablement plan will be reviewed periodically by the same con-
ferees when possible, and that it will be updated when significant
events occur between periods of formal review.

In some respects, the enablement plan resembles other approaches to the provision of services to children and families, including the individual educational plan required by Public Law
94-142, the individual treatment plan required by Medicaid, and

the problem-oriented diagnosis long used in pediatric practice. It also embraces a number of features of "management by objective" strategies.

The liaison teacher-counselor, the Re-ED team, and the foster parents planned together for Mike's enrollment in the Re-ED school: the foster parents were preparing Mike's room at their home, buying clothes he would need at school, getting a medical examination, etc. The foster parents agreed with the Re-ED team that the intervention strategy of primary importance was that of being consistent in interaction with Mike. particularly because of his manipulative behavior. A good example was his use of "needing to go to the bathroom" to get out of doing what he had been instructed to do. A schedule was set up by the Re-ED teacher-counselors, showing when Mike was to go to the bathroom. He went only at those times. If he wet his pants, he wore them wet. The foster parents set a similar schedule for home. During the first two weeks, this behavior diminished rapidly and finally disappeared altogether.

The liaison teacher-counselor kept the foster parents informed about Mike's goals and progress in the Re-ED school. She also shared the information with the welfare worker and the hospital social worker.

Step 3: Monitoring the Reeducation Process. The liaison teacher-counselor is responsible for ensuring that the enablement plan is carried out as well as possible, for revising the plan in response to developments relating to particular items, and for reviewing the whole plan periodically. While the day teacher-counselor and night teacher-counselor are working intensively with the child (and sometimes with parents and teachers as well), the liaison teacher-counselor attends to the functioning of the system as a whole. She meets at least once a week with the reeducation team in a formal review session and also stays in close touch with what is going on by frequent conversations with teacher-counselors, parents, teachers, agency representatives, and other members of the ecosystem. The liaison teacher-counselor is especially attentive to the mobilization of community resources that will be required to make it possible for Re-ED to withdraw from the ecosystem with confidence that the family, neighborhood, school, and community will provide the supports needed to continue the progress made after Re-ED withdraws.

By this time, the liaison teacher-counselor had begun to establish linkages with the public school Mike would attend when he left the Re-ED school. The principal, foster parents, and liaison teacher-counselor met to get acquainted and to review the historical information about Mike and his present academic and social progress. They discussed the kind of program Mike would need in public school. The principal made a commitment to collaborate with the liaison teacher-counselor and with the foster parents in the planning of and preparation for Mike's eventual enrollment in the school, to accept Mike fully as a student, and to provide appropriate programming for him.

We cannot overemphasize the importance of the function of the liaison teacher-counselor in establishing linkages among ecosystem members. Sometimes it is a matter of helping children and parents talk with each other. More often than not, it requires establishment of new communication linkages between home and school. School is central in the life of the child and, not infrequently, the key to overcoming the "emotional disturbance" for which the child was originally referred to Re-ED. The child should not be required to bear the burden of the inability of parents and teachers to talk with each other; the liaison teacher-counselor tries to bridge this communication gap. Unfortunately, communication among components of the ecosystem is not likely to continue after Re-ED withdraws unless some individual in the system accepts responsibility for keeping the communication network going. In other words, the liaison teacher-counselor must teach her role to someone else. The most likely candidate is the mother or father and sometimes both. With the maturing adolescent, it is sometimes possible to transfer the liaison function directly to that person, a happy outcome when successful. Lacking sufficient resources there, a relative might be encouraged to assume the responsibility, or a community agency might move into the role.

The public welfare worker was counseling the foster parents about medical and dental care for Mike; behavior management techniques similar to those of the Re-ED school program; and home chores for Mike, such as making his bed, putting away his toys, and setting the table. Some rules for playing with the neighborhood children were established. The welfare worker encouraged the foster parents to maintain their social life, getting a baby sitter to stay with Mike when they went out.

At this point, the liaison teacher-counselor was asked to consult with the foster mother and the public welfare worker about ways to help the baby sitter manage Mike's behavior when the foster parents were away. After discussing Mike's problem behavior and some possible intervention strategies, the foster mother felt she could teach the baby sitter how to set limits with Mike and follow through with consequences, both positive and negative. The foster mother did succeed in helping the baby sitter with limits and consequences.

As Mike's behavior improved, the weekends became less stressful. An apparent aspect in the ecological system at this time was the increasing adequacy of the foster parents to accept primary responsibility for managing successfully their family life. Mike's behavior at the Re-ED school and at home was more appropriate. He was blooming within his new reality.

An attractive alternative not likely to be realized is to have the public schools take over the liaison function when parents are not up to the responsibility and the child is too young; alas, schools generally define their role so narrowly that they do not readily accept as a responsibility a broad concern for the development of a child. Yet someone must continue to perform the liaison function after a child leaves a Re-ED program. Parents are the preferred choice—or the child himself when he is old enough. Some schools can doubtlessly take on this function when parents are not up to it. Or a social agency case worker may agree to do it. Sometimes it makes sense for a family friend to assume the responsibility. Regardless of who takes on the role, the availability of information will be essential to success. Ecosystems cannot work well without the ready flow of information. All living systems require effective information feedback loops to correct behavior on the basis of the consequences of behavior. Thus, the liaison teacher-counselor must have as a primary objective the building of self-perpetuating information networks in the ecosystems defined by children who are associated with Re-ED programs.

Step 4: Planning Withdrawal of Re-ED from the Ecosystem. In the early days of discovering what we meant by psychological, educational, and ecological strategies in working with seriously disturbed children, we used to talk about "putting the child back into his ecosystem." This reveals our early inadequate grasp of the meaning of ecological concepts. There is no possible way for an agency to return a child to the ecosystem that is, in the first instance, defined by the being of that child. Our early error was an example of the now familiar confusion between "ecosystem" and "environment." At any one time, the ecosystem is composed of the people and places, including the child, that contribute to the variance in what happens to the child. Re-ED becomes a part of that system for as brief a period of time as possible and then withdraws from the system, remaining attentive to it should reentry appear desirable in the interest of the child. For convenience, we sometimes refer to this process as "discharge," but it must be clear that in so doing we are borrowing an inadequate term from medicine. A better term is "graduation"; we much prefer that. It bespeaks the normal process of growing up, maturing, accomplishing objectives.

An ecological conference was scheduled by the liaison teacher-counselor with all members from the key social systems. They would review the strategies in progress and project a graduation date from the Re-ED school for Mike. The graduation date was a far earlier date than anyone would have anticipated when Mike was first enrolled at the Re-ED school. At this conference, the foster parents said that they had decided to apply for the adoption of Mike. They had discussed their desire to adopt him with their own parents, who were claimed by Mike as his foster grandparents. They supported the adoption.

The liaison teacher-counselor intensified her contacts with the public school personnel, and enrollment planning became specific. The appropriate teacher was selected. The teacher and principal visited the Re-ED school to observe Mike and talk with the teaching teacher-counselors. Mike visited the public school with his foster mother and the liaison teacher-counselor. The teacher-counselors began to prepare Mike for meeting the expectations of a public school classroom where there were thirty children instead of eight.

We have noted elsewhere the importance of ritual and ceremony in the lives of children, as in the lives of us all. Graduation, an especially happy time in a Re-ED program, is such a ritual. It is an important rite of passage, affirming the progress the child and others have made, and it adds an affirmative note to an experience of separation, about which most children are likely to have ambivalent feelings. The liaison teacher-counselor works with the Re-ED team to plan the graduation ceremony and to be sure that all important members of the ecosystem are there to share in the occasion.

Graduation occurs when the major participants in the ecosystem judge that the probability of continued effective functioning of the system exceeds the probability that a new state of intolerable discord will develop. The liaison teacher-counselor arranges for the graduation of the child by working with families and schools, especially, to smooth the transition. For example, as a child begins to make progress toward graduation, visits to his new school may be arranged; sometimes a child may attend a regular school while remaining in the Re-ED program for a limited period of time. Sometimes special tutors are required. With adolescents, the inevitable transition from dependency on parents to autonomous living is sometimes facilitated by arrangements for the young person to live in a group home, some of which are affiliated with Re-ED programs. It may be desirable to alert a foreman to the transitional stresses that an adolescent may face in adjusting to his first job. An agency caseworker, a community center recreation worker, a public health nurse, or even a neighbor may be enlisted to ensure the continued satisfactory functioning of the ecosystem after Re-ED withdraws.

We reiterate here our emphasis on time and geography. It seems to us enormously important for children and adolescents to be involved in a Re-ED program for the shortest sensible period of time; any day beyond this minimum means that the child or adolescent is deprived of a day of living in normal circumstances. Some residential treatment centers hold on to children longer than is necessary in order that they can be discharged at a convenient time for reentry into public schools. Our view is that an unnecessarily prolonged stay in a residential program is likely to do far more damage to the child and the ecosystem than is likely to come about as a result of reentering a regular school at an unconventional time. It seems to us equally important that the ecosystem be contained within geographical limits that can sustain face-to-face communication among the people ultimately responsible for making the system work. A fifty-mile radius may well define the outer limits of programming effectiveness when ecosystem management is a major strategy.

The liaison teacher-counselor is responsible for arranging a final evaluation of the child. This makes it possible to check on the achievement of goals specified earlier in the enablement plan as well as to provide a reference point for assessing gains after discharge.

Mike was enrolled in public school seven months after he came to the Re-ED school. The liaison teacher-counselor monitored the process, staying in close touch with the teacher, the foster parents, and the welfare worker.

As Mike's adjustment progressed, the liaison teacher-counselor gradually phased out her self-initiating contacts. She gave assurance to all members of the key social environmental systems that she was as near as the telephone. Systematic follow-up by the liaison teacher-counselor continued monthly, quarterly, and finally every six months.

Mike's ecological system included at this point a home with foster parents who would eventually adopt him; a regular school; a neighborhood and community with playmates and other available human resources; a participating social agency with a welfare worker; a doctor, foster grandparents, a dentist, a minister, a baby sitter, family friends, and others (Figure 7). Mike's whole system

**Figure 7. Mike's Ecological System at the End of Seven Months
from the Point of Entry by the Liaison Specialist**

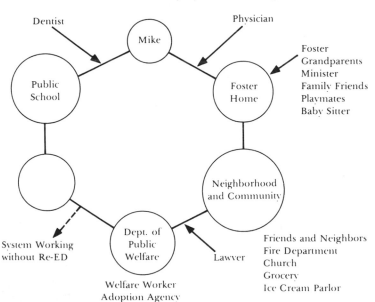

was functioning adequately, no longer needing the Re-ED school
or the liaison teacher-counselor to perform facilitating and col-
laborating functions. Individual and social system development
was in process.

Step 5: Follow-Up. Re-ED programs normally follow children for eighteen months after graduation. The degree of attention
is sufficient to enable members of the ecosystem to take advantage
of Re-ED resources if needed but not so assiduous as to inhibit the
system's working satisfactorily on its own. Practice varies from
program to program, but normally the liaison teacher-counselor
makes contact with the family several times during the eighteen-
month period. At the end of the period, some programs arrange
for a follow-up assessment of the child and the ecosystem. Sometimes it is necessary during this and subsequent periods for the liaison teacher-counselor to assist in making the ecosystem work
without having the child or adolescent reenter the program formally.

Children who have been in Re-ED programs often maintain
their ties over the years. Some schools have annual reunions of
graduates and their families. Frequently graduates will come back
individually to visit. These are ordinarily very happy times for
everyone.

About a year later, Mike and his foster mother were killed
in an automobile accident. The foster father was seriously injured.
The liaison teacher-counselor attended the double funeral at the
home church of the foster grandparents. After the service, the foster grandmother came to the liaison teacher-counselor, thanked
her for all her help, and said, "We gave Mike a good funeral, didn't
we?" The liaison teacher-counselor replied, "What is more important, Mrs. Smith, you gave him a good life." Death came tragically
to Mike, but it came in the midst of a caring and nurturing environment.

9

Working with
Individual Children

*Psychological and Educational
Principles*

Now let us turn to the young
person, to our relationships with him or her, and to what is meant
operationally by the process of reeducation. Here are an even
dozen underlying concepts that seem important to us as we try to
talk about psychological and educational strategies in working
with individuals in Re-ED programs.

Life Is to Be Lived Now

*Principle: Life is to lived now, not in the past, and lived in
the future only as a present challenge.*

We start with the assumption that each day is of great importance to young people; when an hour is neglected, allowed to
pass without reason and intent, teaching and learning go on nevertheless, and the child or adolescent may be the loser. In Re-ED,

no one waits for a special therapeutic hour. We try, as best we can, to make all hours special. We strive for immediate and sustained involvement in purposive and consequential living. We constantly test the optimistic hypothesis that if children and adolescents are challenged to live constructively, if they are given an opportunity for a constructive encounter with other young people and with decent adults, they will turn out well—and they do, most of the time.

It is hard to convey a sense of the pace of a day and a week in a Re-ED school. Living is intense; there is always something engaging at hand and something coming up that is intriguing. The short attention span of the troubled child or adolescent is explicitly recognized, and schedules are planned accordingly. There is breakfast and room cleaning and then, perhaps, responsibility for the morning assembly of the school, a community event. Later, goals for the day are discussed and set for each group member and the group as a whole. Then for two hours in the morning, when students are still fresh, attention turns to the demanding and sometimes fearsome tasks of reading, writing, and arithmetic, of history, literature, and science. Before fatigue and repetition bring boredom and failure, while success is still sweet in the air, there is a change of pace: a morning snack, a softball game, an excursion to get supplies, a questionnaire to be designed for a poll of neighbors regarding after-school jobs. As the day moves into the afternoon, the schedule becomes more varied and more physical, less demanding of disciplined attention. The arts and crafts center is always good for an hour or two of engrossed, purposeful activity, and a game on the playing field, carefully handled, can be a glorious experience. Neither crafts nor games are encumbered by special therapeutic intent; they are not "occupational therapy" or "recreational therapy" but a normal part of creative and even exuberant living. They are therapeutic in the sense that engaged living is therapeutic, so that the traditional labels "O.T." and "R.T." are patently tautological. That crafts and play are singled out for special "therapeutic" labels in traditional programs implies that residual activities of living are not expected to provide a therapeutic thrust. In Re-ED programs, the opposite assumption is made—namely, that every moment makes a difference, that therapy and living are the same thing, and that there is no need at all for these specialized and precious terms.

Afternoons may bring wider-ranging events: possibly a trip to the YMCA for swimming, a cookout at camp, a kite-flying expedition, a trip to a brick yard to get clay for crafts, a trial launching of new rockets, a rehearsal for a puppet show, a visit to the Museum of Science, a shopping trip to get decorations for a party, a visit to a hospital to see a sick friend, or an expedition to hunt fossils or arrowheads, and, for adolescents, a car wash to get money to buy clothes, an automobile driving lesson, a rehearsal for a radio show, or a project to clean a playground, and so on, in an infinite variety of things to do that are satisfying, instructive, and fun. The pace of the day may be broken several times for a pow-wow or group conference to settle some problem. In the late afternoon, television often provides a welcomed interlude in a Re-ED group just as in families, a time-out period before the renewal of body and spirit that comes with the evening meal.

After supper, there may be a time for study, carefully coordinated with the day's schoolwork, and longer for older groups than for younger. Then there may come a time for reading aloud, for story telling, for group singing, for planning for the next day, or for a special trip. Most groups use this time for a formal and regularly scheduled pow-wow or rap session. The group meets in a place set aside for serious purposes to review the day, to assess what went well and what not so well, to consider special problems (such as a growing feud between two group members) and what can be done to straighten things out, to plan for the next day so that it may be more satisfying, and to give each person an opportunity to talk about special feelings and about his or her progress in achieving goals set for the day or week.

At bedtime, going-to-bed rituals get established, and private talks with a friend or the teacher-counselor occur with increasing frequency. By this time, usually everyone is exhausted, the teacher-counselor included, and sleep comes readily. Re-ED schools have remarkably few problems at night (such as seem to plague more confined institutions and require them to make extensive use of drugs), simply because the students are thoroughly tired and, when things have gone well, thoroughly satisfied with the day they have just lived.

Discordant behaviors occur in Re-ED schools, of course, and measures for the control of disruptive behavior are available to meet emergencies. But the dominant strategy is to make the daily program so interesting, so forward moving, that there is neither time nor inclination for the students to engage in much discordant behavior. When the program is going well, it is difficult for a Re-ED student to behave disturbed; there is no need for it.

The Re-ED day is planned (with the help of students) by the team of teacher-counselors, whose schedules are arranged to provide time for a daily conference, thus making possible an articulation of the day and night programs, the achievement of consistent strategies in working with particular children, and, through the liaison teacher-counselor, a responsiveness to the requirements of the child or adolescent's ecosystem. It is not possible, of course, to have a fixed curriculum or schedule of activities or unit of work for even a single group of children, much less for a school. Every day has to be planned anew, and then, in the course of a day, plans must be altered to respond to unpredictable developments. The goal is clear, however, and that is to give each student in the course of every day a large number of successful and instructive experiences in living. We try to reverse the success-failure ratio in the lives of the children and adolescents. Failure has been their most constant companion; we do everything possible to help them get the feel of success. This requires, of course, that each day's activities be tuned to the needs and capacities of individuals, and that the course of events in each day be modulated to keep success rates high. This is where the artistry of the teacher-counselor comes into full play. In a Re-ED school, young people learn, here and now, that life can be lived on terms satisfactory to society and satisfying to themselves. To paraphrase Taft (1937, p. 17): "In the mastery of this day, the child or adolescent learns, in principle, the mastery of all days."

Trust Is Essential

Principle: Trust between child and adult is essential, the foundation on which all other principles rest, the glue that holds teaching and learning together, the beginning point for reeducation.

The development of trust is the first step in the process of reeducation. Disturbed children and adolescents are conspicuously impaired in their ability to learn from adults. The mediation process is blocked or distorted by the young person's experience-based conviction that adults are deceptive, that they are an unpredictable source of hurt and help. The disturbed child or adolescent faces most adults with an expectation of punishment, rejection, derision, withdrawal of love, or indifference. He is acutely impaired in the very process by which mature ways of living may be acquired. A first step, then, in the reeducation process is the development of trust between child and adult. Trust, coupled with understanding, is the beginning point of a new learning experience, an experience that helps a child or an adolescent know that he can use an adult to learn many things: how to read, how to be affectionate, how to be one's self without fear or guilt. Trust is the glue that holds teaching and learning together.

Most children grow up with the set: "Most adults are usually loving and willing to be helpful." The disturbed child or adolescent makes the opposite assumption: "Most adults cannot be trusted." The first step in the reeducation process is to help the young person make a new and very important distinction: that some adults indeed cannot be trusted, while other adults can be counted on as predictable sources of support, understanding, and affection, as well as of help in such practical matters as learning to read or getting a job.

There is nothing to be gained by trying to persuade a child or an adolescent that this difference among adults exists before he has experienced both kinds of relationships, and especially not before he has known a trustworthy adult. Even then, talking about the general idea of trust will probably be of little help. The core experience is that of being genuinely close to an adult without getting hurt. Intimacy with safety is the cardinal requirement. Perhaps human intimacy is a biologically based requirement, a derivative, in the species, of natural selection. But even if genetic factors are not involved, experience in infancy is sufficient to create a learned need for human closeness.

We are sometimes asked how one goes about the building of trust, and we have to say that we don't know, explicitly; yet the ability is apparent in a marked degree in successful teacher-counselors. Some guidelines suggest themselves. A teacher-counselor should be steady in her concern for a child, and her concern must be genuine. She must do what she says she will do; that is, she must be reasonably predictable in important areas. But predictability and consistency are not altogether sufficient because her behavior must be sensitively tuned to the uncertainties of a particular child or adolescent at a particular time. On occasion, and in areas manageable by a child, an unexpected bit of behavior may be a source of surprised delight. How can one rule on such a subtlety? Only artistry can help. A teacher-counselor must be able to define appropriate limits for a particular student at a particular period of growing and to require the student to live within the limits but, again, drawing the limits sensibly and not rigidly. Predictable boundaries are a major source of security for a boy who is discovering the dimensions of himself and his world, and the adult who can provide secure perimeters will gain in his trust.

The teacher-counselor, to nurture trust, must be a whole person, not a detached therapist. She must know intuitively just how much of her own life she should bring into her relationships with her students; she must not burden them heavily with her cares, yet she should not seem aloof from cares and commitments. She will nurture trust further by keeping communication with a child at an optimum level, being neither aloof nor inquisitive, but clearly concerned. How can such sensitivity be prescribed? And she gains a child's confidence through her own competence, quietly shared, through her ability to shape a pot, scull a canoe, wield an ax, make clear the intricacies of arithmetic or algebra. And so on. But how unsatisfactory are all such formulations! The sentences skirt the problem and never truly get to its heart. There is a precise rule for riding a bicycle. To preserve balance, the front wheel must be turned in the direction of imbalance in an amount inversely proportional to the square of the speed of travel. Yet if someone tried consciously to apply this rule in riding a bicycle, he would probably break his neck. So it is with being a teacher-counselor. You just have to know how to do it. With a little practice, some people seem to know what to do. Others will never learn.

Linda Ann cried frequently and fought bitterly. She sometimes seemed to be in a state of panic; at other times, she seemed to be using these tactics knowingly to control the behavior of others—notably, her mother and also the staff at Wright School. After about six weeks in the program, she began to make progress in trusting adults and in controlling her outbursts. On her return from a weekend at home, she cried for forty-five minutes. The assistant principal stayed with her, supporting her in her struggle for self-control but insisting that she stop crying before joining the other children. She told her teacher-counselor later: "I did the best I've ever done. I didn't bite or kick." On Monday night, she sat very close to her teacher-counselor and said: "It is . . . could it be like you are my mother here . . . I mean, you know, like I have a mother here too." The teacher-counselor said: "You certainly do. You can count on me."

The next night, Linda Ann said to the teacher-counselor: "You know, crying makes me feel worse. It hurts me inside. It hurts my feelings when I cry." And later: "I don't know what happens to me. I get upset and then I get real mean. I don't like it." She seemed to be reaching out for help, with a new attitude, that of trying to understand herself and alleviate some pain. The next evening, Linda Ann was quiet and calm. She asked for some construction paper and made a cut-out figure which she gave to the teacher-counselor. She said: "You can put this in your room. It's for you." This was the first time that she had made anything and not put it immediately in her suitcase. The two teacher-counselors and the assistant principal all drew clear lines between acceptable and unacceptable behavior and supported her strongly in her tentative reaching out in a new mode. On Thursday, she had an exceptionally good day in school, showing a level of ability that had not been suspected. On the last morning of the week, she slept until 7:00 and did not cry at all before going home.

The complexities of the problem of creating trust and the artistry required for its solution are well illustrated in the following comments by a teacher-counselor:*

One of the most difficult distinctions for some new staff (myself included) is between "like" and "trust." The teacher-counselor plays an adult role and must make some decisions children don't like. Good rapport develops as the child learns that the adult *will* make decisions and will back them up. What seems to confound the new staff member more than anything is the business of fairness. Disturbed children and adolescents are acutely sensitive to fairness whenever they sense that they are on the short end. Their arguments are so convincing that—if the T.C. is not careful—he will find himself caught up in frantic oscillations of

*David Friedlein, teacher-counselor at Wright School.

position. But firm "yes" and "no" decisions (that the T.C. will hold to) are a great source of security for the children. At last, adults can be trusted! There is an important exception. While I typically refuse to judge in fairness disputes (though I will always accept verbal expression of the related feelings), I sometimes sense that I've really made a mistake. In such cases, I am never reluctant to admit this to the boys. This is as important as the yes-no business above. Adults are human, and there's no loss when kids know it.

Let me pursue this fairness business a bit further. Frequently, I find it necessary to grant "special privileges" to particular children. For instance, I have loaned one of my boys the school's autoharp. Buddy is interested in music and, knowing that his interest would extinguish if he could not experience some sort of "instant success," I speculated that the autoharp might provide sufficiently rapid gratification. As you might expect, this raised all sorts of group problems. While it would be fair to pass the instrument around, giving each child equal time, it is unlikely that this would be of benefit to anyone. Rather, I let it be known that Buddy is using the autoharp right now. Various group members freely vent their feelings (jealousy, anger toward me). I listen, and discussion centers on how the group should handle the "problem." Meanwhile, Buddy has pieced together a few chords into songs, another boy is working at the guitar, and two other boys have improvised some drums. A combo (called "The Teacher's Pets") has evolved. Buddy, who was not previously motivated to learn chords on his electric guitar, has demonstrated a renewed interest. Easily frustrated, he will practice on his own instrument and then return to the autoharp. The periods of guitar practice, however, are lengthening, and I expect that Buddy will soon make a complete transition. Special privileges are varied and numerous, and ultimately even out. One boy usually helps me set up the movie projector, another uses the school's guitar, another feeds Stormy (our mascot) her evening meal, and another is a Museum Aide.

Gaining and holding the trust of an adolescent boy or girl requires a special skill and understanding. It is frequently hard to do, since the adolescent has two tasks, one general and one particular, that inhibit the development of trust. There is first the general need of all adolescents to establish their independence; thus, they are more likely to turn to each other for counsel than to reach out or respond to an older person. Then there are individual past experiences that make some adolescents especially wary of older people. An important beginning point for the adult is to accept genuinely the adolescent's need for privacy, autonomy, and idiosyncratic selfhood. Patience, a reserved availability, and a dependable acceptance are part of the adult's needed response pattern. Something external for adolescent and adult to engage in together—shooting baskets, repairing a car, weaving, macrame, playing chess—can reduce anxiety and make open talk easier. Backpacking, rock climbing, and white-water canoeing require a mutual commitment for safety. Competence in whatever the task is and enthusiasm for it are all-important. Finally, for the adult to let himself be dependent on the adolescent in appropriate circumstances is to nurture respect and trust.

Ronald A., at home for his first weekend after admission to Crockett Academy, threatened his father with a butcher knife. The father, who was out of work and drinking heavily, had been badgering the boy for two days. When Ronald threatened him with the knife, the father called the police. A terrified Ronald was taken to the juvenile detention center and put in a locked cell. Ronald's mother called his teacher-counselor, a man, who went to the center, initiated arrangements for his "diversion" from the court, and stayed with him for fourteen hours until he was released. The trust thus engendered was pivotal in helping Ronald modify his own behavior and make plans to move into a group home and get a job while completing his senior year in high school.

What does it take, this building of trust between teacher and child? First of all, if one wants to gain the trust of a child, it is necessary to believe that the problem of trust is real and that progress toward its solution will mean progress toward the child's learning. Then one must have time or take time simply to be with the child. One must also be able to recognize the child's distrust and to accept without dismay—or retaliation—his swift and sure thrusts to hurt and keep others away; to recognize that a child's feelings have a validity quite independent of other people's reality; to modulate expectations of a child's achievement until success, however modest, becomes his frequent joy; to be patient, infinitely patient; to be utterly dependable, to keep one's word; to seek help from objective observers of one's own behavior with the child, for one cannot always distance himself properly from a self-defining commitment; to use private resources for personal understanding and support, especially when the going is tough; and to be genuinely content, no, joyous, when a child begins to catch fire with learning, however limited or grand his flame may be. It can be done; we vouchsafe that.

Competence Is Crucial

Principle: Competence makes a difference, and children and adolescents should be helped to be good at something, especially at schoolwork.

The ability to do something well gives a child or an adolescent confidence and self-respect and gains acceptance by peers, by teachers, and, unnecessary as it might seem, even by parents. In a society as achievement oriented as ours, a person's worth is established in substantial measure by the ability to produce or perform. Acceptance without productivity is a beginning point in the process of reeducation, but an early goal is to help the young person become good at something.

What, then, in the process of reeducation, does the acquisition of competence mean? It means first and foremost the gaining of competence in school skills, in reading, writing, and arithmetic (for all ages), and in other subjects as well: algebra, mechanical drawing, secretarial work, computer operations. If a boy feels inadequate in school, inadequacy can become a pervasive theme in his life, leading to a consistent pattern of failure to work up to his level of ability. Underachievement in school is the single most common characteristic of emotionally disturbed children and adolescents. We regard it as sound strategy to attack directly the problem of adequacy in school, for its intrinsic value as well as for its indirect effect on the young person's perception of his worth and his acceptance by people who are important in his world. A direct attack on the problem of school skills does not mean a gross assault in some area of deficiency. On the contrary, it requires utmost skill and finesse on the part of the teacher-counselor to help a disturbed child or adolescent move into an area where defeat has so often been known, where failure is a well-rooted expectancy, where a printed page can evoke flight or protest or crippling anxiety.

A child who overcomes a reading handicap often gains dramatically in general adjustment. The common assumption that emotional disturbance causes reading difficulties leads to the conclusion that the emotional difficulty must be cleared up before progress can be made in the improvement of reading. This is a too-simple conception of the relationship between symptom and cause. All evidence calls at least for an interaction hypothesis to account for the frequent improvement in adjustment following improvement in basic academic skills.

So Re-ED "keeps school." This is an old-fashioned phrase that underscores our old-fashioned emphasis on the importance of school in the life of young people. School is not regarded as something that can wait until the student gets better, as though he were recovering from measles or a broken leg. School is the very stuff of a child's or adolescent's problems, and, consequently, a primary source of instruction in living, in the achievement of competence. Special therapy rooms are not needed; the classroom is a natural setting for a constructive relationship between a disturbed youngster and a competent, concerned adult.

But academic competence is not our only goal. Here are some perceptive observations by a night teacher-counselor* that illuminate briefly the process of helping a child grow in competence:

My personal bias here is to shift the emphasis away from academics per se. This is not to underrate academics but simply to compensate for what, I feel, may be an overemphasis. True, school performance comes first, and I would prefer it no other way. Each afternoon, I review, with my teammate, each child's work. Much of the evening discussion relates to the class day, praise is distributed—in abundance—where appropriate, and children who failed to complete their assignments are required to do so before entering into the evening activities. Many children, formerly not motivated, "get hooked," as we say, and actually become quite excited about their progress in class. This is rewarding to both the day teacher-counselor and myself, since it is our prime goal with most children. Nevertheless, I think that we occasionally lose touch with reality and get caught up in our Utopian classroom, where individual progress is emphasized regardless of where the child is performing academically. The cold truth is that a large majority of

*David Friedlein, teacher-counselor at Wright School.

these children come to us several years behind in school performance. While the child may make terrific gains—and four months' progress in four months' time may represent a 500 percent increase in learning rate—he may be returning to his own school behind his classmates. My suggestion is that competence is not limited to the classroom. We must help the child find other hooks on which to hang his hat. My bias is that this should be a primary goal of the afternoon and evening program. Climbing a mountain, firing a model rocket, learning how to play a musical instrument, planning and taking an extended field trip, building a bookshelf in shop, entering the Soap Box Derby, erecting a teepee, laying a trail, and building a cabin are experiences with a great deal of meaning and sustaining power. While the child may still be unable to read very well, these are experiences that he can share with his parents and peers. The competencies gained are assets which will help keep the child afloat while he tries to overcome the academic gap.

Sometimes it is hard to say what was done to help a particular boy or girl grow in competence and grace. Sometimes we think that we simply get out of their way, removing some of the restraints in their world that have been thwarting their normal growth, and avoiding imposing our own solutions. But even in these instances, the skillful hand and responsive heart of the skilled teacher-counselor show themselves, as they do in this account of the flowering of Dannie.

Dannie, Age Nine*

Dannie was nine on admission to Wright School. His public school teacher and principal described Dannie as an underachieving, hyperactive daydreamer who would not enter into activities with other children. I saw him as a child who seemed to carry a great load of worry. His speech was almost unintelligible. He was quite retarded academically, though apparently of at least normal intelligence. It was almost as if he were too concerned about something to join actively into life.

What we did for Dannie is hard to pinpoint. I can only say that this child unfolded like a flower right before our eyes—day by day—and I don't think we could have stopped it. I can guess at two things we did.

*This account was written by Frances Smith, teacher-counselor at Wright School.

Dannie was placed in a group with adults who said, in effect, "You are nine and a person. Children are here because there are things about themselves that they want to change. We are here to help. Problems in living are not always fun, nor is it fun to be alone with them. We will work with you on these problems. But there are many joys, too, and happiness. These we can find together. Perhaps some of the joys will be in facing and dealing with the problems. As a nine-year-old and a person, you have rights, choices, responsibilities. You may like or dislike, do and not do, give your opinion."

The very first night, we conquered one problem—sleeping pills. Dannie said he didn't like to take them but he must in order to sleep at all. I suggested he try a night without them. The next morning, he had a smiling face.

Dannie seemed unable to resist joining in. When difficulties arose, he learned to talk about them and was soon able to stand up for himself. He was becoming a dirty, daring, self-confident, happy nine-year-old.

The most noticeable thing about Dannie when he came was his infantile speech. His difficulty in communication increased when he was upset or when he asked something he was unsure of. We proposed working on his speech problem, but Dannie at first insisted there was nothing wrong with the way he talked. I therefore chose to attack the problem informally by correcting him when we were more or less alone. After about two months in the group, he came to me and after much grimacing finally asked me to help him talk better. Reason: so people could understand him. We set up a half-hour period after dinner every day, during which we could work on his speech. Our educational consultant and a speech therapist from the Raleigh schools helped set up the program. We made tapes and compared them day by day for signs of progress. Dannie was delighted. What followed was again rather dramatic. He played his tapes for the group. He practiced at home. He asked for corrections after the group sessions. His parents reported that he began going to the store alone. Much to his delight, he was able to ask for things and was understood.

The formal speech sessions dropped out as he became busier being a happy nine-year-old and as he became comfortable being corrected openly by me, by the other children, and especially by himself.

Dannie returned home in many ways the same boy. But most importantly he saw himself as a worthwhile somebody. He saw problems as conquerable rather than conquering, and that living could be exciting and enjoyable rather than burdened, gloomy, and lonely.

I choose to tell about Dannie because he seems to show that

putting problems in perspective and working on them—plus adding the ingredients of love, happiness, excitement, and learning—can help a child see life as something to look forward to rather than to be faced with increasing dread; that recognizing and dealing with the speech problem openly and directly promoted competence and accelerated the growing process; that just living in an atmosphere where life problems are faced and dealt with today makes tomorrow more comfortable and bright; that expectations of being able to be a happy nine-year-old help one be so; that people can be trusted to give and take warmth and help; that life must not be lived entirely alone—that one can share things and feelings; and that one can reach out of unhappiness for help.

What is considered work or play depends on attitudes and labels as much as on what is being done; yet activities regarded as work are important in the achievement of competence for both child and adolescent. Schoolwork is obviously central in Re-ED, and work it is, beyond doubt. But the important component is the outcome in success or failure. Most students in a Re-ED school will hate the classroom at first; books and blackboards, teachers and tests are symbols of failure, humiliation, and inadequacy. The Herculean task of the teacher-counselor is to turn all this on end, to win the confidence of the child or adolescent, to lead him step by step to a successful encounter with learning. The small size of the group in the classroom helps make possible the required individualization of instruction. But the skill of the teacher-counselor in selecting and pacing the work for students so that each will experience both challenge and mastery is the heart of the matter. Teacher-counselors repeatedly report that children get some of their greatest delights from gaining competence in their schoolwork.

The camping program of a Re-ED school provides an opportunity for competence building. Work at camp is especially valuable with disturbed children and adolescents, for the rewards and punishments are contingent on foreseeable, natural outcomes and not simply on the approval of adults. Several schools have extensive camping programs, and Pressley Ridge has a year-round wilderness program for adolescent boys. Students live in the woods in tents or hogans built by themselves and do much of their own cooking. If they secure their tents carefully in preparation for a storm, their beds remain dry; if they do a careless job, they may

well find their bedding wet. If everyone plans well and works together, a splendid meal, flavored with the pride of work well done,
may be the outcome; if people goof off, they eat poorly. If a
canoe trip is planned well, everyone is comfortable and well fed;
if not, the trip can be miserable. Camp is especially productive of
such instructive situations, but they can, of course, be found or
contrived anywhere. (This program is described in more detail in
Chapter Eleven.)

Students may need extra money for some special project,
perhaps for a trip, a movie, or a piece of equipment. They might
decide to raise the necessary money by washing cars. The students
make arrangements for a place and needed supplies and equipment; they work out detailed criteria for an adequate job and set
up an inspection system; they print and sell tickets, keep books on
the operation, do the work, inspect it, and then review the whole
operation to see how it might be improved the next time. There
are many variations on this theme, which, if not overworked, can
be an important and enjoyable source of instruction in responsibility and maturity. Not all work projects need to produce money, of
course. Picking up trash in the neighborhood or collecting old
newspapers can be a rewarding exercise in civic responsibility and
may win appreciation quite as satisfying as money.

Much of the work may involve a direct contribution to the
school or to the program of a particular group. The arts and crafts
program at Cumberland House (described in Chapter Ten) has provided an endless stream of interesting and worthwhile things to do,
projects that were fun at the time and that usually have left something of value to others. A trip to the brick yard means shoveling
hundreds of pounds of clay into containers to be hauled back to
school for processing. The processing itself is a difficult task requiring careful work, but the result is a supply of excellent clay
body that will be used by a number of children in making many
hand-shaped forms. The children have built two studios, nailing
the nails where they really counted and doing the painting that
gave the rooms an inimitable character. The children have also
made tables, wedging boards, easels, a puppet stage, bird houses,
two paddle-wheel boats, and a series of marvelously contrived tree
houses. One of the most satisfactory projects involved cutting out
and mounting the wooden letters that make up the sign in front of

Cumberland House. It is a handsome and useful achievement, one that seems somehow to be owned by group after group of children. Incidentally, one of the by-products of having the children contribute directly to the decoration of the buildings is that they then take better care of everything. There is very little destructive behavior in Re-ED schools.

With adolescents, work moves from the shelter of school or camp to the real world. Jobs are an immediate source of learning and maturing, of increased competence and independence, and of movement toward adult status. The school curriculum puts increasing emphasis on preparation for a job or for further education or training; counseling about such matters grows in importance. As in other aspects of the Re-ED program, clarity about objectives, specificity of means to ends, and concern for outcomes are evident. Group discussions shape attitudes toward work and the future. Practice sessions develop skill in preparing for a job interview. Biographical sketches are written, criticized, and redone. The ecological perspective in Re-ED makes clear that success on a job may be determined by situational factors as well as by the competence of the person. If an adolescent has had some special adjustment problem, the liaison teacher-counselor may discuss the matter with the job supervisor and get him or her to assist in making the job a success experience.

The many competences acquired in the Re-ED experience, accumulated, may permit a child or adolescent to say accurately of himself: "I am a competent person."

Time Is an Ally

Principle: Time is an ally, working on the side of growth in a period of development when life has a tremendous forward thrust.

We have often said that time is an ally in the process of re-education. Time works on our side and in the child's interest at a period of development when life has a tremendous forward thrust. What to make of time may well be the most important practical and theoretical decision confronting a staff responsible for designing a program to help disturbed children and adolescents. Time is a practical commodity; it is stuff to be used in particular ways, to do things to make a difference in the lives of young people. Time is also the concept most relevant to existential being, to beginnings and endings, to comings and departures, to what one is and might become, to birth and death. An awareness of the significance of time in human affairs is one of the most exacting criteria of maturity. Otto Rank, with profound insight into human nature, made the management of time central to his therapeutic theory. The management of time is the management of life.

From childhood through adolescence, the individual grows steadily in stature, in intellectual capacity, in physical skill, in knowledge, in sensitivity. These years may prove to be optimum for providing corrective experiences for children who have been given a poor psychological start in life. We do not assume some mystical growth force as an explanatory principle but simply note descriptively that young people are still open to experience and change, and that they have surplus energy to support the operation. A broken bone knits more rapidly at six and sixteen than at sixty; we assume a comparable vitality in the psychological domain. Reeducation may simply speed up a process that would occur in an unknown percentage of children anyway. A long stay in a treatment center may actually slow down the process of learning to be oneself, to be effective, to be mature. The great tragedy is that children and adolescents can get caught up in institutional arrangements that must inexorably run their course, insensitive to the individuality and special promise of a particular child. In Re-ED, we try at least to avoid getting in the way of the normal restorative processes of life.

In studies of the effectiveness of therapeutic interventions, the intervention is regarded as effective only if the patient improves more than he would have, simply through the passage of time, without treatment. Thus, a control group, a group that receives no therapy, provides a basis for comparisons. Not uncommonly, the control group makes impressive gains, thereby providing evidence that in life things tend to get better rather than worse. A child is most likely to be referred to a mental health facility at a time of crisis in his own development or of breakdown in the functioning of his home or school. A decision to seek professional help is usually made at a low point in the child's behavior and in the family's ability to sustain him; improvement thereafter may often be expected. The child gets a better hold on himself; things at school settle down; the family gets a bit better organized. To provide nothing more than a benign sanctuary for a child at a time of crisis is a worthy endeavor. The reeducation process thus claims time as an ally, not just an effect to be surpassed by some other intervention.

In planning Re-ED, we resolved to do everything possible to cut down the length of stay, to separate children from their families and schools (even for five days a week) only as long as we are clearly helping, and only up to the point where the system can operate in a reasonably satisfactory manner without our assistance. We feel that limited goals are sensible goals and that one must expend penuriously, and account honestly for, each day that a child is kept away from home, school, and community, from the normal arrangements for living in our society. We assume that there will be substantial individual differences in responsiveness of children and adolescents to the Re-ED program. Some may stay in a school a few days or weeks; others may require a number of months, even a year or so. But we have from the outset been determined to avoid the trap of assuming that some finite amount of time is required to let a therapeutic process occur. Experience has shown that our aspirations are soundly based. The average length of stay of a child in a Re-ED school today is from four to eight months, and the variability remains great, as it should.

Many programs admit children for a definite period, but that period can be adjusted if necessary. The time limit gives everyone a definite goal to work toward. The child knows that his task is to get ready to go home and back to school and that he has so many months to do it in, with our help. The parents are made sharply aware at the outset of their continuing responsibility; they cannot abandon their child to an indeterminate future, and they have so many months to do what must be done to provide for him as satisfactory a home as they can. The adolescent knows that he must make it in school or on a job, with the help of his family or independently. Agencies are given a definite deadline; if special arrangements are to be made for the child—if he is to be placed in another home, for example—there is a date for getting arrangements made. The child's regular school knows that he is expected to return and can keep a place open. Perhaps most important of all, our own staff, the teacher-counselors and all supporting people, have a definite goal to work toward, and this makes a big difference in countering a drift toward longer and longer periods of stay.

It is interesting that Wright School, with an explicit four-month-stay policy, has consistently had a somewhat more rapid turnover of children from Cumberland House.

How has Wright School managed to maintain its emphasis on *short-term* residential programming? In the early days, no one was certain what types of disturbed/disturbing children should be accepted into the Wright School program or for what length of time the optimum stay should be. Initially, referrals were very slow in coming. In fact, six children were enrolled during the first six months of operation; it was not until after the second complete fiscal year that full occupancy of twenty-four residents was achieved. Therefore, with observers and evaluators watching closely, we were not about to be too choosy as to which classifications of children (diagnoses) were to be admitted. With only a few exceptions, if a child was of elementary school age, if he had behavioral or learning difficulties, if the parents were willing to have him enroll, and if we believed that we might be of help, he was accepted.

There was some attempt initially to be flexible in determining lengths of stay. However, before the first youngster was enrolled, we decided on four months for an average stay. With few exceptions, that period of time was adhered to, though there were notable exceptions of six, eight, nine, and even twelve months' enrollment in the earlier years.

By 1970 (seven years into our history), these two decisions (taking almost anyone who met our minimum admissions criteria and adhering to a four-month limit) seemed to have proven quite sound. A longitudinal follow-up study (Gregory, Sechinger, and Anderson, 1971) of a randomly selected group from a total of 314 children served indicated that beyond six months no appreciable gains were made either by the child or by his natural support system back home. In similar fashion, no discernible or significant differences in success could be linked with any particular type of child.

Two happy events of no minor consequence also resulted from that liberal admissions policy and arbitrary length-of-stay decision. First, our waiting list never grew to the point of creating extreme frustration for referring agencies in attempts to get children enrolled in a timely fashion; and, second, our reputation for accepting children whom no one else would consider was rapidly built. Success, indeed, bred success and continues with us today.

Symptoms Can and Should Be Controlled

Principle: Self-control can be taught and children and adolescents helped to manage their behavior without the development of psychodynamic insight; and symptoms can and should be controlled by direct address, not necessarily by an uncovering therapy.

It is standard doctrine in psychodynamic theory that symptoms should not be treated, that the symptom removed will simply be replaced by another, and that the task of the therapist is to uncover underlying conflicts against which the symptom is a defense, thus eliminating the need for any symptom at all. In Re-ED, we contend that symptoms are important in their own right and deserve direct attention. The assumption is that children and adolescents get rejected in large part because of identifiable behaviors that are regarded as unacceptable by family, friends, school, or community. Regardless of the person's level of maturity, adjustment, ego strength, or other index of psychological health, some symptoms are more obnoxious than others. For example, the symptoms that maladjusted boys develop are more unacceptable to schools than are the symptoms developed by maladjusted girls. For the moment, we do not concern ourselves with the adequacy of the family, friendship group, school or community but instead accept some accommodation to them as a de facto requirement in the young person's life. Indeed, for all their inadequacies, we see families, friends, schools, and neighborhoods as a more substantial source of psychological nourishment, of the stuff of adequacy and contentment, than a reeducation center could ever be. The problem is to help children and adolescents make effective contact with normal sources of affection, support, instruction, and discipline. A first step in this process is to help them unlearn particular habits that keep high the probability that they will be rejected by people whose support they must have if they are to grow. We also work on a principle of parsimony, which instructs us to give first preference to explanations involving the assumption of minimum pathology, as contrasted to deep explanations and the derogation of all else as superficial.

Hundreds of incidents in Re-ED illustrate the deliberate management of symptoms, some of minor consequence and some of major importance in the young person's life. We have not observed that new symptoms replace the objectionable behavior that has been removed. On the contrary, the students usually seem proud of their achievement, and their satisfaction is often shared by their parents and by others in their group. Symptoms doubtlessly have functional significance in the total economy of the person's life. Something in the system sustains the undesirable behavior. But there are often noxious consequences, too; the symptom may be embarrassing, may deprive the person of opportunities to do things, or may repeatedly create trouble. As a consequence, the mastery of a symptom usually brings substantial gains. But if the person is "hung up" on the symptom, he needs help to get the behavior under control. Many different approaches have been used, as is clear in the following accounts.

Reg, Age Seven

Reg was a very small child, age seven, not much more than half the size of the other children of his age. He had an acute fear of insects, which was the reason for his being referred to Cumberland House: he was afraid to go out of doors without an adult, and he refused to go to school. The symptom may have been indicative of deep conflict, but we decided to ignore this possibility and to treat the symptom directly, through a carefully planned program of desensitization. The symptom had to be removed as a precondition to his full participation in the school program, an experience he needed to gain in competence in order to compensate for his very small size.

A day teacher-counselor designed and carried out the plan. She first gained Reg's confidence. She spent a lot of time with him for a couple of weeks, accompanying him out of doors to protect him from insects. She then directly appealed to Reg to get his support for a plan to overcome his fear. In the first step, the teacher-counselor held Reg on her lap and read to him about bugs and showed him pictures of bugs. Sometimes this was done while Reg was eating (in a classical tactic first described by Watson and Rayner in 1920). Then she introduced a dead bug in a jar, and Reg handled the jar. More dead bugs were added. Then she put a single, small, live bug in the jar; and then more bugs. Reg really enjoyed it all; there was excitement, but the danger never got too great. Finally, the teacher-counselor got Reg to pick up a small dead bug, then a large dead bug, then a small live bug, and finally a larger live bug—the whole process carefully paced, and each success acclaimed. In the meantime, Reg continued to study about bugs, their names and habits and so on. Reg was fascinated and learned well. The whole procedure was started indoors, then moved to a porch, and finally out of doors at camp. Before the summer was over, Reg became an ardent bug collector.

Bert, Age Twelve

Bert was the only child of a long-divorced mother. A mental health center had urged his admission to Cumberland House because he had, at age twelve, begun to develop strong effeminate tendencies. He wore eye shadow and mascara, painted his nails, and postured in an effeminate manner—activities that his mother sometimes encouraged and sometimes censured. When he was admitted, it was agreed that we would work primarily to strengthen the masculine component in his behavior and self-concept. He was assigned to a teacher-counselor team made up of a feminine female and a masculine male. They agreed to ignore his feminine behavior and encourage engagement in masculine activities. The man on the team served as a model for identification, which had been lacking in the child's life, and the woman admired and encouraged his progress toward being an all-around boy. The mental health center worked with the mother to get her interested in things outside herself and her child. Soon after coming to Re-ED, Bert dropped the specific behaviors symbolic of the female role and began gradually to participate successfully in male role activities. He was introduced to the YMCA, and arrangements were made for him to continue his activities there on discharge. Follow-up three years later has shown him to be still somewhat effeminate but well within the range of what society can comfortably accept.

C. B., Age Seven

C. B., age seven, was the child of two busy professional people, one an engineer and the other a physician, who set exacting standards for him. He had a number of adjustment problems, but the one that made the parents willing to send him to a Re-ED school was his soiling. He had begun soiling himself several times a day, which distressed them immensely but did ensure him their attention. The teacher-counselor team decided to try simply ignoring it and leaving him to care for himself but otherwise supporting him in anything he wanted to do. The children avoided him when he smelled bad. The symptom subsided in a couple of weeks. The team then turned its attention to other inappropriate behaviors and to academic work. The liaison teacher-counselor worked with the parents over a period of several months, giving them help in behavior management. They were highly responsive, as was C. B. The parents became proud of him—and of themselves as well.

Tony, Age Nine

Tony was a nine-year-old boy who was unable to stay in his seat long enough to do any work. This kept him in trouble in his regular school. The teacher-counselors felt that Tony's hyperactivity was impulsive and that, if he had a way to restrain himself, he could break the habit of getting out of his seat. This change could lead to more adaptive behavior in other areas. The teacher-counselors and Tony talked about the problem. He came up with the practical suggestion of a seat belt that he could use to remind himself to stay at his desk. A seat belt was provided, and Tony buckled it around the back of his chair and his waist as soon as he entered the classroom. When he finished his work, he would remove it for the freedom he had earned. Tony wore the seat belt at other times during the day by choice. He was very proud of it and would tell everyone why he had it. Tony was prouder, however, a month later, when he returned the seat belt, stating that he no longer needed it.

Velma, Age Seventeen

Velma, age seventeen and quite bright, was greatly overweight. When she was a child, her weight was normal for her age; she began to gain weight at about the time she entered puberty, when her parents were divorced and Velma lived with her mother, who was obese. Velma had struggled mightily to control her weight but without success. She would go on stringent diets, but when frustrated or angry she would gorge herself with rich foods for days; at these times, she seemed always to be eating. She thought of herself as ugly and as "having a weak character." She had been caught shoplifting several times and was finally committed by the juvenile court to a Re-ED school.

The staff worked out a plan for helping her lose weight and gain in self-esteem, with the assistance of staff consultants, a pediatrician, and a psychologist skilled in behavior modification. Velma was assigned to an experimental co-ed unit, with a female day teacher-counselor to serve as a role model. The teacher-counselor was warm, attractive, and physically fit. A number of things were done. Each week, Velma set a goal for loss of weight, and she weighed herself daily. She kept a chart of her weight, privately at first, and then posted on the unit bulletin board, as the other group members began to encourage her, to remind her of her own rules, and to praise her for meeting a goal. She was taught techniques of controlling stimuli to overeating. When she lapsed in her diet—as she did, but with decreasing frequency—everyone ignored it; she got neither sympathy nor blame.

The day teacher-counselor worked with Velma to improve her appearance by attending to grooming, makeup, and dress. Arrangements were made with her mother for Velma to be rewarded for meeting her goals by something Velma wanted that also made her more attractive—a permanent early on and much later a trim pantsuit. The teacher-counselor got Velma to agree to talk with her when she felt frustrated or unhappy (including phone calls on weekends), and then later to share her feelings openly with others; this was perhaps the most important step taken. The teacher-counselor also got Velma to join her in running every morning, to raise her activity level. The liaison teacher-counselor worked with the mother to enlist her help with diet on the weekends and also arranged a part-time job for Velma as a clerk in an insurance office, to help her transition back to high school and to an adult role. These arrangements worked well. A follow-up eighteen months after graduation showed Velma to be controlling her weight, doing well in school, liking her job, and planning to go away to college.

Intelligence Can Be Taught

Principle: The cognitive competence of children and adolescents can be considerably enhanced; they can be taught generic skills in the management of their lives as well as strategies for coping with the complex array of demands placed upon them by family, school, community, or job; in other words, intelligence can be taught.

Re-ED programs are based on the postulate that intelligence can be taught, that children and adolescents can be helped to increase their capacity for problem solving and for making good choices in the living of their lives. We regard as myth the idea, now deeply rooted in American thought, that intelligence is immutable. We assume, instead, that intelligence is a dynamic, evolving, and malleable capacity for making good choices in liv-

ing. We base this unconventional view on research of the past decade on the effectiveness of child development and compensatory
education programs; on the theoretical work of Piaget (1952),
Feuerstein (1979, 1980), Kagan and Klein (1973), Clarke and
Clarke (1976), and others; and, most important, on examining
and reflecting on the Re-ED experience itself.

According to Piaget, childhood is the period in the growth
of the mind when "concrete operations" are learned. Guided by
adults, the child acquires a repertoire of concepts that make communication possible and that provide the tools for the acquisition
of "formal operations," or the ability to engage in abstract thought
and problem solving in adolescence. Children and adolescents coming into a Re-ED program frequently have deficits in both concepts and in problem-solving ability. These deficits grow out of the
adult-child relationships that also produced behaviors called "emotionally disturbed." Thus, we deliberately seek to repair deficits in
intelligence, both in the content of thought and in the process of
thinking.

Responsive to the need to repair deficits in the content of
thought, Re-ED programs are notable for the richness of the experience provided the child or adolescent. Every day is tightly
packed with experiences, and experiences reflected on, in an effort
to provide the student with the cognitive constructs needed for
problem solving. Responsive to the need to repair deficits in the
process of thought, the program provides many formal experiences
in problem solving—especially in interpersonal relationships, where
the students display conspicuous ineptitude. The students learn
that they can think about their behavior, about their relationships
with other people, about their futures. They learn that they do
not need to be victims of impulse or the persuasion of others—in
sum, that they can take thought and control their behavior, here
and now.

Children called emotionally disturbed have had precarious
and unpredictable relationships with their parents or other adults.
Lacking the emotional bonds with deeply caring adults, they lack
as well the benefits of day-by-day, hour-by-hour, minute-by-minute
instruction that more fortunate children have as a matter of course.
Most children, by the time they enter school, have been prepared
for the invitation to learning that is the essence of schooling. The

culture of a home and the culture of the school are harmonious. As the children grow older, learnings at school and learnings at home are mutually reinforcing and have a cumulative effect that defines the difference between competent adults and incompetent adults, and between children who are growing up well and children who are deeply in trouble.

Many of the benefits of growing up with caring adults who value learning are readily apparent in vocabulary development, in quickness to read, in familiarity with numbers, and in good scores on readiness tests. But many other kinds of important learnings are not so obvious—for example, the insight that identifiable methods can be applied to the solution of problems; the ability to delay gratification or to settle for lesser rewards in order to gain greater postponed rewards; the love of books, puzzles, and thinking games; a growing awareness of metaphor and other versatilities of language; and the idea that one can deliberately go about learning something. All these marvelous understandings are a consequence of thousands of transactions between caring adults and receptive children. But children and adolescents referred to as emotionally disturbed often seem conspicuously lacking in these manifestations of intelligence.

Much of the Re-ED program, especially during the morning hours, is devoted to repairing deficits in academic skills and understanding. A comparable investment is made morning, noon, and night in repairing deficits in the ability of children to apply intelligence to the solution of problems of living, here and now. We reject the notion that intelligence is a fixed attribute and maintain, instead, that intelligence can be taught. We see the human organism as far more flexible, far more responsive to opportunities to enhance capacity, than is ordinarily considered possible. Certainly, through the age ranges encompassed by Re-ED programs, from eighteen months to eighteen years, the human organism is highly responsive to environmental restrictions and opportunities. For children whose development has been impaired or diminished by affective and cognitive deprivation, the Re-ED program provides rich opportunities for learning to be intelligent in relationship with caring adults who say to the child, as well as in their own lives, that behaving intelligently is much to be preferred over behaving as though one has no control over his or her options.

Here are some specific ways that routine daily activities in a Re-ED program provide opportunities for the exercise of intelligence:

- In the pow-wow, rap session, huddle, or group conference, students learn that talking things over helps solve problems. Often children influence their families to begin to discuss problems together.
- In goal setting, students learn the advantage of deciding on specific objectives and working toward them.
- In review sessions, students learn the benefits of checking on what has or has not been accomplished.
- In group problem-solving sessions, students learn to define what the problem is; they also learn that there may be several ways to solve a problem and that the merits of each approach can be weighed in advance.
- In an arts and crafts project, students learn to plan the whole project in advance, to be certain that all materials needed are on hand and organized, and to explain steps in the process to others.
- In planning for a job interview, students learn to anticipate questions that might be asked and to prepare themselves to respond.
- In many situations, students learn that their behavior has consequences and that they can control their own behavior to produce desired outcomes.
- In planning a trip or a learning enterprise, students learn how to get information that may be needed to make the undertaking successful.
- In many activities—a backpacking trip, for example—students learn that their individual comfort and safety may depend on mutual assistance willingly given and received.
- In complex undertakings, such as producing an album of folk music, students learn that a process that may seem impossibly complicated can be broken into specific tasks that are both comprehensible and manageable.
- In a discussion of the usefulness of a fallen and rotting tree, students learn to appreciate the complex interactions that occur in all natural systems, including their own lives.
- In preparing to get a driver's license, students can be helped to learn something about the privileges and obligations of citizenship that will be useful in addressing other problems involving themselves and society.
- In various games, role-playing exercises, and dramatic events,

students learn to play with ideas, to be creative in identifying and carrying out alternative solutions to problems.

In many circumstances, older adolescents learn to reflect on their own thought processes, to think about thinking, an important skill and habit in the exercise of intelligence at the highest levels.

Feelings Should Be Nurtured

Principle: Feelings should be nurtured, shared spontaneously, controlled when necessary, expressed when too long repressed, and explored with trusted others.

We are interested in the nurturance and expression of feelings, negative and positive, to help a child or an adolescent own all of herself without guilt. Anger and resentment, fear and anxiety are commonplace in children served by Re-ED schools. Some children need to learn to control their violent impulses; others need to give vent to feelings too long repressed. In Re-ED schools serving younger children, one finds the familiar ratio of four or five boys to one girl, a consequence in part, we believe, of a lack of masculine challenge in public schools and in communities today; thus, we contrive situations of controlled danger, in which children can test themselves, can know fear and become the master of it. Positive feelings are important, too. The simple joy of companionship is encouraged. We are impressed by the meaningfulness of friendships and how long they endure. The annual homecoming is anticipated by many youngsters as an opportunity to walk arm in arm with an old friend associated with a period of special significance in their lives. And we respect the need to be alone, to work things through without intrusion, and to have a private purpose. Children have a way of showing up with animals, and we are glad for this. A child who has known the rejection of adults may find it safest, at first, to express affection to a dog. And a pet can be a source of pride and of sense of responsibility. Feelings also get expressed through many kinds of creative activities that are woven into the fabric of life in a Re-ED school. Throwing clay on a potter's wheel may give a girl a first sense of her potential for shaping her world. A play written by an older boy may permit freer expression of emotion than would ordinarily be tolerable. Drawing and painting can be fun for a whole group. And an object to mold gives something to do to make it safe for an adult and child to be close together.

Most of the young people who come to a Re-ED school are incapacitated in some way in the management of their feelings. Some are overtly fearful or anxious or depressed. Many are tied up inside, controlled, thoroughly contained within themselves. Most are aggressive, hostile, explosive, for it is such young people who are most likely to get into trouble and to be referred for special help. Thus, the goals in working with different children will vary greatly and are often explicitly agreed on by the staff. We are pleased when a girl gains the courage to explore potentially catastrophic areas of her life and when a measure of assurance and spontaneity begins to replace her apprehensiveness. We get great satisfaction from seeing a boy finally speak up for himself, "blow his top," get in a fight, assert himself against his teacher, his brother, his parents. We are pleased, and often relieved as well, when a child who has been persistently belligerent begins to substitute words for fists, or seems no longer to need to fight the world. What we would like to be able to achieve, of course, is for all children and adolescents to have available for experiencing and use the full range of their emotions, under appropriate ego controls, for them to be able to laugh freely, to get angry, to feel sad, to reach out in affection, to be ashamed, to be amused at themselves, to feel sorry, to be homesick, to be quietly contented, to know a fulgent joy. It is mainly the teacher-counselors who help these transformations come about.

The teacher-counselors must be skilled and purposeful in helping children and adolescents become aware of their feelings so that they can own them fully and express them in ways satisfying to themselves, and satisfactory (for the most part) to others. Much of the teacher-counselor's talk with a child will be about the child's feelings. He starts with the assumption that feelings are intrinsically real and that there is no profit in denying their existence. While a child or adolescent may, and often must, inhibit actions based on feelings, trouble begins when the feelings themselves are prohibited, either by the young person or by other people. Persistently denied feelings tend to get expressed eventually, often in ways that are defeating to the person. So the teacher-counselor, in the process of reeducation, is constantly responsive to the feelings the child or adolescent is trying to express, here and now.

The important thing is not how the child came to feel the way she does, but how she feels now, and the teacher-counselor, therefore, has the difficult task of denying his curiosity about *why* the child feels the way she does. The origins of her feelings are of no importance. The teacher-counselor does not ask "Why?"—a useless and often threatening question—but "How do you feel?" or "What happened and how did it feel?" Usually, of course, he has no need to ask such questions but simply to respond, and to respond simply, to the feelings that the young person is trying to communicate through word, gesture, or expression. It seems that the important thing is for the child or adolescent to know that someone else who matters to her knows how she feels, accurately and in depth, and that the person still accepts her and believes in her.

The feelings expressed by a child or an adolescent are not interpreted by the teacher-counselor. There is no need to make psychodynamic sense of feelings; indeed, to do so will more often than not make for difficulties rather than growth. What is to be sought is an empathic sharing of an existential moment, taken for what it is and not for what it is supposed to signify. The child or adolescent learns through an immediate experience of affective sharing that the whole of herself, feelings and all, can be owned without fear of punishment. She becomes more authentically herself.

The teacher-counselor does not probe for feelings that he may suspect are present but that have not in some way been communicated. The child or adolescent is not pushed into sharing feelings that she is not ready to express. She will share her feelings when she feels accepted by the teacher-counselor and in a depth and richness commensurate with the extent to which she feels secure. Probing for feelings, even when they are accurately surmised, simply slows things down. The young person will control the pace of her opening up; if she feels that the teacher-counselor wishes to go faster than she does, she will not cooperate. Thus, the teacher-counselor follows the person, accepting her sense of what she will find manageable.

In the following account, we see a teacher-counselor sensitively helping a girl, through group and individual conversations, to share and accept her feelings.

Betty, Age Fourteen*

Betty, a physically mature fourteen-year-old, was attracted to Stoakley Mann, a visitor for a few days in the older boys' unit. She saved a seat for him at evening class and at assembly. One night, she spent forty-five minutes wrapping a candle and a book, a Christmas present for him. Betty was a bit silly in her remarks to the other girls, but she also showed a great deal of seriousness and determination. When Stoakley left with his parents, Betty stood for a long time staring out the window. After the car had gone, she seemed "lost" and had a sad, pensive look on her face. Afterward she began to act out, to return to her rebellious behavior, to be restless and moody. Part of this might have been due to her menstrual period and part to her fear of returning to public school, but there appeared to be a connection, too, with her feelings for the boy. These feelings seemed to produce a conflict of wanting to become more feminine and, at the same time, to return to her old "wildcat" self. Betty's pajamas had been soiled, and Judy offered to lend her either pajamas or a gown. Betty got upset trying to decide which she wanted, almost chose the gown, but ended up going to bed with the pajamas and a windbreaker on top of them.

At group meeting that night, Judy said that Lisa and Anna had had a "good day." T.C. asked each girl in turn what a good day was like to her and what a bad day was like. Lisa said a good day was "doing lots of things" and a bad day was "like burning inside." Anna said a "good day" was one "that passes quick" and a bad day was "one that passes slow." Betty blocked. A few minutes later, she said: "I didn't have such a hot day today."

T.C.: "Why, Betty?"
Betty: "Stoakley left."
T.C.: "That makes you feel bad, Betty?"
Betty: "I dunno."
T.C.: "It was hard watching him leave? . . . Empty maybe?"
Betty: "Yeah. That's about it."
T.C.: "And sad?"
Betty: "Yeah."
T.C.: "I understand. . . . You know, Betty, he left with some lovely gifts."

*This account was written by a teacher-counselor.

Betty: (Silent, sad.)

T.C.: "And perhaps he will be back."

Betty: "But I'll be gone then."

After the girls had been in bed thirty minutes, T.C. heard sobbing from Betty's room and went to investigate. Betty was really crying, deep heaving sobs, like the crying of a broken-hearted child. T.C. comforted her. Betty couldn't speak for a good while. When she did, she said, through the sobs: "They didn't have to be so mean."

T.C.: "Who was mean?"

Betty: "They called him names all the time (bursts into more sobs). Everybody. Called him 'Stuck-up man.' They didn't have to do that. They didn't have to!"

T.C.: "That's very true, Betty. And I know he is special to you. I also know that you feel it deeply when anyone is hurt. That's a very fine quality of yours, a very good part of you. Are you sad because they called him names, or because he left?"

Betty: "Both."

T.C.: "You must be awfully pleased that you had the lovely gifts, wrapped so nicely, to give Stoakley. He will remember a good friend at Wright School. I think you could think about that, and be very glad."

Betty stopped crying. T.C. left her with the girls quietly reassuring her, particularly Judy. But she did not sleep until nearly 11:00. T.C. heard Betty say to Judy: "He ran away because he was homesick, and there's nothing wrong with feeling homesick."

And here is what was done to help a boy with strong feelings of inadequacy express his feelings:

Mitchell, Age Fifteen*

Mitchell came to a Re-ED school with the belief that he was brain damaged and could not participate in sports and other normal activities of a fifteen-year-old. As he expressed it, "My brain is cracked." Mitchell's behavior seemed to be a reflection of his feeling incomplete, inferior, and not valuable at all. He was constantly late to meals, to group meetings, to class, to anything, and he left the impression of not caring if he missed them altogether. Much of the time, he seemed emotionless, staring blankly and dropping

*This account was written by Dean Richey, former teacher-counselor at Cumberland House and currently on the faculty of Tennessee Technological University in the department of educational psychology.

things. But there were indications of nervousness and tension; Mitchell bit his fingernails whenever he had the opportunity and was overpolite to adults. His aversive behavior was limited to things done when adults were not around (like picking on a smaller student). One of the most obvious things about Mitchell was that he seemed incapable of expressing anger, or emotion of any sort, for that matter. One got the feeling that he was keeping everything inside for fear that he could get hurt by expressing himself. For the longest time, we never saw Mitchell cry or lose his temper; as a matter of fact, these two things soon became important goals for him.

We used several methods to encourage Mitchell to express and deal with his feelings. It was not enough simply to assure him that we would accept his anger and hostility and that he should show them. The old patterns of expressing anger in passive ways (joking, ignoring, "bugging" people) had worked too well too long. We decided to intervene when we saw Mitchell expressing his feelings inappropriately and to confront him with them by saying, "You're angry, Mitch." This was a way of allowing Mitchell to recognize and verbalize his anger, if not express it otherwise. We structured situations in the group that would provide for Mitchell's needs. We went so far as to put him with a roommate who we felt would create conflicts that Mitchell would have to deal with overtly. In addition, we labeled Mitchell's feelings in the presence of the group at pow-wow sessions and on other occasions. Mitchell was able to set goals for himself, such as "Not to act like I don't hear the teachers or the other students." "To say what I feel and not be overly nice." Essentially, then, we used three strategies: structuring situations that would provide for expression, confronting Mitchell in a nonthreatening way with his anger, and labeling his feelings through the group sessions.

Here is an honest account by a teacher-counselor who was caught in a psychodynamic trap by responding to the content of a child's message rather than to the feelings involved.

Ted, Age Twelve*

Ted, age twelve, was the only child in a well-educated family. I worked with Ted as his night teacher-counselor. Ted's father was away from home most of the time, working overseas for an

---

*This account was written by James Paul, formerly teacher-counselor at Wright School and currently chairman of the department of special education, University of North Carolina.

oil company. The public school had completely given up on helping Ted, saying that he could not be contained in a regular class.
Ted had a history of difficulty and during the early years of his
life had been in child analysis in Europe. He had superior intelligence (IQ 135) but had always been unmanageable in school. On
the second day that Ted was at Re-ED, he told me he would like
to "sit down and talk about some of my problems." With this began a long series of conversations with Ted in which he said such
things as "Daddy's gone most all the time and, you know, I'm
kind of glad because while he's away I can sleep with Mother.
When Daddy comes home, I have to sleep in the other room because he sleeps with Mother. I love him and want him home and
all that, but I guess I have to say I'm kind of glad when he goes
back." Over a period of a few days, Ted covered most of the major
topics that a psychoanalytic lecture would include. Freud would
indeed have been pleased with the material as documentation of
some of his basic concepts.

Being a neophyte in understanding child behavior, I was
completely taken in. Everything Ted said rang true to the psychoanalytic model. I felt so pleased with myself "making this child
feel comfortable enough to talk about his problems" and I did not
dare interrupt this "therapeutic process." Consequently, restrictions on Ted's behavior were minimized. Almost from day one,
Ted was a major behavioral problem in the unit. I tried to deal
with these behavior problems by the "let's talk about it" method.
Ted's talk was always so rich in dynamic material that anyone who
had read an article on Freud from a popular magazine could have
brought some interpretation to what he was saying. What I did not
realize was that Ted knew as much psychoanalytic jargon as I did
and that he was much more sophisticated in gamesmanship than I.
The sophisticated talks continued, and limits were not set.

It was after several weeks that, with the help of our consultants, I began to listen to the words Ted was saying and hear the
absence of affect. When my error in working with Ted became
clear to me, it was something of a jolt and, when fully understood,
it hurt. By this time, it was difficult to begin again with Ted. We
were unable to find ways to correct the mistake that had already
been made. The error in working with Ted, when added to the
pathology in the family, made further efforts seem futile. Eventually Ted had to be discharged from the school.

Strongly hostile feelings may get expressed in antisocial behavior, overt hostility, tantrums, profanity, stealing, running away,
aggressive attacks on other children and adults, and destruction of
property. Sometimes we are delighted when a child or an adoles-

cent can express hostility openly. It can be a sure sign of progress. However, a more frequent problem involves the management of hostility by the staff and ultimately by the student himself. There are complications in both theory and method.

At the level of theory, there are two formulations of the problem that enjoy strong support, sometimes even by the same theorist. One formulation of the sources of hostility may be called the need theory and the other the habit theory, the former drawing sustenance from psychodynamic theory and the latter from the psychology of learning. The *need* orthodoxy maintains that there is a given quantity of hostility in a child, some of which simply has to be vented and some of which should be sublimated or otherwise converted into socially tolerable activities. The *habit* orthodoxy maintains that hostile behavior is a product of reward contingencies in the environment and that changing the contingencies in appropriate ways will eliminate the hostility. To true believers of either persuasion, the problem is simple. For us, it remains complicated because we find that both formulations have merit and it can be hard to know which one to draw on in a particular instance. As a consequence, we tend to rely on both.

At the level of tactics, there are other complications. Often the unacceptable behavior cannot be ignored, and coping with it through restraint or punishment may simply evoke more hostility. Furthermore, it is extremely difficult to handle hostility directly without becoming hostile oneself. Teacher-counselors struggle with the problem and with themselves but never cease to be human beings; thus, they remain vulnerable. Other students, of course, may be incited to hostility by hostility, or they may act with little restraint to punish the offender. So solutions about the handling of hostility and of antisocial behavior are not easy to come by.

However, some tactics can be suggested. First of all, there should be clear guidelines about what kind of behavior is expected. Expectations will be violated but not nearly so frequently as when the rules are not made explicit. Whenever possible, the aggressive behavior should be ignored and behavior incompatible with hostility reinforced. And all experiences of the day should be made as engrossing and rewarding as possible, to keep frustration down and to minimize opportunities for destructive behavior.

One procedure for handling highly aggressive and destructive behavior calls for the use of an isolation room, commonly referred to as a "quiet room," though it is seldom quiet when occupied. We are gradually working our way toward consensus on how such a room should be used. We started out with the unrealistic position that there would be no such room. Then we built isolation rooms but said they must be used on a voluntary basis by the student. But this was not sufficient, so then we said a person might be confined for a limited period of time but only when there was an adult with him. This arrangement, however, sustained undesirable behavior by predictably rewarding it. So we have moved a step beyond and do occasionally confine a child or an adolescent when he is out of control and likely to do damage to himself or others or to so disrupt things that too many people suffer. Sometimes a child or an adolescent will ask to go to the quiet room voluntarily to get himself under control, and we are always pleased at this evidence of foresight and purposefulness. But then there are slam-bang and angry times when a student has forcibly to be locked in a room alone. We are not comfortable with this even now, although we recognize it as a necessity in dealing with some disturbed young people, as with adults. We try to release the student as soon as his acting-out subsides and to welcome him back warmly into the group. The adult who puts a child in the room is responsible for him and puts aside all else to handle the situation with as much skill as he can. We do not think the quiet room helps children much; it simply gets the child into a position where we can help him. And it is never used for punishment, only for the containment of otherwise unmanageable behavior. We do not think the quiet room procedure has been abused and it is indeed used sparingly; but its availability for use when all else fails has made it possible for us to accept much more disturbed children and adolescents than we would otherwise have been able to do.

The Group Is Important to Young People

Principle: The group is very important to young people, and it can be a major source of instruction in growing up.

In programs for both children and adolescents, students are organized in groups of eight or ten, with three teacher-counselors in charge. The group is kept intact for nearly all activities and becomes an important source of motivation, instruction, and control. When a group is functioning well, it is difficult for an individual student to behave in a disturbing way. Even when the group is functioning poorly, the frictions and the failures can be used constructively. The pow-wow or rap session, involving discussion of difficulties or planning of activities, can be a most maturing experience. And the sharing of adventure, of vicissitudes, and of victories provides an experience in human relatedness to which most of our students have been alien. The group is so important in the process of reeducation that it is treated at length in Chapter Eleven.

Ceremony and Ritual Give Order, Stability, and Confidence

Principle: Ceremony and ritual give order, stability, and confidence to troubled children and adolescents, whose lives are often in considerable disarray.

Many Re-ED students have lived chaotic lives, even in their brief compass. They may come from homes where interpersonal disarray is endemic. We have stumbled on and been impressed by the beneficence of ceremony, ritual, and metaphor for young people and have come to plan for their inclusion in the program. The nightly backrub is an established institution with the Whippoorwills, a time of important confidences. Being a Bobcat brings a special sense of camaraderie and has its own metaphorical obligations. And a Christmas pageant can effect angelic transformation of boys whose ordinary conduct is far from seraphic.

Here are several illustrations of ceremonies and rituals that have become important parts of Re-ED programs.

At the Re-ED school in Louisville (for children six to thirteen), every Thursday is "dress-up night." Girls dress in party dresses and boys in jackets and ties (if a child cannot afford to dress up, the school unobtrusively provides suit or dress). The ceremony is formal, the dinner a special treat. There are candles and music from a record player. Then awards are given out—to every child (there is no child who in the course of a week does not do something worthy of recognition). Never make the mistake of underestimating the power for good of such occasions!

At Pressley Ridge Wilderness School, a very simple but important ritual has evolved. Before the noonday meal every day, the campers gather and sit in groups on "ready-logs." The camp staff (plus visitors) line up at the entrance to the mess hall. When the dinner bell rings, the campers, one group at a time, walk through the line of staff and visitors. There is a handshake, and from the staff a personal, appreciative comment. It is a powerful event, asserting comradeship and community.

Ready-logs themselves have become a part of the ritual and ceremony of Re-ED programs, especially at camp but in other settings as well. Experienced workers with young people (and disturbed youngsters especially) know that, in order to start a new activity, it is first necessary to bring old activities to an end. Ready-logs (and their many functional analogs) serve this purpose. Before any new activity at camp, groups gather and sit in a circle on logs. Quiet is expected. Then with attentions focused on what is coming up, appropriate behavior can be expected.

Whippoorwills go regularly and on special days to sing for the people at the "Old Folks' Home" a few blocks from Cumberland House. At Christmas each year, the old people give a party for the Whippoorwills. Each child receives a stocking filled with goodies. This has become an annual affair, rewarding to children and old folks alike.

The daily Assembly at Wright School is an important event guided by ritual that is now as predictable as ancient orders of service. It is regarded by the staff as a major contributor to morale and to a feeling of unity in the school as a whole. The Assembly is a fifteen- to twenty-minute period after breakfast, just prior to the beginning of classroom activities. This aspect of the Re-ED day came about as a result of a need to develop a sense of community in the school as a whole. Just as each group of children formed a whole with unique identity, so, it seemed, the school itself should have a corporate identity. The physical setting for Assembly is the dining hall, a simple, cheerful, and comfortable room equipped with cloth-covered tables and sturdy chairs, movable to suit the occasion, and with a piano, record player, and song charts. Each group of children is responsible for Assembly one morning a week. What actually happens is quite simple; what results is often complex. A member of the group introduces the program: "Unit II will start our program with the Pledge to the Flag and the singing of 'America.' " (All stand, with the audience participating.) Then: "Joe, Pete, Larry, and Chris will have a skit about 'Billy Goats Gruff' " (with simplest of costuming and props, the short story is acted out dramatically). And then: "We will conclude the program by singing the Wright School Song." Another program might include a show of the older boys' mastery of tumbling or a once shy and clumsy child's reading a simple verse. Certainly not all Assembly endeavors are successful; yet, amazingly, the children seldom indicate a failure but seem to recognize that, as the staff is patient and appreciative, so they themselves can wait and try harder next time.

The Body Is the Armature of the Self

Principle: The body is the armature of the self, the physical self around which the psychological self is constructed.

We are intrigued by the idea that the physical self is the armature around which the psychological self is constructed and that a clearer experiencing of the body should lead to a clearer definition of the self, and thus to greater psychological fitness and enhanced effective functioning. We actually have no data and but scant theory to support the notion; yet it has its appeal, it can do no harm, and it might actually be beneficial. Let us review where the idea came from and what support it does have in fact and theory before we describe what it means in practice in the process of reeducation.

The Outward Bound Schools, established first in England and now in operation in many parts of the world, were created to give a brief and intensive experience to young men to help them overcome the anomie that is the product of living in an industrial, urbanized civilization. These programs were first studied in England in 1956 by a senior member of the Re-ED staff and then experienced directly in the Peace Corps training program in Puerto Rico, which incorporated Outward Bound concepts. The Peace Corps program involved rock climbing, survival treks, surf kyaking, physical fitness exercises, and other similar activities designed not to train volunteers to do this sort of thing on their jobs but to give them a greater awareness of themselves and to extend the range of what they thought they were capable of doing. It was an exercise in self-discovery. The basic notions seemed applicable to work with young children and especially with adolescents. Outward Bound activities are fun in their own right, and they seemed more attuned to the nature of young people than the lethargic, passive, and proper activities provided for patients in traditional residential treatment centers. We thought them worth trying.

Subsequently, we have found support in research and in theory for the practice of emphasizing physical experiences in the Re-ED program. There is instruction to be had, for example, in the characteristics of extremely disturbed, autistic children. These youngsters seem to be acutely alienated from other people, to have developed but the fragments of selfhood, and sometimes to be involved in intricate, private, and metaphorical constructions of themselves and the world. Often they do not speak, or they have a private language. Their greatest skill perhaps is in preventing any kind of personal intrusion into their world. It is significant to our present concerns that these children often seem not to own their bodies at all, to have somehow sealed off, or to have never developed, an awareness of bodily functions. They are frequently insensitive to temperature and pain. When picked up or helped in some task, they may seem to respond no more than inanimate material would. The crucial idea for our purpose here is that the beginnings of growth often involve the slow discovery by the child of his body, of his physical separateness from the rest of the world, and of his most primitive body functions—eating, urinating, and defecating. It is as though the rudiments of selfhood are to be found in the experiencing of the body and its functions. Few children are so profoundly disturbed as those called autistic; yet we are inclined to believe that the principles illuminated by autistic children apply by extension to more moderately disturbed youngsters. Perhaps at all levels of ego development, there is enrichment and elaboration of the self to be obtained through physical experience and a heightened awareness of the body.

The question presents itself as to what is cause and what is consequence. Is a poor or ill-defined body concept the result of inadequate ego development or a partial cause of it? We would surmise an interaction effect. Although it is not yet clear that activities designed to promote a heightened sense of the physical body will result in further healthy development of the ego, we assume so and have designed our program accordingly. A Re-ED school has a much more physically involving program than one will find in traditional treatment programs or in public schools. A list of activities through which the idea here presented is realized would be too long, varied, and changeable to be significant, but we would mention such things as swimming, jogging, dancing, clay modeling, canoeing, tumbling, tree climbing, cutting wood, playing dodge ball, riding a bicycle, backpacking for ten days, getting a back rub, building a tree house, walking a monkey bridge, scuba diving, technical rock climbing, horseback riding, surfing, spelunking, felling a tree, and building a winter shelter.

Here are some illustrations of program activities designed to develop a heightened awareness of the body or to create a more favorable body image.

Once or twice a year, the day teacher-counselors devote a part of several days to an activity that the children find intensely absorbing, probably because it evokes a heightened awareness of their bodies. A sheet of heavy, brown wrapping paper about 3 feet by 5 feet is put on the floor. A child lies still on his back on the paper. Another child, usually with the verbal assistance of several demanding critics, draws with a heavy pencil an outline of the body of his reclining friend. The picture is then hung on a wall at the height of the child. It never fails to evoke the intense interest of the subject, usually accompanied by expressions of amazement and pleasure. The subject then paints his own picture within the outline.

Rick came to Wright School at age thirteen. Following an accident, he had undergone surgery for a hernia and had subsequently been overprotected by his parents. He had been warned against vigorous activity and kept away from the "danger of active games." Rick did not trust his own body. At Wright School, over a period of time, Rick became part of an aggressive physical activities program. He began to feel much better about himself and, in fact, to take pride in his athletic abilities. Because of family difficulties, Rick went to a military school. He did very well there, achieving several honors. The liaison teacher-counselor and social worker visited him several months after he left Wright School. He stood straight and tall and talked confidently about his activities at the military school.

Part of the significance of the body for personal development is its social stimulus value, the kind of response it elicits from other people. A fat, pudgy, awkward boy is found to be the butt of jokes and to have a difficult time gaining acceptance or even feeling himself to be acceptable. So we often work out a special program for physical development for a boy of this kind. One seriously disturbed girl had conspicuously protruding teeth that detracted greatly from her appearance. She made excellent progress at Cumberland House and was able to return to a regular school, where she continued to make progress. About a year after discharge, and with evidence that she was getting along well, we worked with the family to obtain corrective braces for her teeth. (We should have done it earlier!) We believe her improved appearance will modestly but perceptibly increase the chances that she will continue to make a good adjustment.

A very bright, academically promising fifteen-year-old girl, for lack of better role models than were available in her unpromising environment (her two older sisters were school dropouts and prostitutes), dressed, used makeup, and did her hair in ways that invited a similar future for her. She became close to two teacher-counselors, a married couple. While neither teacher-counselor could accurately be called "square," both had lively intellectual interests, a strong commitment to young people, and a sufficient connection with mainstream society to make their way in it. She became attached to the couple, identified strongly with the wife, and began to alter her view of herself. Most evident was the gradual change in her appearance. She became an attractive young woman with pride in her appearance. She was graduated from a community college and has a steady job as a hairdresser. At this writing, she is planning to be married. While she is at present far from realizing her intellectual potential, she is far from where she would have been if two teacher-counselors had never entered her life.

Communities Are Important

Principle: Communities are important for children and youth, but the uses and benefits of community must be experienced to be learned.

The systems concept in Re-ED leads to an examination of the relationship of children to their home communities. Many children and adolescents who are referred to our schools come from families that are alienated or detached from community life or are not sufficiently well organized or purposeful to help children develop a sense of identity with neighborhood, town, or city. They have little opportunity to discover that communities exist for people. While the goodness of fit between the two may often leave much to be desired, an important part of growing up is to learn that community agencies and institutions exist for the welfare of all and that each individual has an obligation as a citizen to contribute to their effective functioning. This is especially true for many of the boys referred to Re-ED, whose energy, aggressiveness, lack of control, and resentment of authority dispose them to behaviors that get labeled delinquent. This idea has a number of implications for program planning. Field trips to the fire, police, and health departments are useful. Memberships in the YMCA, a children's museum, a playground group, or a community center may be worked out. Church attendance may be encouraged and a clergyman persuaded to take special interest in a family, or a library card can be a proud possession and a tangible community tie.

One of the most successful projects that has nurtured the concept of community for a large number of children at Wright School is its Museum Project. A group of older boys and girls serve as guides at the open-air children's museum in Durham, located not far from the school. Afternoons are a busy time at the museum, and this is when the Re-ED students serve. Before being assigned as guide, a new student must learn facts about the exhibits, how to dress properly, how to greet and say goodbye to visitors, and what to do in an emergency. The guides wear arm bands and are proud of their special status. Not all children in the unit can be assigned to guide duty on admission to Wright School, but it is a goal toward which they can work. A teacher-counselor is always present to supervise. There have been few difficulties because the students live up to the role expectations in this community project.

Re-ED programs for adolescents have worked out dozens of ways for students to participate in community projects, including painting a house for an elderly couple, operating a "roadblock" to solicit funds for a hospital, serving as ushers at a park concert, serving under close supervision as voluntary fire fighters in a woods fire near a Re-ED camp, distributing boxes of food and toys to needy families at Christmas, gathering migrating birds injured by flying into a television tower at night and taking the birds to a shelter, participating in a neighborhood clean-up day, and so on.

Of course, all these projects require advanced arrangements, usually by the liaison teacher-counselor. They also require careful planning by the group, unobtrusive supervision, and daily evaluations by the group of its performance.

A Child Grows on Joy

Principle: In growing up, a child should know some joy in each day and look forward to some joyous event for the morrow.

We have often speculated about the lack of a psychology of well-being. There is an extensive literature on anxiety, guilt, and dread, but little that is well developed on joy. Most psychological experiments rely for motivation on avoidance of pain or hunger or some other aversive stimuli; positive motivations are limited to the pleasure that comes from minute, discrete rewards ("reinforcers"). This poverty with respect to the most richly human of motivations leads to anemic programming for youngsters. We thus go beyond most contemporary psychology to touch one of the most vital areas of human experiencing. We try to become skillful at developing joy in the young people we work with. We believe that a joyous experience is immensely important, that it is immediately therapeutic (if further justification is required) for young people to know some joy in each day and to look forward with eagerness to at least some joy-giving event that is planned for tomorrow.

Joyous experiences can cluster around a sequence of events that unfold as some enterprise develops. For example, a Cherokee Indian project at Cumberland House generated hundreds of moments of satisfaction as children worked hard to make its realization possible. However, we could not have anticipated all the satisfying experiences it brought to the children as each day was anticipated and then lived. Many subjects, some of them noxious to the children in other contexts, such as reading and arithmetic, geography and history, were swept forward on the current of well-being that flowed from a core idea. The folk music project at Pine Breeze (described in Chapter Ten) provided a steady stream of joyous events for the adolescents involved.

Teacher-counselors are in substantial agreement about what it takes to produce the joyous spirit that can infuse a group and enrich the day of a child or an adolescent. They repeatedly say that it is the teacher-counselor's attitude that makes things happen, and it is simple things that work best.

At camp one summer, a teacher-counselor devised a game called "Peanuts." Early each morning, every member of the Bobcats group received a small piece of brown cardboard, cut in the shape of a peanut. On the peanut was written the name of some person at camp: the cook, the director, the counselor in charge of the water program, or a child in another group. There were eight children in the group, and each had the name of a different person who was his "Peanut" for the day. During the day, the child had to do something that would make his Peanut happy, without revealing why it was being done. Everything had to be kept secret—the names of the Peanuts, what was done, and so on. Then each night, before going to bed, the group would meet, and each child would reveal the name of his Peanut for the day and what he had done to make him happy. After this fascinating recital, each child was given a felt letter, one each day for six days, the letters spelling BOBCAT. The letters were sewn on T-shirts as they were received. It is hard to imagine the effect of this simple game on the Bobcats that summer. While the game was going on, excitement ran high, the group was very closely knit, conduct was excellent, and everyone had a good time. It was all but impossible for a Bobcat to behave disturbed that week.

A similar game has been worked out for older groups. It is called "Secret Agent" or "Hit Man."

Teacher-counselors must retain an appreciation of simple joys in life, for they set the stage for everyone else as they react to some specific situation in a way that engages a student in their own enjoyment. And there are individual differences in style among teacher-counselors. One teacher-counselor carefully plans to make important things happen for a particular child. Knowing how much a child needs the support of his father, she arranges for the father to have a job to do in connection with a group cookout, so that he will be sure to show up. The child is delighted. Another teacher-counselor has a fine sense of play; he is marvelous to watch work with a group of children. He assembles a group in the evening and gives each child a "thinking pill" (a piece of green candy) and a picture to study. He then asks each child to tell a story about his picture. All this is done with a light touch that somehow brings immense pleasure to the group. Getting an ice-cream cone can be an event of little meaning or an occasion for all kinds of joyous associations. Going to the corner store together as a self-administered reward for good work can transform an evening. Love of the out-of-doors is an infectious quality of yet another teacher-counselor. Able to make the most of the unexpected, she takes her group for a walk in the rain. Everyone gets thoroughly soaked outside and thoroughly warmed within. Yet another counselor is great with the guitar; quiet excitement is evident in the faces of a group around a fire as they sing favorite songs and make up new ones. Another teacher-counselor has an affinity for gentle laughter; the group catches on, and much of the day gets transformed into humorous and pleasurable happenings, all of a gentle character. Another teacher-counselor has said, "To start a Re-ED school, you first need a creek." The children at Wright School, which is so fortunate, spend enchanted hours building dams, digging caves, and catching crayfish. Teacher-counselors agree that some of the most satisfying moments are generated by successful achievement in school. To do well in spelling or arithmetic, especially for students who expect and dread failure, is to know a sharp delight. It is like spitting from the top of a windmill.

Teacher-counselors also agree that joy should be reciprocal; teacher-counselors must have fun, too. They should have the freedom to do what they like to do, so that they can do it with enthusiasm and satisfaction. Opportunities are endless, materials are abundant, occasions are beyond definition for the teacher-counselor to light the life of a child with joy. But the techniques cannot be prescribed; they depend on the style, the *joie de vivre*, the world view of the teacher-counselor.

10

Helping Children
Learn to Learn

Our experience over the years has taught us how important school achievement is in the lives of children and adolescents. Emotional disturbance in children surely has its origins in multiple sources; however, school figures more frequently than any other setting, even the family itself, as the place where adjustment difficulties first become manifest. Though school is not the sole causal agent, school is often the beginning point of a downward spiral with behavioral repercussions in home, school, and community. As school pressures mount and failure becomes more frequent (often around the fourth grade but with evidence always of earlier academic difficulties), discord builds in the ecosystem. While parents may have been discontented with the behavior of their child for some years, the first public confirmation of their dissatisfaction comes most often from the school. Teachers, principals, school psychologists, and others either create or validate parental dissatisfactions. Already subject to criticism at school, the child now experiences growing disapproval at home. The child may respond to concerted criticism in a number of ways but seldom by doing better schoolwork. He may avoid school tasks, become aggressive and abusive at school and at home, and retaliate by antisocial behavior in the community. Or he may withdraw further and further into himself. There are numerous transactional scenarios, all different, but the general pattern is very familiar to all who work with children. Failure breeds failure. The disparity between the child's behavior and the expectations of adults grows, and, by adolescence, he will often have worked out an almost intractable pattern of learned incompetence. At the same time, many of the significant adults in the child's life will have adopted an attitude of intransigent rejection, thus foreclosing new opportunities to learn. By this time, the child or adolescent has acquired a concept of self with incompetence a central feature, and he seeks experiences that confirm his definitions of himself as an incompetent person.

The child or adolescent who has difficulty in learning and in learning to learn probably cannot be helped much by conventional methods of teaching. Indeed, additional pressure on the child to read or cipher may only compound the learning difficulty. Here is the situation. Through low aptitude, poor teaching in school, or inadequate learning experiences prior to school, the child begins to experience failure early, in simple things like learning words, reading, subtracting and multiplying, and understanding how a sentence works. Failure is often followed by disapproval from teachers and parents and sometimes by derision from other children. In time, the prospect of doing any school task raises the child's anxiety level until she discovers ways of avoiding all school tasks. She becomes inattentive, hyperactive, sullen, aggressive toward other children, and hostile toward teachers, schools, and anything that smacks of schooling. To teach such a child, expectations of failure must be replaced by experiences of success.

Sometimes initial successes in learning come not from school subjects but from less fearsome tasks, like throwing a pot on a potter's wheel, learning to tie knots, or getting good at a game like checkers or chess. For school learning, the task must often be greatly simplified, reduced to most rudimentary operations. In braving the threat of a new effort to learn, the child may need at the outset the closest and most understanding support of teacher-counselors, day and night. The learning task must be designed so that the probability of success is very high, and success must be rewarded externally. Gradually, as the child learns, the exercise of the new-found competence will itself be intrinsically rewarding—as the following account of a boy at Pressley Ridge illustrates.

A ten-year-old boy of approximately normal intelligence could not read, write, or do arithmetic. We tried to teach him these skills by conventional methods and failed. His disruptive behavior became intolerable. It was finally necessary for a special program to be worked out to teach him to differentiate between paired digits and paired letters of the alphabet—as rudimentary as that. Success came, and the difficulty of the task was slowly increased, with each increment modulated to assure a favorable outcome. Within about six months, he learned to read. And he did exercises in arithmetic workbooks by the hour. His behavior in school and at home improved dramatically, and he was soon returned to a regular school.

In the wilderness camping programs for teenage boys at Pressley Ridge and in other programs, there is no formal academic instruction. Many of the youngsters have given up all intentions of learning the skills that are absolutely essential for even marginal success in our society, and many have dropped out of or been expelled by schools. Although formal academic work is not a part of the camping program, there is a great investment in teaching academic skills and subject matter. Teaching and learning occur in the context of valued activities, such as building a shelter, planning and budgeting for a trip, keeping personal accounts, discussing history, publishing a camp newspaper, and so on. Several studies have demonstrated that the adolescents in the wilderness camping program improve their own rates of learning and achieve more than comparable students in regular schools (Ziegler and others, 1980).

Research evidence validates our repeated observations that, for children with academic deficits, the mastery of basic learning skills is a prerequisite to overcoming emotional problems. Weinstein (1974), in her study of children completing Re-ED programs and children who remained in public schools and got only such special assistance as happened to be provided, found that the children in both groups who overcame deficits in academic skills also overcame their emotional problems. More Re-ED children overcame their problems than did public school children, to be sure, but the relationship between learning competence and general adjustment was clear in both groups.

Psychodynamic theory treats learning difficulties as a symptom of some underlying pathology that must be cleared up before the child can begin to learn again. We take an interaction view: learning difficulties contribute to behavioral problems, and behavioral problems interfere with learning. While general discord in the ecosystem may make it difficult for a child to learn, learning difficulties are a frequent source of discord in the system. Learning deficits should therefore be addressed promptly and directly. The traditional view of the relationship between emotional disturbance and learning difficulties can lead to a subordination of the school program in traditional residential treatment centers. Teachers may have marginal status and not be included in the treatment team, especially when teachers are assigned by the public schools. Classrooms are often dispirited and dispiriting places that by their appearance proclaim how little education is valued. The negative attitude toward school learning is not lost on the children, who respond with minimum enthusiasm to such teaching as may be offered.

In Re-ED programs, teachers with special preparation for work with troubled and troubling children constitute the professional staff. Other professional people have roles supportive to the teacher-counselors. An emphasis on teaching and learning, and on learning to learn, flows readily from these resources.

Enhancement of Teaching and Learning

Authorities have various schemes for laying out factors to be considered in the enhancement of teaching and learning. We elect to organize our ideas around eleven concepts.

Trust. Most teacher-counselors have had successful academic careers, and it is often difficult for them, when first working with troubled children, to appreciate the anxiety felt by a child or an adolescent when confronted with academic tasks. These children are good learners in other situations, on the athletic field or in the potter's shop, and they have learned well how to avoid facing school tasks. When forced to face school tasks anyway, they exhibit the behavior (depression, withdrawal, hyperactivity, disruptive conduct) that has led them to be labeled "emotionally disturbed." In truth, their behavior is an adaptive response to the punishment they have received and have come to anticipate from inadequate schools or incompetent teachers. The teacher-counselor must fine-tune new learning tasks so that success is possible and the child set off on a rewarding learning experience. However, fine-tuning the task is not enough; the teacher-counselor must help the child deal with the anxiety directly. The teacher-counselor must accept the child completely, without reservation, and the child must come to trust the teacher-counselor. Building a two-way trusting relationship may require hours outside the classroom, preliminary to introducing the new learning task. In those first fearful minutes of facing the page of a book, a column of figures, a sentence to diagram, the teacher-counselor should probably be physically close to the student, and he may well want to recognize the student's feelings of dread: "Bill, you really hate to get started on this, right?" or "This algebra really bugs you, Grace." It is remarkable how frequently such simple acceptance removes the need for the student to do something to avoid the task. At least, someone important understands.

In schoolwork, as in other areas of the student's life, when progress is being made, when good work has been done, it is greatly rewarding for the student to have a teacher-counselor inquire about his project, to express genuine interest in it.

All significant learnings require some self-reorganization, and self-reorganization is inherently anxiety producing. The effective teacher-counselor knows this and is there to help the student manage the transformation, from being a militant nonlearner, for example, to being a child who likes school. Once the process of self-transformation is under way, it tends to gain momentum. We have heard children squeal for joy at reading a page or seen them work algebra problems by the hour for the sheer joy of it.

Motivation. Motivation is largely a pseudoproblem in teaching and learning. Classical texts emphasized its prior importance, and one frequently hears in explanation of a child's failure to learn such comments as "Billy is simply not motivated," "Susan is lazy," and "Children from such backgrounds simply do not appreciate the importance of learning." We consider such statements misguided; they cover up, probably unintentionally, the inadequacy of the instructional program being presented to the student. The truth is that young people love to learn. Learning is an intrinsically gratifying process that is engaged in spontaneously and avidly by people of all ages and all levels of intelligence. The problem is that students are frequently not interested in learning particular kinds of things that adults insist on their knowing. Ironically, their reluctance itself has been learned. It is the product of poor teaching, at home and in school. But the problem is not lack of motivation. Children called emotionally disturbed often exhibit extremely high levels of motivation to avoid engagement with "school learning" while mastering skills not approved of by adults, such as how to control the behavior of adults by having temper tantrums, how to break into a house without leaving evidence, and how to get drugs without getting caught. Healthy living organisms are by definition motivated. So, we believe, if one teaches skillfully, motivation will take care of itself. The task is to engineer situations so that motivation can be channeled in the direction agreed on as essential for the healthy development of the child.

Individualized Programming. All learning, without exception, is individualized learning. Good instruction recognizes this fact. There are individual differences not only in intelligence and readiness for academic learning but also in learning style, pace of work, and preference for rewards. Our emphasis on individualized programming springs from a recognition of the paramount importance of individual differences.

Regular schools can provide instruction in groups because the students' skill in learning compensates for the inadequacies of a generalized instructional program. Children in Re-ED schools do not have this extra margin of skill, and they can learn only if instructional programs are meticulously designed to meet individual needs. Fortunately, the small size of Re-ED groups permits individualized instruction, and the level of individualization will depend on the purposefulness and ingenuity of the teacher-counselor. Ideally, there should be a specific learning program for every child every day and for every formal learning task he will encounter.

Context and Meaning. Learning occurs best in meaningful contexts. Evidence for this principle is abundant in the research literature of the past fifty years and in daily experience either as teacher or learner. The popularity of programmed instruction based on operant conditioning principles has diverted attention from the importance of structure, meaning, relevance, and the general interconnectedness of knowing. Programmed instruction is a powerful engineering tool, but it can also trivialize learning and deprive the learner of equally powerful but less well-understood aids to understanding and the acquisition of knowledge and skills.

Much that happens in Re-ED is designed to provide a meaningful structure to support specific learnings. Many times a day, there are undertakings (planning a car wash, building a tree house, rehearsing for a play) that provide rich and meaningful contexts for specific learnings, ranging from the multiplication table to double-entry bookkeeping. Several learning enterprises last for months, even years, and make specific learnings come alive and reinforce each other in the pursuit of a long-term goal. In the wilderness camping program at Pressley Ridge School, there is no didactic instruction at all. All academic teaching and learning are associated with the meaningfulness of each day's tasks (siting a salt lick to attract night animals, whose tracks can then be learned; ordering canvas to construct a hogan; building a gravity-flow water supply from spring to camp).

In adolescence, as students begin to move into the stage of formal operations described by Piaget, the achievement of structure, context, and meaning may become more abstract. The reaction of an elderly, white Appalachian man to having a black, adolescent girl sitting on his front porch (a rarity in those parts) triggered a lively discussion of American history, the roots of prejudice and acceptance, and the exploration of other hypothetical settings where a similar tension and reconciliation might occur. Often the teacher-counselor must provide the intellectual background for her students to make sense of particular experiences, but the teacher-counselor's explanations must be delicately positioned at the growing edge of cognitive structures brought to the task by each student. It is not easy.

Active Engagement. Learning occurs best in active, purposeful doing. This is manifestly observable in young children. It is also true for older students, especially those for whom learning has not yet become a comfortable task confidently approached. Indeed, it is true for all learners, even M.D.s or Ph.D.s, who learn best when they recite to themselves or share new knowledge with others.

Yet it is striking how much of traditional teaching requires a passive response. Children are supposed to learn by being quiet, paying attention, listening, reading—with no provision for practice. But without practice one cannot learn to distinguish between right and wrong responses, to make generalizations and differentiations, and to bring into play all the senses, not just hearing or seeing. Teacher-counselors have learned hundreds of ways to elicit active learning. For example, instead of calling on one child to answer a question while others sit passively by, the teacher can arrange for all children to select and hold up cards with the correct response. In teaching chess to a junior high school student, a teacher may explain briefly the nature of the game and then have the student start playing immediately with a few pieces. As moves are mastered, pieces are added, and the game continues with an increasingly precise explanation of rules, strategies, and outcomes. We know, further, that children learn more from television if there is an adult present to engage them in thinking and talking about what they have seen than they do if they simply view and listen to a program.

Re-ED has a tremendous advantage over schools and hospitals in the application of this learning principle, since there are fewer children in groups than in regular schools, and there is more space suitable for varied and vigorous activity than is normally true in hospitals. Active engagement in learning, then, is a fundamental principle to which teacher-counselors themselves should be actively attentive.

Specificity of Task and Outcome. Learning occurs best when objectives are specific and when the tasks leading to the objective are clear, precisely delineated, and appropriate to the student's growing level of understanding. It is not enough to say that the objective is to teach a child to read or play the snare drums or operate a keypunch and verifier. These distal goals can define a general domain of work, but more proximal steps are necessary for learning to progress efficiently. For example, a proximal goal may be to help a child understand that one part of a sentence tells who or what is the doer and another part what the doer does. That sentences are so constructed can be a delightful discovery. Further, to help a student become a computer programmer, an early objective would be to help him understand a number system using base 2, or a binary system, in addition to the familiar system using base 10. And the process should be active. When the student understands the binary system, a teacher can fortify that understanding by asking the student to produce his own set of numbers and, later, of messages.

Frequently, when a student is having difficulty in understanding a task, it may be necessary to break the task down into smaller or more elementary units. The teacher-counselor should never be reluctant to give a child an opportunity to master the pieces of a mosaic before the whole is put together. Some professionally designed programmed texts provide a highly sophisticated ordering of sequential steps in mastering some larger task, such as long division or diagramming sentences or solving geometric theorems. The teacher-counselor can gain much by studying these texts. Occasionally they may be directly useful, but learning by a particular child is often a more complex enterprise than can be built into a standard learning program. The teacher-counselor must then be ready to trace back to find the branching point where difficulties first arose and then to provide a sequence of specific learning tasks to enable the child to move through the difficult spot and reach a higher level of comprehension.

Knowledge of Results. For decades, psychologists have known that learning is greatly facilitated by immediate knowledge of results. Yet in secondary schools, teachers often grade papers and return them days later; and younger children are allowed to practice without knowledge of results. The teacher-counselor should become highly sensitive to each child's particular need for guidance, for knowledge that he is on the right track, in mastering some learning task. To return to the example of teaching chess: In the early stages of learning, each correct movement of a piece should be followed immediately by a quiet "Right." Errors may be interrupted by "Better try that one again," until the right response is made, which should be identified by a positive signal. As the student catches on to the movements of each piece, external signals are not needed and should be reduced in frequency but not altogether eliminated until the movements are mastered. In many activities, like playing the piano or catching a ball, the action itself produces immediate knowledge of results. Even then, the instructor can speed learning by immediately signaling when a superior move occurs. Interestingly, even punishment for being on the right track is superior to no information in learning some tasks. For example, in a classical psychological experiment, subjects who were given a mild shock when making a correct turn in learning a maze did much better than subjects who got no information at all.

Incidentally, teacher-counselors who are trying to improve their own teaching skills also need immediate knowledge of results. Sometimes the children themselves can supply such guidance by their responses, but a supervisor can often greatly speed the process of learning to teach.

Reward and Punishment. Rewards and punishments are especially important ways of providing knowledge of results. Thanks to B. F. Skinner and the research he inspired, we now have a tremendous amount of information about these two influences on learning. First of all, a reward (or "reinforcer") is defined as an event subsequent to some behavior that increases the probability of that behavior occurring again. This seemingly circular definition simply means that it is hard to tell in advance what will be an effective reward for any particular child; therefore, some casting about for appropriate reinforcers may be necessary, especially with younger children. Some children respond to candy, others to praise; some to tokens, others to marks on a paper. Activities themselves may be reinforcing. For example, doing arithmetic problems and finishing work on time can be rewarded by activities, such as recess, for which the child previously may have had a strong preference. The timing of rewards also is important. Immediate rewards usually are more potent than delayed ones. In part they serve a guidance function ("I am on the right track"), but they also generate a pleasurable state that seems positively associated with learning. And spacing of rewards for right responses is important, too. In the early stages of learning, rewards should be frequent and then phased out as mastery occurs. But to ensure retention, rewards should be given from time to time anyway. When given on a random schedule, they sustain retention better than if given on a predictable schedule.

How difficult should learning tasks be? There is no precise answer, of course, but for such young people as come to Re-ED, the ratio of success to failure should be set very high, perhaps 90 percent or even higher.

Punishment is a different matter, and we know less of its effects than we do of the effects of positive reinforcers. Punishment can disrupt learning. As frequently administered, punishment identifies what is wrong but is not accompanied by instruction in what is right, or by rewards for right behavior. Punishment can and often does lead to unanticipated learnings, such as resentment of the punisher and the institutions with which he is associated. But punishment is not without instructive value when used gently and sparingly. By far the best procedure to encourage learning is to ignore unwanted responses and reinforce wanted responses. But sometimes this does not work, and behavior must be disrupted by punishment. In such circumstances, it seems best for the punishment to be mild and of brief duration and immediately followed by opportunities to alter behavior in desired ways, with rewards following quickly upon the occurrence of a desired response.

In time, the exercise of competence becomes its own reward. Thus, the achievement of competence tends to be cumulative. That is why, in Re-ED, we sometimes start with the achievement of competence in managing a canoe before presenting a challenge to become competent in reading. Many of the children who come to Re-ED have had long histories of failure. Re-ED seeks planfully to reverse this downward spiral and start it upward again on the basis of competence acquired in well-modulated tasks. Indeed, once a student is on an upward trajectory of competence, her major progress in academic work as in other areas of living may occur after she returns to her regular school or moves on to a job placement.

Review. Review early and often and then less frequently is a sound strategy for promoting learning. Most forgetting occurs immediately after learning but is seldom complete. A modest amount of effort invested in review soon after learning can restore peak performance. Fifty minutes of distributed review is likely to be more effective than an hour of concentrated practice, for most (but not all) learning tasks.

It is useful, if not precisely accurate, to think of two types of memory: short-term memory and long-term memory. Short-term memory refers to the retention of information for immediate use, such as looking up and remembering a telephone number long enough to get a call made. Long-term memory refers to the retention of information that has been processed. Short-term memory has a finite capacity; most people can retain in short-term memory about seven items, plus or minus two. Long-term memory, on the other hand, is theoretically infinite. The problem in long-term memory is to get the right cue to call up the previously learned material. Information is transferred from short-term to long-term memory by a process involving a number of factors, including intending to remember, reviewing materials learned, putting materials in larger contexts, and using various devices, such as mental images, to aid retrieval. The twenty-four-hour, five-days-a-week program in Re-ED provides an unusually favorable circumstance for the processing of information to improve retention.

Generalization. Learning tends to be remarkably specific and strongly tied to particular circumstances of time and place and people. But learning is useful only when it can be readily applied in new situations; that is, when it can be generalized. There is substantial experimental evidence that deliberate teaching for generalization can increase the utility of knowledge, making it more widely applicable than it might be otherwise, even to situations with little explicit similarity to that in which the initial learning occurred. Re-ED, with its twenty-four-hour investment, its small groups of children, and its good communication among teacher-counselors, children, parents, teachers, and agency people, can efficiently facilitate generalization. The principal strategy is to point out at the time of learning how what is learned can be applied in different situations. The learning can be further generalized by having people in new situations point out the applicability of the newly acquired learning. In time, the student himself can deliberately generalize by asking himself: "What have I learned in other situations that I can apply in this one?"

Work Style. As elaborated on elsewhere, learning can be greatly facilitated by learning how to learn. Inexperienced learners in general, and "emotionally disturbed" learners in particular, approach new learning tasks in an almost random fashion, making

little use of what they have learned before, and with little appreciation that they can govern their own learning performance.
Many college students have not acquired this fundamental understanding. Learnable strategies for improving one's own learning
and problem-solving skills are myriad. They range from such simple matters as lining figures up straight, to avoid errors in adding
or subtracting, to algorithms for checking on complex calculations. Students can be taught to assemble all materials prior to
starting a macramé project; to be sure to know what the problem
is before trying to solve it; to lay out available information systematically and to ask whether additional information is needed; to
check work for errors (how frequently this simple step is neglected!); to ask if what is being learned makes sense in the light
of what is already known; to draw diagrams to clarify relationships; to recite to one's self and share new learnings with other
people; to get an overview of a chapter to be learned, using all
markers provided by the author; to keep notes; to skim when material is already known; to use mental images to facilitate memory.
Through such techniques, one can improve his ability as a learner
and problem solver.

Educational Assessment

The kind of precision teaching done in a Re-ED program requires a thorough appraisal of the child's educational status. Information for the appraisal is obtained from the child's school, from
diagnostic tests, and from continuing observation in the Re-ED
program.

As described earlier, the liaison teacher-counselor visits the
child's school and talks with all those involved in planning for the
referral of the child, including always the child's teacher and sometimes the principal, the school psychologist, the school social
worker. With older children, several teachers may be involved and
perhaps a guidance counselor. The objective is to get precise information that can be used in designing an individual teaching and
learning plan for the child on entry into the Re-ED program. Information may be obtained from the child's cumulative record or
from current observations by school personnel. The inquiry may
be organized around six major concerns:

1. *Reasons for referral.* What specifically are the child's difficulties? What past efforts have been made to help him? What changes would need to be brought about for the child to be acceptable to the school? What person at the school would be assigned responsibility for working with the liaison teacher-counselor to plan and carry out a program for the child?

2. *Academic deficits and strengths.* From achievement records and the results of tests administered by the school, what are the specific deficits in the child's academic performance, especially with respect to mastery of basic skills in reading, writing, spelling, and arithmetic? Are data available on level of achievement in each of these functions? In what areas does the child show special academic competence? What is his level of intellectual functioning? Of vocabulary development? Does the child have special talents, such as musical talent? Does he have interests or hobbies that could provide a foundation for an instructional program? Does the child participate in extracurricular activities having academic implications? What are the child's work habits in school? At home?

3. *Behavioral deficits and strengths.* To what extent are behavioral problems involved in the referral? Specifically, what kinds of behaviors need to be remedied before the child would be acceptable to the school? What is the history of the behavior? What is the child's general attitude toward school? What is the child's attendance history? Does he get along better with some teachers than with others? Are there situations that evoke unacceptable behavior or commendable behavior? Have teachers discovered ways of managing the behavior of the child? How does the child's behavior in school compare with his behavior out of school? For older children, are there known problems with juvenile authorities? How does the child relate to other children? To teachers? Is unacceptable behavior relatively constant, or is it episodic? If it is episodic, is it related to particular circumstances?

4. *Health.* Do school records or observation of the child provide information about his health status that may be useful in planning a program at Re-ED? Is the child on medication or a special regimen? Does the school need to make special provisions for the health needs of the child, such as privacy for urine testing, supervision for taking medication, or provision of special diets? What is known of the child's general nutritional status? Of his eating habits? Are there any specific health problems that need to be remedied before the child could be returned to the school?

5. *Family support.* What is the child's family background? How supportive are the parents in the efforts of the school to teach

and to deal with the child's behavior? Are there particular members of the family who can be counted on to concern themselves with the well-being of the child? Does the family situation itself generate problems that carry over into school performance or conduct? Who in the family is most likely to be able to provide support and guidance for the child during his stay at Re-ED and after graduation?

6. *Placement after Re-ED.* What arrangements should be made for school placement of the child after graduation from Re-ED? Can he return to the same school? If so, what would be the proper grade placement? What changes in conduct or academic achievement must be effected during the child's stay in Re-ED to make possible his readmission to the school? If a change of schools is indicated, is it possible at this time to indicate which school it should be? If an adolescent, should plans be made for him to attend college or to go early into a vocational training program? Does he have interests or talents that suggest directions for vocational planning?

The educational diagnostician may give an array of tests to identify strengths and weaknesses in academic performance to obtain information needed to plan a highly specific instructional program. The tests naturally vary widely according to the age of the child, the general nature of her problem, the shape of plans that may be made for her future. Projective tests and personality tests are seldom used, since they provide little information of use in designing a plan to help the child. A general intelligence test may be given or scores obtained from the school or mental health center, but, again, such information is sought only when it can make a difference in program planning. Routine testing is discouraged.

Not infrequently, the educational diagnostician or the teacher-counselor may develop special tests to assess progress in highly specific areas. In most instances, the educational diagnostician and the teacher-counselors are interested primarily in the child's performance with respect to some criterion established by the child's own strengths and deficits. This is sometimes referred to as "criterion-referenced testing." There is relatively little interest in comparing the child's performance with respect to national norms.

Educational assessment is an ongoing process, with teacher-counselors making daily and weekly observations on academic performance. Again, the emphasis is not on achievement with respect to group norms but on how the child performs with respect to her previous performance. Frequently the teacher-counselor will establish "baseline data" on some specific aspect of academic performance and use this reference point to determine whether or not instructional procedures are working. Tests are repeated following instruction, and teaching procedures are changed or new baselines established. Of special interest to teacher-counselors are behaviors that impede learning and that can be worked on in both the day and night programs. Sometimes observation can provide information that tests do not reveal. For example, a child may have some idiosyncratic and inaccurate method of addition or subtraction or some peculiar way of analyzing a sentence. Observations may lead to highly specific plans for helping the child overcome that deficit.

Educational programming in Re-ED is always highly specific. An educational plan is developed for each child and modified as frequently as necessary. "To teach a child to read" is far too general a statement of objectives. Instead, the teacher-counselor concentrates on specific intermediate steps that must be mastered in order for the child to be able to read effectively. And so, too, for other subjects, whether, for younger children, it is arithmetic, reading, spelling, pronunciation of words, or handwriting, or, for older students, algebra, sentence construction, drafting, or the writing of a short story.

Each week, usually on Monday mornings, each child sets goals for himself for the week, usually in discussion with teacher-counselors and other students. While the goals, three or four in number, may touch various aspects of the child's life, goals involving academic performance are nearly always included. Goal achievement is assessed daily and at the end of the week. The specificity of goals and of methods agreed on to achieve the goals facilitates the integration of the day and night programs.

Special Instruction

Depending in part on available funds and available talent, Re-ED programs use specialized instructors to supplement the work of regular teacher-counselors and enrich the learning experiences of students. Special instructors may be full time or part time. From time to time and from school to school, special instruction has been provided in music, dance, theater, painting, pottery, weaving, silk screen, chess, technical rock climbing and caving, astronomy, health, woodworking, nature study, auto mechanics, hairdressing, childcare, family planning, music recording, secretarial skills, computer operations, computer programming, and bookkeeping.

As is true throughout the Re-ED curriculum, special instructors are interested in teaching children and adolescents to be competent in something, and they are equally interested in teaching them to be effective people capable of managing their lives and gaining satisfaction in living.

Here is an account of a special instructor in arts and crafts who emphasizes both goals.

Arts and Crafts Studio
Cumberland House*

In one way or another, most children come to Cumberland House because they have, by some definition, failed. The arts and crafts studio provides a setting in which children can succeed, where they can explore, invent, discover, create, laugh, listen to music, sing, dance, feel bad, talk, and be still. It is a place that is very special, respected by children and adults alike. Few of its furnishings lack the involvement of children's hands; its walls of light yellow, under close inspection, reveal the many runs and pinholes where children have had too much or too little paint in their brush; the gay mural done in oil paint on the rough rock wall is a reminder of group struggles as each child in the school wanted to leave as big a mark as possible to show the work of his hands. In this sense, the children own the studio.

Ownership implies responsibility on the part of the child for the management of his belongings. A child at Re-ED is responsible for taking care of the things he has made. Each child has his own shelf in the studio for his products. One might expect that many objects would be broken or missing; however, a child soon grows to value and to care for his own possessions and to respect the work of others. Tools, equipment, and materials belong to every

---

*This account was written by Billie J. Garrison, instructor in arts and crafts at Cumberland House, Nashville, Tennessee.

child. Their proper care and use constitutes a major teaching emphasis in the studio. The children as a group maintain a vigil among themselves to care for these things properly. Occasionally a tool may disappear, but, as soon as the disappearance is discovered by the group, the tool usually finds its way back to its proper place. Sometimes a child will misuse a tool, but his group will be quick to bring it to his attention.

When a child develops a sense of pride in accomplishment, there seems to be a change in his evaluation of himself. He no longer is content to be last to get his materials to begin work, and he enjoys studying and handling the things he has made. These seem to indicate feelings of self-worth that were weak indeed upon enrollment in Re-ED.

When a child first comes to art class and is faced with a set of drawing materials, he might be asked to draw, for example, a picture of a child rolling a tire down a sidewalk. Various reactions include burying his head in his arms on the table, sitting quietly with his head down and his hands hidden under the table, or violently opposing the teacher. His behavior indicates that, for one reason or another, he does not want to try. Support for this child varies. There have been times when the color-book approach has been used, and the child will simply be required to fill in what has been drawn for him. Or there may be a gentle encouragement from the teacher-counselor for him to try freehand drawing. The group usually explains that individuals do not have to draw a certain way and that honest efforts are always valued. Sometimes, however, there may be a demand by the teacher that the child make the effort to draw. The important thing is that the child participate in some way with an individual contribution. During these first tentative efforts, the child begins to form a basis for a self-evaluative, noncompetitive approach to his work in the arts and crafts class.

Leaving a child alone with stimulating materials is an important part of his development in creative problem solving. Opportunity to feel his way through a task with little or no attention can give him confidence as well as great satisfaction in the experience. As a child involves himself and works independently, he is praised and receives some kind of responsibility in setting up class materials for the next art period.

While overteaching is an ever present threat to the child's development in creative problem solving, failure to recognize the child's need for help when he feels himself reaching a dead end can be equally harmful.

Time seems to be that intangible precious commodity which delights children when they have some control over it. "Can we use our class time for working in clay today?" is a frequent question. Sometimes the teacher asks "How would you like to sit and talk this period?" Sometimes the students react negatively to the teacher's plan for the arts and crafts activity for the day; in such instances, they themselves assume responsibility for coming up with a good activity.

Teaching a child to work on the potter's wheel provides an entré that moves the child quickly to the point where he is willing to trust an adult for help. This experience is not for selected children but is part of the curriculum in the arts and crafts program. At first, a child may refuse to try the potter's wheel; soon, however, the magic of what happens to a piece of clay in the hands of its shaper is too appealing for him to resist. Even the most fearful child at camp one season, on the very last day, requested an opportunity to try. She did and was so pleased with her experience that she brought the maintenance man, a valued friend, to view her creation. She also asked to work on the wheel again.

The single most important factor in teaching a disturbed child how to throw on the potter's wheel is constant support during the introductory lessons, support to the point of the teacher's taking the child's hands in his and performing the entire throwing operation through the hands of the child. During these lessons, verbal interaction occurs with ease; questions, answers, and laughter come naturally. As the child's need of support begins to fade, there usually remains a relationship which permits the child to come to the adult for help when he needs it.

Frequently a child will request evaluation of work he has just finished. It is recognized that a child must have approval and guidance, but, at the same time, measures are initiated to teach him to rely on his own judgment of what is satisfying. In arts and crafts, the degrees of freedom in allowing a child to evaluate his own work are much greater than in most areas in elementary school. It seems an appropriate area to begin teaching individuals to evaluate their own experiences as well as to learn that some things in life are satisfying not because they meet certain objective criteria but because they are pleasurable to do.

To guide an idea from inception to realization is an exciting and satisfying experience for a child in the arts and crafts program. When a child's idea becomes a reality, he grows. Furthermore, he is motivated to continue to realize ideas. A group was making a bicycle paddle-wheel boat. A child suggested mounting the paddle wheels on the sides of the boat rather than on the rear of the transom. The suggestion simplified an otherwise complex task. From that point on, the child was alert to find other ways of making the craft better and more efficient. Experiments with glaze colorants can be used to recognize worthwhile ideas. When a child discovers an interesting glaze color, the recipe is saved for others to use, and the color is named for the child. For example, it might be called a "Todd Green" or a "Smith Brown." When a child knows that his thinking can influence something in a meaningful way, he is alert to take part in serious planning. It gives him real purpose for participation; it gives him a knowledge of his essential function in the group; and it gives him courage to face other areas of learning with more assurance.

Cherokee Enterprise
Cumberland House*

The Bobcats (boys, ages eight to ten) had found a small wooden shelter, originally a storage house for athletic equipment, and decided to use it as a clubhouse. The boys were told that the house could be theirs to use if they could think of some way to make it especially interesting as a clubhouse. The group talked it over and decided that the house could be made into a Northwest Indian stilthouse. The interest in Indians gathered momentum rapidly, and they moved into an enterprise that lasted several months and provided a vehicle for learning that ranged from spelling and arithmetic to art, music, and dancing. The goals of the group and those of the teacher-counselors were not always the same as the project developed. The boys, needless to say, were interested in learning about Indians. The teachers, in addition to wanting the group to learn about Indians, hoped to use this subject as a vehicle for teaching basic skills (arithmetic, reading, spelling, and writing).

After beginning work on their Indian stilthouse, the group became interested in the types of shelters used by other Indians. Encyclopedias and other reference books gave pictures and descriptions of many different Indian lodgings. The boys decided to make small reproductions of several of these shelters and mount them on blocks of wood. One made a southern teepee, another a Navajo adobe hut (using mud and clay he mixed himself), another a hogan frame out of small willow twigs, and another a Pueblo adobe hut, with "bear skin" (cut from a fur glove) inside the hut as furnishing.

The task of decorating the stilthouse led into a study of Indian designs. Though most of the boys had not been at all interested in art previously, they became excited by the colors and geometric shapes in Indian art. They sketched the designs on the stilt-

*This account was written by Robert Slagle, formerly a teacher-counselor at Cumberland House, Nashville, Tennessee, and currently program coordinator in the Division of Children and Youth Services, Department of Mental Health and Mental Retardation, State of Tennessee.

house, chose the colors, and spent much of the afternoon time during one week painting the house in vivid colors and authentic designs. The thunderbird designs especially fascinated the boys (probably because they had just heard the folk tale about the magical thunderbird), and several evening periods were spent in drawing original thunderbird designs on construction paper and then taping them together into a paper totem pole, which decorated the unit wall for the rest of the month.

The block patterns found on vases and sometimes in Indian weaving were easy for the boys to reproduce on graph paper. At the time the boys were making these graph designs, each worked on a dictionary of Indian names and words and made an original cover for his book with a graph design.

It came time for the Bobcats to have their turn at presenting an assembly program for the rest of the school. Being well into their study of Indians, they chose to give an Indian program. They planned an exhibit. They would show the totem poles they had made, the models of Indian houses, their book covers, and their reference books about Indians. The boys were proud of what they had done but realized that this was not enough for a program. They decided to put on "Indian" entertainment. From scrap leather pieces, feathers, lacing, and scissors, they produced belts, necklaces, headbands, and decorations for the leggings. Loin cloths were made out of burlap and sheeting. For entertainment, an Indian dance (in the costumes the boys had made) was planned, with Indian songs accompanied by drums made from cans and rubber sheets.

At this point, the group had been studying Indians for almost a month. The Cherokee Indians, a tribe that had once inhabited the area, had become the focus of greatest interest in the group. This interest grew through the use of Cherokee folklore as bedtime stories and class reading assignments. Their favorite Cherokee story was "The Trail of Tears," the story of the removal of the Cherokee Nation to Oklahoma and of the eventual granting of a reservation in North Carolina.

With this background, the boys were presented with the idea of spending a week camping with Indian boys on the Cherokee Reservation. The suggestion met with excited approval, and the work and plans that led to the trip became the vehicle for teaching many skills during the following weeks. Motivation was higher at this point than it had been at any previous time.

The boys were told that, before they could make the trip, many arrangements would have to be made with the Indians whom they would be visiting. They decided to make the arrangements by writing letters. Since none of the boys had ever written a letter, the classroom instruction would contribute directly, and quite visibly, to the evening activity. The classroom teacher instructed the boys on the basic form of a letter, and that night they composed a letter to be sent to the agent on the Cherokee reservation. After the letter was composed and written on the blackboard, each boy made his own copy of the letter and added a personal note of his own.

In response to their letters, the agent at the reservation sent each boy additional addresses to which he could write. During the week, the boys wrote to a teacher in the Indian school and to the classroom they hoped to visit. Each boy also wrote a letter and sent a picture of himself to be given to a friend in the classroom who would be the host for that boy during the visit. The week of letter writing was concluded by a visit to a post office, where the boys saw what a letter goes through before it is mailed and how mail is sorted when it reaches its destination.

The next step in preparation for the trip was to study several sets of maps to determine the most interesting route. Maps were procured from airlines, travel bureaus, and gas stations. The trip was to lead from Nashville through Chattanooga into the Smoky Mountains. The boys outlined the route on each of the maps, and finally each made a map of his own. The boys were fascinated with the fact that they would be passing into another time zone (from Central to Eastern at a point near Chattanooga), and this added more interest to map study as each boy carefully drew in the line marking the point at which the time would change by an hour.

The boys had been saving money for several weeks, but they realized that they did not have enough for the trip, so they planned a budget. Travel expenses were estimated on the basis of the number of miles they would travel, the number of meals they would need to buy, the side trips they would take, and the amount needed for each boy to spend for refreshments and souvenirs. Some of these plans were made in the classroom, some of them during the evening study periods.

None of the boys could tell time, and, though several had watches, there was little motivation for learning. Time telling was introduced in the classroom as the boys were planning their daily schedules for the trip, hour by hour. The bulletin board in the unit was covered by an extensive one-week schedule; each time in the schedule was designated by the face of a clock drawn in the margin, with the hands drawn in at the appropriate times. By the end of the week, each of the boys could tell time from a clock, some very well, others at least to the point that they would be able to proceed on their own in learning to tell time.

Reading was among the skills stressed during the planning sessions. The group members were eager to study all the available information on the Cherokee people and their reservation. They became familiar with the story of Sequoia, who gave the alphabet to the Cherokees; with Junaluska, who once saved the life of Andrew Jackson; with Tsali, the chief who loved peace. They learned several Cherokee words: *Nantahala,* meaning land of the noon-day sun; *Hiawassee,* beautiful river; *Konaheeta,* beautiful valley; *Cheoah,* land of the fox. The boys were reading because they wanted to know and reading was a way of finding out.

Early on the appointed morning, the boys were in the car ready to leave on the long-awaited trip. The journey to the Smokies was accompanied by excited chatter as the boys wondered how their Indian friends would like them and whether they could be recognized by their pictures. They watched for the marker where they could set their watches ahead an hour, and tried to hold their breath "for an hour" as they crossed from one time zone to another. The car had to be backed up so they could cross the line again because one boy missed it and didn't hold his breath.

The Indian school was ready for the boys. An Indian man explained how blowguns are made and used, and he guided a tour through each classroom of Indian children who were to serve as their hosts during the stay. The week was full of hikes, fishing, games, and trips with the Indian boys who were chosen to be hosts to our boys. There were visits to Indian homes and industries near the reservation. But the most fun of all was going to school with the Indian boys.

The trip taught each of the boys from school, and possibly the Indian boys, an important lesson. They learned that boys are not different just because their skin happens to be white or red. They learned that Indian boys play many of the same games as boys in Nashville, that the same things cause joy in the Smokies that cause joy in any other place. Maybe they even learned that every person deserves respect regardless of creed or color.

In the context of pursuing group goals in the Cherokee Enterprise, there was opportunity to work toward individual goals at all three levels mentioned in the earlier analysis. Pete, for example, was seen as a serious motivational problem, defiant and withdrawn much of the time, unable to engage himself with school-related tasks. He was given to occasional, and not very predictable, outbursts of temper, which, because of his size and strength, were dangerous to anyone within his reach. The incentives provided by the enterprise—working on the clubhouse and the Indian ceremonies and planning the trip—were powerful enough to entice him into participation. Tentatively at first, he initiated individual tasks, but later he was able to express enthusiasm and to begin seeing himself as a fully functioning member of the group. All the boys, of course, had some history of problems in taking constructive roles in a peer group, and the enterprise gave a sense of common purpose and group unity that allowed experimentation in role taking and realistic feedback from peers. From the description of activities like writing a letter and learning to tell time, it is apparent that level of attainment in school was low for the entire group and that individual programs in basic educational skills were required so that each boy could make a realistic contribution toward the achievement of group goals.

Folk Music Enterprise
Pine Breeze Center*

Chattanooga lies nestled between the southern end of Walden's Ridge and the Smoky Mountains. It is often used as the southern boundary of "Appalachia." And, like other communities of Appalachia, remnants of the traditional culture of the Southern Highlands remain in the valleys and ridges around Chattanooga.

In the fall of 1975, I set out with several of my students at Pine Breeze Center to locate and document one aspect of our fast-disappearing traditional culture—the traditional music of our area.

Ballads, songs, and fiddle tunes that have been handed down from generation to generation have long interested collectors who have visited the Southern Highlands. Back at the turn of the century, collectors such as Cecil Sharp had found ballads that were directly descended from seventeenth-century English ballads. The Library of Congress did extensive field recording of traditional musicians in the 1930s, but the Chattanooga area had been neglected by all of them. We were the first to do field recordings of traditional music in our area.

While certain that traditional musicians were still around, we first had to locate them. The answer was close to school. Paul Skiles, one of our maintenance men, told me of his brother who played fiddle. After talking to Raymond Skiles, we set up a time to record him at the school. We borrowed recording equipment from individuals and a local music store, called up one of the local newspapers, and set up the equipment. Raymond Skiles arrived, but he brought with him a fiddler from Soddy, Tennessee (about fifteen miles north of the school), named Eldia Barbee. The fiddle came alive in Eldia's hands with the hard-driving music of earlier times.

We took our tapes to Charles Wolfe at Middle Tennessee State University, who is a nationally known expert on string band

*This account was written by Ronald Williams, teacher-counselor at Pine Breeze Center, Chattanooga, Tennessee, who conceived and directed the enterprise.

music. He said we had a gem of an old-time fiddler and ought to do a record. A year later, after we received a $600 grant from the Tennessee Arts Commission, "The Eldia Barbee Tapes," an album of old-time fiddle tunes, came out on the Pine Breeze label. We sold the records both locally and by mail. With the profits from the sales, we bought recording equipment and produced another record—and another, and, as of 1979, the students at Pine Breeze had produced six albums of local traditional music. The project is self-supporting, and the record albums are recorded, mixed, edited, and produced by students.

The equipment that the students learn to operate is fairly complex. Basically, they run a four-channel tape recorder during the field recording sessions (done at the musicians' homes). Back at Pine Breeze, they mix the four-channel recordings into stereo by using a mixer and a two-channel recorder. They also have to edit and splice and tape into a final mix. The students have been responsible for writing liner notes, laying out jacket designs, and taking and developing photographs. They are also responsible for keeping the books on record sales (a quite complex system set up by the state auditors), filling orders, and mailing out our project newsletters.

The kids get a lot of benefits out of the project. Sometimes the "therapeutic" value of the project directly relates to their problem. One girl who was in the project came to us severely abused. She didn't talk for months. We visited the Foxfire Project group in Rabun's Gap, Georgia, where they were beginning a music project similar to ours. The girl sat silently on the front porch of their cabin for three days. For the next couple of months, she began to interact more on the trips that we made. I asked her to write a couple of paragraphs for the liner notes of the third album. In the middle of the article, she wrote that the music "brings people together, and it makes you wanna dance, clap your hands, stomp your feet, and yell as loud as you can. It lifts up your spirits and makes you wanna talk so much; it would be a shame to let the songs go and never give an interest to them."

The interaction between the kids and the old folks—the meeting of cultures and generations—is always fascinating. Ezell, a black kid from the city, was the first black person ever inside Payne Jones's home on Flattop Mountain. Payne had been a moonshiner and had spent years in Brushy Mountain Prison for a murder that involved some illegal whiskey. Ezell started sketching Payne. Payne, enthralled by Ezell's deft hand, suddenly forgot the differences in color and age. Ezell is now a young adult working with younger children at a youth program in the city; his sketch of Payne still is tacked to the walls of Payne's mountain cabin.

The project has enabled both the students and the folk musicians to go to places they would not have been able to go without it. The Barbee family from Soddy and several of my students have been to Washington, D.C., twice. The Barbees have played at the National Folk Festival there two years in a row. But the trips to the ridges and valleys are more important than the trips to faraway places. Listening to eighty-year-old Ella Hughes sing old English ballads that have been handed down in her family for five generations; or walking with Eldia Barbee through the fields and picking poke sallet, lambs quarters, and wild mustard; or watching Jim Speir carefully carve a coondog out of a piece of chestnut; or listening to Homer Chastain play a tune centuries old on a fiddle he exquisitely crafted—these are the trips and experiences that will be valuable as these traditions die off.

The greatest immediate benefit for the students is a great feeling of success and pride that comes from seeing their names on an album cover, or reading a review in a national magazine complimenting their work. They know that it was their fingers that controlled the machines that made the recordings.

In four years, about fifty students have been involved in the project. They have produced (as of September 1979) six record albums and are working on a seventh. Orders have been received from all fifty states and four foreign countries. Net income for the project for record orders has been about $5,000. The community has had the music from over thirty of their traditional musicians preserved, and we believe the students have learned a little about their roots and how much they can accomplish.

Below are two revealing passages, one by teacher-counselor Ron Williams, who created "The Folk Music Enterprise," and the other by one of his students, an adolescent girl whose *Diagnostic and Statistical Manual* classification is "Childhood Schizophrenia, Simple Type." The passages say a lot about each.

Pine Breeze Teacher-Counselor: Late one night, as we were driving back from a state park in Georgia where we had played, Eldie began talking—more reflectively than usual. He said that his education had ended in the fourth grade but that he still considered himself educated. He knew when to plant, how to grow, and when to harvest every crop grown in this area. He knew how to raise stock, and he knew how to survive with little or no money. His only regret was that he didn't know the words to describe or how to write his knowledge. He said that he would like to write a book—for the kids—so that they could learn the knowledge that comes from living a hard life, without having to go through the actual struggle. If sixty-seven years of hard work and living could be written down, what an encyclopedia it would make.

The albums of old-time music my students have produced will affect people different ways. The folklorist may wonder what a twenty-five-year-old social studies teacher is doing playing with a sixty-seven-year-old fiddler. They will not know that Eldie's music is one of the few things he has to share and that he would be deeply offended if I refused to play along—even for the sake of the "purity"of his music. (They will not know, also, the many times Eldie has taken my banjo away from me to show me the *right* way to play a tune. I'm beginning to feel a part of the traditional process.)

People who are not familiar with old-time music may like the idea of the project but may wonder at the "roughness" of the music. They will not know the integral part the music has played in the lives of Eldie or Blaine or Florrie and the rest of their friends. Or the several generations through which the music has traveled. Then the roughness takes on a beauty.

My hope for the records is to share what I've hoped my students have learned. The lack of pretension, the honesty, the sense of community and family—all those things that Eldie would have liked to write about—that is what I hope they have learned. These folks are the last generation of traditional Appalachians. When my students have children, there will be no Eldie Barbees, no Blaine Smiths or Florrie Stewarts, and we will still need their qualities.

Pine Breeze Student: The trips are really great. There is a wide chance of meeting interesting people who make their work of playing music something worth hearing.

The songs have background history that will not be forgotten because the songs are being passed down to people who want to make something out of songs. And some do, by recording, selling records, and tuning people in to how good the music sounds.

I wish I had the chance to be stuck on the mountain, getting out my fiddle and playing all day.

But I guess it's okay just to watch and listen to what messages are being brought out of the songs. Also it is interesting to hear personally what people think of traditional music.

The music is entertaining and educational, and it brings people together and it makes you wanna dance, clap your hands, stomp your feet and yell as loud as you can. It lifts up your spirits, and makes you wanna talk so much; it would be a shame to let the songs go and never give an interest to the songs.

It's also a cinch to square dance and listen to the music both at the same time, they can really go together.

To me, traditional music is something to come home to. Listening and playing music can keep a smile on your face all day.

When we have nothing to do, nowhere to go, or even if it's raining outdoors, you can always stay inside and listen.

Model Rocketry Enterprise
Wright School*

I would not attempt to outline specifically what I've done with the boys in the area of model rockets for the purpose of providing another teacher-counselor with a course program. Although this was my ambition at one point, I have become more and more convinced that the program must come from the teacher-counselor. A unit in music can, I feel, be as effective as a mountain climbing experience, if the teacher-counselor is interested, enthusiastic, and fairly competent in the chosen area. My personal interests lean toward science and the outdoors. These are areas in which I am comfortable and, most important, I feel *happy*. Needless to say, my program over the past three years has reflected these interests. Fortunately, my supervisors have allowed me the freedom to pursue them with the boys. I might add that I do not feel uncomfortable tackling an area in which I am interested but know very little.

The rocketry enterprise came about when, a couple of years ago, some of the boys in my group caught me industriously working on my first model. One of my favorite professional journals is *Boy's Life* magazine, and I couldn't resist the introductory offer of a model rocket firm in Colorado. With my personal interest at a peak, I easily interested the boys in my new discovery. The model rocket enterprise which followed was something of a battle to see if I could stay one step ahead of the boys. Enthusiasm ran high, and frustrations were many. We had a lot of fun and learned a great deal through the trial-and-error solution of very real problems. For example, we failed to consider weather conditions until, one day, we lost sight of a parachute and payload section (containing a live mouse) after chasing it down range for almost two miles. Subsequently, launchings were postponed when there was sufficient wind to deflect smoke. We learned by experience, however, that a sea-level calm was not always indicative of the conditions at 2,500 feet.

We learned, too, the value of good craftsmanship. A boy who is anxious to complete his model may glue a fin off center. While the teacher-counselor can point this out at the time, the advice may not be taken seriously. But let a boy see his model wob-

*This account was written by David Friedlein, former teacher-counselor at Wright School, Durham, North Carolina.

ble to a 250-foot altitude and burn out, and you can bet he'll straighten out that fin before the next launch date! Another child learned the value of following directions. Model rocket engines come with different thrust and burning time characteristics. With each model, the manufacturer has specified which engines are most suitable. One boy selected a more powerful engine than that suggested, in hopes of achieving a higher altitude. At 25 feet, the model exploded, and only a few parts were ever recovered. He concluded that the engine was faulty and wrote a letter explaining the incident to the manufacturer. A kind response pointed out that the structural characteristics of the particular model were not sufficient to survive the tremendous speed produced by the engine and that the model probably shed a fin, thus upsetting the stability and causing the rocket to fly to pieces. A lesson learned.

The debut of the camping program forced us to wrap up our rocket program for the year. The following spring, however, Jane (my teammate) and I decided to include both boys' groups in a similar program. We planned for the unit to cover a sixteen-week period. Each week, the two groups met together for a class. The lesson considered both real and model rockets and was usually accompanied by a film or demonstration. Later in the week, the groups met separately. This class began with a simple quiz covering the material that had been covered in the joint meeting, and the rest of the time was used for building models. Occasional afternoons were taken for launchings. This went fairly well, but Jane and I shared our dissatisfactions. The program seemed too structured; spontaneity was not as apparent as in the earlier effort. Building the models together and step by step as a class produced some attractive models but handicapped those boys who were eager and able to move at a faster pace. We dropped the classroom quiz after eight weeks, convinced that the children were learning no more by it. With some reluctance, we continued the launching data sheet (a lengthy form filled out by each child for each rocket fired: date, weather, type of rocket, and so on). It was evident that the child wanted to see his rocket fly, recover it, and know how high it went. He did not care about the date, launch site, and humidity! There were some positives, however. The older boys built an ingenious, eight-pad, remote-control launch system. Jane and I saw miles of instructional film and have a much better idea of what is available and what is useful. Also, we have a better idea of what to expect from different children in terms of ability. We found that some of the younger or more disturbed children were simply not capable of building the model, much less grasping any of the more complex concepts.

The second rocketry experience was certainly not a failure, but I am convinced that it could have been handled more effectively. I think that, in our enthusiasm, we lost sight of the individuality of the children. The projects we have worked out can be categorized as "independent" or "group." Group projects may involve building a cabin, erecting a tepee, or planning for a week-long trip to the Outer Banks on the coast of North Carolina. They require unified planning, and all the boys must meet certain expectations. Model rockets, on the other hand, represent a more independent sort of activity. There is no common goal, no natural motivation toward cooperation.

Having tried both independent and group activities, I have come to favor the latter. My reason is simply that most of the day is spent at independent activities and that most of our children are terribly deficient in the social area. With so little evening activity time available, I feel that group involvement is the best investment. This is not the easy way out. On the contrary, I could probably sit down to an evening of reading if the boys were all building models or working in the shop. Group projects precipitated all sorts of problems, which only strengthens my conviction. All this is not to discount my general positive feelings about model rocketry. I've not found a better single stimulation for interest and motivation. The problem facing me now is how to incorporate it into some larger context of group goals.

I wish I could report that the rocket enterprise was packed with educational gems, but I didn't really feel that was the case. One of the problems is that the child needs to get over the sheer thrill of seeing his model go up. Once this novelty wears off, he must, of necessity, become more involved in the technical aspects. He begins to wonder about how high, how fast, how stable. He begins to design and build his own models, static test them in a wind tunnel, make refinements, and fly them. Unfortunately, few children are here long enough to get past the thrill stage, and many of the technical aspects are beyond our children academically.

I would maintain that the program does two very constructive things. First, it creates interest in real space travel and exploration. The child can now watch a live launching on television with some understanding of what has gone before, and what is meant by such terms as *thrust, staging,* and *orbit.* He leaves the program with an interest in model rocketry, which he may pick up sometime after discharge from Wright School. I have been pleased to see several fathers pick up on this hobby. In several cases, it has become a mutual enterprise between a father and son who formerly shared no common interests. Second—and, I suspect, more important—this program almost always results in the child's experiencing joy and satisfaction from the accomplishment of a demanding and exciting task.

11

Helping Children Learn to Behave

In discussing the ecological perspective that undergirds the Re-ED approach to working with troubled and troubling children and youth, we made the point that the child or adolescent, in almost every instance, contributes to the discord that leads to the breakdown of the ecosystem. A transactional process is assumed. Possibly in response to environmental pressures or expectations, a child begins to behave in ways that are unacceptable to important people in her life—to her mother, father, teacher, or some other high-valence person, usually an adult. The adult may respond to the child's unacceptable behavior in ways that ensure the perpetuation of the behavior; reinforcement unwittingly given increases the likelihood that the "bad" behavior will be repeated, and possibly intensified. As a child gets older, the transactional situation becomes more complex, extending far beyond these simple interactions. The adult begins to generalize about the child, thinking of her as "a troublemaker," "a person not to be trusted," and so on. The child may also generalize and incorporate these expectations in her self-concept: "I am a mean or unworthy person." Re-ED seeks to interrupt this escalating process. One part of the task is to help high-valence adults change their behavior and their expectations of the child. The other part of the task is to help the child change her own behavior. The fundamental learning principles in each instance are the same. Furthermore, the principles elucidated in Chapter Ten on "Learning to Learn" apply with equal force to "Learning to Behave." The principles are continuous; what changes are objectives, strategies, and methods.

Helping children learn to behave demands a high level of understanding of and sensitivity to normal patterns of development as well as individual departures therefrom. Procedures that work for a six-year-old are likely to fail with a sixteen-year-old. Furthermore, variability will be great among six-year-olds and among sixteen-year-olds. The age and developmental level of the child or adolescent will provide only general guidance for program planning. Individual differences will be substantial. In Re-ED, as in other effective treatment programs, intervention strategies are highly individualized.

In academic learning, developmental tasks are reasonably well defined by familiar expectations: to be able to read, write, and do arithmetic at a specified age or grade level; to have a knowledge of history, mathematics, and other subjects related to entry into work or into further education. Developmental patterns and sequences in *behavior,* however, are much less well known than are those in academic development. It is imperative, then, that teacher-counselors have a good understanding of normal child and adolescent development, as is emphasized in our earlier discussion of the training of teacher-counselors (see Chapter Four). Initially, to simplify programming by restricting the developmental range to be dealt with, Re-ED programs were designed for children ages six to twelve; even within this truncated range, developmental differences were large and demanded constant and informed attention. Today Re-ED programs serve children from eighteen months to eighteen years of age, thus greatly increasing the need for teacher-counselors and supervisors to understand normal child and adolescent development as well as individual deviations therefrom.

Although academic learning and behavioral learning are inextricably intertwined (requiring equal skill in the management of both by the day teacher-counselor and the night teacher-counselor), it is useful to consider the management of behavior as a separate topic. Sometimes it is necessary to concentrate on behavior changes before academic work, or any other goal-oriented task, can be addressed effectively.

Generally speaking, there are two formal approaches to the management of behavior in Re-ED programs. One is founded in operant conditioning or behavior modification, in the tradition of Wolpe and Skinner. The other emphasizes group process. However, there is great variability in emphasis on these two generic approaches from program to program and even from group to group within a program. One or two programs are thoroughgoing in their commitment to behavior modification and make little deliberate use of group process; other programs emphasize group process and have no formal structure embracing behavior modification principles. Most programs fall between these extremes. There is, however, an emerging consensus that operant principles are more effective with younger children and group process principles are more effective with older children and adolescents. Actually, all programs inevitably use both behavior modification and group process; they differ in how deliberate they are in doing so.

Goal Setting

An integral part of both general approaches to behavior change is goal setting—a procedure widely used in Re-ED programs. It involves having each child define goals for a day, a week, or a weekend, declaring the goals to the group and its teacher-counselors and checking up to see whether or not goals have been met. Goals should generally be hard enough to be challenging but also easy enough for success in their achievement to occur often, at least at first, with difficulty increasing as the child gains confidence in his competence. Goals are ordinarily arrived at in group meetings, usually at the beginning of the week and of each day, and are posted in the classroom or in the living unit. Various arrangements are made to monitor and reward goal achievement.

What are some typical goals?

For children

> To learn the multiplication table.
> To stay out of fights.
> To not pick on Billy. (Positive: to be kind to Billy.)
> To finish classwork on time.
> To not use vulgar language. (Positive: to use proper language.)
> To avoid arguments with my sister on the weekend.
> To help my mother by emptying the trash.
> To stay in my seat in class.
> To finish my work on time.
> To take "time out" when I am about to lose my temper.

For adolescents

> To prepare a job application.
> To lose a pound a week for ten weeks.
> To quit smoking.
> To read Conrad's *Heart of Darkness.*
> To avoid entanglements with my father.
> To improve my grooming.
> To avoid being sarcastic.
> To prepare for the written examination to get a driver's license.
> To write a note to my friend in the hospital.
> To pay back the money I stole from a neighbor's house.

What are the characteristics of good goal statements? These attributes seem important:

First of all, good goal statements are highly specific. Not "To be good" but "To take time out when about to lose my temper." Not "To study hard" but "To learn to multiply and divide fractions." In general, positively stated are preferable to negatively stated goals.

Second, goals should involve overt behavior, not private thoughts. It should be possible for the student as well as group members and teacher-counselors to agree when a goal has been accomplished.

Third, the goal should be appropriate to the level of development of the child and the circumstances of his ecosystem. Not "To persuade my father to quit drinking" but "To stay out of arguments at the table at home."

Fourth, the goals should be few in number. We are concerned

not so much about what goals are achieved but about the habit of specifying and achieving particular goals. Two to three goals at a time are quite enough.

Finally, goals should be shareable with the group, with teacher-counselors, and with members of the family—at least initially. In time, goals can become private and their achievement a matter of private pride or disappointment.

Sometimes other members of the child's ecosystem, including even teacher-counselors, can appropriately be encouraged to set specific goals for themselves, to share these, and to check up to assess accomplishment.

Operant Conditioning and Behavior Modification

Operant conditioning maintains that behavior is a function of its antecedents and consequences. Below, we elaborate briefly on this idea and describe some of the central concepts employed in the theory and its practice.

Behavior is anything a child does that can be observed and counted. This definition encompasses the range of behaviors of rats and pigeons better than of children; nonetheless, observing and counting behavior is a powerful instrument in helping children learn to behave.

Antecedent conditions refer to environmental events that elicit or trigger behavior. They are the stimuli in the stimulus-response paradigm. Most behavior modification programs recommended for the treatment of emotionally disturbed children and adolescents give primary attention to the consequences of behavior and insufficient attention to the circumstances that evoke behavior. In Re-ED programs, a great deal of emphasis is put on arranging circumstances that are favorable to constructive responses.

Cueing is a specific application of the principle that antecedent events elicit particular responses. Since disturbed children and adolescents are often distractable (they pay attention to stimuli other than those desired by an adult), the teacher-counselor can give a cue to get the student ready for a desired response. For example, to get a group to be quiet, the teacher-counselor may raise his hand to signal quiet; members of the group raise their hands in a ritual that becomes so compelling in time that the most distractible child follows suit. In Campbell Loughmiller's camping program, campers sit on a circle of logs prior to any new activity. This enables them to change attention sets and to enter the new activity with appropriate responses. The campers named the logs, quite appropriately, "ready-logs."

A *reinforcer* is any event following behavior that increases the probability that the behavior will be repeated. The definition is obviously circular, but once the efficacy of a reinforcer has been established, it can then be used to change the frequency of occurrence of other behaviors, thus breaking out of the circularity. Reinforcers are referred to sometimes as contingencies, sometimes as rewards and punishments.

A *primary reinforcer* is directly related to some physiological function, such as eating or avoiding pain; a *secondary reinforcer* is a symbolic representation derived from pairing words or other symbols with a primary reinforcer. Thus, the word *good* when paired with a primary reinforcer comes in time to be a reinforcer in its own right. A smile, a pat on the back, even a checkmark on a piece of paper can acquire reinforcing properties.

Positive reinforcers can generally be used with greater certainty of outcome than negative reinforcers.

The function of punishment in learning is complicated. Punishment can disrupt behavior and stop an undesired response, at least temporarily. However, it does not signal what the correct response is, thus leaving the learner without constructive guidance. Avoidance of anticipated punishment can lead to a reduction of stress and thus to reinforcement of the punishment-avoiding behavior. However, it is often difficult to control the response a child selects to avoid punishment. Thus, lying, running away, daydreaming, and the like may be reinforced unintentionally. Furthermore, punishment may often teach the child or adolescent to resent or hate the punisher, and thus, through generalization, all authority figures. If punishment is used to disrupt behavior, the proper response must be made clear promptly, allowed to occur, and reinforced. In general, by far the best strategy is to ignore undesired behavior and reward desired behavior.

Reinforcers can be *extrinsic* or *intrinsic*. Extrinsic reinforcers are ordinarily not directly related to the learning experience itself, and in behavior modification programs are frequently

provided arbitrarily by other people. Intrinsic reinforcers are inherent in the achievement itself and represent a level of maturity
that should be the goal of all learning. Thus, satisfaction with
one's private estimate of a task well done is much to be preferred
over a reward arbitrarily administered from an external source.

Rewards can be of many kinds. A reward embraced by the
Premack principle is that preferred activities, such as going out to
recess or to a meal, can be used to reinforce prior, and possibly
less valued, activities. Daily schedules are usually built with this
principle in mind: an arithmetic lesson is followed by arts and
crafts, a daily planning session by a trip to an ice cream parlor.

Skinner and his associates have established the importance
of *schedules of reinforcement*—schedules indicating the frequency
and timing of reinforcement in establishing a desired behavior. As
noted, rewarded responses tend to get established; unrewarded responses tend to drop out. The permanency of a response is a function of reinforcement schedules, and different schedules are called
for in different phases of acquisition of a new behavior. At the beginning of learning, every correct response should be rewarded and
all incorrect responses ignored. In time, however, reinforcement of
the desired response should be given intermittently. Otherwise, the
response will drop out as soon as reinforcement is no longer forthcoming. As behavior becomes established, reinforcements should
be spaced further and further apart, and on an irregular basis. Behavior thus learned will persist for long periods of time with only
occasional reinforcement.

Extinction occurs when a behavior goes unrewarded. Extinction is a valuable tool in programming for disturbed children,
especially for eliminating irrational fears, temper tantrums, and
other forms of maladaptive behavior. Extinction occurs most rapidly when the undesired behavior is paired with a new reinforced
response that is incompatible with the response to be extinguished.
In a classical example, a child was taught to fear a rabbit when the
appearance of the rabbit was paired with a loud and unpleasant
noise. Soon the rabbit alone produced a fear response, and the response generalized to other furry objects. The fear response was
extinguished when the rabbit was gradually reintroduced in a situation (eating while being held) that elicited a response incompatible with fear.

By combining positive reinforcement of one response with ignoring of an undesired response, one can teach *discrimination*. The learner can be helped to establish quite fine differentiations—learning, for example, that joking behavior is appropriate in some settings but not in others.

In order to ensure that desired behaviors developed in a treatment program are transferred to other situations, such as home and regular school, the learning experience should be designed to ensure *generalization*. Within a behavior modification paradigm, it is necessary to ensure that the desired response is reinforced in diverse settings, including, if possible, deliberate reinforcement by parents or teachers in accordance with a prearranged plan.

Although operant principles can be powerful in shaping behavior, they have severe limitations both theoretically and practically. In its pure form, behavior modification concerns itself with inputs and outputs and not with the intervening processing of information. It has been called an "empty organism" theory. While contemporary interpreters of the theory have moved far beyond this simple position to incorporate cognitive processes, most of the available texts on the use of operant principles in work with disturbed children lag behind these theoretical developments. As a consequence, behavior modification programs for disturbed children and adolescents tend to be highly mechanistic and tightly bound to the achievement of a limited repertoire of behavioral responses. They underemphasize the ability of children and adolescents to think, to solve problems, to create novel solutions not likely to be found in program guides or devised by teacher-counselors. Furthermore, as is emphasized in Chapter Ten, learning occurs best in meaningful contexts that are charged with intent and purpose and that bring rewards or disappointments far more complex and consequential than those associated with the rattle of an M & M down a dispenser chute or the racking up of 900 points signifying nothing more than that the child or adolescent is conforming to the expectations defined and imposed by other people.

On the practical side, treatment programs based on operant principles can become so enmeshed in the mechanics of programming that more meaningful activities get sidetracked. Joy, adventure, private purpose, and unexpected opportunity can be squeezed out, leaving each day drab and forlorn, even when judged "success-ful" on the basis of points won or levels achieved by the students. Paradoxically, the more effective an operant conditioning pro-gram is, the more confining it can become. Teacher-counselors would do well to reflect on a cartoon in the Harvard *Lampoon* a number of years ago. A Harvard rat says to a rat friend: "Boy, do I have that psychologist conditioned! Every time I press this bar, he gives me a pellet."

It is not necessary to accept the constrictions implied by a strict application of operant principles in helping youngsters change their behavior. As often reiterated in this book, learning proceeds best in meaningful contexts. In other words, children and adolescents think, and they derive guidance from precept and example as well as from experienced rewards and punishments. It is important, we think, to explain to students exactly what is going on in an operant conditioning program, and to enlist their help in putting the learning experience into larger and more mean-ingful contexts than is possible in a Re-ED program, rich as it is in variety of experience. Furthermore, it is important to help the young person move beyond the need for formal operant instruc-tional programs and to derive intrinsic rewards from the unpredict-able consequences of committing oneself to new experiences. Operant conditioning may be thought of as a sometimes necessary procedure to get a child into a position where he can engage in learnings that transcend the possibilities of predesigned learning programs. Operant principles will doubtlessly continue to operate but at a level of complexity, subtlety, and privacy that overleap any possible learning experience engineered by others.

Around 1965, behavior modification began to take hold in Re-ED schools. Skinner's thinking has greatly enriched the process of reeducation. We are especially attracted to the position that when a child fails to learn, the fault is in the program, not in the child. We do not discount the child's or adolescent's contribution to a defeating life situation, nor are we inclined to play down his sense of responsibility for doing something about it, but we are strongly disposed to the idea that adults have a special responsibil-ity for young people, a responsibility to get the contingencies right so that they can grow in competence, freedom, responsibility, and self-respect.

Our current view is that behavior modification, powerful as it is, is not a sufficient theoretical base for helping disturbed children and adolescents. It pays insufficient attention to the evocative power of identification with an admired adult, to the rigorous demands of expectancies stated and implicit in situations, and to the fulfillment that comes from the exercise of competence.

Behavior modification works best with younger children. Almost inevitably, adolescents, with their growing intelligence, make formal behavior modification programs into a game of "Who's conning whom?" except perhaps when operant conditioning techniques are made available to an adolescent to help him or her control some undesired behavior, such as smoking. But to nurture general development, the best we can do is to devise situations for children and adolescents in which completely unpredictable contingencies have a high probability of reinforcing behaviors that are generally considered desirable. This is not an unimportant achievement. In the near-perfect expression of the idea, young people learn to discriminate among options and to commit themselves to new situations in which (to preserve the Skinnerian idiom) the contingencies are likely to sustain the kind of persons they would like to become. But on the way to this goal, sometimes referred to as maturity, operant techniques become elusive if not trivial, leaving only the Skinnerian metaphor, to which we subscribe with a full appreciation of its power as well as an acute awareness of its limitations.

Token Economy
Re-ED School of Kentucky*

For all groups, various forms of reinforcement for participation and acceptable behavior are earned during any activity. A daily record of chips earned is kept and charted weekly. When a child has earned a percentage of chips, he is graduated from chips and is rewarded primarily through verbal praise. Chips are ex-

---

*The Re-ED School of Kentucky, described in Chapter Three, operates on the basis of an imaginatively conceived and well-executed token economy. The children, ages six to twelve, earn chips for good behavior and a panoply of special awards (badgets, trophies, jackets) for special achievements. The description here is provided by Brewer and Lackey (1978, pp. 105-110).

changed for free time, special activities, and treats. At the end of the week, any child having earned an appropriate level that particular week earns a specified amount of money to spend during a shopping expedition. The money can be spent or saved for future use as desired, to help delay gratification. For example, a Buckskin who earned 85 to 95 chips during one week would have 20¢ to spend; for each 10 chips over 85, another nickel is added. The amounts may vary according to the age and developmental level of each group.

In conjunction with the token reinforcers, a levels system has been organized to focus on individual behaviors. There are four steps, beginning with the targeting of specific behaviors noted by individual teachers of the referring school and observation made upon entry. A shaping process is begun on level one. As the child moves through the program, the goals in the higher levels aim toward group integration and development of an internal reinforcement system. This will provide the child with the self-reinforcing skills to function in a regular school program.

Specifically for the Buckskin group (boys six to nine), the following system is utilized. For each 200 chips earned, a cooperation badge is painted and given to the child to be sewn on his vest. A vest is earned when a child has exhibited cooperative and acceptable behavior for one week. A special ceremony is held when one or more boys earn a vest. During the ceremony, all Buckskins with a vest recite the pledge and motto. Bonus chips are given spontaneously for commendable behavior in all groups. Buckskins are given verbal praise at every chance. Some of the consequences for inappropriate behavior are payment of chips earned, time out (usually taken outside classroom door), and loss of activity participation. The quiet room is used when the child exhibits excessive loss of behavior control. Awarding badges is part of our program, used as positive reinforcement for the learning and application of specific skills. Various badges are earned and given to be sewn on the vest. When a Buckskin earns his vest, he automatically receives his Moon Month badge, which is the Indian symbol for the child's birth month. Any other badges previously earned are also distributed. There are three swimming badges, each successive one requiring more complex skills. Many of the children are afraid of or don't like the water, and these badges provide incentive for learning how to swim and enjoy the water.

All groups engage in physical exercises several times a week to promote muscular strength and to provide an appropriate outlet for excess energy. These exercises are many and varied. They include the following: situps, pushups, 50-yard dash, 220-yard dash, broad jump, softball throw, and cross-country or obstacle course. The exercises, distances, and time limits are fixed for the particular group. The Physical Fitness badge is earned when a child successfully completes the requirements for this badge.

Most of the children referred have poor peer relationships. Many do not know how to initiate friendship. The Good Friend Award was designed to teach the children appropriate ways of interacting with peers. The award varies with each group, but a Buckskin earns a necklace which can be worn when a child displays positive peer interaction. Inviting another to share something of his own is an example of how a child may earn this award.

These badges provide good incentive for participation and cooperation within many of the afternoon activities. They promote good peer relationships and a positive interaction with authority. The badges also enhance a positive self-concept within the child.

Pine Breeze Motivational System

A teacher-counselor at Pine Breeze, a program for adolescents, said: "If you can't get behavior under control, you simply can't get anything else accomplished." The control of behavior was a serious problem at Pine Breeze for its first two or three years. Today, however, the day proceeds in orderly fashion, marred occasionally but not often by disruptive behavior, and much is being accomplished with a group of severely disturbed boys and girls. The staff at Pine Breeze agree that the change occurred following the introduction of the Pine Breeze Motivational System.

During the first few years, the staff attempted to control behavior by a contract system that led to rewards when individual contracts were fulfilled. While contracting may work well elsewhere, it did not work at Pine Breeze. The negotiating sessions—involving the adolescent, her parents perhaps, and teacher-counselors—were long, complicated, and often contentious. It was difficult for staff to keep in mind the requirements of all the contracts. Each adolescent became the world's authority on his own contract and could often con his way out of responsibilities or into undeserved rewards. Since behavior expectations were defined for individuals, it was difficult to establish group expectations integral with individual contracts. Thus, there tended to be two sets of rules: one set for the school at large and one set made up of a number of individual contracts. In any event, the system did not work well, and tension ran high in the school for a long time. Interestingly, however, the program did succeed in helping a number of adolescents, largely through the work of a highly effective liaison program.

The Pine Breeze Motivational System is designed to require

conformity of all students to a uniform and explicit behavioral code. Points are gained or lost on the basis of behavior, and accrued points are used to buy privileges. There are two kinds of privileges, those that are associated with status and those that are discrete. There are four status levels, designated by Roman numerals:

Level I severely restricts the freedom of the adolescent. Level I residents live in a large room and may leave it only with permission of a teacher-counselor. They must eat in a designated area, turn in personal cash and personal items when returning on Sunday evening, and wear clothes issued by teacher-counselors.

Level II residents can buy a number of privileges, including carrying their own money up to $1, buying snacks and cigarettes, watching television, using the gymnasium or the recreation room, attending campus social activities, making telephone calls, going off campus, and so on.

Level III residents have free many of the privileges that must be purchased at Levels I and II. They can also buy additional privileges not available to Levels I and II students, including, for example, an off-campus date. They may have a private room and are allowed to decorate it, and they become eligible to be elected group leaders.

Level IV residents have free all the privileges of Levels I, II, and III. Level IV students are responsible for the American flag, and they meet weekly with the program director to suggest changes in the program. They may stay up until 1:00 A.M., engaged in quiet activities. Most important of all, they are free from the point system and are expected to govern their conduct on their own.

Students enter at Level II and may be demoted to Level I or promoted to Levels III or IV after appropriate intervals. Students at any level, including Level IV, may lose their status through misbehavior but may gain it back through good behavior.

Behaviors that earn points include taking a shower, doing a load of laundry, keeping point balance sheet correctly, not smoking, being on time, maintaining good grooming, achieving target behaviors specified in goal-setting sessions, keeping a weekend diary, and, most important of all, doing well in academic work. Each student carries with him all the time a daily point sheet, on which he enters gained or lost points. The sheet is initialed by a teacher-counselor at the end of each activity period.

Behaviors that get penalties include negative comments, not following instructions, making disruptive noises, smoking in restricted areas, being out of bedroom after hours, being late for meals, carrying a weapon of any kind, engaging in inappropriate sexual behavior, lying, violating shop rules, cheating, and wearing dirty clothes or going ungroomed. The heaviest penalties are imposed for running away.

From a distance, the system has many unattractive features. It is reminiscent of merits and demerits at summer camps and military schools. The motivations are heavily extrinsic (though the expectation is that they will become intrinsic). The process, the keeping of records, would presumably consume much time. In practice, however, these negative features are not apparent. The system is neither intrusive nor time consuming. It is there always in the background, but it does not inhibit other activities; indeed, it appears to make other activities possible.

The setting of clear expectations for behavior is extremely important for children and adolescents who have grown up in settings where expectations have been ill defined, highly variable, unpredictably rewarded or punished, or at sharp variance with the expectations of the larger community. The system provides security and instruction, so that the students can internalize expectations and develop a personal code of conduct harmonious with the basic requirements of society. Having acquired this elementary foundation, the student can subsequently incorporate principles of conduct responsive to moral and ethical promptings that transcend the simple regulatory function of the Pine Breeze system.

The system derives its strength from the fact that it makes clear at the outset what kinds of behaviors are expected of all students in the program. It is highly specific, so debate over appropriate conduct is seldom possible. It provides the adolescent with immediate knowledge of results, essential in learning to behave as in all other learning. It provides a continuous charting of progress. The students like it, and it works.

We want to emphasize that the motivational procedures at Pine Breeze are much in the background. While they provide the structure necessary for a student to learn to behave, their primary function is to make it possible to carry out a rich, experiential program involving the acquisition of basic academic skills; prescriptive instruction in secondary school subjects; highly creative experiences in arts, crafts, and music; a vigorous program of physical fitness, including camping, backpacking, and spelunking; specific vocational training and preparation for getting and holding a job; and imaginative learning experiences (see Chapter Ten for a description of the Folk Music Enterprise). The motivational system is a means-to-ends, including not only the control of behavior, the importance of which should not be diminished, but also the experiencing of the full array of events in Re-ED that prepare the young person to take over the management of his own life.

Group Process

From the beginning of the Re-ED program, we have emphasized the importance of the group in helping each member of the
group grow in competence, confidence, self-esteem, and ability to
meet the demands of living in home, school, and community. By
group process, we mean the planned use of identifiable and com-
municable ways of working so that the group does indeed perform
the functions expected of it.

In Re-ED programs, groups are continuous; they are ordinarily not made up anew for particular purposes or periods of
time. As one or two students graduate, one or two new students
are brought into the group. This continuity permits the building of
a group culture that powerfully influences the behavior of everyone associated with it. Each Re-ED group has a distinctive culture.
The culture is modified over time in response to new members,
new teacher-counselors, or new circumstances, but its essential
character remains remarkably stable. The constant challenge in a
Re-ED program is to help groups build cultures that sustain children and adolescents in their efforts to manage their lives in ways
satisfying to themselves and satisfactory to others.

One of the early groups at Cumberland House, a group of
older boys age ten to thirteen, called itself the "Confederate Aviators." The group worked very well for several years. Then, for reasons we do not understand, it began to go sour. The culture of the
group began to encourage internal dissension, to support the domi-
nation of the group by two members, and to reward antisocial activities on and off the campus. Unacceptable standards, which
might have been dealt with early by a skillful teacher-counselor,
came to dominate the culture. The interesting thing is that no one
was happy with the situation. The staff were perplexed and frustrated, and the children were miserable.

A number of steps were taken to remedy the situation, but
none worked. Finally it was decided that drastic measures had to
be taken. The group was disbanded. Arrangements were made for
other agencies to work with individual children. The name "Confederate Aviators" was retired, and an entirely new group was con-
stituted and given a new name. The new group shaped up quite
well and has lasted for a dozen or more years. To this day, we do
not know what went wrong with the Confederate Aviators. But we
came to appreciate the power of the culture of a group and to in-

vest heavily in helping groups build cultures that work well in the interest of their members.

How does the culture of a group come into being? And what can be done to ensure that a group develops a culture that sustains Re-ED objectives? We actually do not know enough about the process to make prescriptions or to write a How to Do It manual. But we do have some concepts that teacher-counselors can use in discovering ways to utilize for good cause the enormous influence groups can have in the lives of young people, as they do in the lives of us all.

First of all, a culture cannot be imposed on a group. There is simply no sense in making a lot of rules and regulations, in devising names, in working out schedules, in creating rituals and ceremonies from above. Group cultures emerge out of life as it is lived on a day-by-day basis. It thus takes time to build a group culture, and the process cannot be rushed. In the early stages of the life of a group, teacher-counselors may have to provide structure and direction, but these should be loosely linked and easily reassembled by the group and the teacher-counselors as they live and try to make sense of each day.

The character of a group grows out of ordinary living reflected upon. There is always a temptation for teacher-counselors to believe that some spectacular group achievement would be more valuable in building a group than would be the ordinary routines of getting up in the morning, cleaning up, going to school, going to meals, playing a softball game, watching television, evaluating the day, and going to bed. Not so. It is the little things that count. Remember, the objective of Re-ED is not to prepare a child to cross the North Pole by dogsled but rather to manage well at home, at school, and in the community, where success or failure depends not on a noble exploit but on handling well and getting satisfaction from hundreds of commonplace experiences.

But grand adventures have their place as well. Once a group has built a culture that encourages its members to behave in ways essential to their subsequent success, special achievements can have both immediate and enduring value. The "Iron Men" of the Lexington program successfully and happily completed a 200-mile hike on the Appalachian Trail. A group of students at Pine Breeze School made and distributed a half-dozen folk music albums. The Keystones, a group of girls at Cumberland House, salvaged a sunken pontoon boat, repaired and painted it, raised money to buy an outboard motor, and now enjoy venturesome voyages on the Cumberland River. When a group already has in place values, standards, expectations that give stability, guidance, and pleasure in the living of each day, these out-of-the-ordinary accomplishments are enormously productive. They not only open up for the students new visions of the possible and a new sense of personal competence; they also can redefine at a higher level expectations for daily living, for doing better schoolwork, for being better school citizens, for having the neatest living unit, for doing better on weekends, and so on. Furthermore, the legends last and influence the character of generations that follow.

Various Re-ED programs have developed different patterns of formal group meetings with all students and staff present. Descriptions of "group process" often refer mainly to these formal meetings. Actually, group process operates all the time, and it may well be that most of its usefulness occurs in the living out of ordinary events of the day, from the informal exchanges that occur spontaneously at meals, in the classroom, on the playing field, in quarters at night. Minor conflicts arise and are quietly resolved; modest triumphs (throwing a fine pot, getting a self-made kite to fly, mastering an algebra problem, presenting a good report on a trip, and so on) are shared. One child helps another with a problem. Two older girls talk through similar difficulties they are having at home. A group on a backpacking trip get caught in a storm and together find shelter. A group on a trip by land come across a stranded elderly couple in a car, and they work out a plan to get help. And so on in thousands of variations on a theme. Teacher-counselors, and in time group members themselves, comment on the events in ways that help students generalize on their meaning. The point being made here is that group process is not something special; it occurs all the time.

The Alpha Omega Group*
Pine Breeze High School

One means of describing how processes within the group are developed and directed is to present an example, drawn from the

---

*This account is modified from *Group Process in the Re-Education School,* edited by Steve Weinberg and published by the Tennessee Department of Mental Health, 1971.

experience of the Younger Boys group at Pine Breeze High School, the adolescent reeducation center in Chattanooga, Tennessee. This example illustrates how the team of teachers began with ten individual students and built them into a group that was highly self-directed, and one in which the group members were highly sophisticated as behavioral change agents. The group was composed of ten boys, ages thirteen to sixteen. Most of the boys had already been enrolled at Pine Breeze.

Creating the Group. The first major problem confronted by the teacher-counselors was to bring together ten individuals and help them become a group. Merely placing ten individual students together was no guarantee that they would act and feel and think as a group. The first task, then, was to establish a common identity, to foster a feeling of "groupness."

Initially, it was very difficult for the group members to accept the notion of "groupness," largely because most of the members had been enrolled in the school under a highly individualistic system before entering the group system. The group system represented a drastic change. No longer was the student responsible solely for his own behavior; he was responsible also for the behavior of nine other individuals, and he was responsible to the whole group.

Group cohesiveness was fostered through a few basic rules imposed at the outset by the teacher-counselors. Five rules helped to structure the early group processes: (1) Every student is a member of the group. (2) Group decisions are group responsibilities. (3) All problems are group problems. (4) Groups must be responsible. (5) Teacher-counselors have veto power (largely in matters of health and safety).

The structure for the Alpha Omegas consisted of the initial rules imposed by the teacher-counselors and those evolved by the group; rituals, which were largely group evolved; the daily and weekly group schedule; formal roles within the group, such as the leadership or "cook" role; norms, values, and standards for behaviors, which were often codified as group rules; and planning, problem-solving, and evaluation meetings. These structural characteristics of the group defined the group process; that is, they defined how the members would interact with each other. Initially, rules were enforced by the teacher-counselors. As the group began to grow and to accept the structure defined by its own rules, the teacher-counselors gradually withdrew their directive role and acted to support the group and be a resource to it.

Cohesiveness and group identity were fostered by various other means. The group chose for itself the name "Alpha Omega," or "the first and best." The connotations of the name helped to identify how the members would act and interact; that is, they would strive to be "number one" in their activities.

Throughout the process of establishing the group structure,

the teacher-counselors had some notion of how they wanted to meet the needs of the group in line with the goals of the school; however, the structure needed to come from the students themselves, for two important reasons. First, to impose structure on the group could deprive the members of a valuable learning experience. The task of building a group was one that required a great deal of social interaction, cooperation, and problem solving to meet the needs of the members. The students, often for the first time, had to be aware of the needs of someone other than themselves, and they had to tackle complex social situations and find solutions which would satisfy all group members. Second, a structure imposed on the group could be regarded as just another arbitrary restriction devised by adults to monitor the lives of children. The youths would be "spoon-fed" another list of do's, don'ts, whens and hows. Meaning and relevance would be absent. On the other hand, a group allowed to evolve its own structure, to be responsible for its own choices, to experience the problems of social living, and to develop a structure out of the needs demonstrated by that experience would become highly concerned about the group's structure.

Planning Meetings. Group meetings were held to plan daily and weekly activities. All group members participated, and all ideas were considered. By consensus, the group decided what it was going to do, who would do what task (arrange for transportation, make a phone call, write a letter, buy supplies, schedule a room), what the schedule would be, and so on. The group's decisions were placed on a blackboard, so that every member could see what had been decided and what assignments had been made.

The schedule of activities for each week was drawn up on Sunday evening and Monday morning. The Sunday-night meeting was used to plan for the evening activities and was conducted by the night teacher-counselor. This meeting usually lasted only about fifteen minutes, since the students, expecting the meeting, had already thought out the kinds of things they wanted to be doing for the next week. The Monday-morning meeting, conducted by the day teacher-counselor, was used to plan daytime activities. As situations arose and there was a need to plan some other activity or to expand on plans formulated earlier, the group would call additional planning sessions.

The enterprise unit, which occurred each afternoon during a two-hour block of time, was planned each day. An enterprise unit was a group activity designed to make learning relevant and meaningful. The unit often grew out of the interest of the group members and provided an opportunity for teacher-counselors to plug in academic subjects. For example, the Alpha Omegas became interested in Early American architecture through social science instruction. As their interest evolved, the group members decided to build a foundry at the school to use in arts and crafts classes. Though the students were highly interested in the activity because it seemed to be a fun project, it was also an opportunity to bolster the students' academic skills and attitudes toward learning. To build the foundry required the students to read books, use math skills, write letters, and order equipment. The unit gave the students an opportunity to use skills they had learned in the classroom and also helped to demonstrate the relevance of developing new skills. Because the task was meaningful, learning became exciting. To carry out the enterprise unit, the group members had to plan each day what they were going to accomplish the next day. They might plan to devote the next day to "digging out the footage." They might also set up group goals they wished to accomplish during the unit, such as to work as a group, to cut down on cursing, or even to get through early so the group members could work on another activity.

Gradually the Alpha Omegas became foresightful enough to anticipate many of the problems, obstacles, or needs that had to be met in engaging in a group activity. Skills in planning developed largely through the group's experiencing the consequences of not anticipating needs. In the early stages, the group often neglected to arrange for a vehicle to transport the group; within a few weeks, the first question asked in planning a trip was "Do we have a vehicle?"

A problem-solving meeting was held at any time group members felt that they needed to discuss a problem. In most cases, the students defined the problem on their own. In some cases, the teacher-counselor had to redefine the problem when the group was floundering. The format for the problem-solving meeting was as follows: (1) the problem is stated, (2) the problem is discussed, (3) a conclusion is reached from group consensus, and (4) the consensus is summarized.

One day, a group member decided to leave the group early to wash his clothes. The boys immediately started looking for the missing student, whom they found already at the dorm. The group then convened for a problem-solving meeting. A student's leaving the group violated the second basic group rule: "Every student is a member of the group." The offending group member defined the problem as a "misunderstanding"; he had misunderstood what the group had planned to do. After he stated his position, the rest of the group discussed it. The group decided that the problem as stated was not accurate. Instead, the group felt that even though he had misunderstood, he had left the group and had been aware that he wasn't with it. The group redefined the problem as "R. S. left the group." A discussion then followed on the problem as redefined. Since this was a recurring problem, something for which the student had been found guilty before, the group imposed a penalty on him. Prior to this, the group had not established any consequences for his behavior. This one occasion, however, had made the group members aware of a serious problem, one which threatened the group's functioning. So this time, they took steps to stop the behavior from recurring. The group decided that if the student left the group in the future he would lose one meal. After the group members expressed their feelings, the student was allowed to comment, which he chose not to do. The problem and consensus were then summarized. Several days later, the student again left the group, and the group decided to take away his privilege of eating the dinner meal. He had to go to dinner with the group but was not allowed to eat.

Each member of the group was obligated to call a problem-solving meeting whenever he spotted or was involved in a problem. He could call the meeting at any time by saying "problem-solving meeting." Whenever any member said this, everything stopped and the group convened. Though it might appear under this format that the group would be continually convening for problem-solving meetings, the experience with the Alpha Omega group indicated that this does not happen. The students were proud of the fact that they could go a whole day without having to meet to discuss a problem. Not needing a problem-solving meeting indicated that the group was progressing and that its members were working well together. The need for the group not to call a problem-solving meeting was often so great that merely the threat of having to call such a meeting served to encourage the students to deal with a problem quickly, before the group was convened.

Initially, the teacher-counselors made the rule that "problems must be solved." After examining this rule, the group changed it to "problem-solving meetings must reach closure." They realized that, although many problems could not be solved immediately, closure could be reached even if closure was that "there is no solution." It was rare that a given problem did not have a solution. It was common, however, that problems could not be solved immediately "on the spot" but needed to be worked on for several days.

At no time was a group member ostracized from the group. If there was a need for punishment, there was a group problem which had to be dealt with. The group might decide to ignore the student, but he had to be physically present. Every group member had the responsibility to let every other group member know where he was at all times. The group could be separated only when the group had planned for different members to be apart.

The problem-solving meeting seldom led to punishment. If a member created a problem, the group would seek an experimental solution to help the student deal with his problem. The group would rarely decide that the student must give up something positive or accept some negative consequences.

Evaluation Meetings. In the Alpha Omega group, there were two evaluation meetings daily, one before dinner (to evaluate the day's activities) and one before bedtime (to evaluate the evening activities). At the meeting, each member would say (1) what he felt was "positive" during the day, (2) what he felt was "negative," and (3) how the day could have been better.

In the early phase of the group's development, evaluations were largely self-oriented. Each group member viewed what was good or bad about the day largely in terms of himself. After the first week or so, after the group had grown accustomed to the format of the evaluation meeting and was beginning to become a group, there were seldom any references to "I" in the evaluation. Instead, the members talked about what happened, good or bad, to the group. When the members criticized one another, they did it indirectly. They would not mention the names of the individuals they were discussing but would say "one of our group members . . ." This procedure of not referring directly to a group member evolved from the group and was not a device of the teacher-counselors. The members found that criticizing group members personally caused members to "cut" each other in retaliation.

The opportunity to reinforce attitudes conducive to productive group processes often arose during the evaluation meeting. A group member would express a positive attitude toward the group or commend the behavior of an individual member. When this happened, the teacher-counselor supported the affirmative behavior.

In the evaluation meeting, the teacher-counselor also had the opportunity to evaluate the day's activities. He had the opportunity to reinforce both behaviors and attitudes demonstrated by the group members throughout the day. Since the group functioned closely, the opportunity to reinforce the behavior or attitude of one student helped other students identify acceptable behaviors and attitudes.

Group Goals. A group goal was a task that the group as a whole would strive to achieve. The one overriding, all-pervasive goal was to become a well-functioning group. This goal applied to every group member during every moment with the group. If the group were to attain its primary goal, each member had to be responsible for both his own behavior and the behavior of his fellow group members. Problem behavior on the part of any one individual worked against the group's goal. Thus, not only was each member responsible for himself, but other group members were responsible to help him. If Jim were "acting out," it became his responsibility to control his aggressiveness, since this behavior interfered with the group's primary goal; it was also the group's responsibility to help Jim control his behavior. Group members might do this by getting him out of frustrating situations, by giving him support when he demonstrated control, or by ignoring him when he started to be aggressive.

Each group member was aware of the academic needs of every other group member. Academic needs were defined as deficits which the student must remedy to return to regular school. Almost all of the Alpha Omegas were highly motivated to get back into high school and eventually graduate. Thus, each group member accepted responsibility for helping other group members make academic progress. Students more skilled would tutor less skilled students. Students prodded each other when they became frustrated, praised each other when they were progressing, and reinforced the need to get back into school when a member was about to give up.

Experience with the Alpha Omegas demonstrated that the group approached the problems of each individual member with a great deal of concern, understanding, and tolerance. Group members realized that each student at Pine Breeze was there because he had problems. The students took the attitude that the individual was not "bad" and that they had the responsibility to help him behave in a more competent and appropriate manner.

Leadership. In the development of the Alpha Omega group, the teacher-counselors expected a power struggle to develop for leadership. This never happened. One boy attempted to assume leadership by being physically aggressive. But, as one teacher-counselor put it, "The group problem-solved him to death." The group gave him a contract which stated that if he attempted to assume leadership by force he would be sent home immediately to reconsider his commitment to Re-ED. The contract was drawn up by all of the group members and signed. Early one morning, shortly after the contract had been drawn up, the student broke it and was immediately sent home. He returned that afternoon, willing to renew his contract and his commitment to the group and to the school. This procedure was not devised by the teacher-counselors but by the group members themselves during a problem-solving meeting.

In a well-functioning group, there was no way that anyone, including the teacher-counselors, could take over the group and become its leader. As one teacher-counselor for the Alpha Omegas described it: "You can take the rottenest apple and put him in a well-functioning group and the kids will shape him up."

Leadership in the Alpha Omega group was a changing thing. In academic activities, there was one leader, in camping another, in canoeing another, and so on. In most situations, a leader emerged with the support of group members because they felt he was the most capable to direct a particular activity. Each group member was thus responsible for evaluating objectively not only his own skills but those of others, if the group was to choose the most appropriate leader for each task. Within this structure, each member gained experience in evaluating the needs of a given situation, evaluating his own skills and the skills of others, selecting a leader, supporting the leader, and following his leadership. Since there was in the group a diversity of skills among the group members, each member would at some time or another have the opportunity to assume the leadership role and lead the group toward one of its goals. He assumed the leadership role not on the basis of popularity or power but on the basis of strengths and abilities.

Early in the group's development, the members would not talk about personal problems. They felt that such problems were nobody's business but their own. As the group developed, the students began to share problems which did not directly affect the group. At a group meeting, one student brought up the problem of his not having much spending money because his father drank heavily. The group suggested ways that he could earn spending money without having to rely on his father to give him an allowance. Though the group members could not change the student's home situation, they could and did give him sympathy, support, and helpful suggestions.

Once the group had developed group skills and techniques for controlling the behavior of group members, group process was ongoing within the group. Since there was rarely, if ever, a completely new group established—that is, since the group members did not all graduate at once—there was always a majority of group members who were skilled in the group techniques and who would carry on the group's rules, values, procedures, and structure.

A Weekend Goal-Setting Meeting*

Setting: It is Friday morning. The All-Stars, a group of seven adolescent boys (ages fifteen to seventeen), are holding their Friday-morning rap session. They are in the dining room. Cut-out letters stating "Love Is Being Together" are pasted on the window.

Purpose: To review weekend goals for the boys' visits home. In addition, a review of what has been accomplished during the week will be held.

---

*Frank M. Hewitt visited several Re-ED programs during the summer of 1981. This is his account of a group session at a school serving adolescent boys and girls.

Cast: Bill—a sixteen-year-old very street-wise youth who is the most respected boy in the group.

Conrad—a fifteen-year-old immature boy who is easily angered by the teasing of the group when he clowns around seeking attention.

Paul—a sixteen-year-old quiet, sullen youth who seldom initiates conversation.

Greg—a large, muscular sixteen-year-old who delights in "pushing any and all of the other boys' buttons."

Mike—a quiet, conforming fifteen-year-old who keeps to himself.

Charles—an intense, lonely fifteen-year-old who is the weakest member of the group. He takes several types of medication to control his seizure disorder.

Don—a husky seventeen-year-old who is the newest member of the group.

T-C—the morning teacher-counselor.

We enter shortly after the group has started reviewing the goals each boy will work on when he goes home for the weekend. Conrad has started to state his goals when he angrily lashes out at Greg.

Conrad: You did it again! You're always putting me down. (Conrad relates how Greg taunted him when he was emptying the garbage can. Greg told him he could not go outside the dorm without getting permission. Conrad gets more and more upset.)

T-C: Why did you let Greg get you so upset? It really wasn't such a big deal.

Conrad: It's just he never lets up.

T-C: Never lets up like your brother who you'll see this weekend. Is that it?

Conrad: That's right. (Conrad says that his twelve-year-old brother never misses an opportunity to tease and hassle him. He tells how his brother often piles objects on his (Conrad's) bed and refuses to remove them, causing Conrad to sleep on the couch because he refuses to remove them himself.)

T-C: But your brother really wants your company, doesn't he?

Conrad: Yes, he does. But I won't give it to him when he hassles me.

Bill: Why don't you hit him in the mouth?

Conrad: I tried that once but never again. I don't like to make my little brother cry.

(T-C reminds Conrad of the contract approach they had discussed some weeks before.)

T-C: Why don't you set up a contract again? Tell your brother you won't spend time with him if he hassles you.

Conrad: I tried that. He was OK until Sunday afternoon. Then he hassled me for two hours.

T-C: You can handle two hours of hassling. Nobody can handle two days, though.

(The boys chime in that Conrad should give the contract another try.)

T-C: You can't change your brother any more than you can change Greg. But you can change how you react. You could have handled Greg differently, couldn't you?

(The group discusses how Conrad could have directly told Greg to leave him alone or could have ignored him. T-C gets the garbage can, and Greg and Conrad replay the incident several times, with Conrad ignoring the taunts.)

T-C: All right, Bill. What are your weekend goals?

Bill: (reading from goal sheet) I'm not going to raise Hell, come home drunk or high, or hassle the neighbors. I'll have at least one meal with my father.

(T-C challenges Bill's drinking, since he is only sixteen but eases up, saying, "Lots of people aren't perfect." But he cautions Bill about "moderation." The members of the group take turns defining the term *moderation* for Bill.)

T-C: OK. Paul, you're next.

Paul: I'll try and talk more at home. I really can talk a lot, you know. I just don't do it. When I was in school, I used to look around the room and say to myself, "Why should I talk to any of you?"

T-C: Mike?

Mike: I will clean my room, do any other chores, not tease my sister, and come home early.

T-C: Fine. What about you, Charles?

Charles: I'll spend some time with one friend.

Bill: One friend? Is that all you've got? I've got hundreds of friends.

Charles: I know I spend too much time with my parents. I have to start getting out more. Spending time with one friend is pretty good for me.

T-C: Bill, Charles is working on being away from home more often while maybe you should be working on spending more time at home, especially with your father.

(The other boys state their weekend goals.)

T-C: Now, before we finish the rap, let's review what we each learned or accomplished this week. The state spends $525 a week on each of you to keep you here in the school. What did the state get for its money this week? Bill, how did you earn your keep?

Bill: I decided this isn't such a bad place after all. Two weeks ago, I wanted to get out of here any way I could. But I like it now.

T-C: You earned your keep, Charles?

Charles: I learned you should never let yourself care too much about anybody. If you do, you'll only be hurt when they are gone.

T-C: You're talking about Bob?

Charles: Yes, I tried to talk him out of signing himself out of the school, but he wouldn't listen.

T-C: You and Bob were close friends.

Charles: We were very close. He said he was going to sign himself out at least ten times before, and I always talked him out of it. But now he's gone.

T-C: You don't think you should ever really get close to anybody?

Charles: That's right. I'll only get hurt again.

Bill: (leaning across the table) You're wrong, Charles. You should get as close to everybody as you can. Just because Bob is gone doesn't mean he's not still your friend. You'll see him on weekends.

Greg: When someone you are close to leaves, they can stay close friends in your head. You *should* get close to them. They'll always stay close in your head.

T-C: Bob didn't leave because he stopped being your friend, Charles. He left because he felt he had to. You can't control your friends and because you can't doesn't mean they still aren't your friends. Greg, were you worth $525 this week?

Greg: I learned I spend more time paying attention to other people's goals than to my own goals. I gotta start working on my own goals. I also learned I can do anything I want. I wanted to lift 200 pounds and now I can. I wanted to get better grades in school and I have been.

T-C: Right on, Greg! Don, you've only been here one week. What did you learn?

Don: There's good people here. I learned I can trust them. I never had anybody in my life I trusted before. I could never count on anybody before. (stops and smiles slightly) I learned this place loves me.

(The boys smile. Greg claps his hand on Don's shoulder. The teacher-counselor does the same. The boys finish the rap and prepare to return home for the weekend.)

*Pressley Ridge Wilderness School Program**

The therapeutic camping process at Pressley Ridge Wilderness School removes the child from the environment that contrib-

---

*This account was prepared by Clark Luster, executive director of Pressley Ridge School, and J. P. Sakey, Wilderness School program director.

uted to his disturbance and places him in a new, Spartan environment—one that is physically and emotionally secure. There he participates in a therapeutic process in small groups. This treatment
emphasizes a real living situation in which each group member is a
necessary, contributory partner and participant. It involves creative experiences, group and self-analysis, goal development, interpersonal communications, and close relationships with positive
adult role models. The program is designed to promote a therapeutic environment centered around the small, balanced, continuous
peer group experience. The educational process for each child is an
individualized experience-based curriculum. An education continuum exists, beginning with the learning of basic academic skills
and ending with the development of motivation for seeking formalized instruction. Each child is exposed to planned situations requiring the development and application of concrete learning. Activities are selected to accentuate success and lead gradually to
more abstract learning with the same focus on attainment.

The Pressley Ridge Wilderness School serves boys, ages eight
to fifteen, who have developed emotional problems or deviant behavior. The continuous groups are surrounded only by the outdoors and caring adults. Teacher-counselors work with the children (campers)—five campers per teacher-counselor, ten campers
per treatment group—on a twenty-four-hour-a-day basis. Through
living and learning together, the campers practice becoming worthwhile, productive members of society.

The Autonomous Treatment Group. The campers live and
work in autonomous groups at the Wilderness School. Each group
builds, maintains, and lives in a semipermanent campsite; plans
and cooks about a third of its meals; and works out and executes
its daily plans, which are derived from its weekly plans, which are
derived from its monthly plans, which are derived from the long-
range six-month plans.

Outdoor living of this sort naturally leaves with the individual and his group the main responsibilities for their comfort and
well-being. The group must construct its shelters, cut its firewood,
repair its equipment, arrange its own recreation, maintain its trail
system, and do all the things necessary for safe and responsible living. These practices, in themselves, provide a sort of objective discipline and play a significant role in helping children develop a
better sense of social and personal responsibility.

The group is continuous. The group structure provides a stable framework that facilitates the experience and communication
of group values and the strengthening of group purpose and cohesiveness in living within the daily schedule of work and play. A
child develops confidence and skill in a group that provides a feeling of familiarity and security in the face of everyday problems. A
child's progress toward rehabilitation at the Wilderness School can

frequently be attributed to his acceptance by and identification with his fellow campers and their collective ideas and goals.

From the time a child first arrives at the Wilderness School, emphasis is on helping him make changes in his behavior and attitude that will enable him to return to his home, school, and community. This is accomplished through the use of group process and individual and group counseling techniques implemented in the wilderness environment.

The program teaches causal reasoning in every task, small or large. The campers learn a great deal about how to relate to other people and come to see how they have helped create conflicts and difficulties for themselves. More importantly, the campers develop insight into the needs and feelings of others, and learn how to compromise. They learn how to control themselves rather than to have to be controlled by others. They learn to verbalize their feelings, rather than to have to act them out. Immediate feedback is a prime concept. Difficulties arise frequently among the campers. One child or an entire group may become angry, upset, fearful, uncooperative, or irresponsible. When this happens, the group interrupts its activities and, with the guidance of its teacher-counselors, focuses attention on the problem until it is resolved.

At the end of the day, the campers discuss the day's activities, pinpointing strengths and weaknesses in their actions, setting a positive note on their accomplishments. Emphasis is on discovering, as a group, the relationships between action and the consequences of those actions; on eliminating disruptive, problem-causing, discordant behavior; and on fostering constructive, functional, and problem-solving behavior.

The continuous experience a child gets in a small peer group can be a powerful therapeutic and educational influence. He is forced constantly to evaluate his experience. Every project and task is planned, accomplished, and evaluated.

The Education Program. The primary goal of the educational program of studies is to develop fundamental skills through an experience-based curriculum. The program seeks to enhance competence in language arts and mathematics. Language arts activities include plan writing, menu writing, letters home, newspaper articles, trip experiences, and personal as well as group goal statements. Also included in language activities are concepts related to science, social studies, and creative expression. Mathematics activities include menu calculations and tent building, which require such skills as reading numbers, ordering to size, calculating, and measuring. These subject matter areas are integrated into the daily life experience of each camper. For example, since the group members must write menus for six meals a week and build every shelter in their campsite, mathematical computations are constantly taught and reinforced. Here, as in all teaching, it is the fulfillment of basic human needs—food, shelter, and recreation —which supplies the impetus and structure.

The education program will progress and be effective only if there is a strong relationship between teacher-counselor and child. A child cannot be taught unless he wants to learn, and this desire is stimulated initially by the teacher-counselor, who is the role model for the group. Only as a child identifies with a healthy adult can a learning attitude be cultivated and encouraged. Because of the mobility of personnel and the ease with which information flows throughout the organization, an atmosphere of trust and openness is created—an atmosphere that allows creativity to flourish. The outdoor setting, which puts everything at a child's level and pace and combines cause and effect with the fulfillment of basic needs, provides a comprehensive model for the development of fundamental skills, critical thinking skills, democratic process skills, and interpersonal relationship skills. Learning opportunities surround each camper and become a part of everyone's life.

The Liaison-Counselor Component. One of the principles of Pressley Ridge's Wilderness School is that the end product always sought will be a return of the camper to his home and family or an appropriate substitute family. The Wilderness School liaison staff maintains family, community, and agency contact, from referral past ultimate discharge to follow-up. It is the liaison unit's conviction and practice that total families should participate in the helping process, that the results are more favorable when parents can be helped to grow and change as their children do.

Pressley Ridge offers dual means for helping parents to be involved. The first is frequent contacts between parent and child, both at home and at the Wilderness School during initial visits, home days, school visits, family conferences, parent group meetings, and the like. The other is the assignment of full-time liaison-counselors, who work intensively with the family of every child.

In this setting, parents are seen as an additional force for growth, and every effort is extended to see that children are not sent to the program and forgotten. Children are nurtured and loved at the Wilderness School, but the concept always in mind is that home is wherever the family is and that eventually the child will return there.

Program Results. How well does the program serve? This is a constant question in any treatment program. Since 1976, Pressley Ridge, with consultation from West Virginia University, has undergone an intensive evaluation project. The academic data demonstrate that the program improves the youths' rate of learning over their previous base rate. This represents an average 19 percent increase in their rate of learning. A summary of the annual evaluation reports indicates that the major benefits of the program for the child are: learning to function in a community, ego building, developing positive relationships, improved self-concepts, modifying inappropriate behavior, and improved school adjustment.

Follow-up data continue to be gathered and are very positive: Most camp graduates are enrolled in regular schools and have not had major school problems.

12

Epilogue:
Observations
and Recommendations
of a Panel of Visitors

Eli M. Bower, Wayne H. Holtzman,
Reginald S. Lourie, Charles R. Strother

In 1969, four members of a "Panel of Visitors" set out to take a final look at a new program for helping emotionally disturbed children.* The program was an eight-year demonstration project supported by the National Institute of Mental Health, known as "Project Re-ED," or "A Project for the Reeducation of Emotionally Disturbed Children." It was one of the first demonstration or pilot study programs funded by NIMH. All of the Panel members had been closely associated with

*The work here reported was made possible by a grant from the Spencer Foundation. The views expressed are those of the authors and are not necessarily those of the foundation.

Re-ED ideas, concepts, and problems and had been anxious on-lookers as the staffs at Cumberland House, George Peabody College for Teachers, the Nashville community, and the state of Tennessee began the program in 1961. Cumberland House was followed shortly by the opening of Wright School in Durham, under the sponsorship of the state of North Carolina. When the panel members made their first visits (during the demonstration years from 1961 to 1969), Cumberland House and Wright School, plus a training program at Peabody College, *were* the Re-ED program. The schools served children ages six to twelve in short-term, residential settings. By 1980, the programs had grown to twenty in number, had spread across the country, and had produced several promising new forms to serve children from early childhood to eighteen years of age.

As it turned out, happily, the 1969 "final look" was not the last one. In 1980, the panel took another look at Project Re-ED. The original panel was composed of Eli M. Bower, educational psychologist; Reginald S. Lourie, psychiatrist; Charles R. Strother, clinical psychologist; and Robert L. Sutherland, sociologist. Dr. Sutherland died in 1976, leaving us saddened and the panel incomplete. At the time of the first panel's work, Dr. Sutherland was president of the Hogg Foundation for Mental Health and professor of sociology at the University of Texas. Wayne H. Holtzman, professor of psychology at Texas, succeeded Robert Sutherland as president of the Hogg Foundation, and we were fortunate that he responded readily to our invitation to join the panel.

The report of the first panel of visitors to Re-ED was published in 1969. Since that report is an important prelude to this one, a few comments carrying forward the spirit of that report may be useful. Both reports begin with a caveat to the reader. In our visits then and now, we found no Re-ED program which considered itself the magic solution to the treatment of emotionally disturbed children nor the sole source of truth. Staff members referred favorably to other treatment programs, based on other treatment philosophies, which they felt provided effective services to emotionally disturbed children. Re-ED is one approach to helping children, but certainly not the only one. We concentrate on Re-ED because we were invited to do so and because it is a program of demonstrated effectiveness in an area of great human need. It has proven its effectiveness over a twenty-year period, and it is today being replicated over the country.

If this quartet of panelists has a bias, it is to develop, enhance, and encourage effective and economical programs for emotionally disturbed children. Our interest in Re-ED is one of professional concern and curiosity: To what extent can such a program be of service to children, families, and communities? What are its assets, its problems, its future? We attempt in this report to make a candid response to such questions.

The staff of any program, old or new, should have unbounded faith and enthusiasm for what they do and hope to accomplish for the people they serve. But, at the same time, they must accept with equal enthusiasm mechanisms to correct, adjust, balance, or support judgments about the effectiveness of their work. This panel of visitors is one of these mechanisms. During our visits, staffs and community personnel, including parents and members of governing boards, shared with us not only their enthusiasm but also their doubts, questions, anxieties, and confusions. We were open to any problem which anyone wished to share. We actively initiated hard-nosed confrontations on concepts and operations when such seemed appropriate. Panel members visited programs individually, collected our thoughts, noted our observations, and came together in Nashville on July 28-29, 1980, to share our conclusions. What follows are individual and group reflections and response to what we saw and what we thought.

The original panel had only two schools to visit over an eight-year period. Thus, panel members in those more leisurely days made repeated visits to both Cumberland House and Wright School. The current panel, with limited time and travel resources, as well as a large number of programs to choose from, had to divide responsibilities and select programs to visit. All members of the panel visited Cumberland House and Crockett Academy in Nashville, and some members visited Wright School in Durham, the Positive Education Program in Cleveland, Pressley Ridge School in Pittsburgh, and the Regional Intervention Program in Nashville. Though the selection of programs to visit had to be limited, we believe the observations of the panel are generally pertinent to all of the programs. Where exceptions are evident, these are mentioned in the text.

The original panel of visitors, in its 1969 report, recorded the following summary of its observations and conclusions (Bower, Lourie, Struther, and Sutherland, 1969, p. 23):

The panel of visitors of Project Re-ED, having followed the development of the program with due skepticism, growing involvement, and now considerable enthusiasm, has reached the following conclusions: that Re-ED represents a conceptually sound, economically feasible, and demonstrably effective approach to helping emotionally disturbed children, including the moderately disturbed and some seriously disturbed; that it does make available an important new source of mental health manpower and extends the effectiveness of highly trained and scarce mental health specialists; that it has developed concepts applicable to other educational and mental health programs for children; and that it has passed the crucial test of professional, public, and legislative scrutiny and acceptance. We therefore recommend the adoption of the Re-ED program as a primary resource for the help of emotionally disturbed children of the nation.

In 1980, after visiting several programs, reading about others, and debating the strengths and weaknesses of Re-ED today, the panel finds these earlier judgments to be sound and adds its current endorsement to them. Having done that, it seems to us important to add our observations about Re-ED twelve years later, to record its development into maturity, to commend when commendation is due and prod where deficiencies are observed, and, finally, to make observations that may be useful in the shaping of public policy in the interest of emotionally disturbed children and their families. The task of the panel appears to us to take on added significance in these days of financial stringency and of increased responsibility of the states for program planning and management.

As the panel pooled its observations, a number of positive features stand out as particularly impressive about the programs visited. These, as well as the negative observations, have been verified by consultants who are familiar with the programs not visited by panel members.

Many demonstration projects fade away after federal monies are withdrawn or after the initial favorable attention has been diverted elsewhere. By contrast, when the federal demonstration grant terminated, both Tennessee and North Carolina, impressed by the cost-effectiveness of their programs, assumed full support of Cumberland House and Wright School, and, indeed, in both states the program has been expanded in subsequent years. Cumberland House continues to enjoy high visibility both near and far. The steady stream of visitors, the general public awareness of Cumberland House, and the apparent pride in Cumberland House exhibited by the administrative staff within the state Department of Mental Health and Mental Retardation could not have continued all these years if the program were not in fact successful. The same could be said of Wright School. Other programs, especially those with unique features (such as Pressley Ridge with its camping program; the Regional Intervention Program with its emphasis on preschool children and their families; and the Positive Education Program in Cleveland (a day program that operates from 8:30 A.M. to 4:00 P.M. five days a week, eleven months a year), enjoy similar attention from people from around the world.

There continues to be a high degree of personal commitment, high morale, and enthusiasm on the part of all staff interviewed. Obviously, this dedication to the task and commitment to the principles of Re-ED are invaluable assets that should be highly prized. An analysis of current staff in one school indicates that, of the fifteen full-time workers who are providing direct services for children in the four groups, the average length of stay in the job is 2.6 years; at another school, the average for this group was three years. By contrast, the average length of stay among personnel serving in administrative capacities is 8.1 years of service. Many of these individuals are former teacher-counselors who moved on to positions of higher responsibility after several years of direct service activities. These statistics indicate that young, idealistic men and women should not be expected to remain in direct service activities for more than three or four years before moving on in their careers to other professional roles, either within Re-ED programs or elsewhere. Consequently, a continuous training program and special efforts to maintain the enthusiastic involvement of young people are critical to the continuing success of Re-ED programs. The director of Wright School reports that experienced teacher-counselors are eagerly sought by school systems and other agencies because they know they are extremely well trained. School systems offer a ten-month working year rather than an eleven-month year, and they can frequently supplement the basic state salary, which Wright School is not permitted to do.

Schools vary considerably in admissions policies. The continued high rate of voluntary admissions to Cumberland House and Wright School (explainable in part by their working with younger children) is indeed unusual, given the many pressures from various sources in the community to take children under court orders or transfers from other institutions. At Cumberland House, nine out of ten children are admitted voluntarily after extensive negotiations involving the liaison teacher-counselor with the family, school, social agencies, and, most importantly, with the individual child prior to admission. The fact that many parents and children genuinely want to be enrolled in the program is clearly a major strength. Programs for adolescents, such as Crockett Academy, Pine Breeze, and Pressley Ridge, come under heavier pressure from the courts to admit children. In some instances, acceptance of a court-referred child is mandatory; in other instances, the program retains control over admissions. All of the programs, however, have a reputation for providing services to the truly difficult children and youth of the communities they serve.

Cumberland House, Wright School, the Regional Intervention Program, the Positive Education Program, Pressley Ridge, and others are apparently regarded by most members of the community as educational enterprises, special schools rather than mental health treatment centers, in spite of the fact that most (but not all) programs come under the state or local mental health authority. For example, Cumberland House is an integral part of the Middle Tennessee Mental Health Institute and all of the staff members are employees of the Tennessee Department of Mental Health and Mental Retardation. Even so, the Cumberland House students and alumni continue to regard it as a school, with all of the positive features associated with such an image (including an annual reunion of graduates and their families). Re-ED programs located on mental hospital grounds are burdened by the negative public perception of such settings.

The original proposal for Project Re-ED called for settings and facilities that would metaphorically represent the character of the program, with its emphasis on school, on family relationships, on the normal activities of childhood and adolescence, on health rather than pathology, and on close community ties. An extraordinary amount of effort was expended to find appropriate locations for Cumberland House and Wright School. Pressley Ridge, Pine Breeze, the Positive Education Program, and others carry forward the design with notable success. However, a number of compromises have been made when the choice seemed between having no Re-ED program at all or having it in a less than ideal setting. These decisions reflected the confidence of the staffs in the sturdiness of Re-ED ideas; indeed, it was thought that they might even have a salubrious effect on hospital programs.

Many of the schools make highly effective use of advisory committees, both lay and professional. Pressley Ridge has a prestigious board of trustees made up of outstanding citizens who are responsible for the trust funds that help defray the cost of the program. A new organization, "The Friends of Cumberland House," has just been started to raise funds in support of enrichment programs at Cumberland House, an encouraging sign of the extent and depth of good will that has been built up over the years concerning the Cumberland House program. Similar examples could be drawn from other programs, but it must be pointed out that some of the programs operate without the evident benefits of advisory groups.

Re-ED programs have demonstrated their strength by weathering a number of crises that might not have been survived by programs with a less dedicated staff. Cumberland House faced a serious crisis in 1975, when there was a strong effort to move Cumberland House from its pleasant community setting to state hospital grounds. The staff rose in unison in defending the current program. The crisis came to a head when the principal resigned rather than give in to administrative authority on this major issue. The resulting publicity and closing of ranks by parents, citizens, and staff quickly reversed the situation, permitting Cumberland House to remain in its present quarters. But this victory was only partial, since a negotiated settlement resulted in loss of half the land at Cumberland House for the construction of Crockett Academy, a residential treatment program for disturbed adolescents. The nascent Re-ED program in California came close to being nipped in the bud by an adviser who was not fully knowledgeable about Re-ED, having been informed that it served only mildly disturbed children. Much to his credit, he reversed his position when accurate information was provided concerning the actual range of children served by Re-ED. His fairness led to the restoration of the California Re-ED program, now vigorously growing.

In Tennessee, the decision of state authorities to use Title XIX (Medicaid) funds for its Re-ED program resulted in a requirement that the Tennessee schools comply with the standards of both Medicaid and the Joint Commission on Accreditation of Hospitals. The burden of this change can be seen as a grave threat to the integrity of the Tennessee Re-ED program. It requires a layer of supervisory personnel who have no essential functions in the program; it requires diagnostic procedures that are not relevant to the program; and it imposes an alien treatment philosophy that tends to be demoralizing to the staff and to require extraordinary efforts on the part of Re-ED administrators to protect the program from severe distortion. Most serious of all, it substantially increases the cost of Re-ED, which elsewhere is especially appreciated because of its low cost and high effectiveness. Added costs arising from inappropriate accreditation requirements are difficult to justify.

While salaries of the professional teacher-counselors and liaison teacher-counselors may still be lower than they should be, the salaries are equal to if not higher than comparable salaries for other master's level professional workers, such as social workers or master's teachers within the state system. Tennessee apparently has a sufficiently large critical mass of Project Re-ED programs that it has revamped its personnel descriptions and salary levels to recognize the special skills involved. This recognition is itself unusual and speaks well for the future of the program, at least in Tennessee. The state of California will certify teacher-counselors on the basis of a two-year graduate training program (or its equivalent) now being designed at the University of California at Berkeley and the University of California at Los Angeles. North Carolina certifies teacher-counselors and provides a salary scale generally deemed to be competitive with that of professional groups of comparable training and experience.

Determining the costs of a Re-ED program presents a formidable undertaking, since there is no "model" Re-ED program and since cost-accounting practices vary from state to state and even from program to program. The issue is discussed in detail in Chapter Three of this book. It is important not to overemphasize that Project Re-ED is cheaper than other programs, since indeed it may not be on a per-day cost. Rather, one needs to stress the positive features of the program and how much one can get for the money invested. It is also important to note that the length of stay per child at Cumberland House is shorter than in most other residential treatment centers (though longer than in some other Re-ED programs), so that the actual total cost per child may indeed be less than elsewhere. The panel judges that a per-day cost of $80 for a Re-ED residential program would be a good approximation. Day programs cost less, of course. The estimate includes all overhead costs assigned by the state, and it assumes five-day-a-week programming. A seven-day-a-week assumption would more accurately reflect the continuing responsibilities of the staff.

Re-ED programs vary considerably in their ties to universities, initially a central feature of their structure. In California, the Re-ED program, La Cheim, is closely linked to the University of California at Berkeley; and the programs at Camarillo and Hobbs Landing are linked to the University of California at Los Angeles. Wright School has maintained close contacts with both Duke University and the University of North Carolina, with some consultants having served for twenty years, and with students from education and psychiatry, especially, frequently involved. The Positive Education Program has started an Institute for Research and Training in conjunction with Cleveland State and Kent State universities; they jointly employ two professorial-level staff members. Pressley Ridge has an affiliation with the University of West Virginia, but the focus here seems to be primarily on research. Centennial School is actually operated by Lehigh University. Other programs have more tenuous affiliations with universities.

The ties of Cumberland House to universities and training programs, particularly at Peabody, were strong in the early days of the project. Over the years, these have diminished to the point where few formal ties exist. To be sure, some internship and clerkship types of training do go on, but this is a far cry from the systematic kind of training program that ought to be continued at Cumberland House as well as in the other Project Re-ED facilities. An even more important advantage to be gained from continued formal ties with nearby universities is the steady stream of new ideas, intellectual debate, and ferment that accompany such ties when properly implemented. Closer ties to some of the universities in Nashville should greatly improve the likelihood of continued evolution and improvement at Cumberland House. The university programs have much to gain from such ties with Re-ED programs.

As Re-ED programs began to move their coverage upward through the adolescent years, there was a veritable explosion of inventiveness, so great are the pressures to provide services for this difficult group of youngsters. Pine Breeze made the pioneering effort in 1969. It had an ideal setting, on a Blue Ridge mountaintop close to Chattanooga; and the Moccasin Bend Hospital continued to operate a ward for adolescents, thus taking immediate pressure off Pine Breeze for the first several years. Nonetheless, there were many difficulties in adapting Re-ED ideas to this older group. Now the program is operating about as smoothly as any program for adolescents, and the hospital has closed down its adolescent ward. Wright School initiated a highly successful program for younger adolescents in conjunction with a community elementary school (the Braggtown Project). Pressley Ridge School established its wilderness camping program for (among others) severely antisocial adolescent boys. The Positive Education Program in Cleveland treats severely disturbed adolescents in its regular day program and has worked out an alliance with a residential substance abuse program to operate the educational program for adolescents. The first of several halfway houses for disturbed adolescents will be opened by the Positive Educational Program in 1982. The Lakeshore Mental Health Institute in Knoxville has created Cooper House, a residential program housed in a commodious dwelling in a neighborhood in North Knoxville. Cooper House serves fourteen boys, ages around fifteen and sixteen, in a homelike setting that has had an excellent record in returning boys to their own homes and regular schools. Initially (in 1973) Cooper House could accept only adjudicated delinquents, but today this requirement no longer obtains and Cooper House serves boys "who can't get along at home or in school, who have probably gotten in trouble with the police, or who may be facing a sentence to a correctional facility" (Fitzgerald, 1978).

Because all the members of the 1980 panel visited Crockett Academy, more extensive observations were made of it than of other programs for adolescents. Unlike Cumberland House, Crockett Academy has been in existence for only a few years and may not be a genuine high-fidelity model of Project Re-ED. It falls somewhere between such a model and some of the more traditional ways of handling difficult adolescents. In fact, Crockett Academy was converted from a state hospital adolescent ward, now closed.

On the positive side, Crockett Academy is engaged in a heroic struggle to cope effectively with the most difficult and neglected age group in our society. Many of the staff are dedicated to implementing the principles of Project Re-ED and indeed are mostly successful in their struggle to maintain such principles. On the negative side, in *some* instances, there are too many compromises of Project Re-ED principles. Perhaps a hybrid model is emerging, and the staff are still searching for the ideal mixture of the old and the new principles.

Crockett Academy is at a turning point. Most of the problems encountered in the shakedown of the past several years are now behind it, and it can look forward to a more vigorous, positively implemented program in the future.

Cumberland House was singled out for observations about the adequacy of follow-up, though comparable criticisms might be made of other programs. In spite of the attention given conceptually to the follow-up of individual children after they leave Cumberland House, the actual degree of follow-up is disturbingly superficial. Granted that it would take additional funds and resources to do a first-class job, it strikes the panel that such follow-up is just as important as, or perhaps even more important than, the extensive preadmission liaison work that is done effectively for every case except the emergency admissions. Even a child who functions well in the school and appears to have gained a great deal from his residential experience can get into serious difficulty and sharply regress if the environment to which he is discharged is not dealt with effectively for many months after discharge.

The relative neglect of evaluative research in Re-ED programs should be remedied. While such neglect is commonplace in mental health treatment programs, their negligence is no excuse for a program that strongly asserted its commitment to research in the early days and that, indeed, has produced one of the most significant investigations of the effects of educationally oriented treatment on seriously disturbed children.

Laura Weinstein (1974) studied 122 boys, ages six to twelve, who attended one of the schools over a five-year period and compared their progress with that of a group of untreated disturbed children and a group of randomly selected peers. Quay (1970), summarizing the at-discharge data, concludes that "the project led to a more positive self-concept, more internal locus of control, decreased motor and cognitive impulsivity, and more constructive family relationships as perceived by the child. Over the same period, there was no significant improvement in these areas among the untreated disturbed group" (p. 396). "In terms of the care, thoughtfulness, and effort which went into the evaluation, this project might well serve as a model for the evaluation of residential treatment" (p. 398).

Other data have been collected through the years, but they remain unexamined. Trend analyses from statistical reports can provide information of value. More systematic follow-up of graduates from Re-ED schools is clearly an urgent need, not only from a point of view of evaluation research but simply from the point of view of providing a more effective and lasting service. The specialized skills needed for ongoing operations research as well as periodic evaluation research are quite different from those present in the service staff. Nearly a thousand children have graduated from Cumberland House in the past eighteen years, providing a precious reservoir of useful information if wisely tapped by an experienced researcher. Certainly, closer ties to Vanderbilt or some other interested university could easily result in a first-class evaluation research project. The existing program needs to be documented more accurately and verified with respect to its processes and impacts. Follow-up studies of children and follow-up studies of the workers themselves should be high on the agenda for evaluation. The earlier work of Weinstein especially should be reexamined and extended.

Although research has lagged, the panel learned of a number of heartening developments that indicate a renewed commitment to this area. In Tennessee, Wilbert Lewis, one of the founders of Re-ED, has been appointed full-time director of research for the children and youth program of the Middle Tennessee Mental

Health Institute; this program includes Cumberland House, Crockett Academy, and the Regional Intervention Program. The Positive Education Program in Cleveland has appointed (jointly with Cleveland State and Kent State universities) Robert Cantrell to its staff, with responsibility for mounting a systematic evaluation program. Pressley Ridge School is continuing its contract for research studies with Robert Hawkins and William Fremouw of the University of West Virginia.

For the past four years, Wright School has had an arrangement with the department of special education of the University of North Carolina in support of research on various aspects of the school's program. There is a Wright School–University of North Carolina research committee that meets regularly. Its initial objective, now accomplished, was to develop a computer-based information system that will permit comparative analyses of the program year by year. In addition, a full-time-equivalent staff position has been committed to research; the funds provide half-time support for Betty Epanchin, assistant professor of special education at the University of North Carolina, plus support for one doctoral student a year to do a dissertation, under her supervision, on some aspect of the Wright School program. These arrangements should begin to yield substantial results in the near future.

With increased national attention to the need for masters' level professional direct-service providers in the mental health field, especially those employing educational models such as Project Re-ED, it is clearly now time to embark on a nationally significant systematic evaluation of such programs, wherever they may be implemented. Such research is expensive and may take several years to complete. Nevertheless, if it is not begun immediately, we will still have the same unanswered questions three years from now, when the answers are even more urgently needed.

When established twenty years ago, Re-ED had some distinct characteristics in providing effective services to emotionally disturbed children. It created a new type of institution, essentially educational in nature, in which children who would otherwise be in psychiatric, correctional, or social welfare facilities might be cared for. The central responsibility for the children was placed in the hands of teacher-counselors rather than traditional mental health professional personnel, and substantial resources were allocated to a broadly conceived liaison with the child's ecosystem: family, neighborhood, and school, and, for older students, the work place.

Conceptually, this involved the creation of a new social institution, a therapeutic residential school, and a new profession—the teacher-counselor. Furthermore, it opened up new roles for mental health and other highly trained medical and educational specialists as consultants to teacher-counselors, thus extending their knowledge and talents and providing a sturdy structure for offering mental health services to children and youth and their families. In some instances and for some periods of time, Re-ED programs were allowed to develop without conforming to the conventional constraints of a service system such as mental health, corrections, or education. This was evident in the early days of its development, when it was supported professionally and financially by the National Institute of Mental Health and had the aura of an experimental program. However, pressures toward conformity to requirements of the host institution or agency have increased and are forcing changes in Re-ED procedures. Whether these changes are significant to the integrity and survival of Re-ED remains to be seen.

It is difficult to get first-rate mental health services for children and adolescents. Many of our best-trained psychiatrists and clinical psychologists prefer private practice over service in community agencies; the Comprehensive Community Mental Health Centers have been repeatedly faulted for their neglect of children and adolescents; and state residential treatment programs for seriously disturbed children and youth are frequently staffed by foreign-trained physicians, who have difficulty with the language and little understanding of the culture.

Consequently, childcare agencies and federal and state policy makers are now beginning to look for different patterns of service for these children and are readier than they have been in the past to consider the possibility of a Re-ED type of program.

Some criticisms of such programs have come from children and youth services agencies. Juvenile judges generally have been well satisfied and strongly support the programs because they are obviously superior to any of the alternatives. These judges are delighted with any agency that can deliver the results that a Re-ED program can deliver. But the people in children and youth services have been suspicious of the Re-ED agencies, partly because in some ways they seem to deviate from the traditional social work concepts. Some of the casework functions and community social work functions that are provided by social workers are provided in Re-ED by people who have no social work training. Psychiatrists and clinical psychologists, on the other hand, are often unfamiliar with contemporary concepts and procedures in education; they have for the most part been trained as clinicians and scientists, and some of them find uncongenial the role of consultant in Re-ED, which would permit them to multiply their effectiveness by sharing their knowledge and skills with teacher-counselors and thereby increase the effectiveness of these excellent but less extensively trained people. Therein lie the seeds of contention about professional territorial rights.

Another problem that stems from the placement of a Re-ED program under the auspices of a mental health agency is that it can result in the exclusion of children who do not demonstrate "observable" mental health problems. These are primarily the delinquent children and status offenders, many of whom need the Re-ED program and for whom experience has shown such a program to be effective. A child must show some evidence of "disease" or "emotional problems" before the mental health agency would have any jurisdiction over the child. Such jurisdictional and conceptual disputes are unfortunate, and unless something can be done to bring about greater freedom in the admission policy of Re-ED programs or to coordinate the mental health and correctional programs, independent programs are going to have to be developed under the auspices of different agencies.

One may need to explore the possibility of Re-ED development within the juvenile court and related child welfare agencies. There is a very obvious and increasingly urgent need for more effective programs for the management of juvenile delinquents and predelinquents. Re-ED programs have a great deal to offer in this respect, particularly camping and wilderness programs of the type maintained by Pressley Ridge and others like it. One of the great advantages of these wilderness camps is that they isolate the child completely from the type of environment in which his delinquent behavior occurred. It places him under close twenty-four-hour observation and under highly effective peer pressures.

One of the shortcomings of juvenile programs has been their

inability to repair the deficiencies in their clients' basic academic skills. Also, many of these juveniles have a major difficulty in impulse control. Unless supervision and contact are sufficiently close, the child has little opportunity to learn and practice impulse control. Another effective element of such a program, at least as exemplified at Pressley Ridge camp, was the substitution of problem solving and discussion for the child's acting-out behavior. If an instance of loss of control is terminated promptly, and a cooling-off period is provided, the child then has an opportunity for reflection, not only about the conditions that instigated this behavior but about alternative nonaggressive, or at least nonphysical, ways of dealing with the situation. Consequently, the opportunity both for control and for the rapid acquisition of effective and acceptable social skills is greatly improved.

It is difficult to understand why the liaison teacher-counselor concept has not been more broadly accepted and utilized. It is one of the most innovative and useful concepts in the Re-ED formulation. In the multiple-agency context which almost all troubled children are exposed to, the parents often get differing versions of what is wrong and what needs to be done. Interpretations, suggestions, and treatment from various sources may differ and even conflict with each other, increasing the family's anxiety and confusion. One area in which the liaison teacher-counselor has been effective is in clarifying for the family and the agencies involved what an integration of all their ideas, observations, and orientations looks like. This then becomes a basis for future planning, particularly when the child is returned to the community with a commitment worked out by the liaison teacher-counselor and the support of the other agencies.

The most useful and successful direct interveners with the children have been found to be young, energetic, interested people who are not trained in any of the traditional mental health disciplines. They are bright and optimistic and, above all, flexible and able to incorporate principles from other disciplines in their own work. As young and innovative workers begin to translate the Re-ED concepts in new directions, other payoffs become possible. What is learned in a Re-ED preschool program becomes valuable in parent education. The techniques developed for basic approaches to parent involvement and the use of parents as "therapists" (as in the Regional Intervention Program) suggest a promising approach to work with parents of older children in other Re-ED programs.

There is always the danger that any newcomer such as Re-ED will become a threat to the established disciplines. To reduce the possibility of such inhospitality, trainees from other programs and disciplines have been invited to observe, air doubts, ask questions, pursue confusions, and then to find the answers that will allow them to understand why a program like Re-ED works and for whom it works. This is being done at the Wright School program in collaboration with Duke University.

In summary, the panel of visitors of Project Re-ED, having concluded its second round of visits to programs twelve years after its first report and twenty years after the project was initiated, makes the following judgments about Re-ED today:

1. In its beginnings, Project Re-ED was a bold experiment in the field of mental health of children. Based as much on hope as on a desperate need for expanded services, the project has been transformed from a set of general aspirations to a substantial body of concepts and procedures that can be precisely stated, communicated to others, and used as a basis for day-by-day work with moderately and severely disturbed children and youth. The panel judges the demonstration project to have been notably successful. The panel suggests that continuing to refer to Re-ED as a "project" is no longer appropriate and that, except in casual reference, even the term "Re-ED" is not entirely felicitous.

2. Among the most significant achievements of Project Re-ED is the creation of an entirely new profession within the mental health field, that of the teacher-counselor. The new profession has many attractive features: it draws on an abundant pool of talented and caring young adults; it requires less extensive and expensive graduate training than does psychiatry or clinical psychology; it provides a rich experience in socially valuable and personally rewarding work for those who stay in the role, if only for a few years; and it is a stepping stone to longer-term administrative and instructional positions in reeducation or to further graduate study. Panel members were especially impressed by the competence and high morale of the teacher-counselors in the schools visited.

3. Reeducation depends on psychiatrists, pediatricians, special educators, psychologists, social workers, and other highly

trained specialists, but it has devised an arrangement that permits these knowledgeable and skillful professional people to multiply their effectiveness many times over by working, in the role of consultant, through the teacher-counselors. Extended, the arrangement could greatly expand the overall effectiveness of the nation's mental health program.

4. The development of ecological concepts in working with emotionally disturbed children, with its elaboration into the liaison function, appears to the panel to be a major contribution that is readily adaptable to other human services programs for children and youth. This point of view recognizes the centrality of parents (or surrogate parents) in the lives of children and seeks to support them in carrying out the arduous tasks of which they cannot ever truly be relieved. It also emphasizes the importance of families, schools, churches, neighborhoods, and other socializing agencies and strives to enhance their effectiveness in helping young people grow up well.

5. Among other innovations associated with reeducation (though not necessarily invented in that context) are: the insistence on removing of the child from home, school, and community for the shortest possible period consistent with achieving a favorable outcome; the five-day residential week, with children going home every weekend to maintain and nurture family ties; the insistence on small size in programs—not more than forty or fifty residents; the limitation of services to a restricted geographical area, to permit constant engagement with the ecosystem of which the child is the defining member; the emphasis on the achievement of competence, especially in basic educational skills so necessary for effective living; the training of parents to work positively with younger children; the preparation of adolescents for further education or for work; the incorporation of wilderness camping for highly antisocial adolescents; the emphasis on adventure for all children. The panel was especially impressed by the fact that reeducation is not a grim process but one that is infused with an affirmative spirit and a deep appreciation of people, of children especially, and of life's simple satisfactions.

6. The panel is concerned about the role of reeducation in the nation's human services systems. Re-ED properly belongs in the mental health system, where it started and where it is meet-

ing a great need. However, there are large numbers of emotionally disturbed children and youth who are not touched by the mental health system, either directly or indirectly. These children, who could benefit greatly from reeducation, are to be found in the public schools, in the general health system, in social services, in developmental disabilities programs, and in corrections. The panel urges that authorities in these several systems explore the feasibility of incorporating principles of reeducation in their programs and, further, that they take steps to evaluate the effectiveness of reeducation in these new settings.

7. The panel finds the costs of reeducation programs reasonable. On a cost per-child per-day basis, reeducation is more expensive than custodial programs and less expensive than traditionally staffed residential treatment programs. However, it compares most favorably with other programs in the total cost of restoring a child to his home, school, and community.

8. The panel has grave concerns about programs where sources of funding, usually through third-party payment arrangements, have been allowed to distort the fundamental philosophy of reeducation, to impose on programs alien expectations as well as superfluous personnel, and to run up costs unconscionably. Where such situations exist, they should be rectified as rapidly as possible, and the mistake should not be repeated in the establishment of new programs around the country.

9. The panel was divided on the issue of dissemination of reeducation programs. After twenty years, there are twenty programs. Is this good or bad? Is the glass half empty or half full? However, the panel was unanimous in its opinion that efforts at disseminating the concepts of reeducation should be greatly stepped up and that states especially should initiate pilot programs to test reeducation in a variety of settings to meet the service needs of emotionally disturbed children and youth.

10. The panel is disappointed in the failure of some existing Re-ED programs to follow up adequately on the children and youth they have served. Follow-up should be much more than a perfunctory assessment of status of children and their families; it should be a natural extension in time of the reeducation process.

11. The panel is also disappointed in the failure of Re-ED programs to evaluate satisfactorily the results of their work. Al-

though one exemplary study has been published and a number of assessments of children's progress have been made, these efforts fall far short of what might reasonably be expected of a program that started out with a strong commitment to research and evaluation. Every reeducation center should be a center for research in the interest of program improvement and as a model for other approaches to the treatment of emotionally disturbed children and youth. The panel found several indicators of a revival of interest in research and evaluation and recommends that all possible support be given to this emergent development, both within Re-ED and on the part of funding agencies.

12. The panel was disappointed to observe that several of the existing Re-ED programs appear to have neglected their traditionally close ties to universities from which new ideas can be drawn and to which important training opportunities can be offered. Some programs have highly productive relationships with universities, but others do not. The panel urges that this deficiency be remedied promptly as one way of ensuring the continuing vitality of reeducation. Advisory groups, present in some programs but not in others, can serve much the same purpose.

13. The panel urges that new training programs for teacher-counselors be established in universities around the country. It applauds the development in California of Re-ED training programs at the University of California at Berkeley and at Los Angeles and, in Pennsylvania, at Lehigh University. This effort needs to be expanded greatly to prepare teacher-counselors not only for Re-ED schools but for a number of other settings, such as psychiatric hospitals and clinics, public schools, social service agencies, and correctional institutions, where, under congenial circumstances, their services could be of great value.

14. The panel strongly reaffirms the conclusions recorded in its 1969 report as well as its recommendation that reeducation programs be developed as a primary resource for serving the nation's emotionally disturbed children and youth. But this restrained statement fails to communicate the enthusiasm expressed by all members of the panel as they assessed the status of reeducation in 1980. We have found Re-ED twenty years after its beginnings to be an exciting, zestful enterprise, at once idealistic yet practical, stable yet ever evolving. It has been adapted to a variety of settings

and circumstances without losing its essential character. It serves really difficult children, including those often turned down by other agencies, and it does a good job with them, not always succeeding but ever ready to try. It is cost-conscious and economical, though not cheap. It gives staff members a rewarding, growth-filled experience that most appear to cherish. It enjoys the strong support of administrators of mental health programs that have adopted the model. It has wavered in some of its commitments, as pointed out above, and it faces tough problems; but the Re-ED leaders seem to know that the flip side of adversity is opportunity. The panel judges Re-ED to be worthy of public and professional trust and support. The members of the panel take satisfaction from having been associated with reeducation for so many years, from having perhaps contributed modestly to its success. The panel members are grateful to all those who shared generously of their time, thoughts, and feelings in making its work possible.

Bibliography

Albee, G. W. *Mental Health Manpower Trends.* New York: Basic Books, 1959.

Bower, E. M. *Early Identification of Emotionally Handicapped Children in School.* Springfield, Ill.: Thomas, 1960.

Bower, E. M., and others. *Learning to Play: Playing to Learn.* Berkeley: School of Education, University of California, 1974.

Bower, E. M., Lourie, R. S., Strother, C. R., and Sutherland, R. L. *Project Re-ED: New Concepts for Helping Emotionally Disturbed Children.* Nashville, Tenn.: The John F. Kennedy Center, George Peabody College, 1969.

Braginsky, B. M., Braginsky, D. D., and King, K. *Methods of Madness: The Mental Hospital as Last Resort.* New York: Holt Rinehart and Winston, 1969.

Brewer, K. L., and Lackey, J. W. "Building Appropriate Peer Interaction: Afternoon Curriculum." *Behavior Disorders,* 1978, *3* 105-110.

Bricker, W. A. "Competence as a Key Factor in the Study of Children's Deviant Behavior." *Mind over Matter.* Nashville: Tennessee Department of Mental Health, 1967.

Cantrell, R. P., and Cantrell, M. L. "Preventive Mainstreaming: Impact of a Supportive Services Program on Pupils." *Exceptional Children,* 1976, *42,* 381-386.

Cantrell, R. P., and Cantrell, M. L. "Evaluation of a Heuristic Approach to Solving Children's Problems." *Peabody Journal of Education,* 1977, *54,* 168-173.

Cantrell, R. P., Stenner, A. J., and Katzenmeyer, W. G. "Teacher Knowledge, Attitudes, and Classroom Correlates of Student Achievement." *Journal of Educational Psychology,* 1977, *69,* 172-179.

Cantrell, R. P., Wood, J. L., and Nichols, C. "Teacher Knowledge of Behavior Principles and Classroom Teaching Patterns." Paper presented at meeting of the American Educational Research Association, Chicago, April 1974.

Children's Defense Fund. *Children Without Homes: An Examination of Public Responsibility to Children in Out-of-Home Care.* Washington, D.C.: Children's Defense Fund, 1978.

Children's Defense Fund. *Children's Mental Health: Preliminary Findings and Issues.* Washington, D.C.: Children's Defense Fund, 1980.

Clarke, A. M., and Clarke, A. D. B. *Early Experience: Myth and Evidence.* New York: Free Press, 1976.

Day, M. *Adolescent Thought: Theory, Research, and Educational Implications.* Houston: University of Houston, 1979.

Dokecki, P. R. "The Liaison Perspective on the Enhancement of Human Development: Theoretical, Historical, and Experiential Background." *Journal of Community Psychology,* 1977, *5,* 13-17.

Fabry, B. D., and others. "Effects of the Pressley Ridge Programs on Youth Personal-Social Behavior: What the Jesness Behavior Checklist Says." Technical report #790720 to Pressley Ridge School, Pittsburgh, July 1979.

Feuerstein, R. *The Dynamic Assessment of Retarded Performers.* Baltimore: University Park Press, 1979.

Feuerstein, R. *Instrumental Enrichment: An Intervention Program for Cognitive Modifiability.* Baltimore: University Park Press, 1980.

Fields, S. "Parents as Therapists." *Innovations,* 1975, *2,* 3-8.

Fitzgerald, W. "Cooper House: An Alternate for Troubled Teen-Agers." *Breakthrough,* Summer 1978, pp. 3-5.

Ginger, S. "Histoire et Geographie de l'Éducateur Spécialisé." *Bulletin de l'Union Mondiale pour la Sauvegarde de l'Enfance et de l'Adolescence,* March 1979, No. 59, pp. 7-14.

Goffman, E. *Asylums.* Chicago: Aldine, 1961.

"Gold Award: A Parent-Implemented Early Intervention Program for Preschool Children—Regional Intervention Program, Nashville, Tennessee." *Hospital and Community Psychiatry,* 1976, *27* (10), 728-731.

Gregory, R. J., Sechinger, E., and Anderson, D. "An Assessment of the Success of Intervention in the Lives of Emotionally Disturbed Children." Unpublished research at Wright School, Durham, N.C., June 30, 1971.

Guindon, J. "(1) The Re-Education Process" and "(2) The Psycho-éducateur Training Program." *International Journal of Mental Health,* 1973, *2,* 15-26, 27-32.

Hawkins, R. P., and others. "Academic, Personal, and Social Growth of Youths in Two Programs." Second quarter report to Buhl Foundation and Pressley Ridge School, Pittsburgh, July 1978.

Heim, K. M., and others. "Juvenile Detention: Another Boundary Issue for Physicians." *Pediatrics,* 1980, *66* (2), 239-245.

Hersh, S. P. "A Report on the Child and Youth Activities of the National Institute of Mental Health: October 1, 1976–September 30, 1977." Internal Document, National Institute of Mental Health, 1977.

Hewitt, F. M. "The Re-Education Process." Unpublished report to the Director of Children and Youth Services, Department of Mental Health, State of California, 1981.

Hobbs, N. "Sources of Gain in Psychotherapy." *American Psychologist,* 1962, *17,* 741-747.

Hobbs, N. "Mental Health's Third Revolution." *American Journal of Orthopsychiatry,* 1964, *34* (5), 822-833.

Hobbs, N. "Helping Disturbed Children: Psychological and Ecological Strategies." *American Psychologist,* 1966, *21,* 1105-1115.

Hobbs, N. *The Futures of Children: Categories, Labels, and Their Consequences.* San Francisco: Jossey-Bass, 1975a.

Hobbs, N. (Ed.). *Issues in the Classification of Children: A Source-*

book on Categories, Labels, and Their Consequences. San Francisco: Jossey-Bass, 1975b.

Hobbs, N. "Perspectives on Re-Education." *Behavior Disorders,* 1978, *3* (2), 65-66.

Hobbs, N. "Adolescent Development and Public Policy." Paper presented at 1981 meeting of the American Psychological Association, Los Angeles, August 25, 1981.

Hobbs, N., and others. *Exceptional Teaching for Exceptional Learning.* New York: Ford Foundation, 1979.

Hubbell, R. *Foster Care and Families: Conflicting Values and Policies.* Philadelphia: Temple University Press, 1981.

Ingalls, R. P. *Results of the Children and Adolescent Level of Care Survey.* Albany: New York State Council on Children and Families, n.d.

Jackson, A. M., Berkowitz, H., and Farley, G. K. "Race as a Variable Affecting the Treatment Involvement of Children." *Journal of the American Academy of Child Psychiatry,* 1974, *13* (1), 20-31.

Joint Commission on Mental Health of Children. *Crisis in Child Mental Health: Challenge for the 1970s.* New York: Harper & Row, 1970.

Joint Commission on Mental Illness and Health. *Action for Mental Health.* New York: Basic Books, 1961.

Kagan, J., and Klein, R. E. "Cross-Cultural Perspectives on Early Development." *American Psychologist,* 1973, *28,* 947-961.

Kirby, T., Wilson, C. T., and Short, M. J. "A Follow-Up Study of Disturbed Children Treated in a Re-ED Program." *Hospital and Community Psychiatry,* Sept. 1977, pp. 694-697.

Kramer, M. "Issues in the Development of Statistical and Epidemiological Data for Mental Health Services Research." *Psychological Medicine,* 1976, *6,* 185-215.

Lafon, R. *Psychopédagogie Médico-Sociale.* Paris: Presses Universitaires de France, 1953.

Lafon, R. *Vocabulaire de Psychopédagogie et de Psychiatrie de l'Enfant.* (3rd ed.) Paris: Presses Universitaires de France, 1973.

LaPaglia, J. *Evaluation of the Social/Emotional Treatment Program at Crockett Academy.* Nashville: Department of Mental Health and Mental Retardation, State of Tennessee, 1978.

Levitt, E. E. "The Results of Psychotherapy with Children: An

Evaluation." *Journal of Consulting Psychology*, 1957, *21*, 189-196.

Lewis, D. O., Balla, D. A., and Shanok, S. S. "Some Evidence of Race Bias in the Treatment of the Juvenile Offender." *American Journal of Orthopsychiatry*, 1979, *49* (1), 53-61.

Lewis, W. W. "Educational Intervention in Emotional Disturbance." In J. Hellmuth (Ed.), *Educational Therapy*. Seattle: Special Child Publications, 1966a.

Lewis, W. W. "Project Re-ED: Re-Education of Emotionally Disturbed Children." In H. P. David (Ed.), *International Resources in Mental Health*. New York: McGraw-Hill, 1966c.

Lewis, W. W. "Project Re-ED: Educational Intervention in Discordant Child Rearing System." In E. L. Cowen, E. A. Gardner, and M. Zax (Eds.), *Emergent Approaches to Mental Health Problems*. New York: Appleton-Century-Crofts, 1967.

Lewis, W. W. "Ecological Planning for Disturbed Children." *Childhood Education*, 1970, *46*, 306-310.

Lewis, W. W. "Project Re-ED: The Program and a Preliminary Evaluation." In H. C. Rickard (Ed.), *Behavioral Intervention in Human Problems*. Elmsford, N.Y.: Pergamon Press, 1971.

Linton, T. E. (Ed.). "The Éducateur: A European Model for the Care of 'Problem' Children." *International Journal of Mental Health*, 1973, *2*, 1-88.

Lorimer, J. I. "A Child's View of Re-ED." *Behavioral Disorders*, 1978, *3* (2), 87-91.

Loughmiller, C. *Wilderness Road*. Austin, Texas: Hogg Foundation for Mental Health, 1965.

Loughmiller, C. *Kids in Trouble: An Adventure in Education*. Tyler, Texas: Wildwood Book Company, 1979.

McGurk, D. "The Effects of Differential Knowledge of Results on Self-Monitoring." Unpublished doctoral dissertation, George Peabody College for Teachers, 1979.

Morris, N., and Hawkins, G. *Letter to the President on Crime Control*. Chicago: University of Chicago Press, 1977.

Newbrough, J. R. "Liaison Services in the Community Context." *Journal of Community Psychology*, 1977, *5*, 24-27.

Piaget, J. *The Origins of Intelligence in Children*. New York: International Universities Press, 1952.

Positive Education Program. *Helping Disturbed Children: A Model for Systematic Treatment.* Cleveland, Ohio: Positive Education Program, 1980.

President's Commission on Mental Health. *Report to the President.* Vol. 1. Washington, D.C.: U.S. Government Printing Office, 1978.

President's Committee on Mental Retardation. *Island of Excellence.* Washington, D.C.: U.S. Government Printing Office, 1973.

Quay, H. C. "Residential Treatment." In H. C. Quay and J. S. Werry (Eds.), *Psychological Disorders of Childhood.* (2nd ed.) New York: Wiley, 1970.

Regier, D. A., and Goldberg, I. D. "The De Facto U.S. Mental Health Services System." *Archives of General Psychiatry,* June 1978, *35,* 685-693.

Rhodes, W. C. "The Disturbing Child: A Problem of Ecological Management." *Exceptional Children,* 1967, *33* (7), 449-455.

Rhodes, W. C. "Ecological Models of Emotional Disturbance." In J. Paul and W. C. Rhodes (Eds.), *Models of Emotional Disturbance.* New York: Wiley, 1971.

Rhodes, W. C. *Behavioral Threat and Community Response.* New York: Behavioral Publications, 1972.

Robins, L. N. *Deviant Children Grown Up: A Sociological and Psychiatric Study of Sociopathic Personality.* Baltimore: Williams & Wilkens, 1966.

Select Panel for the Promotion of Child Health. *Better Health for Our Children: A National Strategy.* (4 vols.) Washington, D.C.: Department of Health and Human Services, 1981.

Short, M. J., Kirby, T., and Wilson, C. T. Internal Document. Greenville, S.C.: Marshall I. Pickens Hospital Children's Program, 1975.

Short, M. J., Kirby, T., and Wilson, C. T. "A Follow-Up Study of Disturbed Children Treated in a Re-ED Program." *Hospital and Community Psychiatry,* 1977, *28* (9), 694-697.

Silver, L. B. "The Special Health–Mental Health Needs of Children." In Select Panel for the Promotion of Child Health, *Better Health for Our Children: A National Strategy.* Vol. IV: *Background Papers.* Washington, D.C.: Department of Health and Human Services, 1981.

Southern Regional Education Board. *Mental Health Training and*

Research in the Southern States. Atlanta: Southern Regional Education Board, 1954.

Sowder, B. J. *Issues Related to Psychiatric Services for Children and Youth: A Review of Selected Literature from 1970-1979.* Bethesda, Md.: Burt Associates, 1980.

Starfield, B., and others. "Psychosocial and Psychosomatic Diagnoses in Primary Care of Children." *Pediatrics,* 1980, *66* (2), 159-167.

Strain, P. S., and others. "Long Term Effects of Oppositional Child Treatment with Mothers as Therapists and Therapists Trainers." *Journal of Applied Behavior Analysis,* in press.

Taft, J. *The Dynamics of Therapy in a Controlled Relationship.* New York: Macmillan, 1937.

Tennessee Department of Mental Health. *Group Process in the Re-education School.* Nashville: Tennessee Department of Mental Health, 1971.

Timm, M. A., and Rule, S. "RIP: A Cost-Effective Parent-Implemented Program for Young Handicapped Children." *Early Child Development and Care,* 1981, *7,* 147-163.

United States Commission on Civil Rights. *The Age Discrimination Study.* Washington, D.C.: U.S. Government Printing Office, 1977.

Watson, J. B., and Rayner, R. "Conditioned Emotional Reactions." *Journal of Experimental Psychology,* 1920, *3* (1), 1-14.

Weinstein, L. *Evaluation of a Program for Re-Educating Disturbed Children: A Follow-Up Comparison with Untreated Children.* Washington, D.C.: Department of Health, Education and Welfare, 1974. (Available through ERIC Document Reproduction Service, ED-141-966.)

Williams, J. S. "Liaison Functions as Reflected in a Case Study." *Journal of Community Psychology,* 1977, *5,* 13-17.

Ziegler, D. R., and others. "Annual Evaluation Report on Two Pressley Ridge School Programs: 1978-1979." Technical report #800601 to Pressley Ridge School, Pittsburgh, June 1980.

Zigler, E., and Bulla, D. A. "Impact of Institutional Experience on the Behavior and Development of Retarded Persons." *American Journal of Mental Deficiency,* 1977, *82,* 1-11.

Index

If you would like to join the association . . .

AREA

Subscribing
Membership

July 1, 199___
to
June 30, 199___

Please send Check or
Money Order
payable to AREA to:

American Re-EDucation Association
1827 East 101st Street
Cleveland, OH 44106
216-231-0401 (ext. 11)

Last
Name _____ First
Name _____ Initial _____

Home Address _____

City, State, Zip _____ Phone (____) ____-_____

Agency Name _____

School / Program Name _____

Address _____

City, State, Zip _____ Phone (____) ____-_____

Position _____

Check One: ☐ First Time Member ☐ Renewal

Membership: $15.00 per person per membership year
$10.00 if employed by a member agency

Feel free to copy . . . and share with a colleague!